THE HARVARD CLASSICS

The Five-Foot Shelf of Books

Listening to a geometrical demonstration by Descartes

Queen Christine of Sweden
Listening to a geometrical demonstration by Descartes
From the painting by Dumesnil

THE HARVARD CLASSICS
EDITED BY CHARLES W. ELIOT, LL.D.

French *and* English
Philosophers

Descartes · Rousseau
Voltaire · Hobbes

With *Introductions and Notes*
Volume 34

P. F. Collier & Son Company
NEW YORK

CONTENTS

CONTENTS

INTRODUCTORY NOTE

René Descartes was born at La Haye in Touraine, March 31, 1596. He came of a landed family with possessions in Brittany as well as in the south. His education was begun at the Jesuit College of La Flèche, continued at Paris, and completed by travel in various countries; and his studies were varied by several years of military service. After he began to devote himself to philosophy, he lived chiefly in Holland; but the last five months of his life were spent in Stockholm, at the court of Queen Christina of Sweden, where he died on February 11, 1650.

While still young, Descartes had become profoundly dissatisfied with the scholastic philosophy, which still survived in the teaching of the Jesuits from whom he received his early training; and adopting a skeptical attitude he set out on his travels determined "to gain knowledge only from himself and the great book of the world, from nature and the observation of man." It was in Germany, as he tells us, that there came to him the idea which proved the starting point of his whole system of thought, the idea, "I think, therefore I exist," which called a halt to the philosophical doubt with which he had resolved to regard everything that could conceivably be doubted. On this basis he built up a philosophy which is usually regarded as the foundation of modern thought. Not that the system of Descartes is accepted to-day; but the sweeping away of presupposition of all kinds, and the "method" which he proposed for the discovery of truth, have made possible the whole modern philosophic development. It was in the "Discourse" here printed, originally published in 1637, that this method was first presented to the world.

Descartes was distinguished in physics and mathematics as well as in philosophy; and his "Geometry" revolutionized the study of that science.

[PREFATORY NOTE BY THE AUTHOR.]

IF this Discourse appear too long to be read at once, it may be divided into six parts: and, in the first, will be found various considerations touching the Sciences; in the second, the principal rules of the Method which the Author has discovered; in the third, certain of the rules of Morals which he has deduced from this Method; in the fourth, the reasonings by which he establishes the existence of God and of the Human Soul, which are the foundations of his Metaphysic; in the fifth, the order of the Physical questions which he has investigated, and, in particular, the explication of the motion of the heart and of some other difficulties pertaining to Medicine, as also the difference between the soul of man and that of the brutes; and, in the last, what the Author believes to be required in order to greater advancement in the investigation of Nature than has yet been made, with the reasons that have induced him to write.

DISCOURSE ON THE METHOD

OF RIGHTLY CONDUCTING
THE REASON AND SEEKING THE TRUTH
IN THE SCIENCES

By René Descartes

PART I

GOOD SENSE is, of all things among men, the most equally distributed; for every one thinks himself so abundantly provided with it, that those even who are the most difficult to satisfy in everything else, do not usually desire a larger measure of this quality than they already possess. And in this it is not likely that all are mistaken: the conviction is rather to be held as testifying that the power of judging aright and of distinguishing Truth from Error, which is properly what is called Good Sense or Reason, is by nature equal in all men; and that the diversity of our opinions, consequently, does not arise from some being endowed with a larger share of Reason than others, but solely from this, that we conduct our thoughts along different ways, and do not fix our attention on the same objects. For to be possessed of a vigorous mind is not enough; the prime requisite is rightly to apply it. The greatest minds, as they are capable of the highest excellencies, are open likewise to the greatest aberrations; and those who travel very slowly may yet make far greater progress, provided they keep always to the straight road, than those who, while they run, forsake it.

For myself, I have never fancied my mind to be in any respect more perfect than those of the generality; on the contrary, I have often wished that I were equal to some others in promptitude of thought, or in clearness and distinctness of imagination, or in fulness and readiness of memory. And besides these, I know of no other qualities that contribute to the perfection of the mind; for as to the Reason or

Sense, inasmuch as it is that alone which constitutes us men, and distinguishes us from the brutes, I am disposed to believe that it is to be found complete in each individual; and on this point to adopt the common opinion of philosophers, who say that the difference of greater and less holds only among the *accidents,* and not among the *forms* or *natures* of *individuals* of the same *species*.

I will not hesitate, however, to avow my belief that it has been my singular good fortune to have very early in life fallen in with certain tracks which have conducted me to considerations and maxims, of which I have formed a Method that gives me the means, as I think, of gradually augmenting my knowledge, and of raising it by little and little to the highest point which the mediocrity of my talents and the brief duration of my life will permit me to reach. For I have already reaped from it such fruits that, although I have been accustomed to think lowly enough of myself, and although when I look with the eye of a philosopher at the varied courses and pursuits of mankind at large, I find scarcely one which does not appear vain and useless, I nevertheless derive the highest satisfaction from the progress I conceive myself to have already made in the search after truth, and cannot help entertaining such expectations of the future as to believe that if, among the occupations of men as men, there is any one really excellent and important, it is that which I have chosen.

After all, it is possible I may be mistaken; and it is but a little copper and glass, perhaps, that I take for gold and diamonds. I know how very liable we are to delusion in what relates to ourselves, and also how much the judgments of our friends are to be suspected when given in our favour. But I shall endeavour in this Discourse to describe the paths I have followed, and to delineate my life as in a picture, in order that each one may be able to judge of them for himself, and that in the general opinion entertained of them, as gathered from current report, I myself may have a new help towards instruction to be added to those I have been in the habit of employing.

My present design, then, is not to teach the Method which each ought to follow for the right conduct of his Reason, but solely to describe the way in which I have endeavoured to conduct my own. They who set themselves to give precepts must of course regard themselves as possessed of greater skill than those to whom they prescribe; and if they err in the slightest particular, they subject themselves to censure. But as this Tract is put forth merely as a history, or, if you will, as a tale, in which, amid some examples worthy of imitation, there will be found, perhaps, as many more which it were advisable not to follow, I hope it will prove useful to some without being hurtful to any, and that my openness will find some favour with all.

From my childhood, I have been familiar with letters; and as I was given to believe that by their help a clear and certain knowledge of all that is useful in life might be acquired, I was ardently desirous of instruction. But as soon as I had finished the entire course of study, at the close of which it is customary to be admitted into the order of the learned, I completely changed my opinion. For I found myself involved in so many doubts and errors, that I was convinced I had advanced no farther in all my attempts at learning, than the discovery at every turn of my own ignorance. And yet I was studying in one of the most celebrated Schools in Europe, in which I thought there must be learned men, if such were anywhere to be found. I had been taught all that others learned there; and not contented with the sciences actually taught us, I had, in addition, read all the books that had fallen into my hands, treating of such branches as are esteemed the most curious and rare. I knew the judgment which others had formed of me; and I did not find that I was considered inferior to my fellows, although there were among them some who were already marked out to fill the places of our instructors. And, in fine, our age appears to me as flourishing, and as fertile in powerful minds as any preceding one. I was thus led to take the liberty of judging of all other men by myself, and of concluding that there was no science in existence that was of such a nature as I had previously been given to believe.

I still continued, however, to hold in esteem the studies of the Schools. I was aware that the Languages taught in them are necessary to the understanding of the writings of the ancients; that the grace of Fable stirs the mind; that the memorable deeds of History elevate it; and, if read with discretion, aid in forming the judgment; that the perusal of all excellent books is, as it were, to interview with the noblest men of past ages, who have written them, and even a studied interview, in which are discovered to us only their choicest thoughts; that Eloquence has incomparable force and beauty; that Poesy has its ravishing graces and delights; that in the Mathematics there are many refined discoveries eminently suited to gratify the inquisitive, as well as further all the arts and lessen the labour of man; that numerous highly useful precepts and exhortations to virtue are contained in treatises on Morals; that Theology points out the path to heaven; that Philosophy affords the means of discoursing with an appearance of truth on all matters, and commands the admiration of the more simple; that Jurisprudence, Medicine, and the other Sciences, secure for their cultivators honours and riches; and in fine, that it is useful to bestow some attention upon all, even upon those abounding the most in superstition and error, that we may be in a position to determine their real value, and guard against being deceived.

But I believed that I had already given sufficient time to Languages, and likewise to the reading of the writings of the ancients, to their Histories and Fables. For to hold converse with those of other ages and to travel, are almost the same thing. It is useful to know something of the manners of different nations, that we may be enabled to form a more correct judgment regarding our own, and be prevented from thinking that everything contrary to our customs is ridiculous and irrational,—a conclusion usually come to by those whose experience has been limited to their own country. On the other hand, when too much time is occupied in travelling, we become strangers to our native country; and the over curious in the customs of the past are generally ignorant of those of the present. Besides, fictitious narratives lead us to imagine the possibility of many events that are impossible; and even the most faithful histories, if they do not wholly misrepresent matters, or exaggerate their importance to render the account of them more worthy of perusal, omit, at least, almost always the meanest and least striking of the attendant circumstances; hence it happens that the remainder does not represent the truth, and that such as regulate their conduct by examples drawn from this source, are apt to fall into the extravagances of the knight-errants of Romance, and to entertain projects that exceed their powers.

I esteemed Eloquence highly, and was in raptures with Poesy; but I thought that both were gifts of nature rather than fruits of study. Those in whom the faculty of Reason is predominant, and who most skilfully dispose their thoughts with a view to render them clear and intelligible, are always the best able to persuade others of the truth of what they lay down, though they should speak only in the language of Lower Brittany, and be wholly ignorant of the rules of Rhetoric; and those whose minds are stored with the most agreeable fancies, and who can give expression to them with the greatest embellishment and harmony, are still the best poets, though unacquainted with the Art of Poetry.

I was especially delighted with the Mathematics, on account of the certitude and evidence of their reasonings: but I had not as yet a precise knowledge of their true use; and thinking that they but contributed to the advancement of the mechanical arts, I was astonished that foundations, so strong and solid, should have had no loftier superstructure reared on them. On the other hand, I compared the disquisitions of the ancient Moralists to very towering and magnificent palaces with no better foundation than sand and mud: they laud the virtues very highly, and exhibit them as estimable far above anything on earth; but they give us no adequate criterion of virtue, and frequently that which they designate with so fine a name is but apathy, or pride, or despair, or parricide.

I revered our Theology, and aspired as much as any one to reach heaven: but being given assuredly to understand that the way is not less open to the most ignorant than to the most learned, and that the revealed truths which lead to heaven are above our comprehension, I did not presume to subject them to the impotency of my Reason; and I thought that in order competently to undertake their examination, there was need of some special help from heaven, and of being more than man.

Of philosophy I will say nothing, except that when I saw that it had been cultivated for many ages by the most distinguished men, and that yet there is not a single matter within its sphere which is not still in dispute, and nothing, therefore, which is above doubt, I did not presume to anticipate that my success would be greater in it than that of others; and further, when I considered the number of con-

flicting opinions touching a single matter that may be upheld by
learned men, while there can be but one true, I reckoned as well-nigh
false all that was only probable.

As to the other Sciences, inasmuch as these borrow their principles
from Philosophy, I judged that no solid superstructures could be
reared on foundations so infirm; and neither the honour nor the gain
held out by them was sufficient to determine me to their cultivation:
for I was not, thank Heaven, in a condition which compelled me to
make merchandise of Science for the bettering of my fortune; and
though I might not profess to scorn glory as a Cynic, I yet made very
slight account of that honour which I hoped to acquire only through
fictitious titles. And, in fine, of false Sciences I thought I knew the
worth sufficiently to escape being deceived by the professions of an
alchemist, the predictions of an astrologer, the impostures of a magi-
cian, or by the artifices and boasting of any of those who profess to
know things of which they are ignorant.

For these reasons, as soon as my age permitted me to pass from
under the control of my instructors, I entirely abandoned the study
of letters, and resolved no longer to seek any other science than the
knowledge of myself, or of the great book of the world. I spent the
remainder of my youth in travelling, in visiting courts and armies,
in holding intercourse with men of different dispositions and ranks,
in collecting varied experience, in proving myself in the different
situations into which fortune threw me, and, above all, in making
such reflection on the matter of my experience as to secure my
improvement. For it occurred to me that I should find much more
truth in the reasonings of each individual with reference to the affairs
in which he is personally interested, and the issue of which must
presently punish him if he has judged amiss, than in those conducted
by a man of letters in his study, regarding speculative matters that
are of no practical moment, and followed by no consequences to
himself, farther, perhaps, than that they foster his vanity the better
the more remote they are from common sense; requiring, as they
must in this case, the exercise of greater ingenuity and art to render
them probable. In addition, I had always a most earnest desire to
know how to distinguish the true from the false, in order that I might

be able clearly to discriminate the right path in life, and proceed in it with confidence.

It is true that, while busied only in considering the manners of other men, I found here, too, scarce any ground for settled conviction, and remarked hardly less contradiction among them than in the opinions of the philosophers. So that the greatest advantage I derived from the study consisted in this, that, observing many things which, however extravagant and ridiculous to our apprehension, are yet by common consent received and approved by other great nations, I learned to entertain too decided a belief in regard to nothing of the truth of which I had been persuaded merely by example and custom: and thus I gradually extricated myself from many errors powerful enough to darken our Natural Intelligence, and incapacitate us in great measure from listening to Reason. But after I had been occupied several years in thus studying the book of the world, and in essaying to gather some experience, I at length resolved to make myself an object of study, and to employ all the powers of my mind in choosing the paths I ought to follow; an undertaking which was accompanied with greater success than it would have been had I never quitted my country or my books.

PART II

IWAS then in Germany, attracted thither by the wars in that country, which have not yet been brought to a termination; and as I was returning to the army from the coronation of the Emperor, the setting in of winter arrested me in a locality where, as I found no society to interest me, and was besides fortunately undisturbed by any cares or passions, I remained the whole day in seclusion,[1] with full opportunity to occupy my attention with my own thoughts. Of these one of the very first that occurred to me was, that there is seldom so much perfection in works composed of many separate parts, upon which different hands have been employed, as in those completed by a single master. Thus it is observable that the buildings which a single architect has planned and executed, are generally more elegant and commodious than those which several have attempted to improve, by making old walls serve for purposes for which they were not originally built. Thus also, those ancient cities which, from being at first only villages, have become, in course of time, large towns, are usually but ill-laid out compared with the regularly constructed towns which a professional architect has freely planned on an open plain; so that although the several buildings of the former may often equal or surpass in beauty those of the latter, yet when one observes their indiscriminate juxtaposition, there a large one and here a small, and the consequent crookedness and irregularity of the streets, one is disposed to allege that chance rather than any human will guided by reason, must have led to such an arrangement. And if we consider that nevertheless there have been at all times certain officers whose duty it was to see that private buildings contributed to public ornament, the difficulty of reaching high perfection with but the materials of others to operate on, will be readily acknowledged. In the same way I fancied that those nations which, starting from a semi-barbarous state and advancing to civili-

[1] Literally, in a room heated by means of a stove.—*Tr.*

sation by slow degrees, have had their laws successively determined, and, as it were, forced upon them simply by experience of the hurtfulness of particular crimes and disputes, would by this process come to be possessed of less perfect institutions than those which, from the commencement of their association as communities, have followed the appointments of some wise legislator. It is thus quite certain that the constitution of the true religion, the ordinances of which are derived from God, must be incomparably superior to that of every other. And, to speak of human affairs, I believe that the past pre-eminence of Sparta was due not to the goodness of each of its laws in particular, for many of these were very strange, and even opposed to good morals, but to the circumstance that, originated by a single individual, they all tended to a single end. In the same way I thought that the sciences contained in books, (such of them at least as are made up of probable reasonings, without demonstrations,) composed as they are of the opinions of many different individuals massed together, are farther removed from truth than the simple inferences which a man of good sense using his natural and unprejudiced judgment draws respecting the matters of his experience. And because we have all to pass through a state of infancy to manhood, and have been of necessity, for a length of time, governed by our desires and preceptors, (whose dictates were frequently conflicting, while neither perhaps always counselled us for the best,) I farther concluded that it is almost impossible that our judgments can be so correct or solid as they would have been, had our Reason been mature from the moment of our birth, and had we always been guided by it alone.

It is true, however, that it is not customary to pull down all the houses of a town with the single design of rebuilding them differently, and thereby rendering the streets more handsome; but it often happens that a private individual takes down his own with the view of erecting it anew, and that people are even sometimes constrained to this when their houses are in danger of falling from age, or when the foundations are insecure. With this before me by way of example, I was persuaded that it would indeed be preposterous for a private individual to think of reforming a state by fundamentally changing it throughout, and overturning it in order to set it up amended; and the same I thought was true of any similar project for reforming the body of the Sciences, or the order of teaching them established in the Schools: but as for the opinions which up to that time I had embraced, I thought that I could not do better than resolve at once to sweep them wholly away, that I might afterwards be in a position to admit either others more correct, or even perhaps the same when they had undergone the scrutiny of Reason. I firmly believed that in this way I should much better succeed in the conduct of my life, than if I built only upon old foundations, and leant upon principles which, in my youth, I had taken upon trust. For although I recognised various difficulties in this undertaking, these were not, however, without remedy, nor once to be compared with such as attend the slightest reformation in public affairs. Large bodies, if once overthrown, are with great difficulty set up again, or even kept erect when once seriously shaken, and the fall of such is always disastrous. Then if there are any imperfections in the constitutions of states, (and that many such exist the diversity of constitutions is alone sufficient to assure us,) custom has without doubt materially smoothed their inconveniences, and has even managed to steer altogether clear of, or insensibly corrected a number which sagacity could not have provided against with equal effect; and, in fine, the defects are almost always more tolerable than the change necessary for their removal; in the same manner that highways which wind among mountains, by being much frequented, become gradually so smooth and commodious, that it is much better to follow them than to seek a straighter path by climbing over the tops of rocks and descending to the bottoms of precipices.

Hence it is that I cannot in any degree approve of those restless and busy meddlers who, called neither by birth nor fortune to take part in the management of public affairs, are yet always projecting reforms; and if I thought that this Tract contained aught which might justify the suspicion that I was a victim of such folly, I would by no means permit its publication. I have never contemplated anything higher than the reformation of my own opinions, and basing them on a foundation wholly my own. And although my own satisfaction with my work has led me to present here a draft of it, I do not by any means therefore recommend to every one else to make a similar attempt. Those whom God has endowed with a larger measure of genius will entertain, perhaps, designs still more exalted; but for the many I am much afraid lest even the present undertaking be more than they can safely venture to imitate. The single design to strip one's self of all past beliefs is one that ought not to be taken by every one. The majority of men is composed of two classes, for neither of which would this be at all a befitting resolution: in the *first* place, of those who with more than a due confidence in their own powers, are precipitate in their judgments and want the patience requisite for orderly and circumspect thinking; whence it happens, that if men of this class once take the liberty to doubt of their accustomed opinions, and quit the beaten highway, they will never be able to thread the byeway that would lead them by a shorter course, and will lose themselves and continue to wander for life; in the *second* place, of those who, possessed of sufficient sense or modesty to determine that there are others who excel them in the power of discriminating between truth and error, and by whom they may be instructed, ought rather to content themselves with the opinions of such than trust for more correct to their own Reason.

For my own part, I should doubtless have belonged to the latter class, had I received instruction from but one master, or had I never known the diversities of opinion that from time immemorial have prevailed among men of the greatest learning. But I had become aware, even so early as during my college life, that no opinion, however absurd and incredible, can be imagined, which has not been maintained by some one of the philosophers; and afterwards in the course of my travels I remarked that all those whose opinions are decidedly repugnant to ours are not on that account barbarians and savages, but on the contrary that many of these nations make an equally good, if not a better, use of their Reason than we do. I took into account also the very different character which a person brought up from infancy in France or Germany exhibits, from that which, with the same mind originally, this individual would have possessed had he lived always among the Chinese or with savages, and the circumstance that in dress itself the fashion which pleased us ten years ago, and which may again, perhaps, be received into favour before ten years have gone, appears to us at this moment extravagant and ridiculous. I was thus led to infer that the ground of our opinions is far more custom and example than any certain knowledge. And, finally, although such be the ground of our opinions, I remarked that a plurality of suffrages is no guarantee of truth where it is at all of difficult discovery, as in such cases it is much more likely that it will be found by one than by many. I could, however, select from the crowd no one whose opinions seemed worthy of preference, and thus I found myself constrained, as it were, to use my own Reason in the conduct of my life.

But like one walking alone and in the dark, I resolved to proceed so slowly and with such circumspection, that if I did not advance far, I would at least guard against falling. I did not even choose to dismiss summarily any of the opinions that had crept into my belief without having been introduced by Reason, but first of all took sufficient time carefully to satisfy myself of the general nature of the task I was setting myself, and ascertain the true Method by which to arrive at the knowledge of whatever lay within the compass of my powers.

Among the branches of Philosophy, I had, at an earlier period, given some attention to Logic, and among those of the Mathematics to Geometrical Analysis and Algebra,—three Arts or Sciences which ought, as I conceived, to contribute something to my design. But, on examination, I found that, as for Logic, its syllogisms and the majority of its other precepts are of avail rather in the communication of what we already know, or even as the Art of Lully, in speaking without judgment of things of which we are ignorant, than in the investigation of the unknown; and although this Science contains indeed a number of correct and very excellent precepts, there are, nevertheless, so many others, and these either injurious or superfluous, mingled with the former, that it is almost quite as difficult to effect a severance of the true from the false as it is to extract a Diana or a Minerva from a rough block of marble. Then as to the Analysis of the ancients and the Algebra of the moderns, besides that they embrace only matters highly abstract, and, to appearance, of no use, the former is so exclusively restricted to the consideration of figures, that it can exercise the Understanding only on condition of greatly fatiguing the Imagination;[2] and, in the latter, there is so complete a subjection to certain rules and formulas, that there results an art full of confusion and obscurity calculated to embarrass, instead of a science fitted to cultivate the mind. By these considerations I was induced to seek some other Method which would comprise the advantages of the three and be exempt from their defects. And as a multitude of laws often only hampers justice, so that a state is best governed when, with few laws, these are rigidly administered; in like manner, instead of the great number of precepts of which Logic is composed, I believed that the four following would prove perfectly sufficient for me, provided I took the firm and unwavering resolution never in a single instance to fail in observing them.

The *first* was never to accept anything for true which I did not clearly know to be such; that is to say, carefully to avoid precipitancy and prejudice, and to comprise nothing more in my judgment than what was presented to my mind so clearly and distinctly as to exclude all ground of doubt.

The *second,* to divide each of the difficulties under examination into as many parts as possible, and as might be necessary for its adequate solution.

The *third,* to conduct my thoughts in such order that, by commencing with objects the simplest and easiest to know, I might ascend by little and little, and, as it were, step by step, to the knowledge of the more complex; assigning in thought a certain order even to those objects which in their own nature do not stand in a relation of antecedence and sequence.

And the *last,* in every case to make enumerations so complete, and reviews so general, that I might be assured that nothing was omitted.

The long chains of simple and easy reasonings by means of which geometers are accustomed to reach the conclusions of their most difficult demonstrations, had led me to imagine that all things, to the knowledge of which man is competent, are mutually connected in the same way, and that there is nothing so far removed from us as to be beyond our reach, or so hidden that we cannot discover it, provided only we abstain from accepting the false for the true, and

[2] The Imagination must here be taken as equivalent simply to the Representative Faculty.—*Tr.*

always preserve in our thoughts the order necessary for the deduction of one truth from another. And I had little difficulty in determining the objects with which it was necessary to commence, for I was already persuaded that it must be with the simplest and easiest to know, and, considering that of all those who have hitherto sought truth in the Sciences, the mathematicians alone have been able to find any demonstrations, that is, any certain and evident reasons, I did not doubt but that such must have been the rule of their investigations. I resolved to commence, therefore, with the examination of the simplest objects, not anticipating, however, from this any other advantage than that to be found in accustoming my mind to the love and nourishment of truth, and to a distaste for all such reasonings as were unsound. But I had no intention on that account of attempting to master all the particular Sciences commonly denominated Mathematics: but observing that, however different their objects, they all agree in considering only the various relations or proportions subsisting among those objects, I thought it best for my purpose to consider these proportions in the most general form possible, without referring them to any objects in particular, except such as would most facilitate the knowledge of them, and without by any means restricting them to these, that afterwards I might thus be the better able to apply them to every other class of objects to which they are legitimately applicable. Perceiving further, that in order to understand these relations I should sometimes have to consider them one by one, and sometimes only to bear them in mind, or embrace them in the aggregate, I thought that, in order the better to consider them individually, I should view them as subsisting between straight lines, than which I could find no objects more simple, or capable of being more distinctly represented to my imagination and senses; and on the other hand, that in order to retain them in the memory, or embrace an aggregate of many, I should express them by certain characters the briefest possible. In this way I believed that I could borrow all that was best both in Geometrical Analysis and in Algebra, and correct all the defects of the one by help of the other.

And, in point of fact, the accurate observance of these few precepts gave me, I take the liberty of saying, such ease in unravelling all the questions embraced in these two sciences, that in the two or three months I devoted to their examination, not only did I reach solutions of questions I had formerly deemed exceedingly difficult, but even as regards questions of the solution of which I continued ignorant, I was enabled, as it appeared to me, to determine the means whereby, and the extent to which, a solution was possible; results attributable to the circumstance that I commenced with the simplest and most general truths, and that thus each truth discovered was a rule available in the discovery of subsequent ones. Nor in this perhaps shall I appear too vain if it be considered that, as the truth on any particular point is one, whoever apprehends the truth, knows all that on that point can be known. The child, for example, who has been instructed in the elements of Arithmetic, and has made a particular addition, according to rule, may be assured that he has found, with respect to the sum of the numbers before him, all that in this instance is within the reach of human genius. Now, in conclusion, the Method which teaches adherence to the true order, and an exact enumeration of all the conditions of the thing sought includes all that gives certitude to the rules of Arithmetic.

But the chief ground of my satisfaction with this Method, was the assurance I had of thereby exercising my reason in all matters, if not with absolute perfection, at least with the greatest attainable by me: besides, I was conscious that by its use my mind was becoming gradually habituated to clearer and more distinct conceptions of its objects; and I hoped also, from not having restricted this Method to any particular matter, to apply it to the difficulties of the other Sciences, with not less success than to those of Algebra. I should not, however, on this account have ventured at once on the examination of all the difficulties of the Sciences which presented themselves to me, for this would have been contrary to the order prescribed in the Method, but observing that the knowledge of such is dependent on principles borrowed from Philosophy, in which I found nothing certain, I thought it necessary first of all to endeavour to establish its principles. And because I observed, besides, that an inquiry of this kind was of all others of the greatest moment, and one in which precipitancy and anticipation in judgment were most to be dreaded, I thought that I ought not to approach it till I had reached a more mature age, (being at that time but twenty-three,) and had first of all employed much of my time in preparation for the work, as well by eradicating from my mind all the erroneous opinions I had up to that moment accepted, as by amassing variety of experience to afford materials for my reasonings, and by continually exercising myself in my chosen Method with a view to increased skill in its application.

PART III

AND, finally, as it is not enough, before commencing to rebuild the house in which we live, that it be pulled down, and materials and builders provided, or that we engage in the work ourselves, according to a plan which we have beforehand carefully drawn out, but as it is likewise necessary that we be furnished with some other house in which we may live commodiously during the operations, so that I might not remain irresolute in my actions, while my Reason compelled me to suspend my judgment, and that I might not be prevented from living thenceforward in the greatest possible felicity, I formed a provisory code of Morals, composed of three or four maxims, with which I am desirous to make you acquainted.

The *first* was to obey the laws and customs of my country, adhering firmly to the Faith in which, by the grace of God, I had been educated from my childhood, and regulating my conduct in every other matter according to the most moderate opinions, and the farthest removed from extremes, which should happen to be adopted in practice with general consent of the most judicious of those among whom I might be living. For, as I had from that time begun to hold my own opinions for nought because I wished to subject them all to examination, I was convinced that I could not do better than follow in the meantime the opinions of the most judicious; and although there are some perhaps among the Persians and Chinese as judicious as among ourselves, expediency seemed to dictate that I should regulate my practice conformably to the opinions of those with whom I should have to live; and it appeared to me that, in order to ascertain the real opinions of such, I ought rather to take cognizance of what they practised than of what they said, not only because, in the corruption of our manners, there are few disposed to speak exactly as they believe, but also because very many are not aware of what it is that they really believe; for, as the act of mind by which a thing is believed is different from that by which we know that we believe it, the one act is often found without the other. Also, amid many opinions held in equal repute, I chose always the most moderate, as much for the reason that these are always the most convenient for practice, and probably the best, (for all excess is generally vicious,) as that, in the event of my falling into error, I might be at less distance from the truth than if, having chosen one of the extremes, it should turn out to be the other which I ought to have adopted. And I placed in the class of extremes especially all promises by which somewhat of our freedom is abridged; not that I disapproved of the laws which, to provide against the instability of men of feeble resolution, when what is sought to be accomplished is some good, permit engagements by vows and contracts binding the parties to persevere in it, or even, for the security of commerce, sanction similar engagements where the purpose sought to be realized is indifferent: but because I did not find anything on earth which was wholly superior to change, and because, for myself in particular, I hoped gradually to perfect my judgments, and not to suffer them to deteriorate, I would have deemed it a grave sin against good sense, if, for the reason that I approved of something at a particular time, I therefore bound myself to hold it for good at a subsequent time, when perhaps it had ceased to be so, or I had ceased to esteem it such.

My *second* maxim was to be as firm and resolute in my actions as I was able, and not to adhere less steadfastly to the most doubtful opinions, when once adopted, than if they had been highly certain; imitating in this the example of travellers who, when they have lost their way in a forest, ought not to wander from side to side, far less remain in one place, but proceed constantly towards the same side in as straight a line as possible, without changing their direction for slight reasons, although perhaps it might be chance alone which at first determined the selection; for in this way, if they do not exactly reach the point they desire, they will come at least in the end to some place that will probably be preferable to the middle of a forest. In the same way, since in action it frequently happens that no delay is permissible, it is very certain that, when it is not in our power to determine what is true, we ought to act according to what is most probable; and even although we should not remark a greater probability in one opinion than in another, we ought notwithstanding to choose one or the other, and afterwards consider it, in so far as it relates to practice, as no longer dubious, but manifestly true and certain, since the reason by which our choice has been determined is itself possessed of these qualities. This principle was sufficient thenceforward to rid me of all those repentings and pangs of remorse that usually disturb the consciences of such feeble and uncertain minds as, destitute of any clear and determinate principle of choice, allow themselves one day to adopt a course of action as the best, which they abandon the next, as the opposite.

My *third* maxim was to endeavour always to conquer myself rather than fortune, and change my desires rather than the order of the world, and in general, accustom myself to the persuasion that, except our own thoughts, there is nothing absolutely in our power; so that when we have done our best in respect of things external to us, all wherein we fail of success is to be held, as regards us, absolutely impossible: and this single principle seemed to me sufficient to prevent me from desiring for the future anything which I could not obtain, and thus render me contented; for since our will naturally seeks those objects alone which the understanding represents as in some way possible of attainment, it is plain, that if we consider all external goods as equally beyond our power, we shall no more regret the absence of such goods as seem due to our birth, when deprived of them without any fault of ours, than our not possessing the kingdoms of China or Mexico; and thus making, so to speak, a virtue of necessity, we shall no more desire health in disease, or freedom in imprisonment, than we now do bodies incorruptible as diamonds, or the wings of birds to fly with. But I confess there is need of prolonged discipline and frequently repeated meditation to accustom the mind to view all objects in this light; and I believe that in this chiefly consisted the secret of the power of such philosophers as in former times were enabled to rise superior to the influence of fortune, and amid suffering and poverty, enjoy a happiness which their gods might have envied. For, occupied incessantly with the consideration of the limits prescribed to their power by nature, they became so entirely convinced that nothing was at their disposal except their own thoughts, that this conviction was of itself sufficient to prevent their entertaining any desire of other objects; and over their thoughts they acquired a sway so absolute, that they had some ground on this account for esteeming themselves more rich and more powerful, more free and more happy, than other men who, whatever be the favours heaped on them by nature and fortune, if destitute of this philosophy, can never command the realization of all their desires.

In fine, to conclude this code of Morals, I thought of reviewing the different occupations of men in this life, with the view of making choice of the best. And, without wishing to offer any remarks on the employments of others, I may state that it was my conviction that I could not do better than continue in that in which I was engaged, viz., in devoting my whole life to the culture of my Reason, and in making the greatest progress I was able in the knowledge of truth, on the principles of the Method which I had prescribed to myself. This Method, from the time I had begun to apply it, had been to me the source of satisfaction so intense as to lead me to believe that more perfect or more innocent could not be enjoyed in this life; and as by its means I daily discovered truths that appeared to me of some importance, and of which other men were generally ignorant, the gratification thence arising so occupied my mind that I was wholly indifferent to every other object. Besides, the three preceding maxims were founded singly on the design of continuing the work of self-instruction. For since God has endowed each of us with some Light of Reason by which to distinguish truth from error, I could not have believed that I ought for a single moment to rest satisfied with the opinions of another, unless I had resolved to exercise my own judgment in examining these whenever I should be duly qualified for the task. Nor could I have proceeded on such opinions without scruple, had I supposed that I should thereby forfeit any advantage for attaining still more accurate, should such exist. And, in fine, I could not have restrained my desires, nor remained satisfied, had I not followed a path in which I thought myself certain of attaining all the knowledge to the acquisition of which I was competent, as well as the largest amount of what is truly good which I could ever hope to secure. Inasmuch as we neither seek nor shun any object except in so far as our understanding represents it as good or bad, all that is necessary to right action is right judgment, and to the best action the most correct judgment,—that is, to the acquisition of all the virtues with all else that is truly valuable and within our reach; and the assurance of such an acquisition cannot fail to render us contented.

Having thus provided myself with these maxims, and having placed them in reserve along with the truths of Faith, which have ever occupied the first place in my belief, I came to the conclusion that I might with freedom set about ridding myself of what remained of my opinions. And, inasmuch as I hoped to be better able successfully to accomplish this work by holding intercourse with mankind, than by remaining longer shut up in the retirement where these thoughts had occurred to me, I betook me again to travelling before the winter was well ended. And, during the nine subsequent years, I did nothing but roam from one place to another, desirous of being a spectator rather than an actor in the plays exhibited on the theatre of the world; and, as I made it my business in each matter to reflect particularly upon what might fairly be doubted and prove a source of error, I gradually rooted out from my mind all the errors which had hitherto crept into it. Not that in this I imitated the Sceptics who doubt only that they may doubt, and seek nothing beyond uncertainty itself; for, on the contrary, my design was singly to find ground of assurance, and cast aside the loose earth and sand, that I might reach the rock or the clay. In this, as appears to me, I was successful enough; for, since I endeavoured to discover the falsehood or incertitude of the propositions I examined, not by feeble conjectures, but by clear and certain reasonings, I met with nothing so doubtful as not to yield some conclusion of adequate certainty, although this were merely the inference, that the matter in question contained nothing certain. And, just as in pulling down an old house, we usually reserve the ruins to contribute towards the erection, so, in destroying such of my opinions as I judged to be ill-founded, I made a variety of observations and acquired an amount of experience of which I availed myself in the establishment of more certain. And further, I continued to exercise myself in the Method I had prescribed; for, besides taking care in general to conduct all my thoughts according to its rules, I reserved some hours from time to time which I expressly devoted to the employment of the Method in the solution of Mathematical difficulties, or even in the solution likewise of some questions belonging to other Sciences, but which, by my having detached them from such principles of these Sciences as were of inadequate certainty, were rendered almost Mathematical: the truth of this will be manifest from the numerous examples contained in this volume.[1] And thus, without in appearance living otherwise than those who, with no other occupation than that of spending their lives agreeably and innocently, study to sever pleasure from vice, and who, that they may enjoy their leisure without ennui, have recourse to such pursuits as are honourable, I was nevertheless prosecuting my design, and making greater progress in the knowledge of truth, than I might, perhaps, have made had I been engaged in the perusal of books merely, or in holding converse with men of letters.

These nine years passed away, however, before I had come to any determinate judgment respecting the difficulties which form matter of dispute among the learned, or had commenced to seek the principles of any Philosophy more certain than the vulgar. And the examples of many men of the highest genius, who had, in former times, engaged in this inquiry, but, as appeared to me, without success, led me to imagine it to be a work of so much difficulty, that I would not perhaps have ventured on it so soon had I not heard it currently rumoured that I had already completed the inquiry. I know not what were the grounds of this opinion; and, if my conversation contributed in any measure to its rise, this must have happened rather from my having confessed my ignorance with greater freedom than those are accustomed to do who have studied a little, and expounded, perhaps, the reasons that led me to doubt of many of those things that by others are esteemed certain, than from my having boasted of any system of Philosophy. But, as I am of a disposition that makes me unwilling to be esteemed different from what I really am, I thought it necessary to endeavour by all means to render myself worthy of the reputation accorded to me; and it is now exactly eight years since this desire constrained me to remove from all those places where interruption from any of my acquaintances was possible, and

---

[1] The Discourse on Method was originally published along with the Dioptrics, the Meteorics, and the Geometry.—*Tr.*

betake myself to this country,[2] in which the long duration of the war
has led to the establishment of such discipline, that the armies maintained seem to be of use only in enabling the inhabitants to enjoy
more securely the blessings of peace; and where, in the midst of a
great crowd actively engaged in business, and more careful of their
own affairs than curious about those of others, I have been enabled
to live without being deprived of any of the conveniences to be had
in the most populous cities, and yet as solitary and as retired as in
the midst of the most remote deserts.

[2] Holland; to which country he withdrew in 1629.—*Tr.*

PART IV

I AM in doubt as to the propriety of making my first meditations in the place above mentioned matter of discourse; for these are so metaphysical, and so uncommon, as not, perhaps, to be acceptable to every one. And yet, that it may be determined whether the foundations that I have laid are sufficiently secure, I find myself in a measure constrained to advert to them. I had long before remarked that, in (relation to) practice, it is sometimes necessary to adopt, as if above doubt, opinions which we discern to be highly uncertain, as has been already said; but as I then desired to give my attention solely to the search after truth, I thought that a procedure exactly the opposite was called for, and that I ought to reject as absolutely false all opinions in regard to which I could suppose the least ground for doubt, in order to ascertain whether after that there remained aught in my belief that was wholly indubitable. Accordingly, seeing that our senses sometimes deceive us, I was willing to suppose that there existed nothing really such as they presented to us; and because some men err in reasoning, and fall into paralogisms, even on the simplest matters of Geometry, I, convinced that I was as open to error as any other, rejected as false all the reasonings I had hitherto taken for demonstrations; and finally, when I considered that the very same thoughts (presentations) which we experience when awake may also be experienced when we are asleep, while there is at that time not one of them true, I supposed that all the objects (presentations) that had ever entered into my mind when awake, had in them no more truth than the illusions of my dreams. But immediately upon this I observed that, whilst I thus wished to think that all was false, it was absolutely necessary that I, who thus thought, should be somewhat; and as I observed that this truth, *I think, hence I am,* was so certain and of such evidence, that no ground of doubt, however extravagant, could be alleged by the Sceptics capable of shaking it, I concluded that I might, without scruple, accept it as the first principle of the Philosophy of which I was in search.

In the next place, I attentively examined what I was, and as I observed that I could suppose that I had no body, and that there was no world nor any place in which I might be; but that I could not therefore suppose that I was not; and that, on the contrary, from the very circumstance that I thought to doubt of the truth of other things, it most clearly and certainly followed that I was; while, on the other hand, if I had only ceased to think, although all the other objects which I had ever imagined had been in reality existent, I would have had no reason to believe that I existed; I thence concluded that I was a substance whose whole essence or nature consists only in thinking, and which, that it may exist, has need of no place, nor is dependent on any material thing; so that "I," that is to say, the mind by which I am what I am, is wholly distinct from the body, and is even more easily known than the latter, and is such, that although the latter were not, it would still continue to be all that it is.

After this I inquired in general into what is essential to the truth and certainty of a proposition; for since I had discovered one which I knew to be true, I thought that I must likewise be able to discover the ground of this certitude. And as I observed that in the words *I think, hence I am,* there is nothing at all which gives me assurance of their truth beyond this, that I see very clearly that in order to think it is necessary to exist, I concluded that I might take, as a general rule, the principle, that all the things which we very clearly and distinctly conceive are true, only observing, however, that there is some difficulty in rightly determining the objects which we distinctly conceive.

In the next place, from reflecting on the circumstance that I doubted, and that consequently my being was not wholly perfect, (for I clearly saw that it was a greater perfection to know than to doubt,) I was led to inquire whence I had learned to think of something more perfect than myself; and I clearly recognised that I must hold this notion from some Nature which in reality was more perfect. As for the thoughts of many other objects external to me, as of the sky, the earth, light, heat, and a thousand more, I was less at a loss to know whence these came; for since I remarked in them nothing which seemed to render them superior to myself, I could believe that, if these were true, they were dependencies on my own nature, in so far as it possessed a certain perfection, and, if they were false, that I held them from nothing, that is to say, that they were in me because of a certain imperfection of my nature. But this could not be the case with the idea of a Nature more perfect than myself; for to receive it from nothing was a thing manifestly impossible; and, because it is not less repugnant that the more perfect should be an effect of, and dependence on the less perfect, than that something should proceed from nothing, it was equally impossible that I could hold it from myself: accordingly, it but remained that it had been placed in me by a Nature which was in reality more perfect than mine, and which even possessed within itself all the perfections of which I could form any idea; that is to say, in a single word, which was God. And to this I added that, since I knew some perfections which I did not possess, I was not the only being in existence, (I will here, with your permission, freely use the terms of the schools); but, on the contrary, that there was of necessity some other more perfect Being upon whom I was dependent, and from whom I had received all that I possessed; for if I had existed alone, and independently of every other being, so as to have had from myself all the perfection, however little, which I actually possessed, I should have been able, for the same reason, to have had from myself the whole remainder of perfection, of the want of which I was conscious, and thus could of myself have become infinite, eternal, immutable, omniscient, all-powerful, and, in fine, have possessed all the perfection which I could recognise in God. For in order to know the nature of God, (whose existence has been established by the preceding reasonings,) as far as my own nature permitted, I had only to consider in reference to all the properties of which I found in my mind some idea, whether their possession was a mark of perfection; and I was assured that no one which indicated any imperfection was in him, and that none of the rest was awanting. Thus I perceived that doubt, inconstancy, sadness, and such like, could not be found in God, since I myself would have been happy to be free from them. Besides, I had ideas of many sensible and corporeal things; for although I might suppose that

I was dreaming, and that all which I saw or imagined was false, I could not, nevertheless, deny that the ideas were in reality in my thoughts. But, because I had already very clearly recognised in myself that the intelligent nature is distinct from the corporeal, and as I observed that all composition is an evidence of dependency, and that a state of dependency is manifestly a state of imperfection, I therefore determined that it could not be a perfection in God to be compounded of these two natures, and that consequently he was not so compounded; but that if there were any bodies in the world, or even any intelligences, or other natures that were not wholly perfect, their existence depended on his power in such a way that they could not subsist without him for a single moment.

I was disposed straightway to search for other truths; and when I had represented to myself the object of the geometers, which I conceived to be a continuous body, or a space indefinitely extended in length, breadth, and height or depth, divisible into divers parts which admit of different figures and sizes, and of being moved or transposed in all manner of ways, (for all this the geometers suppose to be in the object they contemplate,) I went over some of their simplest demonstrations. And, in the first place, I observed, that the great certitude which by common consent is accorded to these demonstrations, is founded solely upon this, that they are clearly conceived in accordance with the rules I have already laid down. In the next place, I perceived that there was nothing at all in these demonstrations which could assure me of the existence of their object: thus, for example, supposing a triangle to be given, I distinctly perceived that its three angles were necessarily equal to two right angles, but I did not on that account perceive anything which could assure me that any triangle existed: while, on the contrary, recurring to the examination of the idea of a Perfect Being, I found that the existence of the Being was comprised in the idea in the same way that the equality of its three angles to two right angles is comprised in the idea of a triangle, or as in the idea of a sphere, the equidistance of all points on its surface from the centre, or even still more clearly; and that consequently it is at least as certain that God, who is this Perfect Being, is, or exists, as any demonstration of Geometry can be.

But the reason which leads many to persuade themselves that there is a difficulty in knowing this truth, and even also in knowing what their mind really is, is that they never raise their thoughts above sensible objects, and are so accustomed to consider nothing except by way of imagination, which is a mode of thinking limited to material objects, that all that is not imaginable seems to them not intelligible. The truth of this is sufficiently manifest from the single circumstance, that the philosophers of the Schools accept as a maxim that there is nothing in the Understanding which was not previously in the Senses, in which however it is certain that the ideas of God and of the soul have never been; and it appears to me that they who make use of their imagination to comprehend these ideas do exactly the same thing as if, in order to hear sounds or smell odours, they strove to avail themselves of their eyes; unless indeed that there is this difference, that the sense of sight does not afford us an inferior assurance to those of smell or hearing; in place of which, neither our imagination nor our senses can give us assurance of anything unless our Understanding intervene.

Finally, if there be, still persons who are not sufficiently persuaded of the existence of God and of the soul, by the reasons I have adduced, I am desirous that they should know that all the other propositions, of the truth of which they deem themselves perhaps more assured, as that we have a body, and that there exist stars and an earth, and such like, are less certain; for, although we have a moral assurance of these things, which is so strong that there is an appearance of extravagance in doubting of their existence, yet at the same time no one, unless his intellect is impaired, can deny, when the question relates to a metaphysical certitude, that there is sufficient reason to exclude entire assurance, in the observation that when asleep we can in the same way imagine ourselves possessed of another body and that we see other stars and another earth, when there is nothing of the kind. For how do we know that the thoughts which occur in dreaming are false rather than those other which we experience when awake, since the former are often not less vivid and distinct than the latter? And though men of the highest genius study this question as long as they please, I do not believe that they will be able to give any reason which can be sufficient to remove this doubt, unless they presuppose the existence of God. For, in the first place, even the principle which I have already taken as a rule, viz., that all the things which we clearly and distinctly conceive are true, is certain only because God is or exists, and because he is a Perfect Being, and because all that we possess is derived from him: whence it follows that our ideas or notions, which to the extent of their clearness and distinctness are real, and proceed from God, must to that extent be true. Accordingly, whereas we not unfrequently have ideas or notions in which some falsity is contained, this can only be the case with such as are to some extent confused and obscure, and in this proceed from nothing, (participate of negation,) that is, exist in us thus confused because we are not wholly perfect. And it is evident that it is not less repugnant that falsity or imperfection, in so far as it is imperfection, should proceed from God, than that truth or perfection should proceed from nothing. But if we did not know that all which we possess of real and true proceeds from a Perfect and Infinite Being, however clear and distinct our ideas might be, we should have no ground on that account for the assurance that they possessed the perfection of being true.

But after the knowledge of God and of the soul has rendered us certain of this rule, we can easily understand that the truth of the thoughts we experience when awake, ought not in the slightest degree to be called in question on account of the illusions of our dreams. For if it happened that an individual, even when asleep, had some very distinct idea, as, for example, if a geometer should discover some new demonstration, the circumstance of his being asleep would not militate against its truth; and as for the most ordinary error of our dreams, which consists in their representing to us various objects in the same way as our external senses, this is not prejudicial, since it leads us very properly to suspect the truth of the ideas of sense; for we are not unfrequently deceived in the same manner when awake; as when persons in the jaundice see all objects yellow, or when the stars or bodies at a great distance appear to us much smaller than they are. For, in fine, whether awake or asleep, we ought never to allow ourselves to be persuaded of the truth of anything unless on the evidence of our Reason. And it must be noted that I say of our Reason, and not of our imagination or of our senses: thus, for example, although we very clearly see the sun, we ought not therefore to determine that it is only of the size which our sense of sight presents; and we may very distinctly imagine the head of a lion joined to the body of a goat, without being therefore shut up to the conclusion that a chimæra exists; for it is not a dictate of Reason that what we thus see or imagine is in reality existent; but it plainly tells us that all our ideas or notions contain in them some truth; for otherwise it could not be that God, who is wholly perfect and veracious, should have placed them in us. And because our reasonings are never so clear or so complete during sleep as when we are awake, although sometimes the acts of our imagination are then as lively and distinct, if not more so than in our waking moments, Reason further dictates that, since all our thoughts cannot be true because of our partial imperfection, those possessing truth must infallibly be found in the experience of our waking moments rather than in that of our dreams.

PART V

I WOULD here willingly have proceeded to exhibit the whole chain of truths which I deduced from these primary; but as with a view to this it would have been necessary now to treat of many questions in dispute among the learned, with whom I do not wish to be embroiled, I believe that it will be better for me to refrain from this exposition, and only mention in general what these truths are, that the more judicious may be able to determine whether a more special account of them would conduce to the public advantage. I have ever remained firm in my original resolution to suppose no other principle than that of which I have recently availed myself in demonstrating the existence of God and of the soul, and to accept as true nothing that did not appear to me more clear and certain than the demonstrations of the geometers had formerly appeared; and yet I venture to state that not only have I found means to satisfy myself in a short time on all the principal difficulties which are usually treated of in Philosophy, but I have also observed certain laws established in nature by God in such a manner, and of which he has impressed on our minds such notions, that after we have reflected sufficiently upon these, we cannot doubt that they are accurately observed in all that exists or takes place in the world: and farther, by considering the concatenation of these laws, it appears to me that I have discovered many truths more useful and more important than all I had before learned, or even had expected to learn.

But because I have essayed to expound the chief of these discoveries in a Treatise which certain considerations prevent me from publishing, I cannot make the results known more conveniently than by here giving a summary of the contents of this Treatise. It was my design to comprise in it all that, before I set myself to write it, I thought I knew of the nature of material objects. But like the painters who, finding themselves unable to represent equally well on a plain surface all the different faces of a solid body, select one of the chief, on which alone they make the light fall, and throwing the rest into the shade, allow them to appear only in so far as they can be seen while looking at the principal one; so, fearing lest I should not be able to comprise in my discourse all that was in my mind, I resolved to expound singly, though at considerable length, my opinions regarding light; then to take the opportunity of adding something on the sun and the fixed stars, since light almost wholly proceeds from them; on the heavens since they transmit it; on the planets, comets, and earth, since they reflect it; and particularly on all the bodies that are upon the earth, since they are either coloured, or transparent, or luminous; and finally on man, since he is the spectator of these objects. Further, to enable me to cast this variety of subjects somewhat into the shade, and to express my judgment regarding them with greater freedom, without being necessitated to adopt or refute the opinions of the learned, I resolved to leave all the people here to their disputes, and to speak only of what would happen in a new world, if God were now to create somewhere in the imaginary spaces matter sufficient to compose one, and were to agitate variously and confusedly the different parts of this matter, so that there resulted a chaos as disordered as the poets ever feigned, and after that did nothing more than lend his ordinary concurrence to nature, and allow her to act in accordance with the laws which he had established. On this supposition, I, in the first place, described this matter, and essayed to represent it in such a manner that to my mind there can be nothing clearer and more intelligible, except what has been recently said regarding God and the soul; for I even expressly supposed that it possessed none of those forms or qualities which are so debated in the Schools, nor in general anything the knowledge of which is not so natural to our minds that no one can so much as imagine himself ignorant of it. Besides, I have pointed out what are the laws of nature; and, with no other principle upon which to found my reasonings except the infinite perfection of God, I endeavoured to demonstrate all those about which there could be any room for doubt, and to prove that they are such, that even if God had created more worlds, there could have been none in which these laws were not observed.

Thereafter, I showed how the greatest part of the matter of this chaos must, in accordance with these laws, dispose and arrange itself in such a way as to present the appearance of heavens; how in the meantime some of its parts must compose an earth and some planets and comets, and others a sun and fixed stars. And, making a digression at this stage on the subject of light, I expounded at considerable length what the nature of that light must be which is found in the sun and the stars, and how thence in an instant of time it traverses the immense spaces of the heavens, and how from the planets and comets it is reflected towards the earth. To this I likewise added much respecting the substance, the situation, the motions, and all the different qualities of these heavens and stars; so that I thought I had said enough respecting them to show that there is nothing observable in the heavens or stars of our system that must not, or at least may not appear precisely alike in those of the system which I described. I came next to speak of the earth in particular, and to show how, even though I had expressly supposed that God had given no weight to the matter of which it is composed, this should not prevent all its parts from tending exactly to its centre; how with water and air on its surface, the disposition of the heavens and heavenly bodies, more especially of the moon, must cause a flow and ebb, like in all its circumstances to that observed in our seas, as also a certain current both of water and air from east to west, such as is likewise observed between the tropics; how the mountains, seas, fountains, and rivers might naturally be formed in it, and the metals produced in the mines, and the plants grow in the fields; and in general, how all the bodies which are commonly denominated mixed or composite might be generated: and, among other things in the discoveries alluded to, inasmuch as besides the stars, I knew nothing except fire which produces light, I spared no pains to set forth all that pertains to its nature,—the manner of its production and support, and to explain how heat is sometimes found without light, and light without heat; to show how it can induce various colours upon different bodies and other diverse qualities; how it reduces some to a liquid state and hardens others; how it can consume almost all bodies, or convert them into ashes and smoke; and finally, how from these ashes, by the mere intensity of its action, it forms glass: for as this transmutation of ashes into glass appeared to me as wonderful as any other in nature, I took a special pleasure in describing it.

I was not, however, disposed, from these circumstances, to conclude that this world had been created in the manner I described; for it is much more likely that God made it at the first such as it was to be. But this is certain, and an opinion commonly received among theologians, that the action by which he now sustains it is the same with that by which he originally created it; so that even although he had from the beginning given it no other form than that of chaos, provided only he had established certain laws of nature, and had lent it his concurrence to enable it to act as it is wont to do, it may be believed, without discredit to the miracle of creation, that, in this way alone, things purely material might, in course of time, have become such as we observe them at present; and their nature is much more easily conceived when they are beheld coming in this manner gradually into existence, than when they are only considered as produced at once in a finished and perfect state.

From the description of inanimate bodies and plants, I passed to animals, and particularly to man. But since I had not as yet sufficient knowledge to enable me to treat of these in the same manner as of the rest, that is to say, by deducing effects from their causes, and by showing from what elements and in what manner Nature must produce them, I remained satisfied with the supposition that God formed the body of man wholly like to one of ours, as well in the external shape of the members as in the internal conformation of the organs, of the same matter with that I had described, and at first placed in it no Rational Soul, nor any other principle, in room of the Vegetative or Sensitive Soul, beyond kindling in the heart one of those fires without light, such as I had already described, and which I thought was not different from the heat in hay that has been heaped together before it is dry, or that which causes fermentation in new wines before they are run clear of the fruit. For, when I examined the kind of functions which might, as consequences of this supposition, exist in this body, I found precisely all those which may exist in us independently of all power of thinking, and consequently without being in any measure owing to the soul; in other words, to that part of us which is distinct from the body, and of which it has been said above that the nature distinctively consists in thinking,—functions in which the animals void of Reason may be said wholly to resemble us; but among which I could not discover any of those that, as dependent on thought alone, belong to us as men, while, on the other hand, I did afterwards discover these as soon as I supposed God to have created a Rational Soul, and to have annexed it to this body in a particular manner which I described.

But, in order to show how I there handled this matter, I mean here to give the explication of the motion of the heart and arteries, which, as the first and most general motion observed in animals, will afford the means of readily determining what should be thought of all the rest. And that there may be less difficulty in understanding what I am about to say on this subject, I advise those who are not versed in Anatomy, before they commence the perusal of these observations, to take the trouble of getting dissected in their presence the heart of some large animal possessed of lungs, (for this is throughout sufficiently like the human,) and to have shewn to them its two ventricles or cavities: in the first place, that in the right side, with which correspond two very ample tubes, viz., the hollow vein, (*vena cava,*) which is the principal receptacle of the blood, and the trunk of the tree, as it were, of which all the other veins in the body are branches; and the arterial vein, (*vena arteriosa,*) inappropriately so denominated, since it is in truth only an artery, which, taking its rise in the heart, is divided, after passing out from it, into many branches which presently disperse themselves all over the lungs; in the second place, the cavity in the left side, with which correspond in the same manner two canals in size equal to or larger than the preceding, viz., the venous artery, (*arteria venosa,*) likewise inappropriately thus designated, because it is simply a vein which comes from the lungs, where it is divided into many branches, interlaced with those of the arterial vein, and those of the tube called the windpipe, through which the air we breathe enters; and the great artery which, issuing from the heart, sends it branches all over the body. I should wish also that such persons were carefully shewn the eleven pellicles which, like so many small valves, open and shut the four orifices that are in these two cavities, viz., three at the entrance of the hollow vein, where they are disposed in such a manner as by no means to prevent the blood which it contains from flowing into the right ventricle of the heart, and yet exactly to prevent its flowing out; three at the entrance to the arterial vein, which, arranged in a manner exactly the opposite of the former, readily permit the blood contained in this cavity to pass into the lungs, but hinder that contained in the lungs from returning to this cavity; and, in like manner, two others at the mouth of the venous artery, which allow the blood from the lungs to flow into the left cavity of the heart, but preclude its return; and three at the mouth of the great artery, which suffer the blood to flow from the heart, but prevent its reflux. Nor do we need to seek any other reason for the number of these pellicles beyond this that the orifice of the venous artery being of an oval shape from the nature of its situation, can be adequately closed with two, whereas the others being round are more conveniently closed with three. Besides, I wish such persons to observe that the grand artery and the arterial vein are of much harder and firmer texture than the venous artery and the hollow vein; and that the two last expand before entering the heart, and there form, as it were, two pouches denominated the auricles of the heart, which are composed of a substance similar to that of the heart itself; and that there is always more warmth in the heart than in any other part of the body; and, finally, that this heat is capable of causing any drop of blood that passes into the cavities rapidly to expand and dilate, just as all liquors do when allowed to fall drop by drop into a highly heated vessel.

For, after these things, it is not necessary for me to say anything more with a view to explain the motion of the heart, except that when its cavities are not full of blood, into these the blood of necessity flows,—from the hollow vein into the right, and from the venous artery into the left; because these two vessels are always full of blood, and their orifices, which are turned towards the heart, cannot then be closed. But as soon as two drops of blood have thus passed, one into each of the cavities, these drops which cannot but be very large, because the orifices through which they pass are wide, and the vessels from which they come full of blood, are immediately rarefied, and dilated by the heat they meet with. In this way they cause the whole heart to expand, and at the same time press home and shut the five small valves that are at the entrances of the two vessels from which they flow, and thus prevent any more blood from coming down into the heart, and becoming more and more rarefied, they push open the six small valves that are in the orifices of the other two vessels, through which they pass out, causing in this way all the branches of the arterial vein and of the grand artery to expand almost simultaneously with the heart—which immediately thereafter begins to contract, as do also the arteries, because the blood that has entered them has cooled, and the six small. valves close, and the five of the hollow vein and of the venous artery open anew and allow a passage to other two drops of blood, which cause the heart and the arteries again to expand as before. And, because the blood which thus enters into the heart passes through these two pouches called auricles, it thence happens that their motion is the contrary of that of the heart, and that when it expands they contract. But lest those who are ignorant of the force of mathematical demonstrations, and who are not accustomed to distinguish true reasons from mere verisimilitudes, should venture, without examination, to deny what has been said, I wish it to be considered that the motion which I have now explained follows as necessarily from the very arrangement of the parts, which may be observed in the heart by the eye alone, and from the heat which may be felt with the fingers, and from the nature of the blood as learned from experience, as does the motion of a clock from the power, the situation, and shape of its counter-weights and wheels.

But if it be asked how it happens that the blood in the veins, flowing in this way continually into the heart, is not exhausted, and why the arteries do not become too full, since all the blood which passes through the heart flows into them, I need only mention in reply what has been written by a physician[1] of England, who has the honour of having broken the ice on this subject, and of having been the first to teach that there are many small passages at the extremities of the arteries, through which the blood received by them from the heart passes into the small branches of the veins, whence it again returns to the heart; so that its course amounts

[1] Harvey.

precisely to a perpetual circulation. Of this we have abundant proof in the ordinary experience of surgeons, who, by binding the arm with a tie of moderate straitness above the part where they open the vein, cause the blood to flow more copiously than it would have done without any ligature; whereas quite the contrary would happen were they to bind it below; that is, between the hand and the opening, or were to make the ligature above the opening very tight. For it is manifest that the tie, moderately straitened, while adequate to hinder the blood already in the arm from returning towards the heart by the veins, cannot on that account prevent new blood from coming forward through the arteries, because these are situated below the veins, and their coverings, from their greater consistency, are more difficult to compress; and also that the blood which comes from the heart tends to pass through them to the hand with greater force than it does to return from the hand to the heart through the veins. And since the latter current escapes from the arm by the opening made in one of the veins, there must of necessity be certain passages below the ligature, that is, towards the extremities of the arm through which it can come thither from the arteries. This physician likewise abundantly establishes what he has advanced respecting the motion of the blood, from the existence of certain pellicles, so disposed in various places along the course of the veins, in the manner of small valves, as not to permit the blood to pass from the middle of the body towards the extremities, but only to return from the extremities to the heart; and farther, from experience which shows that all the blood which is in the body may flow out of it in a very short time through a single artery that has been cut, even although this had been closely tied in the immediate neighbourhood of the heart, and cut between the heart and the ligature, so as to prevent the supposition that the blood flowing out of it could come from any other quarter than the heart.

But there are many other circumstances which evince that what I have alleged is the true cause of the motion of the blood: thus, in the first place, the difference that is observed between the blood which flows from the veins, and that from the arteries, can only arise from this, that being rarefied, and, as it were, distilled by passing through the heart, it is thinner, and more vivid, and warmer immediately after leaving the heart, in other words, when in the arteries, than it was a short time before passing into either, in other words, when it was in the veins; and if attention be given, it will be found that this difference is very marked only in the neighbourhood of the heart; and is not so evident in parts more remote from it. In the next place, the consistency of the coats of which the arterial vein and the great artery are composed, sufficiently shows that the blood is impelled against them with more force than against the veins. And why should the left cavity of the heart and the great artery be wider and larger than the right cavity and the arterial vein, were it not that the blood of the venous artery, having only been in the lungs after it has passed through the heart, is thinner, and rarefies more readily, and in a higher degree, than the blood which proceeds immediately from the hollow vein? And what can physicians conjecture from feeling the pulse unless they know that according as the blood changes its nature it can be rarefied by the warmth of the heart, in a higher or lower degree, and more or less quickly than before? And if it be inquired how this heat is communicated to the other members, must it not be admitted that this is effected by means of the blood, which, passing through the heart, is there heated anew, and thence diffused over all the body? Whence it happens, that if the blood be withdrawn from any part, the heat is likewise withdrawn by the same means; and although the heart were as hot as glowing iron, it would not be capable of warming the feet and hands as at present, unless it continually sent thither new blood. We likewise perceive from this, that the true use of respiration is to bring sufficient fresh air into the lungs, to cause the blood which flows into them from the right ventricle of the heart, where it has been rarefied and, as it were, changed into vapours, to become thick, and to convert it anew into blood, before it flows into the left cavity, without which process it would be unfit for the nourishment of the fire that is there. This receives confirmation from the circumstance, that it is observed of animals destitute of lungs that they have also but one cavity in the heart, and that in children who cannot use them while in the womb, there is a hole through which the blood flows from the hollow vein into the left cavity of the heart, and a tube through which it passes from the arterial vein into the grand artery without passing through the lung. In the next place, how could digestion be carried on in the stomach unless the heart communicated heat to it through the arteries, and along with this certain of the more fluid parts of the blood, which assists in the dissolution of the food that has been taken in? Is not also the operation which converts the juice of food into blood easily comprehended, when it is considered that it is distilled by passing and repassing through the heart perhaps more than one or two hundred times in a day? And what more need be adduced to explain nutrition, and the production of the different humours of the body, beyond saying, that the force with which the blood, in being rarefied, passes from the heart towards the extremities of the arteries, causes certain of its parts to remain in the members at which they arrive, and there occupy the place of some others expelled by them; and that according to the situation, shape, or smallness of the pores with which they meet, some rather than others flow into certain parts, in the same way that some sieves are observed to act, which, by being variously perforated, serve to separate different species of grain? And, in the last place, what above all is here worthy of observation, is the generation of the animal spirits, which are like a very subtle wind, or rather a very pure and vivid flame which, continually ascending in great abundance from the heart to the brain, thence penetrates through the nerves into the muscles, and gives motion to all the members; so that to account for other parts of the blood which, as most agitated and penetrating, are the fittest to compose these spirits, proceeding towards the brain, it is not necessary to suppose any other cause, than simply, that the arteries which carry them thither proceed from the heart in the most direct lines, and that, according to the rules of Mechanics, which are the same with those of Nature, when many objects tend at once to the same point where there is not sufficient room for all, (as is the case with the parts of the blood which flow forth from the left cavity of the heart and tend towards the brain,) the weaker and less agitated parts must necessarily be driven aside from that point by the stronger which alone in this way reach it.

I had expounded all these matters with sufficient minuteness in the Treatise which I formerly thought of publishing. And after these, I had shewn what must be the fabric of the nerves and muscles of the human body to give the animal spirits contained in it the power to move the members, as when we see heads shortly after they have been struck off still move and bite the earth, although no longer animated; what changes must take place in the brain to produce waking, sleep, and dreams; how light, sounds, odours, tastes, heat, and all the other qualities of external objects impress it with different ideas by means of the senses; how hunger, thirst, and the other internal affections can likewise impress upon it divers ideas; what must be understood by the common sense (*sensus communis*) in which these ideas are received, by the memory which retains them, by the fantasy which can change them in various ways, and out of them compose new ideas, and which, by the same means, distributing the animal spirits through the muscles, can cause the members of such a body to move in as many different ways, and in a manner as suited, whether to the objects that are presented to its senses or to its internal affections, as can take place in our own case apart from the guidance of the will. Nor will this appear at all strange to those who are acquainted with the variety of movements performed by the different automata, or moving machines fabricated by human industry, and that with help of but few pieces compared with the great multitude of bones, muscles, nerves, arteries, veins, and other parts that are found in the body of each animal. Such persons will look upon this body as a machine made by the hands of God, which is incomparably better arranged, and adequate to movements more admirable than is any machine of human invention. And here I specially stayed to show that, were there such machines exactly resembling in organs and outward form an ape or any other irrational animal, we could have no means of knowing that they were in any respect of a different nature from these animals; but if there were machines bearing the image of our bodies, and capable of imitating our actions as far as it is morally possible, there would still remain two most certain tests whereby to know that they were not therefore really men. Of these the first is that they could never use words or other signs arranged in such a manner as is competent to us in order to declare our thoughts to others: for we may easily conceive a machine to be so constructed that it emits vocables, and even that it emits some correspondent to the action upon it of external objects which cause a change in its organs; for example, if touched in a particular place it may demand what we wish to say to it; if in another it may cry out that it is hurt, and such like; but not that it should arrange them variously so as appositely to reply to what is said in its presence, as men of the lowest grade of intellect can do. The second test is, that although such machines might execute many things with equal or perhaps greater perfection than any of us, they would, without doubt, fail in certain others from which it could be discovered that they did not act from knowledge, but solely from the disposition of their organs: for while Reason is an universal instrument that is alike available on every occasion, these organs, on the contrary, need a particular arrangement for each particular action; whence it must be morally impossible that there should exist in any machine a diversity of organs sufficient to enable it to act in all the occurrences of life, in the way in which our reason enables us to act. Again, by means of these two tests we may likewise know the difference between men and brutes. For it is highly deserving of remark, that there are no men so dull and stupid, not even idiots, as to be incapable of joining together different words, and thereby constructing a declaration by which to make their thoughts understood; and that on the other hand, there is no other animal, however perfect or happily circumstanced which can do the like. Nor does this inability arise from want of organs: for we observe that magpies and parrots can utter words like ourselves, and are yet unable to speak as we do, that is, so as to show that they understand what they say; in place of which men born deaf and dumb, and thus not less, but rather more than the brutes, destitute of the organs which others use in speaking, are in the habit of spontaneously inventing certain signs by which they discover their thoughts to those who, being usually in their company, have leisure to learn their language. And this proves not only that the brutes have less Reason than man, but that they have none at all: for we see that very little is required to enable a person to speak; and since a certain inequality of capacity is observable among animals of the same species, as well as among men, and since some are more capable of being instructed than others, it is incredible that the most perfect ape or parrot of its species, should not in this be equal to the most stupid infant of its kind, or at least to one that was crack-brained, unless the soul of brutes were of a nature wholly different from ours. And we ought not to confound speech with the natural movements which indicate the passions, and can be imitated by machines as well as manifested by animals; nor must it be thought with certain of the ancients, that the brutes speak, although we do not understand their language. For if such were the case, since they are endowed with many organs analogous to ours, they could as easily communicate their thoughts to us as to their fellows. It is also very worthy of remark, that, though there are many animals which manifest more industry than we in certain of their actions, the same animals are yet observed to show none at all in many others: so that the circumstance that they do better than we does not prove that they are endowed with mind, for it would thence follow that they possessed greater Reason than any of us, and could surpass us in all things; on the contrary, it rather proves that they are destitute of Reason, and that it is Nature which acts in them according to the disposition of their organs: thus it is seen, that a clock composed only of wheels and weights can number the hours and measure time more exactly than we with all our skill.

I had after this described the Reasonable Soul, and shewn that it could by no means be educed from the power of matter, as the other things of which I had spoken but that it must be expressly created; and that it is not sufficient that it be lodged in the human body exactly like a pilot in a ship, unless perhaps to move its members, but that it is necessary for it to be joined and united more closely to the body, in order to have sensations and appetites similar to ours, and thus constitute a real man. I here entered, in conclusion, upon the subject of the soul at considerable length, because it is of the greatest moment: for after the error of those who deny the existence of God, an error which I think I have already sufficiently refuted, there is none that is more powerful in leading feeble minds astray from the straight path of virtue than the supposition that the soul of the brutes is of the same nature with our own; and consequently that after this life we have nothing to hope for or fear, more than flies and ants; in place of which, when we know how far they differ we much better comprehend the reasons which establish that the soul is of a nature wholly independent of the body, and that consequently it is not liable to die with the latter; and, finally, because no other causes are observed capable of destroying it, we are naturally led thence to judge that it is immortal.

PART VI

THREE years have now elapsed since I finished the Treatise containing all these matters; and I was beginning to revise it, with the view to put it into the hands of a printer, when I learned that persons to whom I greatly defer, and whose authority over my actions is hardly less influential than is my own Reason over my thoughts, had condemned a certain doctrine in Physics, published a short time previously by another individual,[1] to which I will not say that I adhered, but only that, previously to their censure, I had observed in it nothing which I could imagine to be prejudicial either to religion or to the state, and nothing therefore which would have prevented me from giving expression to it in writing, if Reason had persuaded me of its truth; and this led me to fear lest among my own doctrines likewise some one might be found in which I had departed from the truth, notwithstanding the great care I have always taken not to accord belief to new opinions of which I had not the most certain demonstrations, and not to give expression to aught that might tend to the hurt of any one. This has been sufficient to make me alter my purpose of publishing them; for although the reasons by which I had been induced to take this resolution were very strong, yet my inclination, which has always been hostile to writing books, enabled me immediately to discover other considerations sufficient to excuse me for not undertaking the task. And these reasons, on one side and the other, are such, that not only is it in some measure my interest here to state them, but that of the public, perhaps, to know them.

I have never made much account of what has proceeded from my own mind; and so long as I gathered no other advantage from the Method I employ beyond satisfying myself on some difficulties belonging to the speculative sciences, or endeavouring to regulate my actions according to the principles it taught me, I never thought myself bound to publish anything respecting it. For in what

---

[1] Galileo.—*Tr.*

regards manners, every one is so full of his own wisdom, that there might be found as many reformers as heads, if any were allowed to take upon themselves the task of mending them, except those whom God has constituted the supreme rulers of his people, or to whom he has given sufficient grace and zeal to be prophets; and although my speculations greatly pleased myself, I believed that others had theirs, which perhaps pleased them still more. But as soon as I had acquired some general notions respecting Physics, and beginning to make trial of them in various particular difficulties, had observed how far they can carry us, and how much they differ from the principles that have been employed up to the present time, I believed that I could not keep them concealed without sinning grievously against the law by which we are bound to promote, as far as in us lies, the general good of mankind. For by them I perceived it to be possible to arrive at knowledge highly useful in life; and in room of the Speculative Philosophy usually taught in the Schools, to discover a Practical, by means of which, knowing the force and action of fire, water, air, the stars, the heavens, and all the other bodies that surround us, as distinctly as we know the various crafts of our artizans, we might also apply them in the same way to all the uses to which they are adapted, and thus render ourselves the lords and possessors of nature. And this is a result to be desired, not only in order to the invention of an infinity of arts, by which we might be enabled to enjoy without any trouble the fruits of the earth, and all its comforts, but also and especially for the preservation of health, which is without doubt, of all the blessings of this life, the first and fundamental one; for the mind is so intimately dependent upon the condition and relation of the organs of the body, that if any means can ever be found to render men wiser and more ingenious than hitherto, I believe that it is in Medicine they must be sought for. It is true that the science of Medicine, as it now exists, contains few things whose utility is very remarkable: but without any wish to depreciate it, I am confident that there is no one, even among those whose profession it is, who does not admit that all at present known in it is almost nothing in comparison of what remains to be discovered; and that we could free ourselves from an infinity of maladies of body as well as of mind, and perhaps also even from the debility of age, if we had sufficiently ample knowledge of their causes, and of all the remedies provided for us by Nature. But since I designed to employ my whole life in the search after so necessary a Science, and since I had fallen in with a path which seems to me such, that if any one follow it he must inevitably reach the end desired, unless he be hindered either by the shortness of life or the want of experiments, I judged that there could be no more effectual provision against these two impediments than if I were faithfully to communicate to the public all the little I might myself have found, and incite men of superior genius to strive to proceed farther, by contributing, each according to his inclination and ability, to the experiments which it would be necessary to make, and also by informing the public of all they might discover, so that, by the last beginning where those before them had left off, and thus connecting the lives and labours of many, we might collectively proceed much farther than each by himself could do.

I remarked, moreover, with respect to experiments, that they become always more necessary the more one is advanced in knowledge; for, at the commencement, it is better to make use only of what is spontaneously presented to our senses, and of which we cannot remain ignorant, provided we bestow on it any reflection, however slight, than to concern ourselves about more uncommon and recondite phænomena: the reason of which is, that the more uncommon often only mislead us so long as the causes of the more ordinary are still unknown; and the circumstances upon which they depend are almost always so special and minute as to be highly difficult to detect. But in this I have adopted the following order: first, I have essayed to find in general the principles, or first causes of all that is or can be in the world, without taking into consideration for this end anything but God himself who has created it, and without educing them from any other source than from certain germs of truths naturally existing in our minds. In the second place, I examined what were the first and most ordinary effects that could be deduced from these causes; and it appears to me that, in this way I have found heavens, stars, an earth, and even on the earth, water, air, fire, minerals, and some other things of this kind, which of all others are the most common and simple, and hence the easiest to know. Afterwards, when I wished to descend to the more particular, so many diverse objects presented themselves to me, that I believed it to be impossible for the human mind to distinguish the forms or species of bodies that are upon the earth, from an infinity of others which might have been, if it had pleased God to place them there, or consequently to apply them to our use, unless we rise to causes through their effects, and avail ourselves of many particular experiments. Thereupon, turning over in my mind all the objects that had ever been presented to my senses, I freely venture to state that I have never observed any which I could not satisfactorily explain by the principles I had discovered. But it is necessary also to confess that the power of nature is so ample and vast, and these principles so simple and general, that I have hardly observed a single particular effect which I cannot at once recognize as capable of being deduced in many different modes from the principles, and that my greatest difficulty usually is to discover in which of these modes the effect is dependent upon them; for out of this difficulty I cannot otherwise extricate myself than by again seeking certain experiments, which may be such that their result is not the same, if it is in the one of these modes that we must explain it, as it would be if it were to be explained in the other. As to what remains, I am now in a position to discern, as I think, with sufficient clearness what course must be taken to make the majority of those experiments which may conduce to this end: but I perceive likewise that they are such and so numerous, that neither my hands nor my income, though it were a thousand times larger than it is, would be sufficient for them all; so that, according as henceforward I shall have the means of making more or fewer experiments, I shall in the same proportion make greater or less progress in the knowledge of nature. This was what I had hoped to make known by the Treatise I had written, and so clearly to exhibit the advantage that would thence accrue to the public, as to induce all who have the common good of man at heart, that is, all who are virtuous in truth, and not merely in appearance, or according to opinion, as well to communicate to me the experiments they had already made, as to assist me in those that remain to be made.

But since that time other reasons have occurred to me, by which I have been led to change my opinion, and to think that I ought indeed to go on committing to writing all the results which I deemed of any moment, as soon as I should have tested their truth, and to bestow the same care upon them as I would have done had it been my design to publish them. This course commended itself to me, as well because I thus afforded myself more ample inducement to examine them thoroughly, for doubtless that is always more narrowly scrutinized which we believe will be read by many, than that which is written merely for our private use, (and frequently what has seemed to me true when I first conceived it, has appeared false when I have set about committing it to writing;) as because I thus lost no opportunity of advancing the interests of the public, as far as in me lay, and since thus likewise, if my writings possess any value, those into whose hands they may fall after my death may be able to put them to what use they deem proper. But I resolved by no means to consent to their publication during my lifetime, lest either the oppositions or the controversies to which they might give rise, or even the reputation, such as it might be, which they would acquire for me, should be any occasion of my losing the time that I had set apart for my own improvement. For though it be true that every one is bound to promote to the extent of his ability the good of others, and that to be useful to no one is really to be worthless, yet it is likewise true that our cares ought to extend beyond the present; and it is good to omit doing what might perhaps bring some profit to the living, when we have in view the accomplishment of other ends that will be of much greater advantage to posterity. And in truth, I am quite willing it should be known that the little I have hitherto learned is almost nothing in comparison with that of which I am ignorant, and to the knowledge of which I do not despair of being able to attain; for it is much the same with those who gradually discover truth in the Sciences, as with those who when growing rich find less difficulty in making great acquisitions, than they formerly experienced when poor in making acquisitions of much smaller amount. Or they may be compared to the commanders of armies, whose forces usually increase in proportion to their victories, and who need greater prudence to keep together the residue of their troops after a defeat than after a victory to take towns and provinces. For he truly engages in battle who endeavors to surmount all the difficulties and errors which prevent him from reaching the knowledge of truth, and he is overcome in fight who admits a false opinion touching a matter of any generality and importance, and he requires thereafter much more skill to recover his former position than to make great advances when once in possession of thoroughly ascertained principles. As for myself, if I have succeeded in discovering any truths in the Sciences, (and I trust that what is contained in this volume will show that I have found some,) I can declare that they are but the consequences and results of five or six principal difficulties which I have surmounted, and my encounters with which I reckoned as battles in which victory declared for me. I will not hesitate even to avow my belief that nothing further is wanting to enable me fully to realize my designs than to gain two or three similar victories; and that I am not so far advanced in years but that, according to the ordinary course of nature, I may still have sufficient leisure for this end. But I conceive myself the more bound to husband the time that remains, the greater my expectation of being able to employ it aright, and I should doubtless have much to rob me of it, were I to publish the principles of my Physics: for although they are almost all so evident that to assent to them no more is needed than simply to understand them, and although there is not one of them of which I do not expect to be able to give demonstration, yet, as it is impossible that they can be in accordance with all the diverse opinions of others, I foresee that I should frequently be turned aside from my grand design, on occasion of the opposition which they would be sure to awaken.

It may be said, that these oppositions would be useful both in making me aware of my errors, and, if my speculations contain anything of value, in bringing others to a fuller understanding of it; and still farther, as many can see better than one, in leading others who are now beginning to avail themselves of my principles, to assist me in turn with their discoveries. But though I recognise my extreme liability to error, and scarce ever trust to the first thoughts which occur to me, yet the experience I have had of possible objections to my views prevents me from anticipating any profit from them. For I have already had frequent proof of the judgments, as well of those I esteemed friends, as of some others to whom I thought I was an object of indifference, and even of some whose malignity and envy would, I knew, determine them to endeavour to discover what partiality concealed from the eyes of my friends. But it has rarely happened that anything has been objected to me which I had myself altogether overlooked, unless it were something far removed from the subject: so that I have never met with a single critic of my opinions who did not appear to me either less rigorous or less equitable than myself. And further, I have never observed that any truth before unknown has been brought to light by the disputations that are practised in the Schools; for while each strives for the victory, each is much more occupied in making the best of mere verisimilitude, than in weighing the reasons on both sides of the question; and those who have been long good advocates are not afterwards on that account the better judges.

As for the advantage that others would derive from the communication of my thoughts, it could not be very great; because I have not yet so far prosecuted them as that much does not remain to be added before they can be applied to practice. And I think I may say without vanity, that if there is any one who can carry them out that length, it must be myself rather than another: not that there may not be in the world many minds incomparably superior to mine, but because one cannot so well seize a thing and make it one's own, when it has been learned from another, as when one has himself discovered it. And so true is this of the present subject that, though I have often explained some of my opinions to persons of much acuteness, who, whilst I was speaking, appeared to understand them very distinctly, yet, when they repeated them, I have observed that they almost always changed them to such an extent that I could no longer acknowledge them as mine. I am glad, by the way, to take this opportunity of requesting posterity never to believe on hearsay that anything has proceeded from me which has not been published by myself; and I am not at all astonished at the extravagances attributed to those ancient philosophers whose own writings we do not possess; whose thoughts, however, I do not on that account suppose to have been really absurd, seeing they were among the ablest men of their times, but only that these have been falsely represented to us. It is observable, accordingly, that scarcely in a single instance has any one of their disciples surpassed them; and I am quite sure that the most devoted of the present followers of Aristotle would think themselves happy if they had as much knowledge of nature as he possessed, were it even under the condition that they should never afterwards attain to higher. In this respect they are like the ivy which never strives to rise above the tree that sustains it, and which frequently even returns downwards when it has reached the top; for it seems to me that they also sink, in other words, render themselves less wise than they would be if they gave up study, who, not contented with knowing all that is intelligibly explained in their author, desire in addition to find in him the solution of many difficulties of which he says not a word, and never perhaps so much as thought. Their fashion of philosophizing, however, is well suited to persons whose abilities fall below mediocrity; for the obscurity of the distinctions and principles of which they make use enables them to speak of all things with as much confidence as if they really knew them, and to defend all that they say on any subject against the most subtle and skilful, without its being possible for any one to convict them of error. In this they seem to me to be like a blind man, who, in order to fight on equal terms with a person that sees, should have made him descend to the bottom of an intensely dark cave: and I may say that such persons have an interest in my refraining from publishing the principles of the Philosophy of which I make use; for, since these are of a kind the simplest and most evident, I should, by publishing them, do much the same as if I were to throw open the windows, and allow the light of day to enter the cave into which the combatants had descended. But even superior men have no reason for any great anxiety to know these principles, for if what they desire is to be able to speak of all things, and to acquire a reputation for learning, they will gain their end more easily by remaining satisfied with the appearance of truth, which can be found without much difficulty in all sorts of matters, than by seeking the truth itself which unfolds itself but slowly and that only in some departments, while it obliges us, when we have to speak of others, freely to confess our ignorance. If, however, they prefer the knowledge of some few truths to the vanity of appearing ignorant of none, as such knowledge is undoubtedly much to be preferred, and, if they choose to follow a course similar to mine, they do not require for this that I should say anything more than I have already said in this Discourse. For if they are capable of making greater advancement than I have made, they will much more be able of themselves to discover all that I believe myself to have found; since as I have never examined aught except in order, it is certain that what yet remains to be discovered is in itself more difficult and recondite, than that which I have already been enabled to find, and the gratification would be much less in learning it from me than in discovering it for themselves. Besides this, the habit which they will acquire, by seeking first what is easy, and then passing onward slowly and step by step to the more difficult, will benefit them more than all my instructions. Thus, in my own case, I am persuaded that if I had been taught from my youth all the truths of which I have since sought out demonstrations, and had thus learned them without labour, I should never, perhaps, have known any beyond these; at least, I should never have acquired the habit and the facility which I think I possess in always discovering new truths in proportion as I give myself to the search. And, in a single word, if there is any work in the world which cannot be so well finished by another as by him who has commenced it, it is that at which I labour.

It is true, indeed, as regards the experiments which may conduce to this end, that one man is not equal to the task of making them all; but yet he can advantageously avail himself, in this work, of no hands besides his own, unless those of artisans, or parties of the same kind, whom he could pay, and whom the hope of gain (a means of great efficacy) might stimulate to accuracy in the performance of what was prescribed to them. For as to those who, through curiosity or a desire of learning, of their own accord, perhaps, offer

him their services, besides that in general their promises exceed
their performance, and that they sketch out fine designs of which
not one is ever realized, they will, without doubt, expect to be
compensated for their trouble by the explication of some difficulties,
or, at least, by compliments and useless speeches, in which he cannot
spend any portion of his time without loss to himself. And as for
the experiments that others have already made, even although these
parties should be willing of themselves to communicate them to him,
(which is what those who esteem them secrets will never do,) the
experiments are, for the most part, accompanied with so many
circumstances and superfluous elements, as to make it exceedingly
difficult to disentangle the truth from its adjuncts; besides, he will
find almost all of them so ill described, or even so false, (because
those who made them have wished to see in them only such facts
as they deemed conformable to their principles,) that, if in the
entire number there should be some of a nature suited to his purpose,
still their value could not compensate for the time that would be
necessary to make the selection. So that if there existed any one
whom we assuredly knew to be capable of making discoveries of
the highest kind, and of the greatest possible utility to the public;
and if all other men were therefore eager by all means to assist him
in successfully prosecuting his designs, I do not see that they could
do aught else for him beyond contributing to defray the expenses
of the experiments that might be necessary; and for the rest, prevent
his being deprived of his leisure by the unseasonable interruptions
of any one. But besides that I neither have so high an opinion of
myself as to be willing to make promise of anything extraordinary,
nor feed on imaginations so vain as to fancy that the public must
be much interested in my designs; I do not, on the other hand, own
a soul so mean as to be capable of accepting from any one a favour
of which it could be supposed that I was unworthy.

These considerations taken together were the reason why, for
the last three years, I have been unwilling to publish the Treatise
I had on hand, and why I even resolved to give publicity during
my life to no other that was so general, or by which the principles
of my Physics might be understood. But since then, two other
reasons have come into operation that have determined me here

to subjoin some particular specimens, and give the public some account of my doings and designs. Of these considerations, the first is, that if I failed to do so, many who were cognizant of my previous intention to publish some writings, might have imagined that the reasons which induced me to refrain from so doing, were less to my credit than they really are; for although I am not immoderately desirous of glory, or even, if I may venture so to say, although I am averse from it in so far as I deem it hostile to repose which I hold in greater account than aught else, yet, at the same time, I have never sought to conceal my actions as if they were crimes, nor made use of many precautions that I might remain unknown; and this partly because I should have thought such a course of conduct a wrong against myself, and partly because it would have occasioned me some sort of uneasiness which would again have been contrary to the perfect mental tranquillity which I court. And forasmuch as, while thus indifferent to the thought alike of fame or of forgetfulness, I have yet been unable to prevent myself from acquiring some sort of reputation, I have thought it incumbent on me to do my best to save myself at least from being ill-spoken of. The other reason that has determined me to commit to writing these specimens of philosophy is, that I am becoming daily more and more alive to the delay which my design of self-instruction suffers, for want of the infinity of experiments I require, and which it is impossible for me to make without the assistance of others; and, without flattering myself so much as to expect the public to take a large share in my interests, I am yet unwilling to be found so far wanting in the duty I owe to myself as to give occasion to those who shall survive me to make it matter of reproach against me some day, that I might have left them many things in a much more perfect state than I have done, had I not too much neglected to make them aware of the ways in which they could have promoted the accomplishment of my designs.

And I thought that it was easy for me to select some matters which should neither be obnoxious to much controversy, nor should compel me to expound more of my principles than I desired, and which should yet be sufficient clearly to exhibit what I can or cannot accomplish in the Sciences. Whether or not I have succeeded in this it is not for me to say; and I do not wish to forestall the judgments of others by speaking myself of my writings; but it will gratify me if they be examined, and, to afford the greater inducement to this, I request all who may have any objections to make to them, to take the trouble of forwarding these to my publisher, who will give me notice of them, that I may endeavour to subjoin at the same time my reply; and in this way readers seeing both at once will more easily determine where the truth lies; for I do not engage in any case to make prolix replies, but only with perfect frankness to avow my errors if I am convinced of them, or if I cannot perceive them, simply to state what I think is required for defence of the matters I have written, adding thereto no explication of any new matter that it may not be necessary to pass without end from one thing to another.

If some of the matters of which I have spoken in the beginning of the Dioptrics and Meteorics should offend at first sight, because I call them hypotheses and seem indifferent about giving proof of them, I request a patient and attentive reading of the whole, from which I hope those hesitating will derive satisfaction; for it appears to me that the reasonings are so mutually connected in these Treatises, that, as the last are demonstrated by the first which are their causes, the first are in their turn demonstrated by the last which are their effects. Nor must it be imagined that I here commit the fallacy which the logicians call a circle; for since experience renders the majority of these effects most certain, the causes from which I deduce them do not serve so much to establish their reality as to explain their existence; but on the contrary, the reality of the causes is established by the reality of the effects. Nor have I called them hypotheses with any other end in view except that it may be known that I think I am able to deduce them from those first truths which I have already expounded; and yet that I have expressly determined not to do so, to prevent a certain class of minds from thence taking occasion to build some extravagant Philosophy upon what they may take to be my principles, and my being blamed for it. I refer to those who imagine that they can master in a day all that another has taken twenty years to think out, as soon as he has spoken two or three words to them on the subject; or who are the more liable to error and the less capable of perceiving truth in very proportion as they are more subtle and lively. As to the opinions which are truly and wholly mine, I offer no apology for them as new,—persuaded as I am that if their reasons be well considered they will be found to be so simple and so conformed to common sense as to appear less extraordinary and less paradoxical than any others which can be held on the same subjects; nor do I even boast of being the earliest discoverer of any of them, but only of having adopted them, neither because they had nor because they had not been held by others, but solely because Reason has convinced me of their truth.

Though artisans may not be able at once to execute the invention which is explained in the Dioptrics, I do not think that any one on that account is entitled to condemn it; for since address and practice are required in order so to make and adjust the machines described by me as not to overlook the smallest particular, I should not be less astonished if they succeeded on the first attempt than if a person were in one day to become an accomplished performer on the guitar, by merely having excellent sheets of music set up before him. And if I write in French, which is the language of my country, in preference to Latin, which is that of my preceptors, it is because I expect that those who make use of their unprejudiced natural Reason will be better judges of my opinions than those who give heed to the writings of the ancients only; and as for those who unite good sense with habits of study, whom alone I desire for judges, they will not, I feel assured, be so partial to Latin as to refuse to listen to my reasonings merely because I expound them in the vulgar Tongue.

In conclusion, I am unwilling here to say anything very specific of the progress which I expect to make for the future in the Sciences, or to bind myself to the public by any promise which I am not certain of being able to fulfil; but this only will I say, that I have resolved to devote what time I may still have to live to no other occupation than that of endeavouring to acquire some knowledge of Nature, which shall be of such a kind as to enable us therefrom to deduce rules in Medicine of greater certainty than those at present in use; and that my inclination is so much opposed to all other pursuits, especially to such as cannot be useful to some without being hurtful to others, that if, by any circumstances, I had been constrained to engage in such, I do not believe that I should have been able to succeed. Of this I here make a public declaration, though well aware that it cannot serve to procure for me any consideration in the world, which, however, I do not in the least affect; and I shall always hold myself more obliged to those through whose favour I am permitted to enjoy my retirement without interruption than to any who might offer me the highest earthly preferments.

LETTERS ON THE ENGLISH
(LETTRES PHILOSOPHIQUES)

BY

VOLTAIRE

INTRODUCTORY NOTE

FRANÇOIS-MARIE AROUET, known by his assumed name of Voltaire, was born at Paris, November 21, 1694. His father was a well-to-do notary, and François was educated under the Jesuits in the Collège Louis-le-Grand. He began writing verse early, and was noted for his freedom of speech, a tendency which led to his being twice exiled from Paris and twice imprisoned in the Bastile. In 1726 he took refuge in England, and the two years spent there had great influence upon his later development. Some years after his return he became historiographer of France, and gentleman of the king's bedchamber; from 1750 to 1753 he lived at the court of Frederick the Great, with whom he ultimately quarreled; and he spent the last period of his life, from 1758 to 1778, on his estate of Ferney, near Geneva, where he produced much of his best work. He died at Paris, May 30, 1778.

It will be seen that Voltaire's active life covers nearly the whole eighteenth century, of which he was the dominant and typical literary figure. Every department of letters then in vogue was cultivated by him; in all he showed brilliant powers; and in several he reached all but the highest rank. Apart from his "Henriade," an epic on the classical model, and the burlesque "La Pucelle," most of his verse belongs to the class of satire, epigram, and vers de société. Of real poetical quality it has little, but abundant technical cleverness. For the stage he was the most prominent writer of the time, his most successful dramas including "Zaïre," "Œdipe," "La Mort de César," "Alzire," and "Merope." His chief contribution in this field was the development of the didactic and philosophic element. In prose fiction he wrote "Zadig," "Candide," and many admirable short stories; in history, his "Age of Louis XIV" is only the best known of four or five considerable works; in criticism, his commentary on Corneille is notable. His scientific and philosophic interests are to some extent indicated in the following "Letters," which also show his admiration for the tolerance and freedom of speech in England, which it was his greatest service to strive to introduce into his own country.

LETTERS ON THE ENGLISH
(LETTRES PHILOSOPHIQUES)

LETTER I

ON THE QUAKERS

I WAS of opinion that the doctrine and history of so extraordinary a people were worthy the attention of the curious. To acquaint myself with them I made a visit to one of the most eminent Quakers in England, who, after having traded thirty years, had the wisdom to prescribe limits to his fortune and to his desires, and was settled in a little solitude not far from London. Being come into it, I perceived a small but regularly built house, vastly neat, but without the least pomp of furniture. The Quaker who owned it was a hale, ruddy complexioned old man, who had never been afflicted with sickness because he had always been insensible to passions, and a perfect stranger to intemperance. I never in my life saw a more noble or a more engaging aspect than his. He was dressed like those of his persuasion, in a plain coat without pleats in the sides, or buttons on the pockets and sleeves; and had on a beaver, the brims of which were horizontal like those of our clergy. He did not uncover himself when I appeared, and advanced towards me without once stooping his body; but there appeared more politeness in the open, humane air of his countenance, than in the custom of drawing one leg behind the other, and taking that from the head which is made to cover it. "Friend," says he to me, "I perceive thou art a stranger, but if I can do any thing for thee, only tell me." "Sir," said I to him, bending forwards and advancing, as is usual with us, one leg towards him, "I flatter myself that my just curiosity will not give you the least offense, and that you'll do me the honour to inform me of the particulars of your religion." "The people of thy country," replied the Quaker, "are too full of their bows and compliments, but I never yet met with one of them who had so much curiosity as thy self. Come in, and let us first dine together." I still continued to make some very unseasonable ceremonies, it not being easy to disengage one's self at once from habits we have been long used to; and after taking part in a frugal meal, which began and ended with a prayer to God, I began to question my courteous host. I opened with that which good Catholics have more than once made to Huguenots. "My dear sir," said I, "were you ever baptized?" "I never was," replied the Quaker, "nor any of my brethren." "Zounds!" said I to him, "you are not Christians, then." "Friend," replies the old man in a soft tone of voice, "swear not; we are Christians, and endeavour to be good Christians, but we are not of opinion that the sprinkling water on a child's head makes him a Christian." "Heavens!" said I, shocked at his impiety, "you have then forgot that Christ was baptised by St. John." "Friend," replies the mild Quaker once again, "swear not; Christ indeed was baptised by John, but He himself never baptised anyone. We are the disciples of Christ, not of John." I pitied very much the sincerity of my worthy Quaker, and was absolutely for forcing him to get himself christened. "Were that all," replied he very gravely, "we would submit cheerfully to baptism, purely in compliance with thy weakness, for we don't condemn any person who uses it; but then we think that those who profess a religion of so holy, so spiritual a nature as that of Christ, ought to abstain to the utmost of their power from the Jewish ceremonies." "O unaccountable!" said I: "what! baptism a Jewish ceremony?" "Yes, my friend," says he, "so truly Jewish, that a great many Jews use the baptism of John to this day. Look into ancient authors, and thou wilt find that John only revived this practice; and that it had been used by the Hebrews, long before his time, in like manner as the Mahometans imitated the Ishmaelites in their pilgrimages to Mecca. Jesus indeed submitted to the baptism of John, as He had suffered Himself to be circumcised; but circumcision and the washing with water ought to be abolished by the baptism of Christ, that baptism of the Spirit, that ablution of the soul, which is the salvation of mankind. Thus the forerunner said, 'I indeed baptise you with water unto repentance; but He that cometh after me is mightier than I, whose shoes I am not worthy to bear: He shall baptise you with the Holy Ghost and with fire.' Likewise Paul, the great apostle of the Gentiles, writes as follows to the Corinthians, 'Christ sent me not to baptise, but to preach the Gospel;' and indeed Paul never baptised but two persons with water, and that very much against his inclinations. He circumcised his disciple Timothy, and the other disciples likewise circumcised all who were willing to submit to that carnal ordinance. "But art thou circumcised?" added he. "I have not the honour to be so," said I. "Well, friend," continued the Quaker, "thou art a Christian without being circumcised, and I am one without being baptised." Thus did this pious man make a wrong, but very specious application of four or five texts of Scripture which seemed to favour the tenets of his sect; but at the same time forgot very sincerely a hundred texts which made directly against them. I had more sense than to contest with him, since there is no possibility of convincing an enthusiast. A man should never pretend to inform a lover of his mistress's faults, no more than one who is at law of the badness of his cause; nor attempt to win over a fanatic by strength of reasoning. Accordingly I waived the subject.

"Well," said I to him, "what sort of a communion have you?" "We have none like that thou hintest at among us," replied he. "How! no communion?" said I. "Only that spiritual one," replied he, "of hearts." He then began again to throw out his texts of Scripture; and preached a most eloquent sermon against that ordinance. He harangued in a tone as though he had been inspired, to prove that the sacraments were merely of human invention, and that the word "sacrament" was not once mentioned in the Gospel. "Excuse," said he, "my ignorance, for I have not employed a hundredth part of the arguments which might be brought to prove the truth of our religion, but these thou thyself mayest peruse in the Exposition of our Faith written by Robert Barclay. It is one of the best pieces that ever was penned by man; and as our adversaries confess it to be of dangerous tendency, the arguments in it must necessarily be very convincing." I promised to peruse this piece, and my Quaker imagined he had already made a convert of me. He afterwards gave me an account in few words of some singularities which make this sect the contempt of others. "Confess," said he, "that it was very difficult for thee to refrain from laughter, when I answered all thy civilities without uncovering my head, and at the same time said 'thee' and 'thou' to thee. However, thou appearest to me too well read not to know that in Christ's time no nation was so ridiculous as to put the plural number for the singular. Augustus Cæsar himself was spoken to in such phrases as these: 'I love thee,' 'I beseech thee,' 'I thank thee;' but he did not allow any person to call him 'Domine,' sir. It was not till many ages after that men would have the word 'you,' as though they were double, instead of 'thou' employed in speaking to them; and usurped the flattering titles of lordship, of eminence, and of holiness, which mere worms bestow on other worms by assuring them that they are with a most profound respect, and an infamous falsehood, their most obedient humble servants. It is to secure ourselves more strongly from such a shameless traffic of lies and flattery, that we 'thee' and 'thou' a king with the same freedom as we do a beggar, and salute no person; we owing nothing to mankind but charity, and to the laws respect and obedience.

"Our apparel is also somewhat different from that of others, and this purely, that it may be a perpetual warning to us not to imitate them. Others wear the badges and marks of their several dignities, and we those of Christian humility. We fly from all assemblies of pleasure, from diversions of every kind, and from places where gaming is practised; and, indeed, our case would be very deplorable, should we fill with such levities as those I have mentioned the heart which ought to be the habitation of God. We never swear, not even in a court of justice, being of opinion that the most holy name of God ought not to be prostituted in the miserable contests betwixt man and man. When we are obliged to appear before a magistrate upon other people's account (for lawsuits are unknown among the Friends), we give evidence to the truth by sealing it with our yea or nay; and the judges believe us on our bare affirmation, whilst so many other Christians forswear themselves on the holy Gospels. We never war or fight in any case; but it is not that we are afraid, for so far from shuddering at the thoughts of death, we on the contrary bless the moment which unites us with the Being of Beings; but the reason of our not using the outward sword is, that we are neither wolves, tigers, nor mastiffs, but men and Christians. Our God, who has commanded us to love our enemies, and to suffer without repining, would certainly not permit us to cross the seas, merely because murderers clothed in scarlet, and wearing caps two foot high, enlist citizens by a noise made with two little sticks on an ass's skin extended. And when, after a victory is gained, the whole city of London is illuminated; when the sky is in a blaze with fireworks, and a noise is heard in the air, of thanksgivings, of bells, of organs, and of the cannon, we groan in silence, and are deeply affected with sadness of spirit and brokenness of heart, for the sad havoc which is the occasion of those public rejoicings."

LETTER II

ON THE QUAKERS

SUCH was the substance of the conversation I had with this very singular person; but I was greatly surprised to see him come the Sunday following and take me with him to the Quakers' meeting. There are several of these in London, but that which he carried me to stands near the famous pillar called The Monument. The brethren were already assembled at my entering it with my guide. There might be about four hundred men and three hundred women in the meeting. The women hid their faces behind their fans, and the men were covered with their broad-brimmed hats. All were seated, and the silence was universal. I passed through them, but did not perceive so much as one lift up his eyes to look at me. This silence lasted a quarter of an hour, when at last one of them rose up, took off his hat, and, after making a variety of wry faces and groaning in a most lamentable manner, he, partly from his nose and partly from his mouth, threw out a strange, confused jumble of words (borrowed, as he imagined, from the Gospel) which neither himself nor any of his hearers understood. When this distorter had ended his beautiful soliloquy, and that the stupid, but greatly edified, congregation were separated, I asked my friend how it was possible for the judicious part of their assembly to suffer such a babbling? "We are obliged," said he, "to suffer it, because no one knows when a man rises up to hold forth whether he will be moved by the Spirit or by folly. In this doubt and uncertainty we listen patiently to everyone; we even allow our women to hold forth. Two or three of these are often inspired at one and the same time, and it is then that a most charming noise is heard in the Lord's house." "You have, then, no priests?" said I to him. "No, no, friend," replies the Quaker, "to our great happiness." Then opening one of the Friends' books, as he called it, he read the following words in an emphatic tone:—" 'God forbid we should presume to ordain anyone to receive the Holy Spirit on the Lord's Day to the prejudice of the rest of the brethren.' Thanks to the Almighty, we are the only people upon earth that have no priests. Wouldst thou deprive us of so happy a distinction? Why should we abandon our babe to mercenary nurses, when we ourselves have milk enough for it? These mercenary creatures would soon domineer in our houses and destroy both the mother and the babe. God has said, 'Freely you have received, freely give.' Shall we, after these words, cheapen, as it were, the Gospel, sell the Holy Ghost, and make of an assembly of Christians a mere shop of traders? We don't pay a set of men clothed in black to assist our poor, to bury our dead, or to preach to the brethren. These offices are all of too tender a nature for us ever to entrust them to others." "But how is it possible for you," said I, with some warmth, "to know whether your discourse is really inspired by the Almighty?" "Whosoever," says he, "shall implore Christ to enlighten him, and shall publish the Gospel truths, he may feel inwardly, such a one may be assured that he is inspired by the Lord." He then poured forth a numberless multitude of Scripture texts which proved, as he imagined, that there is no such thing as Christianity without an immediate revelation, and added these remarkable words: "When thou movest one of thy limbs, is it moved by thy own power? Certainly not; for this limb is often sensible to involuntary motions. Consequently He who created thy body gives motion to this earthly tabernacle. And are the several ideas of which thy soul receives the impression formed by thyself? Much less are they, since these pour in upon thy mind whether thou wilt or no; consequently thou receivest thy ideas from Him who created thy soul. But as He leaves thy affections at full liberty, He gives thy mind such ideas as thy affections may deserve; if thou livest in God, thou actest, thou thinkest in God. After this thou needest only but open thine eyes to that light which enlightens all mankind, and it is then thou wilt perceive the truth, and make others perceive it." "Why, this," said I, "is Malebranche's doctrine to a tittle." "I am acquainted with thy Malebranche," said he; "he had something of the Friend in him, but was not enough so." These are the most considerable particulars I learned concerning the doctrine of the Quakers. In my next letter I shall acquaint you with their history, which you will find more singular than their opinions.

LETTER III

ON THE QUAKERS

You have already heard that the Quakers date from Christ, who, according to them, was the first Quaker. Religion, say these, was corrupted a little after His death, and remained in that state of corruption about sixteen hundred years. But there were always a few Quakers concealed in the world, who carefully preserved the sacred fire, which was extinguished in all but themselves, until at last this light spread itself in England in 1642.

It was at the time when Great Britain was torn to pieces by the intestine wars which three or four sects had raised in the name of God, that one George Fox, born in Leicestershire, and son to a silk weaver, took it into his head to preach, and, as he pretended, with all the requisites of a true apostle—that is, without being able either to read or write. He was about twenty-five years of age, irreproachable in his life and conduct, and a holy madman. He was equipped in leather from head to foot, and travelled from one village to another, exclaiming against war and the clergy. Had his invectives been levelled against the soldiery only he would have been safe enough, but he inveighed against ecclesiastics. Fox was seized at Derby, and being carried before a justice of peace, he did not once offer to pull off his leathern hat, upon which an officer gave him a great box of the ear, and cried to him, "Don't you know you are to appear uncovered before his worship?" Fox presented his other cheek to the officer, and begged him to give him another box for God's sake. The justice would have had him sworn before he asked him any questions. "Know, friend," says Fox to him, "that I never swear." The justice, observing he "thee'd" and "thou'd" him, sent him to the House of Correction, in Derby, with orders that he should be whipped there. Fox praised the Lord all the way he went to the House of Correction, where the justice's order was executed with the utmost severity. The men who whipped this enthusiast were greatly surprised to hear him beseech them to give him a few more lashes for the good of his soul. There was no need of entreating these people; the lashes were repeated, for which Fox thanked them very cordially, and began to preach. At first the spectators fell a-laughing, but they afterwards listened to him; and as enthusiasm is an epidemical distemper, many were persuaded, and those who scourged him became his first disciples. Being set at liberty, he ran up and down the country with a dozen proselytes at his heels, still declaiming against the clergy, and was whipped from time to time. Being one day set in the pillory, he harangued the crowd in so strong and moving a manner, that fifty of the auditors became his converts, and he won the rest so much in his favour that, his head being freed tumultuously from the hole where it was fastened, the populace went and searched for the Church of England clergyman who had been chiefly instrumental in bringing him to this punishment, and set him on the same pillory where Fox had stood.

Fox was bold enough to convert some of Oliver Cromwell's soldiers, who thereupon quitted the service and refused to take the oaths. Oliver, having as great a contempt for a sect which would not allow its members to fight, as Sixtus Quintus had for another sect, *Dove non si chiavava*,[1] began to persecute these new converts. The prisons were crowded with them, but persecution seldom has any other effect than to increase the number of proselytes. These came, therefore, from their confinement more strongly confirmed in the principles they had imbibed, and followed by their gaolers, whom they had brought over to their belief. But the circumstances which contributed chiefly to the spreading of this sect were as follows:— Fox thought himself inspired, and consequently was of opinion that he must speak in a manner different from the rest of mankind. He thereupon began to writhe his body, to screw up his face, to hold in

[1] "Where there were no clandestine doings."

his breath, and to exhale it in a forcible manner, insomuch that the priestess of the Pythian god at Delphos could not have acted her part to better advantage. Inspiration soon became so habitual to him that he could scarce deliver himself in any other manner. This was the first gift he communicated to his disciples. These aped very sincerely their master's several grimaces, and shook in every limb the instant the fit of inspiration came upon them, whence they were called Quakers. The vulgar attempted to mimic them; they trembled, they spake through the nose, they quaked and fancied themselves inspired by the Holy Ghost. The only thing now wanting was a few miracles, and accordingly they wrought some.

Fox, this modern patriarch, spoke thus to a justice of peace before a large assembly of people: "Friend, take care what thou dost; God will soon punish thee for persecuting His saints." This magistrate, being one who besotted himself every day with bad beer and brandy, died of an apoplexy two days after, the moment he had signed a *mittimus* for imprisoning some Quakers. The sudden death with which this justice was seized was not ascribed to his intemperance, but was universally looked upon as the effect of the holy man's predictions; so that this accident made more converts to Quakerism than a thousand sermons and as many shaking fits could have done. Oliver, finding them increase daily, was desirous of bringing them over to his party, and for that purpose attempted to bribe them by money. However, they were incorruptible, which made him one day declare that this religion was the only one he had ever met with that had resisted the charms of gold.

The Quakers were several times persecuted under Charles II.; not upon a religious account, but for refusing to pay the tithes, for "thee-ing" and "thouing" the magistrates, and for refusing to take the oaths enacted by the laws.

At last Robert Barclay, a native of Scotland, presented to the King, in 1675, his "Apology for the Quakers," a work as well drawn up as the subject could possibly admit. The dedication to Charles II. is not filled with mean, flattering encomiums, but abounds with bold touches in favour of truth and with the wisest counsels. "Thou hast tasted," said he to the King at the close of his epistle dedicatory, "of prosperity and adversity; thou knowest what it is to be banished thy native country; to be overruled as well as to rule and sit upon the throne; and, being oppressed, thou hast reason to know how hateful the oppressor is both to God and man. If, after all these warnings and advertisements, thou dost not turn unto the Lord with all thy heart, but forget Him who remembered thee in thy distress, and give up thyself to follow lust and vanity, surely great will be thy condemnation.

"Against which snare, as well as the temptation of those that may or do feed thee and prompt thee to evil, the most excellent and prevalent remedy will be, to apply thyself to that light of Christ which shineth in thy conscience, which neither can nor will flatter thee nor suffer thee to be at ease in thy sins, but doth and will deal plainly and faithfully with thee, as those that are followers thereof have plainly done.—Thy faithful friend and subject, Robert Barclay."

A more surprising circumstance is, that this epistle, written by a private man of no figure, was so happy in its effects, as to put a stop to the persecution.

LETTER IV

ON THE QUAKERS

ABOUT this time arose the illustrious William Penn, who established the power of the Quakers in America, and would have made them appear venerable in the eyes of the Europeans, were it possible for mankind to respect virtue when revealed in a ridiculous light. He was the only son of Vice-Admiral Penn, favourite of the Duke of York, afterwards King James II.

William Penn, at twenty years of age, happening to meet with a Quaker[1] in Cork, whom he had known at Oxford, this man made a proselyte of him; and William being a sprightly youth, and naturally eloquent, having a winning aspect, and a very engaging carriage, he soon gained over some of his intimates. He carried matters so far, that he formed by insensible degrees a society of young Quakers, who met at his house; so that he was at the head of a sect when a little above twenty.

[1] Thomas Loe.

Being returned, after his leaving Cork, to the Vice-Admiral his father, instead of falling upon his knees to ask his blessing, he went up to him with his hat on, and said, "Friend, I am very glad to see thee in good health." The Vice-Admiral imagined his son to be crazy, but soon finding he was turned Quaker, he employed all the methods that prudence could suggest to engage him to behave and act like other people. The youth made no other answer to his father, than by exhorting him to turn Quaker also. At last his father confined himself to this single request, viz., "that he should wait upon the King and the Duke of York with his hat under his arm, and should not 'thee' and 'thou' them." William answered, "that he could not do these things, for conscience' sake," which exasperated his father to such a degree, that he turned him out of doors. Young Penn gave God thanks for permitting him to suffer so early in His cause, after which he went into the city, where he held forth, and made a great number of converts.

The Church of England clergy found their congregations dwindle away daily; and Penn being young, handsome, and of a graceful stature, the court as well as the city ladies flocked very devoutly to his meeting. The patriarch, George Fox, hearing of his great reputation, came to London (though the journey was very long) purely to see and converse with him. Both resolved to go upon missions into foreign countries, and accordingly they embarked for Holland, after having left labourers sufficient to take care of the London vineyard.

Their labours were crowned with success in Amsterdam, but a circumstance which reflected the greatest honour on them, and at the same time put their humility to the greatest trial, was the reception they met with from Elizabeth, the Princess Palatine, aunt to George I. of Great Britain, a lady conspicuous for her genius and knowledge, and to whom Descartes had dedicated his Philosophical Romance.

She was then retired to The Hague, where she received these Friends, for so the Quakers were at that time called in Holland. This princess had several conferences with them in her palace, and she at last entertained so favourable an opinion of Quakerism, that they confessed she was not far from the kingdom of heaven. The Friends sowed likewise the good seed in Germany, but reaped very little fruit; for the mode of "theeing" and "thouing" was not approved of in a country where a man is perpetually obliged to employ the titles of "highness" and "excellency." William Penn returned soon to England upon hearing of his father's sickness, in order to see him before he died. The Vice-Admiral was reconciled to his son, and though of a different persuasion, embraced him tenderly. William made a fruitless exhortation to his father not to receive the sacrament, but to die a Quaker, and the good old man entreated his son William to wear buttons on his sleeves, and a crape hatband in his beaver, but all to no purpose.

William Penn inherited very large possessions, part of which consisted in Crown debts due to the Vice-Admiral for sums he had advanced for the sea service. No moneys were at that time more insecure than those owing from the king. Penn was obliged to go more than once, and "thee" and "thou" King Charles and his Ministers, in order to recover the debt; and at last, instead of specie, the Government invested him with the right and sovereignty of a province of America, to the south of Maryland. Thus was a Quaker raised to sovereign power. Penn set sail for his new dominions with two ships freighted with Quakers, who followed his fortune. The country was then called Pennsylvania from William Penn, who there founded Philadelphia, now the most flourishing city in that country. The first step he took was to enter into an alliance with his American neighbours, and this is the only treaty between those people and the Christians that was not ratified by an oath, and was never infringed. The new sovereign was at the same time the legislator of Pennsylvania, and enacted very wise and prudent laws, none of which have ever been changed since his time. The first is, to injure no person upon a religious account, and to consider as brethren all those who believe in one God.

He had no sooner settled his government, but several American merchants came and peopled this colony. The natives of the country, instead of flying into the woods, cultivated by insensible degrees a friendship with the peaceable Quakers. They loved these foreigners as much as they detested the other Christians who had conquered and laid waste America. In a little time a great number of these savages (falsely so called), charmed with the mild and gentle disposition of their neighbours, came in crowds to William Penn, and besought him to admit them into the number of his vassals. It was very rare and uncommon for a sovereign to be "thee'd" and "thou'd" by the meanest of his subjects, who never took their hats off when they came into his presence; and as singular for a Government to be without one priest in it, and for a people to be without arms, either offensive or defensive; for a body of citizens to be absolutely undistinguished but by the public employments, and for neighbours not to entertain the least jealousy one against the other.

William Penn might glory in having brought down upon earth the so much boasted golden age, which in all probability never existed but in Pennsylvania. He returned to England to settle some affairs relating to his new dominions. After the death of King Charles II., King James, who had loved the father, indulged the same affection to the son, and no longer considered him as an obscure sectary, but as a very great man. The king's politics on this occasion agreed with his inclinations. He was desirous of pleasing the Quakers by annulling the laws made against Nonconformists, in order to have an opportunity, by this universal toleration, of establishing the Romish religion. All the sectarists in England saw the snare that was laid for them, but did not give into it; they never failing to unite when the Romish religion, their common enemy, is to be opposed. But Penn did not think himself bound in any manner to renounce his principles, merely to favour Protestants to whom he was odious, in opposition to a king who loved him. He had established a universal toleration with regard to conscience in America, and would not have it thought that he intended to destroy it in Europe, for which reason he adhered so inviolably to King James, that a report prevailed universally of his being a Jesuit. This calumny affected him very strongly, and he was obliged to justify himself in print. However, the unfortunate King James II., in whom, as in most princes of the Stuart family, grandeur and weakness were equally blended, and who, like them, as much overdid some things as he was short in others, lost his kingdom in a manner that is hardly to be accounted for.

All the English sectarists accepted from William III. and his Parliament the toleration and indulgence which they had refused when offered by King James. It was then the Quakers began to enjoy, by virtue of the laws, the several privileges they possess at this time. Penn having at last seen Quakerism firmly established in his native country, went back to Pennsylvania. His own people and the Americans received him with tears of joy, as though he had been a father who was returned to visit his children. All the laws had been religiously observed in his absence, a circumstance in which no legislator had ever been happy but himself. After having resided some years in Pennsylvania he left it, but with great reluctance, in order to return to England, there to solicit some matters in favour of the commerce of Pennsylvania. But he never saw it again, he dying in Ruscombe, in Berkshire, in 1718.

I am not able to guess what fate Quakerism may have in America, but I perceive it dwindles away daily in England. In all countries where liberty of conscience is allowed, the established religion will at last swallow up all the rest. Quakers are disqualified from being members of Parliament; nor can they enjoy any post or preferment, because an oath must always be taken on these occasions, and they never swear. They are therefore reduced to the necessity of subsisting upon traffic. Their children, whom the industry of their parents has enriched, are desirous of enjoying honours, of wearing buttons and ruffles; and quite ashamed of being called Quakers they become converts to the Church of England, merely to be in the fashion.

Letter V

ON THE CHURCH OF ENGLAND

England is properly the country of sectarists. *Multæ sunt mansiones in domo patris mei* (in my Father's house are many mansions). An Englishman, as one to whom liberty is natural, may go to heaven his own way.

Nevertheless, though every one is permitted to serve God in whatever mode or fashion he thinks proper, yet their true religion, that in which a man makes his fortune, is the sect of Episcopalians or Churchmen, called the Church of England, or simply the Church, by way of eminence. No person can possess an employment either in

England or Ireland unless he be ranked among the faithful, that is, professes himself a member of the Church of England. This reason (which carries mathematical evidence with it) has converted such numbers of Dissenters of all persuasions, that not a twentieth part of the nation is out of the pale of the Established Church. The English clergy have retained a great number of the Romish ceremonies, and especially that of receiving, with a most scrupulous attention, their tithes. They also have the pious ambition to aim at superiority.

Moreover, they inspire very religiously their flock with a holy zeal against Dissenters of all denominations. This zeal was pretty violent under the Tories in the four last years of Queen Anne; but was productive of no greater mischief than the breaking the windows of some meeting-houses and the demolishing of a few of them. For religious rage ceased in England with the civil wars, and was no more under Queen Anne than the hollow noise of a sea whose billows still heaved, though so long after the storm when the Whigs and Tories laid waste their native country, in the same manner as the Guelphs and Ghibellines formerly did theirs. It was absolutely necessary for both parties to call in religion on this occasion; the Tories declared for Episcopacy, and the Whigs, as some imagined, were for abolishing it; however, after these had got the upper hand, they contented themselves with only abridging it.

At the time when the Earl of Oxford and the Lord Bolingbroke used to drink healths to the Tories, the Church of England considered these noblemen as the defenders of its holy privileges. The lower House of Convocation (a kind of House of Commons) composed wholly of the clergy, was in some credit at that time; at least the members of it had the liberty to meet, to dispute on ecclesiastical matters, to sentence impious books from time to time to the flames, that is, books written against themselves. The Ministry which is now composed of Whigs does not so much as allow those gentlemen to assemble, so that they are at this time reduced (in the obscurity of their respective parishes) to the melancholy occupation of praying for the prosperity of the Government whose tranquillity they would willingly disturb. With regard to the bishops, who are twenty-six in all, they still have seats in the House of Lords in spite of the Whigs,

because the ancient abuse of considering them as barons subsists to
this day. There is a clause, however, in the oath which the Government requires from these gentlemen, that puts their Christian patience to a very great trial, viz., that they shall be of the Church of
England as by law established. There are few bishops, deans, or
other dignitaries, but imagine they are so *jure divino;* it is consequently a great mortification to them to be obliged to confess that
they owe their dignity to a pitiful law enacted by a set of profane
laymen. A learned monk (Father Courayer) wrote a book lately to
prove the validity and succession of English ordinations. This book
was forbid in France, but do you believe that the English Ministry
were pleased with it? Far from it. Those damned Whigs don't care
a straw whether the episcopal succession among them hath been
interrupted or not, or whether Bishop Parker was consecrated (as it
is pretended) in a tavern or a church; for these Whigs are much
better pleased that the Bishops should derive their authority from
the Parliament than from the Apostles. The Lord Bolingbroke
observed that this notion of divine right would only make so
many tyrants in lawn sleeves, but that the laws made so many
citizens.

With regard to the morals of the English clergy, they are more
regular than those of France, and for this reason. All the clergy (a
very few excepted) are educated in the Universities of Oxford or
Cambridge, far from the depravity and corruption which reign in the
capital. They are not called to dignities till very late, at a time of life
when men are sensible of no other passion but avarice, that is, when
their ambition craves a supply. Employments are here bestowed
both in the Church and the army, as a reward for long services; and
we never see youngsters made bishops or colonels immediately upon
their laying aside the academical gown; and besides most of the
clergy are married. The stiff and awkward air contracted by them
at the University, and the little familiarity the men of this country
have with the ladies, commonly oblige a bishop to confine himself to,
and rest contented with, his own. Clergymen sometimes take a
glass at the tavern, custom giving them a sanction on this occasion;
and if they fuddle themselves it is in a very serious manner, and
without giving the least scandal.

That fable-mixed kind of mortal (not to be defined), who is neither of the clergy nor of the laity; in a word, the thing called *Abbé* in France; is a species quite unknown in England. All the clergy here are very much upon the reserve, and most of them pedants. When these are told that in France young fellows famous for their dissoluteness, and raised to the highest dignities of the Church by female intrigues, address the fair publicly in an amorous way, amuse themselves in writing tender love songs, entertain their friends very splendidly every night at their own houses, and after the banquet is ended withdraw to invoke the assistance of the Holy Ghost, and call themselves boldly the successors of the Apostles, they bless God for their being Protestants. But these are shameless heretics, who deserve to be blown hence through the flames to old Nick, as Rabelais says, and for this reason I don't trouble myself about them.

LETTER VI

ON THE PRESBYTERIANS

THE Church of England is confined almost to the kingdom whence it received its name, and to Ireland, for Presbyterianism is the established religion in Scotland. This Presbyterianism is directly the same with Calvinism, as it was established in France, and is now professed at Geneva. As the priests of this sect receive but very inconsiderable stipends from their churches, and consequently cannot emulate the splendid luxury of bishops, they exclaim very naturally against honours which they can never attain to. Figure to yourself the haughty Diogenes trampling under foot the pride of Plato. The Scotch Presbyterians are not very unlike that proud though tattered reasoner. Diogenes did not use Alexander half so impertinently as these treated King Charles II.; for when they took up arms in his cause in opposition to Oliver, who had deceived them, they forced that poor monarch to undergo the hearing of three or four sermons every day, would not suffer him to play, reduced him to a state of penitence and mortification, so that Charles soon grew sick of these pedants, and accordingly eloped from them with as much joy as a youth does from school.

A Church of England minister appears as another Cato in presence of a juvenile, sprightly French graduate, who bawls for a whole morning together in the divinity schools, and hums a song in chorus with ladies in the evening; but this Cato is a very spark when before a Scotch Presbyterian. The latter affects a serious gait, puts on a sour look, wears a vastly broad-brimmed hat and a long cloak over a very short coat, preaches through the nose, and gives the name of the whore of Babylon to all churches where the ministers are so fortunate as to enjoy an annual revenue of five or six thousand pounds, and where the people are weak enough to suffer this, and to give them the titles of my lord, your lordship, or your eminence.

These gentlemen, who have also some churches in England, introduced there the mode of grave and severe exhortations. To them is owing the sanctification of Sunday in the three kingdoms. People are there forbidden to work or take any recreation on that day, in which the severity is twice as great as that of the Romish Church. No operas, plays, or concerts are allowed in London on Sundays, and even cards are so expressly forbidden that none but persons of quality, and those we call the genteel, play on that day; the rest of the nation go either to church, to the tavern, or to see their mistresses.

Though the Episcopal and Presbyterian sects are the two prevailing ones in Great Britain, yet all others are very welcome to come and settle in it, and live very sociably together, though most of their preachers hate one another almost as cordially as a Jansenist damns a Jesuit.

Take a view of the Royal Exchange in London, a place more venerable than many courts of justice, where the representatives of all nations meet for the benefit of mankind. There the Jew, the Mahometan, and the Christian transact together, as though they all professed the same religion, and give the name of infidel to none but bankrupts. There the Presbyterian confides in the Anabaptist, and the Churchman depends on the Quaker's word. At the breaking up of this pacific and free assembly, some withdraw to the synagogue, and others to take a glass. This man goes and is baptized in a great tub, in the name of the Father, Son, and Holy Ghost: that man has his son's foreskin cut off, whilst a set of Hebrew words (quite unintelligible to him) are mumbled over his child. Others retire to their churches, and there wait for the inspiration of heaven with their hats on, and all are satisfied.

If one religion only were allowed in England, the Government would very possibly become arbitrary; if there were but two, the people would cut one another's throats; but as there are such a multitude, they all live happy and in peace.

LETTER VII

ON THE SOCINIANS, OR ARIANS, OR ANTITRINITARIANS

THERE is a little sect here composed of clergymen, and of a few very learned persons among the laity, who, though they don't call themselves Arians or Socinians, do yet dissent entirely from St. Athanasius with regard to their notions of the Trinity, and declare very frankly that the Father is greater than the Son.

Do you remember what is related of a certain orthodox bishop, who in order to convince an emperor of the reality of consubstantiation, put his hand under the chin of the monarch's son, and took him by the nose in presence of his sacred majesty? The emperor was going to order his attendants to throw the bishop out of the window, when the good old man gave him this handsome and convincing reason: "Since your majesty," said he, "is angry when your son has not due respect shown him, what punishment do you think will God the Father inflict on those who refuse His Son Jesus the titles due to Him?" The persons I just now mentioned declare that the holy bishop took a very wrong step, that his argument was inconclusive, and that the emperor should have answered him thus: "Know that there are two ways by which men may be wanting in respect to me—first, in not doing honour sufficient to my son; and, secondly, in paying him the same honour as to me."

Be this as it will, the principles of Arius begin to revive, not only in England, but in Holland and Poland. The celebrated Sir Isaac Newton honoured this opinion so far as to countenance it. This philosopher thought that the Unitarians argued more mathematically than we do. But the most sanguine stickler for Arianism is the illustrious Dr. Clark. This man is rigidly virtuous, and of a mild disposition, is more fond of his tenets than desirous of propagating them, and absorbed so entirely in problems and calculations that he is a mere reasoning machine.

It is he who wrote a book which is much esteemed and little understood, on the existence of God, and another, more intelligible, but pretty much contemned, on the truth of the Christian religion. He never engaged in scholastic disputes, which our friend calls venerable trifles. He only published a work containing all the testimonies of the primitive ages for and against the Unitarians, and leaves to the reader the counting of the voices and the liberty of forming a judgment. This book won the doctor a great number of partisans, and lost him the See of Canterbury but, in my humble opinion, he was out in his calculation, and had better have been Primate of all England than merely an Arian parson.

You see that opinions are subject to revolutions as well as empires. Arianism, after having triumphed during three centuries, and been forgot twelve, rises at last out of its own ashes; but it has chosen a very improper season to make its appearance in, the present age being quite cloyed with disputes and sects. The members of this sect are, besides, too few to be indulged the liberty of holding public assemblies, which, however, they will, doubtless, be permitted to do in case they spread considerably. But people are now so very cold with respect to all things of this kind, that there is little probability any new religion, or old one, that may be revived, will meet with favour. Is it not whimsical enough that Luther, Calvin, and Zuinglius, all of 'em wretched authors, should have founded sects which are now spread over a great part of Europe, that Mahomet, though so ignorant, should have given a religion to Asia and Africa, and that Sir Isaac Newton, Dr. Clark, Mr. Locke, Mr. Le Clerc, etc., the greatest philosophers, as well as the ablest writers of their ages, should scarce have been able to raise a little flock, which even decreases daily.

This it is to be born at a proper period of time. Were Cardinal de Retz to return again into the world neither his eloquence nor his intrigues would draw together ten women in Paris. Were Oliver Cromwell, he who beheaded his sovereign, and seized upon the kingly dignity, to rise from the dead, he would be a wealthy City trader, and no more.

LETTER VIII

ON THE PARLIAMENT

THE members of the English Parliament are fond of comparing themselves to the old Romans.

Not long since Mr. Shippen opened a speech in the House of Commons with these words, "The majesty of the people of England would be wounded." The singularity of the expression occasioned a loud laugh; but this gentleman, so far from being disconcerted, repeated the same words with a resolute tone of voice, and the laugh ceased. In my opinion, the majesty of the people of England has nothing in common with that of the people of Rome, much less is there any affinity between their Governments. There is in London a senate, some of the members whereof are accused (doubtless very unjustly) of selling their voices on certain occasions, as was done in Rome; this is the only resemblance. Besides, the two nations appear to me quite opposite in character, with regard both to good and evil. The Romans never knew the dreadful folly of religious wars, an abomination reserved for devout preachers of patience and humility. Marious and Sylla, Cæsar and Pompey, Anthony and Augustus, did not draw their swords and set the world in a blaze merely to determine whether the flamen should wear his shirt over his robe, or his robe over his shirt, or whether the sacred chickens should eat and drink, or eat only, in order to take the augury. The English have hanged one another by law, and cut one another to pieces in pitched battles, for quarrels of as trifling nature. The sects of the Episcopalians and Presbyterians quite distracted these very serious heads for a time. But I fancy they will hardly ever be so silly again, they seeming to be grown wiser at their own expense; and I do not perceive the least inclination in them to murder one another merely about syllogisms, as some zealots among them once did.

But here follows a more essential difference between Rome and England, which gives the advantage entirely to the latter—viz., that the civil wars of Rome ended in slavery, and those of the English in liberty. The English are the only people upon earth who have been able to prescribe limits to the power of kings by resisting them; and who, by a series of struggles, have at last established that wise Government where the Prince is all powerful to do good, and, at the same time, is restrained from committing evil; where the nobles are great without insolence, though there are no vassals; and where the people share in the Government without confusion.

The House of Lords and that of the Commons divide the legislative power under the king, but the Romans had no such balance. The patricians and plebeians in Rome were perpetually at variance, and there was no intermediate power to reconcile them. The Roman senate, who were so unjustly, so criminally proud as not to suffer the plebeians to share with them in anything, could find no other artifice to keep the latter out of the administration than by employing them in foreign wars. They considered the plebeians as a wild beast, whom it behoved them to let loose upon their neighbours, for fear they should devour their masters. Thus the greatest defect in the Government of the Romans raised them to be conquerors. By being unhappy at home, they triumphed over and possessed themselves of the world, till at last their divisions sunk them to slavery.

The Government of England will never rise to so exalted a pitch of glory, nor will its end be so fatal. The English are not fired with the splendid folly of making conquests, but would only prevent their neighbours from conquering. They are not only jealous of their own liberty, but even of that of other nations. The English were exasperated against Louis XIV. for no other reason but because he was ambitious, and declared war against him merely out of levity, not from any interested motives.

The English have doubtless purchased their liberties at a very high price, and waded through seas of blood to drown the idol of arbitrary power. Other nations have been involved in as great calamities, and have shed as much blood; but then the blood they spilt in defence of their liberties only enslaved them the more.

That which rises to a revolution in England is no more than a sedition in other countries. A city in Spain, in Barbary, or in Turkey, takes up arms in defence of its privileges, when immediately it is stormed by mercenary troops, it is punished by executioners, and the rest of the nation kiss the chains they are loaded with. The French are of opinion that the government of this island is more tempestuous than the sea which surrounds it, which indeed is true; but then it is never so but when the king raises the storm—when he attempts to seize the ship of which he is only the chief pilot. The civil wars of France lasted longer, were more cruel, and productive of greater evils than those of England; but none of these civil wars had a wise and prudent liberty for their object.

In the detestable reigns of Charles IX. and Henry III. the whole affair was only whether the people should be slaves to the Guises. With regard to the last war of Paris, it deserves only to be hooted at. Methinks I see a crowd of schoolboys rising up in arms against their master, and afterwards whipped for it. Cardinal de Retz, who was witty and brave (but to no purpose), rebellious without a cause, factious without design, and head of a defenseless party, caballed for caballing's sake, and seemed to foment the civil war merely out of diversion. The parliament did not know what he intended, nor what he did not intend. He levied troops by Act of Parliament, and the next moment cashiered them. He threatened, he begged pardon; he set a price upon Cardinal Mazarin's head, and afterwards congratulated him in a public manner. Our civil wars under Charles VI. were bloody and cruel, those of the League execrable, and that of the Frondeurs[1] ridiculous.

That for which the French chiefly reproach the English nation is the murder of King Charles I., whom his subjects treated exactly as he would have treated them had his reign been prosperous. After all, consider on one side Charles I., defeated in a pitched battle, imprisoned, tried, sentenced to die in Westminster Hall, and then beheaded. And on the other, the Emperor Henry VII., poisoned by his chaplain at his receiving the Sacrament; Henry III. stabbed by a monk; thirty assassinations projected against Henry IV., several of them put in execution, and the last bereaving that great monarch of his life. Weigh, I say, all these wicked attempts and then judge.

---

[1] *Frondeurs,* in its proper sense *Slingers,* and figuratively *Cavillers,* or lovers of contradiction, was a name given to a league or party that opposed the French Ministry; *i. e.,* Cardinal Mazarin, in 1648.

Letter IX

ON THE GOVERNMENT

THAT mixture in the English Government, that harmony between King, Lords, and Commons, did not always subsist. England was enslaved for a long series of years by the Romans, the Saxons, the Danes, and the French successively. William the Conqueror particularly, ruled them with a rod of iron. He disposed as absolutely of the lives and fortunes of his conquered subjects as an eastern monarch; and forbade, upon pain of death, the English either fire or candle in their houses after eight o'clock; whether he did this to prevent their nocturnal meetings, or only to try, by this odd and whimsical prohibition, how far it was possible for one man to extend his power over his fellow-creatures. It is true, indeed, that the English had Parliaments before and after William the Conqueror, and they boast of them, as though these assemblies then called Parliaments, composed of ecclesiastical tyrants and of plunderers entitled barons, had been the guardians of the public liberty and happiness.

The barbarians who came from the shores of the Baltic, and settled in the rest of Europe, brought with them the form of government called States or Parliaments, about which so much noise is made, and which are so little understood. Kings, indeed, were not absolute in those days; but then the people were more wretched upon that very account, and more completely enslaved. The chiefs of these savages, who had laid waste France, Italy, Spain, and England, made themselves monarchs. Their generals divided among themselves the several countries they had conquered, whence sprung those margraves, those peers, those barons, those petty tyrants, who often contested with their sovereigns for the spoils of whole nations. These were birds of prey fighting with an eagle for doves whose blood the victorious was to suck. Every nation, instead of being governed by one master, was trampled upon by a hundred tyrants. The priests soon played a part among them. Before this it had been the fate of the Gauls, the Germans, and the Britons, to be always governed by their Druids and the chiefs of their villages, an ancient kind of barons, not so tyrannical as their successors. These Druids pretended to be mediators between God and man. They enacted laws, they fulminated their excommunications, and sentenced to death. The bishops succeeded, by insensible degrees, to their temporal authority in the Goth and Vandal government. The popes set themselves at their head, and armed with their briefs, their bulls, and reinforced by monks, they made even kings tremble, deposed and assassinated them at pleasure, and employed every artifice to draw into their own purses moneys from all parts of Europe. The weak Ina, one of the tyrants of the Saxon Heptarchy in England, was the first monarch who submitted, in his pilgrimage to Rome, to pay St. Peter's penny (equivalent very near to a French crown) for every house in his dominions. The whole island soon followed his example; England became insensibly one of the Pope's provinces, and the Holy Father used to send from time to time his legates thither to levy exorbitant taxes. At last King John delivered up by a public instrument the kingdom of England to the Pope, who had excommunicated him; but the barons, not finding their account in this resignation, dethroned the wretched King John and seated Louis, father to St. Louis, King of France, in his place. However, they were soon weary of their new monarch, and accordingly obliged him to return to France.

Whilst that the barons, the bishops, and the popes, all laid waste England, where all were for ruling; the most numerous, the most useful, even the most virtuous, and consequently the most venerable part of mankind, consisting of those who study the laws and the sciences, of traders, of artificers, in a word, of all who were not tyrants—that is, those who are called the people: these, I say, were by them looked upon as so many animals beneath the dignity of the human species. The Commons in those ages were far from sharing in the government, they being villains or peasants, whose labour, whose blood, were the property of their masters who entitled themselves the nobility. The major part of men in Europe were at that time what they are to this day in several parts of the world— they were villains or bondsmen of lords—that is, a kind of cattle bought and sold with the land. Many ages passed away before justice could be done to human nature—before mankind were conscious that it was abominable for many to sow, and but few reap. And was not France very happy, when the power and authority of those petty robbers was abolished by the lawful authority of kings and of the people?

Happily, in the violent shocks which the divisions between kings and the nobles gave to empires, the chains of nations were more or less heavy. Liberty in England sprang from the quarrels of tyrants. The barons forced King John and King Henry III. to grant the famous Magna Charta, the chief design of which was indeed to make kings dependent on the Lords; but then the rest of the nation were a little favoured in it, in order that they might join on proper occasions with their pretended masters. This great Charter, which is considered as the sacred origin of the English liberties, shows in itself how little liberty was known.

The title alone proves that the king thought he had a just right to be absolute; and that the barons, and even the clergy, forced him to give up the pretended right, for no other reason but because they were the most powerful.

Magna Charta begins in this style: "We grant, of our own free will, the following privileges to the archbishops, bishops, priors, and barons of our kingdom," etc.

The House of Commons is not once mentioned in the articles of this Charter—a proof that it did not yet exist, or that it existed without power. Mention is therein made, by name, of the freemen of England—a melancholy proof that some were not so. It appears, by Article XXXII., that these pretended freemen owed service to their lords. Such a liberty as this was not many removes from slavery.

By Article XXI., the king ordains that his officers shall not henceforward seize upon, unless they pay for them, the horses and carts of freemen. The people considered this ordinance as a real liberty, though it was a greater tyranny. Henry VII., that happy usurper and great politician, who pretended to love the barons, though he in reality hated and feared them, got their lands alienated. By this means the villains, afterwards acquiring riches by their industry, purchased the estates and country seats of the illustrious peers who had ruined themselves by their folly and extravagance, and all the lands got by insensible degrees into other hands.

The power of the House of Commons increased every day. The families of the ancient peers were at last extinct; and as peers only are properly noble in England, there would be no such thing in strictness of law as nobility in that island, had not the kings created new barons from time to time, and preserved the body of peers, once a terror to them, to oppose them to the Commons, since become so formidable.

All these new peers who compose the Higher House receive nothing but their titles from the king, and very few of them have estates in those places whence they take their titles. One shall be Duke of D——, though he has not a foot of land in Dorsetshire; and another is Earl of a village, though he scarce knows where it is situated. The peers have power, but it is only in the Parliament House.

There is no such thing here as *haute, moyenne,* and *basse justice*—that is, a power to judge in all matters civil and criminal; nor a right or privilege of hunting in the grounds of a citizen, who at the same time is not permitted to fire a gun in his own field.

No one is exempted in this country from paying certain taxes because he is a nobleman or a priest. All duties and taxes are settled by the House of Commons, whose power is greater than that of the Peers, though inferior to it in dignity. The spiritual as well as temporal Lords have the liberty to reject a Money Bill brought in by the Commons; but they are not allowed to alter anything in it, and must either pass or throw it out without restriction. When the Bill has passed the Lords and is signed by the king, then the whole nation pays, every man in proportion to his revenue or estate, not according to his title, which would be absurd. There is no such thing as an arbitrary subsidy or poll-tax, but a real tax on the lands, of all which an estimate was made in the reign of the famous King William III.

The land-tax continues still upon the same foot, though the revenue of the lands is increased. Thus no one is tyrannised over, and every one is easy. The feet of the peasants are not bruised by wooden shoes; they eat white bread, are well clothed, and are not afraid of increasing their stock of cattle, nor of tiling their houses, from any apprehension that their taxes will be raised the year following. The annual income of the estates of a great many commoners in England amounts to two hundred thousand livres, and yet these do not think it beneath them to plough the lands which enrich them, and on which they enjoy their liberty.

Letter X

ON TRADE

As trade enriched the citizens in England, so it contributed to their freedom, and this freedom on the other side extended their commerce, whence arose the grandeur of the State. Trade raised by insensible degrees the naval power, which gives the English a superiority over the seas, and they now are masters of very near two hundred ships of war. Posterity will very probably be surprised to hear that an island whose only produce is a little lead, tin, fuller's-earth, and coarse wool, should become so powerful by its commerce, as to be able to send, in 1723, three fleets at the same time to three different and far distanced parts of the globe. One before Gibraltar, conquered and still possessed by the English; a second to Porto Bello, to dispossess the King of Spain of the treasures of the West Indies; and a third into the Baltic, to prevent the Northern Powers from coming to an engagement.

At the time when Louis XIV. made all Italy tremble, and that his armies, which had already possessed themselves of Savoy and Piedmont, were upon the point of taking Turin; Prince Eugene was obliged to march from the middle of Germany in order to succour Savoy. Having no money, without which cities cannot be either taken or defended, he addressed himself to some English merchants. These, at an hour and a half's warning, lent him five millions, whereby he was enabled to deliver Turin, and to beat the French; after which he wrote the following short letter to the persons who had disbursed him the above-mentioned sums: "Gentlemen, I received your money, and flatter myself that I have laid it out to your satisfaction." Such a circumstance as this raises a just pride in an English merchant, and makes him presume (not without some reason) to compare himself to a Roman citizen; and, indeed, a peer's brother does not think traffic beneath him. When the Lord Townshend was Minister of State, a brother of his was content to be a City merchant; and at the time that the Earl of Oxford governed Great Britain, his younger brother was no more than a factor in Aleppo, where he chose to live, and where he died. This custom, which begins, however, to be laid aside, appears monstrous to Germans, vainly puffed up with their extraction. These think it morally impossible that the son of an English peer should be no more than a rich and powerful citizen, for all are princes in Germany. There have been thirty highnesses of the same name, all whose patrimony consisted only in their escutcheons and their pride.

In France the title of marquis is given gratis to any one who will accept of it; and whosoever arrives at Paris from the midst of the most remote provinces with money in his purse, and a name terminating in *ac* or *ille,* may strut about, and cry, "Such a man as I! A man of my rank and figure!" and may look down upon a trader with sovereign contempt; whilst the trader on the other side, by thus often hearing his profession treated so disdainfully, is fool enough to blush at it. However, I need not say which is most useful to a nation; a lord, powdered in the tip of the mode, who knows exactly at what o'clock the king rises and goes to bed, and who gives himself airs of grandeur and state, at the same time that he is acting the slave in the ante-chamber of a prime minister; or a merchant, who enriches his country, despatches orders from his counting-house to Surat and Grand Cairo, and contributes to the felicity of the world.

Letter XI

ON INOCULATION

It is inadvertently affirmed in the Christian countries of Europe that the English are fools and madmen. Fools, because they give their children the small-pox to prevent their catching it; and madmen, because they wantonly communicate a certain and dreadful distemper to their children, merely to prevent an uncertain evil. The English, on the other side, call the rest of the Europeans cowardly and unnatural. Cowardly, because they are afraid of putting their children to a little pain; unnatural, because they expose them to die one time or other of the small-pox. But that the reader may be able to judge whether the English or those who differ from them in opinion are in the right, here follows the history of the famed inoculation, which is mentioned with so much dread in France.

The Circassian women have, from time immemorial, communicated the small-pox to their children when not above six months old by making an incision in the arm, and by putting into this incision a pustule, taken carefully from the body of another child. This pustule produces the same effect in the arm it is laid in as yeast in a piece of dough; it ferments, and diffuses through the whole mass of blood the qualities with which it is impregnated. The pustules of the child in whom the artificial small-pox has been thus inoculated are employed to communicate the same distemper to others. There is an almost perpetual circulation of it in Circassia; and when unhappily the small-pox has quite left the country, the inhabitants of it are in as great trouble and perplexity as other nations when their harvest has fallen short.

The circumstance that introduced a custom in Circassia, which appears so singular to others, is nevertheless a cause common to all nations, I mean maternal tenderness and interest.

The Circassians are poor, and their daughters are beautiful, and indeed, it is in them they chiefly trade. They furnish with beauties the seraglios of the Turkish Sultan, of the Persian Sophy, and of all those who are wealthy enough to purchase and maintain such precious merchandise. These maidens are very honourably and virtuously instructed to fondle and caress men; are taught dances of a very polite and effeminate kind; and how to heighten by the most voluptuous artifices the pleasures of their disdainful masters for whom they are designed. These unhappy creatures repeat their lesson to their mothers, in the same manner as little girls among us repeat their catechism without understanding one word they say.

Now it often happened that, after a father and mother had taken the utmost care of the education of their children, they were frustrated of all their hopes in an instant. The small-pox getting into the family, one daughter died of it, another lost an eye, a third had a great nose at her recovery, and the unhappy parents were completely ruined. Even, frequently, when the small-pox became epidemical, trade was suspended for several years, which thinned very considerably the seraglios of Persia and Turkey.

A trading nation is always watchful over its own interests, and grasps at every discovery that may be of advantage to its commerce. The Circassians observed that scarce one person in a thousand was ever attacked by a small-pox of a violent kind. That some, indeed, had this distemper very favourably three or four times, but never twice so as to prove fatal; in a word, that no one ever had it in a violent degree twice in his life. They observed farther, that when the small-pox is of the milder sort, and the pustules have only a tender, delicate skin to break through, they never leave the least scar in the face. From these natural observations they concluded, that in case an infant of six months or a year old should have a milder sort of small-pox, he would not die of it, would not be marked, nor be ever afflicted with it again.

In order, therefore, to preserve the life and beauty of their children, the only thing remaining was to give them the small-pox in their infant years. This they did by inoculating in the body of a child a pustule taken from the most regular and at the same time the most favourable sort of small-pox that could be procured.

The experiment could not possibly fail. The Turks, who are people of good sense, soon adopted this custom, insomuch that at this time there is not a bassa in Constantinople but communicates the small-pox to his children of both sexes immediately upon their being weaned.

Some pretend that the Circassians borrowed this custom anciently from the Arabians; but we shall leave the clearing up of this point of history to some learned Benedictine, who will not fail to compile a great many folios on this subject, with the several proofs or authorities. All I have to say upon it is that, in the beginning of the reign of King George I., the Lady Wortley Montague, a woman of as fine a genius, and endued with as great a strength of mind, as any of her sex in the British Kingdoms, being with her husband, who was ambassador at the Porte, made no scruple to communicate the small-pox to an infant of which she was delivered in Constantinople.

The chaplain represented to his lady, but to no purpose, that this was an un-Christian operation, and therefore that it could succeed with none but infidels. However, it had the most happy effect upon the son of the Lady Wortley Montague, who, at her return to England, communicated the experiment to the Princess of Wales, now Queen of England. It must be confessed that this princess, abstracted from her crown and titles, was born to encourage the whole circle of arts, and to do good to mankind. She appears as an amiable philosopher on the throne, having never let slip one opportunity of improving the great talents she received from Nature, nor of exerting her beneficence. It is she who, being informed that a daughter of Milton was living, but in miserable circumstances, immediately sent her a considerable present. It is she who protects the learned Father Courayer. It is she who condescended to attempt a reconciliation between Dr. Clark and Mr. Leibnitz. The moment this princess heard of inoculation, she caused an experiment of it to be made on four criminals sentenced to die, and by that means preserved their lives doubly; for she not only saved them from the gallows, but by means of this artificial small-pox prevented their ever having that distemper in a natural way, with which they would very probably have been attacked one time or other, and might have died of in a more advanced age.

The princess being assured of the usefulness of this operation, caused her own children to be inoculated. A great part of the kingdom followed her example, and since that time ten thousand children, at least, of persons of condition owe in this manner their lives to her Majesty and to the Lady Wortley Montague; and as many of the fair sex are obliged to them for their beauty.

Upon a general calculation, threescore persons in every hundred have the small-pox. Of these threescore, twenty die of it in the most favourable season of life, and as many more wear the disagreeable remains of it in their faces so long as they live. Thus, a fifth part of mankind either die or are disfigured by this distemper. But it does not prove fatal to so much as one among those who are inoculated in Turkey or in England, unless the patient be infirm, or would have died had not the experiment been made upon him. Besides, no one is disfigured, no one has the small-pox a second time, if the inoculation was perfect. It is therefore certain, that had the lady of some French ambassador brought this secret from Constantinople to Paris, the nation would have been for ever obliged to her. Then the Duke de Villequier, father to the Duke d'Aumont, who enjoys the most vigorous constitution, and is the healthiest man in France, would not have been cut off in the flower of his age.

The Prince of Soubise, happy in the finest flush of health, would not have been snatched away at five-and-twenty, nor the Dauphin, grandfather to Louis XV., have been laid in his grave in his fiftieth year. Twenty thousand persons whom the small-pox swept away at Paris in 1723 would have been alive at this time. But are not the French fond of life, and is beauty so inconsiderable an advantage as to be disregarded by the ladies? It must be confessed that we are an odd kind of people. Perhaps our nation will imitate ten years hence this practice of the English, if the clergy and the physicians will but give them leave to do it; or possibly our countrymen may introduce inoculation three months hence in France out of mere whim, in case the English should discontinue it through fickleness.

I am informed that the Chinese have practised inoculation these hundred years, a circumstance that argues very much in its favour, since they are thought to be the wisest and best governed people in the world. The Chinese, indeed, do not communicate this distemper by inoculation, but at the nose, in the same manner as we take snuff. This is a more agreeable way, but then it produces the like effects; and proves at the same time that had inoculation been practised in France it would have saved the lives of thousands.

LETTER XII

ON THE LORD BACON

NOT long since the trite and frivolous question following was debated in a very polite and learned company, viz., Who was the greatest man, Cæsar, Alexander, Tamerlane, Cromwell, &c.?

Somebody answered that Sir Isaac Newton excelled them all. The gentleman's assertion was very just; for if true greatness consists in having received from heaven a mighty genius, and in having employed it to enlighten our own mind and that of others, a man like Sir Isaac Newton, whose equal is hardly found in a thousand years, is the truly great man. And those politicians and conquerors (and all ages produce some) were generally so many illustrious wicked men. That man claims our respect who commands over the minds of the rest of the world by the force of truth, not those who enslave their fellow-creatures: he who is acquainted with the universe, not they who deface it.

Since, therefore, you desire me to give you an account of the famous personages whom England has given birth to, I shall begin with Lord Bacon, Mr. Locke, Sir Isaac Newton, &c. Afterwards the warriors and Ministers of State shall come in their order.

I must begin with the celebrated Viscount Verulam, known in Europe by the name of Bacon, which was that of his family. His father had been Lord Keeper, and himself was a great many years Lord Chancellor under King James I. Nevertheless, amidst the intrigues of a Court, and the affairs of his exalted employment, which alone were enough to engross his whole time, he yet found so much leisure for study as to make himself a great philosopher, a good historian, and an elegant writer; and a still more surprising circumstance is that he lived in an age in which the art of writing justly and elegantly was little known, much less true philosophy. Lord Bacon, as is the fate of man, was more esteemed after his death than in his lifetime. His enemies were in the British Court, and his admirers were foreigners.

When the Marquis d'Effiat attended in England upon the Princess Henrietta Maria, daughter to Henry IV., whom King Charles I.

had married, that Minister went and visited the Lord Bacon, who, being at that time sick in his bed, received him with the curtains shut close. "You resemble the angels," said the Marquis to him; "we hear those beings spoken of perpetually, and we believe them superior to men, but are never allowed the consolation to see them."

You know that this great man was accused of a crime very unbecoming a philosopher: I mean bribery and extortion. You know that he was sentenced by the House of Lords to pay a fine of about four hundred thousand French livres, to lose his peerage and his dignity of Chancellor; but in the present age the English revere his memory to such a degree, that they will scarce allow him to have been guilty. In case you should ask what are my thoughts on this head, I shall answer you in the words which I heard the Lord Bolingbroke use on another occasion. Several gentlemen were speaking, in his company, of the avarice with which the late Duke of Marlborough had been charged, some examples whereof being given, the Lord Bolingbroke was appealed to (who, having been in the opposite party, might perhaps, without the imputation of indecency, have been allowed to clear up that matter): "He was so great a man," replied his lordship, "that I have forgot his vices."

I shall therefore confine myself to those things which so justly gained Lord Bacon the esteem of all Europe.

The most singular and the best of all his pieces is that which, at this time, is the most useless and the least read, I mean his *Novum Scientiarum Organum*. This is the scaffold with which the new philosophy was raised; and when the edifice was built, part of it at least, the scaffold was no longer of service.

The Lord Bacon was not yet acquainted with Nature, but then he knew, and pointed out, the several paths that lead to it. He had despised in his younger years the thing called philosophy in the Universities, and did all that lay in his power to prevent those societies of men instituted to improve human reason from depraving it by their quiddities, their horrors of the vacuum, their substantial forms, and all those impertinent terms which not only ignorance had rendered venerable, but which had been made sacred by their being ridiculously blended with religion.

He is the father of experimental philosophy. It must, indeed, be confessed that very surprising secrets had been found out before his time—the sea-compass, printing, engraving on copper plates, oil-painting, looking-glasses; the art of restoring, in some measure, old men to their sight by spectacles; gunpowder, &c., had been discovered. A new world has been sought for, found, and conquered. Would not one suppose that these sublime discoveries had been made by the greatest philosophers, and in ages much more enlightened than the present? But it was far otherwise; all these great changes happened in the most stupid and barbarous times. Chance only gave birth to most of those inventions; and it is very probable that what is called chance contributed very much to the discovery of America; at least, it has been always thought that Christopher Columbus undertook his voyage merely on the relation of a captain of a ship which a storm had driven as far westward as the Caribbean Islands. Be this as it will, men had sailed round the world, and could destroy cities by an artificial thunder more dreadful than the real one; but, then, they were not acquainted with the circulation of the blood, the weight of the air, the laws of motion, light, the number of our planets, &c. And a man who maintained a thesis on Aristotle's "Categories," on the universals *a parte rei,* or such-like nonsense, was looked upon as a prodigy.

The most astonishing, the most useful inventions, are not those which reflect the greatest honour on the human mind. It is to a mechanical instinct, which is found in many men, and not to true philosophy, that most arts owe their origin.

The discovery of fire, the art of making bread, of melting and preparing metals, of building houses, and the invention of the shuttle, are infinitely more beneficial to mankind than printing or the sea-compass: and yet these arts were invented by uncultivated, savage men.

What a prodigious use the Greeks and Romans made afterwards of mechanics! Nevertheless, they believed that there were crystal heavens, that the stars were small lamps which sometimes fell into the sea, and one of their greatest philosophers, after long researches, found that the stars were so many flints which had been detached from the earth.

In a word, no one before the Lord Bacon was acquainted with

experimental philosophy, nor with the several physical experiments which have been made since his time. Scarce one of them but is hinted at in his work, and he himself had made several. He made a kind of pneumatic engine, by which he guessed the elasticity of the air. He approached, on all sides as it were, to the discovery of its weight, and had very near attained it, but some time after Torricelli seized upon this truth. In a little time experimental philosophy began to be cultivated on a sudden in most parts of Europe. It was a hidden treasure which the Lord Bacon had some notion of, and which all the philosophers, encouraged by his promises, endeavoured to dig up.

But that which surprised me most was to read in his work, in express terms, the new attraction, the invention of which is ascribed to Sir Isaac Newton.

We must search, says Lord Bacon, whether there may not be a kind of magnetic power which operates between the earth and heavy bodies, between the moon and the ocean, between the planets, &c. In another place he says either heavy bodies must be carried towards the centre of the earth, or must be reciprocally attracted by it; and in the latter case it is evident that the nearer bodies, in their falling, draw towards the earth, the stronger they will attract one another. We must, says he, make an experiment to see whether the same clock will go faster on the top of a mountain or at the bottom of a mine; whether the strength of the weights decreases on the mountain and increases in the mine. It is probable that the earth has a true attractive power.

This forerunner in philosophy was also an elegant writer, an historian, and a wit.

His moral essays are greatly esteemed, but they were drawn up in the view of instructing rather than of pleasing; and, as they are not a satire upon mankind, like Rochefoucauld's "Maxims," nor written upon a sceptical plan, like Montaigne's "Essays," they are not so much read as those two ingenious authors.

His History of Henry VII. was looked upon as a masterpiece, but how is it possible that some persons can presume to compare so little a work with the history of our illustrious Thuanus?

Speaking about the famous impostor Perkin, son to a converted

Jew, who assumed boldly the name and title of Richard IV., King of England, at the instigation of the Duchess of Burgundy, and who disputed the crown with Henry VII., the Lord Bacon writes as follows:—

"At this time the King began again to be haunted with sprites, by the magic and curious arts of the Lady Margaret, who raised up the ghost of Richard, Duke of York, second son to King Edward IV., to walk and vex the King.

"After such time as she (Margaret of Burgundy) thought he (Perkin Warbeck) was perfect in his lesson, she began to cast with herself from what coast this blazing star should first appear, and at what time it must be upon the horizon of Ireland; for there had the like meteor strong influence before."

Methinks our sagacious Thuanus does not give in to such fustian, which formerly was looked upon as sublime, but in this age is justly called nonsense.

LETTER XIII

ON MR. LOCKE

PERHAPS no man ever had a more judicious or more methodical genius, or was a more acute logician than Mr. Locke, and yet he was not deeply skilled in the mathematics. This great man could never subject himself to the tedious fatigue of calculations, nor to the dry pursuit of mathematical truths, which do not at first present any sensible objects to the mind; and no one has given better proofs than he, that it is possible for a man to have a geometrical head without the assistance of geometry. Before his time, several great philosophers had declared, in the most positive terms, what the soul of man is; but as these absolutely knew nothing about it, they might very well be allowed to differ entirely in opinion from one another.

In Greece, the infant seat of arts and of errors, and where the grandeur as well as folly of the human mind went such prodigious lengths, the people used to reason about the soul in the very same manner as we do.

The divine Anaxagoras, in whose honour an altar was erected for his having taught mankind that the sun was greater than Peloponnesus, that snow was black, and that the heavens were of stone, affirmed that the soul was an aërial spirit, but at the same time immortal. Diogenes (not he who was a cynical philosopher after having coined base money) declared that the soul was a portion of the substance of God: an idea which we must confess was very sublime. Epicurus maintained that it was composed of parts in the same manner as the body.

Aristotle, who has been explained a thousand ways, because he is unintelligible, was of opinion, according to some of his disciples, that the understanding in all men is one and the same substance.

The divine Plato, master of the divine Aristotle,—and the divine Socrates, master of the divine Plato,—used to say that the soul was corporeal and eternal. No doubt but the demon of Socrates had instructed him in the nature of it. Some people, indeed, pretend that a man who boasted his being attended by a familiar genius must infallibly be either a knave or a madman, but this kind of people are seldom satisfied with anything but reason.

With regard to the Fathers of the Church, several in the primitive ages believed that the soul was human, and the angels and God corporeal. Men naturally improve upon every system. St. Bernard, as Father Mabillon confesses, taught that the soul after death does not see God in the celestial regions, but converses with Christ's human nature only. However, he was not believed this time on his bare word; the adventure of the crusade having a little sunk the credit of his oracles. Afterwards a thousand schoolmen arose, such as the Irrefragable Doctor, the Subtile Doctor, the Angelic Doctor, the Seraphic Doctor, and the Cherubic Doctor, who were all sure that they had a very clear and distinct idea of the soul, and yet wrote in such a manner, that one would conclude they were resolved no one should understand a word in their writings. Our Descartes, born to discover the errors of antiquity, and at the same time to substitute his own; and hurried away by that systematic spirit which throws a cloud over the minds of the greatest men, thought he had demonstrated that the soul is the same thing as thought, in the same manner as matter, in his opinion, is the same as extension. He asserted, that man thinks eternally, and that the soul, at its coming into the body, is informed with the whole series of metaphysical notions: knowing

God, infinite space, possessing all abstract ideas—in a word, completely endued with the most sublime lights, which it unhappily forgets at its issuing from the womb.

Father Malebranche, in his sublime illusions, not only admitted innate ideas, but did not doubt of our living wholly in God, and that God is, as it were, our soul.

Such a multitude of reasoners having written the romance of the soul, a sage at last arose, who gave, with an air of the greatest modesty, the history of it. Mr. Locke has displayed the human soul in the same manner as an excellent anatomist explains the springs of the human body. He everywhere takes the light of physics for his guide. He sometimes presumes to speak affirmatively, but then he presumes also to doubt. Instead of concluding at once what we know not, he examines gradually what we would know. He takes an infant at the instant of his birth; he traces, step by step, the progress of his understanding; examines what things he has in common with beasts, and what he possesses above them. Above all, he consults himself: the being conscious that he himself thinks.

"I shall leave," says he, "to those who know more of this matter than myself, the examining whether the soul exists before or after the organisation of our bodies. But I confess that it is my lot to be animated with one of those heavy souls which do not think always; and I am even so unhappy as not to conceive that it is more necessary the soul should think perpetually than that bodies should be for ever in motion."

With regard to myself, I shall boast that I have the honour to be as stupid in this particular as Mr. Locke. No one shall ever make me believe that I think always: and I am as little inclined as he could be to fancy that some weeks after I was conceived I was a very learned soul; knowing at that time a thousand things which I forgot at my birth; and possessing when in the womb (though to no manner of purpose) knowledge which I lost the instant I had occasion for it; and which I have never since been able to recover perfectly.

Mr. Locke, after having destroyed innate ideas; after having fully renounced the vanity of believing that we think always; after having laid down, from the most solid principles, that ideas enter the mind through the senses; having examined our simple and complex ideas;

having traced the human mind through its several operations; having shown that all the languages in the world are imperfect, and the great abuse that is made of words every moment, he at last comes to consider the extent or rather the narrow limits of human knowledge. It was in this chapter he presumed to advance, but very modestly, the following words: "We shall, perhaps, never be capable of knowing whether a being, purely material, thinks or not." This sage assertion was, by more divines than one, looked upon as a scandalous declaration that the soul is material and mortal. Some Englishmen, devout after their way, sounded an alarm. The superstitious are the same in society as cowards in an army; they themselves are seized with a panic fear, and communicate it to others. It was loudly exclaimed that Mr. Locke intended to destroy religion; nevertheless, religion had nothing to do in the affair, it being a question purely philosophical, altogether independent of faith and revelation. Mr. Locke's opponents needed but to examine, calmly and impartially, whether the declaring that matter can think, implies a contradiction; and whether God is able to communicate thought to matter. But divines are too apt to begin their declarations with saying that God is offended when people differ from them in opinion; in which they too much resemble the bad poets, who used to declare publicly that Boileau spake irreverently of Louis XIV., because he ridiculed their stupid productions. Bishop Stillingfleet got the reputation of a calm and unprejudiced divine because he did not expressly make use of injurious terms in his dispute with Mr. Locke. That divine entered the lists against him, but was defeated; for he argued as a schoolman, and Locke as a philosopher, who was perfectly acquainted with the strong as well as the weak side of the human mind, and who fought with weapons whose temper he knew. If I might presume to give my opinion on so delicate a subject after Mr. Locke, I would say, that men have long disputed on the nature and the immortality of the soul. With regard to its immortality, it is impossible to give a demonstration of it, since its nature is still the subject of controversy; which, however, must be thoroughly understood before a person can be able to determine whether it be immortal or not. Human reason is so little able, merely by its own strength, to demonstrate the immortality of the soul, that it was absolutely necessary religion should reveal it to us. It is of advantage to society in general, that mankind should believe the soul to be immortal; faith commands us to do this; nothing more is required, and the matter is cleared up at once. But it is otherwise with respect to its nature; it is of little importance to religion, which only requires the soul to be virtuous, whatever substance it may be made of. It is a clock which is given us to regulate, but the artist has not told us of what materials the spring of this clock is composed.

I am a body, and, I think, that's all I know of the matter. Shall I ascribe to an unknown cause, what I can so easily impute to the only second cause I am acquainted with? Here all the school philosophers interrupt me with their arguments, and declare that there is only extension and solidity in bodies, and that there they can have nothing but motion and figure. Now motion, figure, extension and solidity cannot form a thought, and consequently the soul cannot be matter. All this so often repeated mighty series of reasoning, amounts to no more than this: I am absolutely ignorant what matter is; I guess, but imperfectly, some properties of it; now I absolutely cannot tell whether these properties may be joined to thought. As I therefore know nothing, I maintain positively that matter cannot think. In this manner do the schools reason.

Mr. Locke addressed these gentlemen in the candid, sincere manner following: At least confess yourselves to be as ignorant as I. Neither your imaginations nor mine are able to comprehend in what manner a body is susceptible of ideas; and do you conceive better in what manner a substance, of what kind soever, is susceptible of them? As you cannot comprehend either matter or spirit, why will you presume to assert anything?

The superstitious man comes afterwards and declares, that all those must be burnt for the good of their souls, who so much as suspect that it is possible for the body to think without any foreign assistance. But what would these people say should they themselves be proved irreligious? And indeed, what man can presume to assert, without being guilty at the same time of the greatest impiety, that it is impossible for the Creator to form matter with thought and sensation? Consider only, I beg you, what a dilemma you bring yourselves into, you who confine in this manner the power of the

Creator. Beasts have the same organs, the same sensations, the same perceptions as we; they have memory, and combine certain ideas. In case it was not in the power of God to animate matter, and inform it with sensation, the consequence would be, either that beasts are mere machines, or that they have a spiritual soul.

Methinks it is clearly evident that beasts cannot be mere machines, which I prove thus. God has given to them the very same organs of sensation as to us: if therefore they have no sensation, God has created a useless thing; now according to your own confession God does nothing in vain; He therefore did not create so many organs of sensation, merely for them to be uninformed with this faculty; consequently beasts are not mere machines. Beasts, according to your assertion, cannot be animated with a spiritual soul; you will, therefore, in spite of yourself, be reduced to this only assertion, viz., that God has endued the organs of beasts, who are mere matter, with the faculties of sensation and perception, which you call instinct in them. But why may not God, if He pleases, communicate to our more delicate organs, that faculty of feeling, perceiving, and thinking, which we call human reason? To whatever side you turn, you are forced to acknowledge your own ignorance, and the boundless power of the Creator. Exclaim therefore no more against the sage, the modest philosophy of Mr. Locke, which so far from interfering with religion, would be of use to demonstrate the truth of it, in case religion wanted any such support. For what philosophy can be of a more religious nature than that, which affirming nothing but what it conceives clearly, and conscious of its own weakness, declares that we must always have recourse to God in our examining of the first principles?

Besides, we must not be apprehensive that any philosophical opinion will ever prejudice the religion of a country. Though our demonstrations clash directly with our mysteries, that is nothing to the purpose, for the latter are not less revered upon that account by our Christian philosophers, who know very well that the objects of reason and those of faith are of a very different nature. Philosophers will never form a religious sect, the reason of which is, their writings are not calculated for the vulgar, and they themselves are free from enthusiasm. If we divide mankind into twenty parts, it will be found that nineteen of these consist of persons employed in manual labour, who will never know that such a man as Mr. Locke existed. In the remaining twentieth part how few are readers? And among such as are so, twenty amuse themselves with romances to one who studies philosophy. The thinking part of mankind is confined to a very small number, and these will never disturb the peace and tranquillity of the world.

Neither Montaigne, Locke, Bayle, Spinoza, Hobbes, the Lord Shaftesbury, Collins, nor Toland lighted up the firebrand of discord in their countries; this has generally been the work of divines, who being at first puffed up with the ambition of becoming chiefs of a sect, soon grew very desirous of being at the head of a party. But what do I say? All the works of the modern philosophers put together will never make so much noise as even the dispute which arose among the Franciscans, merely about the fashion of their sleeves and of their cowls.

LETTER XIV

ON DESCARTES AND SIR ISAAC NEWTON

A FRENCHMAN who arrives in London, will find philosophy, like everything else, very much changed there. He had left the world a plenum, and he now finds it a vacuum. At Paris the universe is seen composed of vortices of subtile matter; but nothing like it is seen in London. In France, it is the pressure of the moon that causes the tides; but in England it is the sea that gravitates towards the moon; so that when you think that the moon should make it flood with us, those gentlemen fancy it should be ebb, which very unluckily cannot be proved. For to be able to do this, it is necessary the moon and the tides should have been inquired into at the very instant of the creation.

You will observe farther, that the sun, which in France is said to have nothing to do in the affair, comes in here for very near a quarter of its assistance. According to your Cartesians, everything is performed by an impulsion, of which we have very little notion; and according to Sir Isaac Newton, it is by an attraction, the cause of which is as much unknown to us. At Paris you imagine that the earth is shaped like a melon, or of an oblique figure; at London it has an oblate one. A Cartesian declares that light exists in the air; but a Newtonian asserts that it comes from the sun in six minutes and a half. The several operations of your chemistry are performed by acids, alkalies and subtile matter; but attraction prevails even in chemistry among the English.

The very essence of things is totally changed. You neither are agreed upon the definition of the soul, nor on that of matter. Descartes, as I observed in my last, maintains that the soul is the same thing with thought, and Mr. Locke has given a pretty good proof of the contrary.

Descartes asserts farther, that extension alone constitutes matter, but Sir Isaac adds solidity to it.

How furiously contradictory are these opinions!

> "Non nostrum inter vos tantas componere lites."
>
> VIRGIL, Eclog. III.

"'Tis not for us to end such great disputes."

This famous Newton, this destroyer of the Cartesian system, died in March, anno 1727. His countrymen honoured him in his lifetime, and interred him as though he had been a king who had made his people happy.

The English read with the highest satisfaction, and translated into their tongue, the Elogium of Sir Isaac Newton, which M. de Fontenelle spoke in the Academy of Sciences. M. de Fontenelle presides as judge over philosophers; and the English expected his decision, as a solemn declaration of the superiority of the English philosophy over that of the French. But when it was found that this gentleman had compared Descartes to Sir Isaac, the whole Royal Society in London rose up in arms. So far from acquiescing with M. Fontenelle's judgment, they criticised his discourse. And even several (who, however, were not the ablest philosophers in that body) were offended at the comparison, and for no other reason but because Descartes was a Frenchman.

It must be confessed that these two great men differed very much in conduct, in fortune, and in philosophy.

Nature had indulged Descartes with a shining and strong imagination, whence he became a very singular person both in private life and in his manner of reasoning. This imagination could not conceal itself even in his philosophical works, which are everywhere adorned with very shining, ingenious metaphors and figures. Nature had almost made him a poet; and indeed he wrote a piece of poetry for the entertainment of Christina, Queen of Sweden, which however was suppressed in honour to his memory.

He embraced a military life for some time, and afterwards becoming a complete philosopher, he did not think the passion of love derogatory to his character. He had by his mistress a daughter called Froncine, who died young, and was very much regretted by him. Thus he experienced every passion incident to mankind.

He was a long time of opinion that it would be necessary for him to fly from the society of his fellow creatures, and especially from his native country, in order to enjoy the happiness of cultivating his philosophical studies in full liberty.

Descartes was very right, for his contemporaries were not knowing enough to improve and enlighten his understanding, and were capable of little else than of giving him uneasiness.

He left France purely to go in search of truth, which was then persecuted by the wretched philosophy of the schools. However, he found that reason was as much disguised and depraved in the universities of Holland, into which he withdrew, as in his own country. For at the time that the French condemned the only propositions of his philosophy which were true, he was persecuted by the pretended philosophers of Holland, who understood him no better; and who, having a nearer view of his glory, hated his person the more, so that he was obliged to leave Utrecht. Descartes was injuriously accused of being an atheist, the last refuge of religious scandal: and he who had employed all the sagacity and penetration of his genius, in searching for new proofs of the existence of a God, was suspected to believe there was no such Being.

Such a persecution from all sides, must necessarily suppose a most exalted merit as well as a very distinguished reputation, and indeed he possessed both. Reason at that time darted a ray upon the world through the gloom of the schools, and the prejudices of popular superstition. At last his name spread so universally, that the French were desirous of bringing him back into his native country by rewards, and accordingly offered him an annual pension of a thousand crowns. Upon these hopes Descartes returned to France; paid the fees of his patent, which was sold at that time, but no pension was settled upon him. Thus disappointed, he returned to his solitude in North Holland, where he again pursued the study of philosophy, whilst the great Galileo, at fourscore years of age, was groaning in the prisons of the Inquisition, only for having demonstrated the earth's motion.

At last Descartes was snatched from the world in the flower of his age at Stockholm. His death was owing to a bad regimen, and he expired in the midst of some literati who were his enemies, and under the hands of a physician to whom he was odious.

The progress of Sir Isaac Newton's life was quite different. He lived happy, and very much honoured in his native country, to the age of fourscore and five years.

It was his peculiar felicity, not only to be born in a country of liberty, but in an age when all scholastic impertinences were banished from the world. Reason alone was cultivated, and mankind could only be his pupil, not his enemy.

One very singular difference in the lives of these two great men is, that Sir Isaac, during the long course of years he enjoyed, was never sensible to any passion, was not subject to the common frailties of mankind, nor ever had any commerce with women—a circumstance which was assured me by the physician and surgeon who attended him in his last moments.

We may admire Sir Isaac Newton on this occasion, but then we must not censure Descartes.

The opinion that generally prevails in England with regard to these new philosophers is, that the latter was a dreamer, and the former a sage.

Very few people in England read Descartes, whose works indeed are now useless. On the other side, but a small number peruse those of Sir Isaac, because to do this the student must be deeply skilled in the mathematics, otherwise those works will be unintelligible to him. But notwithstanding this, these great men are the subject of everyone's discourse. Sir Isaac Newton is allowed every advantage, whilst Descartes is not indulged a single one. According to some, it is to the former that we owe the discovery of a vacuum, that the air is a heavy body, and the invention of telescopes. In a word, Sir Isaac Newton is here as the Hercules of fabulous story, to whom the ignorant ascribed all the feats of ancient heroes.

In a critique that was made in London on M. de Fontenelle's discourse, the writer presumed to assert that Descartes was not a great geometrician. Those who make such a declaration may justly be reproached with flying in their master's face. Descartes extended the limits of geometry as far beyond the place where he found them, as Sir Isaac did after him. The former first taught the method of expressing curves by equations. This geometry which, thanks to him for it, is now grown common, was so abstruse in his time, that not so much as one professor would undertake to explain it; and Schotten in Holland, and Format in France, were the only men who understood it.

He applied this geometrical and inventive genius to dioptrics, which, when treated of by him, became a new art. And if he was mistaken in some things, the reason of that is, a man who discovers a new tract of land cannot at once know all the properties of the soil. Those who come after him, and make these lands fruitful, are at least obliged to him for the discovery. I will not deny but that there are innumerable errors in the rest of Descartes' works.

Geometry was a guide he himself had in some measure fashioned, which would have conducted him safely through the several paths of natural philosophy. Nevertheless, he at last abandoned this guide, and gave entirely into the humour of forming hypotheses; and then philosophy was no more than an ingenious romance, fit only to amuse the ignorant. He was mistaken in the nature of the soul, in the proofs of the existence of a God, in matter, in the laws of motion, and in the nature of light. He admitted innate ideas, he invented new elements, he created a world; he made man according to his own fancy; and it is justly said, that the man of Descartes is, in fact, that of Descartes only, very different from the real one.

He pushed his metaphysical errors so far, as to declare that two and two make four for no other reason but because God would have it so. However, it will not be making him too great a compliment if we affirm that he was valuable even in his mistakes. He deceived himself, but then it was at least in a methodical way. He destroyed all the absurd chimeras with which youth had been infatuated for two thousand years. He taught his contemporaries how to reason, and enabled them to employ his own weapons against himself. If Descartes did not pay in good money, he however did great service in crying down that of a base alloy.

I indeed believe that very few will presume to compare his philosophy in any respect with that of Sir Isaac Newton. The former is an essay, the latter a masterpiece. But then the man who first brought us to the path of truth, was perhaps as great a genius as he who afterwards conducted us through it.

Descartes gave sight to the blind. These saw the errors of antiquity and of the sciences. The path he struck out is since become boundless. Robault's little work was, during some years, a complete system of physics; but now all the Transactions of the several academies in Europe put together do not form so much as the beginning of a system. In fathoming this abyss no bottom has been found. We are now to examine what discoveries Sir Isaac Newton has made in it.

Letter XV

ON ATTRACTION

The discoveries which gained Sir Isaac Newton so universal a reputation, relate to the system of the world, to light, to geometrical infinities; and, lastly, to chronology, with which he used to amuse himself after the fatigue of his severer studies.

I will now acquaint you (without prolixity if possible) with the few things I have been able to comprehend of all these sublime ideas. With regard to the system of our world disputes were a long time maintained, on the cause that turns the planets, and keeps them in their orbits; and on those causes which make all bodies here below descend towards the surface of the earth.

The system of Descartes, explained and improved since his time, seemed to give a plausible reason for all those phenomena; and this reason seemed more just, as it is simple and intelligible to all capacities. But in philosophy, a student ought to doubt of the things he fancies he understands too easily, as much as of those he does not understand.

Gravity, the falling of accelerated bodies on the earth, the revolution of the planets in their orbits, their rotations round their axis, all this is mere motion. Now motion cannot perhaps be conceived any otherwise than by impulsion; therefore all those bodies must be impelled. But by what are they impelled? All space is full, it therefore is filled with a very subtile matter, since this is imperceptible to us; this matter goes from west to east, since all the planets are carried from west to east. Thus from hypothesis to hypothesis, from one appearance to another, philosophers have imagined a vast whirlpool of subtile matter, in which the planets are carried round the sun: they also have created another particular vortex which floats in the great one, and which turns daily round the planets. When all this is done, it is pretended that gravity depends on this diurnal motion; for, say these, the velocity of the subtile matter that turns round our little vortex, must be seventeen times more rapid than that of the earth; or, in case its velocity is seventeen times greater than that of the earth, its centrifugal force must be vastly greater, and consequently impel all bodies towards the earth. This is the cause of gravity, according to the Cartesian system. But the theorist, before he calculated the centrifugal force and velocity of the subtile matter, should first have been certain that it existed.

Sir Isaac Newton seems to have destroyed all these great and little vortices, both that which carries the planets round the sun, as well as the other which supposes every planet to turn on its own axis.

First, with regard to the pretended little vortex of the earth, it is demonstrated that it must lose its motion by insensible degrees; it is demonstrated, that if the earth swims in a fluid, its density must be equal to that of the earth; and in case its density be the same, all the bodies we endeavour to move must meet with an insuperable resistance.

With regard to the great vortices, they are still more chimerical, and it is impossible to make them agree with Kepler's law, the truth of which has been demonstrated. Sir Isaac shows, that the revolution of the fluid in which Jupiter is supposed to be carried, is not the same with regard to the revolution of the fluid of the earth, as the revolution of Jupiter with respect to that of the earth. He proves, that as the planets make their revolutions in ellipses, and consequently being at a much greater distance one from the other in their Aphelia, and a little nearer in their Perihelia; the earth's velocity, for instance, ought to be greater when it is nearer Venus and Mars, because the fluid that carries it along, being then more pressed, ought to have a greater motion; and yet it is even then that the earth's motion is slower.

He proves that there is no such thing as a celestial matter which goes from west to east since the comets traverse those spaces, sometimes from east to west, and at other times from north to south.

In fine, the better to resolve, if possible, every difficulty, he proves, and even by experiments, that it is impossible there should be a plenum; and brings back the vacuum, which Aristotle and Descartes had banished from the world.

Having by these and several other arguments destroyed the Cartesian vortices, he despaired of ever being able to discover whether there is a secret principle in nature which, at the same time, is the cause of the motion of all celestial bodies, and that of gravity on the earth. But being retired in 1666, upon account of the Plague, to a solitude near Cambridge; as he was walking one day in his garden, and saw some fruits fall from a tree, he fell into a profound meditation on that gravity, the cause of which had so long been sought, but in vain, by all the philosophers, whilst the vulgar think there is nothing mysterious in it. He said to himself, that from what height soever in our hemisphere, those bodies might descend, their fall would certainly be in the progression discovered by Galileo; and the spaces they run through would be as the square of the times. Why may not this power which causes heavy bodies to descend, and is the same without any sensible diminution at the remotest distance from the centre of the earth, or on the summits of the highest mountains, why, said Sir Isaac, may not this power extend as high as the moon? And in case its influence reaches so far, is it not very probable that this power retains it in its orbit, and determines its motion? But in case the moon obeys this principle (whatever it be) may we not conclude very naturally that the rest of the planets are equally subject to it? In case this power exists (which besides is proved) it must increase in an inverse ratio of the squares of the distances. All, therefore, that remains is, to examine how far a heavy body, which should fall upon the earth from a moderate height, would go; and how far in the same time, a body which should fall from the orbit of the moon, would descend. To find this, nothing is wanted but the measure of the earth, and the distance of the moon from it.

Thus Sir Isaac Newton reasoned. But at that time the English had but a very imperfect measure of our globe, and depended on the uncertain supposition of mariners, who computed a degree to contain but sixty English miles, whereas it consists in reality of near seventy. As this false computation did not agree with the conclusions which Sir Isaac intended to draw from them, he laid aside this pursuit. A half-learned philosopher, remarkable only for his vanity, would have made the measure of the earth agree, anyhow, with his system. Sir Isaac, however, chose rather to quit the researches he was then engaged in. But after Mr. Picard had measured the earth exactly, by tracing that meridian which redounds so much to the honour of the French, Sir Isaac Newton resumed his former reflections, and found his account in Mr. Picard's calculation.

A circumstance which has always appeared wonderful to me, is that such sublime discoveries should have been made by the sole assistance of a quadrant and a little arithmetic.

The circumference of the earth is 123,249,600 feet. This, among other things, is necessary to prove the system of attraction.

The instant we know the earth's circumference, and the distance of the moon, we know that of the moon's orbit, and the diameter of this orbit. The moon performs its revolution in that orbit in twenty-seven days, seven hours, forty-three minutes. It is demonstrated, that the moon in its mean motion makes an hundred and fourscore and seven thousand nine hundred and sixty feet (of Paris) in a minute. It is likewise demonstrated, by a known theorem, that the central force which should make a body fall from the height of the moon, would make its velocity no more than fifteen Paris feet in a minute of time. Now if the law by which bodies gravitate and attract one another in an inverse ratio to the squares of the distances be true, if the same power acts according to that law throughout all nature, it is evident that as the earth is sixty semi-diameters distant from the moon, a heavy body must necessarily fall (on the earth) fifteen feet in the first second, and fifty-four thousand feet in the first minute.

Now a heavy body falls, in reality, fifteen feet in the first second, and goes in the first minute fifty-four thousand feet, which number is the square of sixty multiplied by fifteen. Bodies, therefore, gravitate in an inverse ratio of the squares of the distances; consequently, what causes gravity on earth, and keeps the moon in its orbit, is one and the same power; it being demonstrated that the moon gravitates on the earth, which is the centre of its particular motion, it is demonstrated that the earth and the moon gravitate on the sun which is the centre of their annual motion.

The rest of the planets must be subject to this general law; and if this law exists, these planets must follow the laws which Kepler discovered. All these laws, all these relations are indeed observed by the planets with the utmost exactness; therefore, the power of attraction causes all the planets to gravitate towards the sun, in like manner as the moon gravitates towards our globe.

Finally as in all bodies re-action is equal to action, it is certain that the earth gravitates also towards the moon; and that the sun gravitates towards both. That every one of the satellites of Saturn gravitates towards the other four, and the other four towards it; all five towards Saturn, and Saturn towards all. That it is the same with regard to Jupiter; and that all these globes are attracted by the sun, which is reciprocally attracted by them.

This power of gravitation acts proportionably to the quantity of matter in bodies, a truth, which Sir Isaac has demonstrated by experiments. This new discovery has been of use to show that the sun (the centre of the planetary system) attracts them all in a direct ratio of their quantity of matter combined with their nearness. From hence Sir Isaac, rising by degrees to discoveries which seemed not to be formed for the human mind, is bold enough to compute the quantity of matter contained in the sun and in every planet; and in this manner shows, from the simple laws of mechanics, that every celestial globe ought necessarily to be where it is placed.

His bare principle of the laws of gravitation accounts for all the apparent inequalities in the course of the celestial globes. The variations of the moon are a necessary consequence of those laws. Moreover, the reason is evidently seen why the nodes of the moon perform their revolutions in nineteen years, and those of the earth in about twenty-six thousand. The several appearances observed in the tides are also a very simple effect of this attraction. The proximity of the moon, when at the full, and when it is new, and its distance in the quadratures or quarters, combined with the action of the sun, exhibit a sensible reason why the ocean swells and sinks.

After having shown by his sublime theory the course and inequalities of the planets, he subjects comets to the same law. The orbit of these fires (unknown for so great a series of years), which was the terror of mankind and the rock against which philosophy split, placed by Aristotle below the moon, and sent back by Descartes above the sphere of Saturn, is at last placed in its proper seat by Sir Isaac Newton.

He proves that comets are solid bodies which move in the sphere of the sun's activity, and that they describe an ellipsis so very eccentric, and so near to parabolas, that certain comets must take up above five hundred years in their revolution.

The learned Dr. Halley is of opinion that the comet seen in 1680 is the same which appeared in Julius Cæsar's time. This shows more than any other that comets are hard, opaque bodies; for it descended so near to the sun, as to come within a sixth part of the diameter of this planet from it, and consequently might have contracted a degree of heat two thousand times stronger than that of red-hot iron; and would have been soon dispersed in vapour, had it not been a firm, dense body. The guessing the course of comets began then to be very much in vogue. The celebrated Bernoulli concluded by his system that the famous comet of 1680 would appear again the 17th of May, 1719. Not a single astronomer in Europe went to bed that night. However, they needed not to have broke their rest, for the famous comet never appeared. There is at least more cunning, if not more certainty, in fixing its return to so remote a distance as five hundred and seventy-five years. As to Mr. Whiston, he affirmed very seriously that in the time of the Deluge a comet overflowed the terrestrial globe. And he was so unreasonable as to wonder that people laughed at him for making such an assertion. The ancients were almost in the same way of thinking with Mr. Whiston, and fancied that comets were always the forerunners of some great calamity which was to befall mankind. Sir Isaac Newton, on the contrary, suspected that they are very beneficent, and that vapours exhale from them merely to nourish and vivify the planets, which imbibe in their course the several particles the sun has detached from the comets, an opinion which, at least, is more probable than the former. But this is not all. If this power of gravitation or attraction acts on all the celestial globes, it acts undoubtedly on the several parts of these globes. For in case bodies attract one another in proportion to the quantity of matter contained in them, it can only be in proportion to the quantity of their parts; and if this power is found in the whole, it is undoubtedly in the half, in the quarter, in the eighth part, and so on in *infinitum*.

This is attraction, the great spring by which all Nature is moved. Sir Isaac Newton, after having demonstrated the existence of this principle, plainly foresaw that its very name would offend; and, therefore, this philosopher, in more places than one of his books, gives the reader some caution about it. He bids him beware of confounding this name with what the ancients called occult qualities, but to be satisfied with knowing that there is in all bodies a central force, which acts to the utmost limits of the universe, according to the invariable laws of mechanics.

It is surprising, after the solemn protestations Sir Isaac made, that such eminent men as Mr. Sorin and M. de Fontenelle should have imputed to this great philosopher the verbal and chimerical way of reasoning of the Aristotelians; Mr. Sorin in the Memoirs of the Academy of 1709, and M. de Fontenelle in the very eulogium of Sir Isaac Newton.

Most of the French (the learned and others) have repeated this reproach. These are for ever crying out, "Why did he not employ the word *impulsion,* which is so well understood, rather than that of *attraction,* which is unintelligible?"

Sir Isaac might have answered these critics thus:—"First, you have as imperfect an idea of the word impulsion as of that of attraction;

and in case you cannot conceive how one body tends towards the centre of another body, neither can you conceive by what power one body can impel another.

"Secondly, I could not admit of impulsion; for to do this I must have known that a celestial matter was the agent. But so far from knowing that there is any such matter, I have proved it to be merely imaginary.

"Thirdly, I use the word attraction for no other reason but to express an effect which I discovered in Nature—a certain and indisputable effect of an unknown principle—a quality inherent in matter, the cause of which persons of greater abilities than I can pretend to may, if they can, find out."

"What have you, then, taught us?" will these people say further; "and to what purpose are so many calculations to tell us what you yourself do not comprehend?"

"I have taught you," may Sir Isaac rejoin, "that all bodies gravitate towards one another in proportion to their quantity of matter; that these central forces alone keep the planets and comets in their orbits, and cause them to move in the proportion before set down. I demonstrate to you that it is impossible there should be any other cause which keeps the planets in their orbits than that general phenomenon of gravity. For heavy bodies fall on the earth according to the proportion demonstrated of central forces; and the planets finishing their course according to these same proportions, in case there were another power that acted upon all those bodies, it would either increase their velocity or change their direction. Now, not one of those bodies ever has a single degree of motion or velocity, or has any direction but what is demonstrated to be the effect of the central forces. Consequently it is impossible there should be any other principle."

Give me leave once more to introduce Sir Isaac speaking. Shall he not be allowed to say, "My case and that of the ancients is very different. These saw, for instance, water ascend in pumps, and said, 'the water rises because it abhors a vacuum.' But with regard to myself, I am in the case of a man who should have first observed that water ascends in pumps, but should leave others to explain the cause of this effect. The anatomist, who first declared that the motion of the arm is owing to the contraction of the muscles, taught mankind an indisputable truth. But are they less obliged to him because he did not know the reason why the muscles contract? The cause of the elasticity of the air is unknown, but he who first discovered this spring performed a very signal service to natural philosophy. The spring that I discovered was more hidden and more universal, and for that very reason mankind ought to thank me the more. I have discovered a new property of matter—one of the secrets of the Creator—and have calculated and discovered the effects of it. After this, shall people quarrel with me about the name I give it?"

Vortices may be called an occult quality because their existence was never proved. Attraction, on the contrary, is a real thing because its effects are demonstrated, and the proportions of it are calculated. The cause of this cause is among the *Arcana* of the Almighty.

"*Procedes huc, et non amplius.*"

(Thus far shalt thou go, and no farther.)

Letter XVI

ON SIR ISAAC NEWTON'S OPTICS

The philosophers of the last age found out a new universe; and a circumstance which made its discovery more difficult was that no one had so much as suspected its existence. The most sage and judicious were of opinion that it was a frantic rashness to dare so much as to imagine that it was possible to guess the laws by which the celestial bodies move and the manner how light acts. Galileo, by his astronomical discoveries, Kepler, by his calculation, Descartes (at least, in his dioptrics), and Sir Isaac Newton, in all his works, severally saw the mechanism of the springs of the world. The geometricians have subjected infinity to the laws of calculation. The circulation of the blood in animals, and of the sap in vegetables, have changed the face of Nature with regard to us. A new kind of existence has been given to bodies in the air-pump. By the assistance of telescopes bodies have been brought nearer to one another. Finally, the several discoveries which Sir Isaac Newton has made on light are equal to the boldest things which the curiosity of man could expect after so many philosophical novelties.

Till Antonio de Dominis the rainbow was considered as an inexplicable miracle. This philosopher guessed that it was a necessary effect of the sun and rain. Descartes gained immortal fame by his mathematical explication of this so natural a phenomenon. He calculated the reflections and refractions of light in drops of rain. And his sagacity on this occasion was at that time looked upon as next to divine.

But what would he have said had it been proved to him that he was mistaken in the nature of light; that he had not the least reason to maintain that it is a globular body? That it is false to assert that this matter, spreading itself through the whole, waits only to be projected forward by the sun, in order to be put in action, in like manner as a long staff acts at one end when pushed forward by the other. That light is certainly darted by the sun; in fine, that light is transmitted from the sun to the earth in about seven minutes though a cannon-ball, which were not to lose any of its velocity, could not go that distance in less than twenty-five years. How great would have been his astonishment had he been told that light does not reflect directly by impinging against the solid parts of bodies, that bodies are not transparent when they have large pores, and that a man should arise who would demonstrate all these paradoxes, and anatomise a single ray of light with more dexterity than the ablest artist dissects a human body. This man is come. Sir Isaac Newton has demonstrated to the eye, by the bare assistance of the prism, that light is a composition of coloured rays, which, being united, form white colour. A single ray is by him divided into seven, which all fall upon a piece of linen, or a sheet of white paper, in their order, one above the other, and at unequal distances. The first is red, the second orange, the third yellow, the fourth green, the fifth blue, the sixth indigo, the seventh a violet-purple. Each of these rays, transmitted afterwards by a hundred other prisms, will never change the colour it bears; in like manner, as gold, when completely purged from its dross, will never change afterwards in the crucible. As a superabundant proof that each of these elementary rays has inherently in itself that which forms its colour to the eye, take a small piece of yellow wood, for instance, and set it in the ray of a red colour; this wood will instantly be tinged red. But set it in the ray of a green colour, it assumes a green colour, and so of all the rest.

From what cause, therefore, do colours arise in Nature? It is nothing but the disposition of bodies to reflect the rays of a certain order and to absorb all the rest.

What, then, is this secret disposition? Sir Isaac Newton demonstrates that it is nothing more than the density of the small constituent particles of which a body is composed. And how is this reflection performed? It was supposed to arise from the rebounding of the rays, in the same manner as a ball on the surface of a solid body. But this is a mistake, for Sir Isaac taught the astonished philosophers that bodies are opaque for no other reason but because their pores are large, that light reflects on our eyes from the very bosom of those pores, that the smaller the pores of a body are the more such a body is transparent. Thus paper, which reflects the light when dry, transmits it when oiled, because the oil, by filling its pores, makes them much smaller.

It is there that examining the vast porosity of bodies, every particle having its pores, and every particle of those particles having its own, he shows we are not certain that there is a cubic inch of solid matter in the universe, so far are we from conceiving what matter is. Having thus divided, as it were, light into its elements, and carried the sagacity of his discoveries so far as to prove the method of distinguishing compound colours from such as are primitive, he shows that these elementary rays, separated by the prism, are ranged in their order for no other reason but because they are refracted in that very order; and it is this property (unknown till he discovered it) of breaking or splitting in this proportion; it is this unequal refraction of rays, this power of refracting the red less than the orange colour, &c., which he calls the different refrangibility. The most reflexible rays are the most refrangible, and from hence he evinces that the same power is the cause both of the reflection and refraction of light.

But all these wonders are merely but the opening of his discoveries. He found out the secret to see the vibrations or fits of light which come and go incessantly, and which either transmit light or reflect it, according to the density of the parts they meet with. He has presumed to calculate the density of the particles of air necessary between two glasses, the one flat, the other convex on one side, set one upon the other, in order to operate such a transmission or reflection, or to form such and such a colour.

From all these combinations he discovers the proportion in which light acts on bodies and bodies act on light.

He saw light so perfectly, that he has determined to what degree of perfection the art of increasing it, and of assisting our eyes by telescopes, can be carried.

Descartes, from a noble confidence that was very excusable, considering how strongly he was fired at the first discoveries he made in an art which he almost first found out; Descartes, I say, hoped to discover in the stars, by the assistance of telescopes, objects as small as those we discern upon the earth.

But Sir Isaac has shown that dioptric telescopes cannot be brought to a greater perfection, because of that refraction, and of that very refrangibility, which at the same time that they bring objects nearer to us, scatter too much the elementary rays. He has calculated in these glasses the proportion of the scattering of the red and of the blue rays; and proceeding so far as to demonstrate things which were not supposed even to exist, he examines the inequalities which arise from the shape or figure of the glass, and that which arises from the refrangibility. He finds that the object glass of the telescope being convex on one side and flat on the other, in case the flat side be turned towards the object, the error which arises from the construction and position of the glass is above five thousand times less than the error which arises from the refrangibility; and, therefore, that the shape or figure of the glasses is not the cause why telescopes cannot be carried to a greater perfection, but arises wholly from the nature of light.

For this reason he invented a telescope, which discovers objects by reflection, and not by refraction. Telescopes of this new kind are very hard to make, and their use is not easy; but, according to the English, a reflective telescope of but five feet has the same effect as another of a hundred feet in length.

LETTER XVII

ON INFINITES IN GEOMETRY, AND SIR ISAAC NEWTON'S CHRONOLOGY

THE labyrinth and abyss of infinity is also a new course Sir Isaac Newton has gone through, and we are obliged to him for the clue, by whose assistance we are enabled to trace its various windings.

Descartes got the start of him also in this astonishing invention. He advanced with mighty steps in his geometry, and was arrived at the very borders of infinity, but went no farther. Dr. Wallis, about the middle of the last century, was the first who reduced a fraction by a perpetual division to an infinite series.

The Lord Brouncker employed this series to square the hyperbola.

Mercator published a demonstration of this quadrature; much about which time Sir Isaac Newton, being then twenty-three years of age, had invented a general method, to perform on all geometrical curves what had just before been tried on the hyperbola.

It is to this method of subjecting everywhere infinity to algebraical calculations, that the name is given of differential calculations or of fluxions and integral calculation. It is the art of numbering and measuring exactly a thing whose existence cannot be conceived.

And, indeed, would you not imagine that a man laughed at you who should declare that there are lines infinitely great which form an angle infinitely little?

That a right line, which is a right line so long as it is finite, by changing infinitely little its direction, becomes an infinite curve; and that a curve may become infinitely less than another curve?

That there are infinite squares, infinite cubes, and infinites of infinites, all greater than one another, and the last but one of which is nothing in comparison of the last?

All these things, which at first appear to be the utmost excess of frenzy, are in reality an effort of the subtlety and extent of the human mind, and the art of finding truths which till then had been unknown.

This so bold edifice is even founded on simple ideas. The business is to measure the diagonal of a square, to give the area of a curve, to find the square root of a number, which has none in common arithmetic. After all, the imagination ought not to be startled any more at so many orders of infinites than at the so well-known proposition, viz., that curve lines may always be made to pass between a circle and a tangent, or at that other, namely, that matter is divisible in *infinitum*. These two truths have been demonstrated many years, and are no less incomprehensible than the things we have been speaking of.

For many years the invention of this famous calculation was denied to Sir Isaac Newton. In Germany Mr. Leibnitz was considered as the inventor of the differences or moments, called fluxions, and Mr. Bernoulli claimed the integral calculus. However, Sir Isaac is now thought to have first made the discovery, and the other two have the glory of having once made the world doubt whether it was to be ascribed to him or them. Thus some contested with Dr. Harvey the invention of the circulation of the blood, as others disputed with Mr. Perrault that of the circulation of the sap.

Hartsocher and Leuwenhoek disputed with each other the honour of having first seen the *vermiculi* of which mankind are formed. This Hartsocher also contested with Huygens the invention of a new method of calculating the distance of a fixed star. It is not yet known to what philosopher we owe the invention of the cycloid.

Be this as it will, it is by the help of this geometry of infinites that Sir Isaac Newton attained to the most sublime discoveries. I am now to speak of another work, which, though more adapted to the capacity of the human mind, does nevertheless display some marks of that creative genius with which Sir Isaac Newton was informed in all his researches. The work I mean is a chronology of a new kind, for what province soever he undertook he was sure to change the ideas and opinions received by the rest of men.

Accustomed to unravel and disentangle chaos, he was resolved to convey at least some light into that of the fables of antiquity which are blended and confounded with history, and fix an uncertain chronology. It is true that there is no family, city, or nation, but endeavours to remove its original as far backward as possible. Besides, the first historians were the most negligent in setting down the eras: books were infinitely less common than they are at this time, and, consequently, authors being not so obnoxious to censure, they therefore imposed upon the world with greater impunity; and, as it is evident that these have related a great number of fictitious particulars, it is probable enough that they also gave us several false eras.

It appeared in general to Sir Isaac that the world was five hundred years younger than chronologers declare it to be. He grounds his opinion on the ordinary course of Nature, and on the observations which astronomers have made.

By the course of Nature we here understand the time that every generation of men lives upon the earth. The Egyptians first employed this vague and uncertain method of calculating when they began to write the beginning of their history. These computed three hundred and forty-one generations from Menes to Sethon; and, having no fixed era, they supposed three generations to consist of a hundred years. In this manner they computed eleven thousand three hundred and forty years from Menes's reign to that of Sethon.

The Greeks before they counted by Olympiads followed the method of the Egyptians, and even gave a little more extent to generations, making each to consist of forty years.

Now, here, both the Egyptians and the Greeks made an erroneous computation. It is true, indeed, that, according to the usual course of Nature, three generations last about a hundred and twenty years; but three reigns are far from taking up so many. It is very evident that mankind in general live longer than kings are found to reign, so that an author who should write a history in which there were no dates fixed, and should know that nine kings had reigned over a nation; such a historian would commit a great error should he allow three hundred years to these nine monarchs. Every generation takes about thirty-six years; every reign is, one with the other, about twenty. Thirty kings of England have swayed the sceptre from William the Conqueror to George I., the years of whose reigns added together amount to six hundred and forty-eight years; which, being divided equally among the thirty kings, give to every one a reign of twenty-one years and a half very near. Sixty-three kings of France have sat upon the throne; these have, one with another, reigned about twenty years each. This is the usual course of Nature. The ancients, therefore, were mistaken when they supposed the durations in general of reigns to equal that of generations. They, therefore, allowed too great a number of years, and consequently some years must be subtracted from their computation.

Astronomical observations seem to have lent a still greater assistance to our philosopher. He appears to us stronger when he fights upon his own ground.

You know that the earth, besides its annual motion which carries it round the sun from west to east in the space of a year, has also a singular revolution which was quite unknown till within these late years. Its poles have a very slow retrograde motion from east to west, whence it happens that their position every day does not correspond exactly with the same point of the heavens. This difference which is so insensible in a year, becomes pretty considerable in time; and in threescore and twelve years the difference is found to be of one degree, that is to say, the three hundred and sixtieth part of the circumference of the whole heaven. Thus after seventy-two years the colure of the vernal equinox which passed through a fixed star, corresponds with another fixed star. Hence it is that the sun, instead of being in that part of the heavens in which the Ram was situated in the time of Hipparchus, is found to correspond with that part of the heavens in which the Bull was situated; and the Twins are placed where the Bull then stood. All the signs have changed their situation, and yet we still retain the same manner of speaking as the ancients did. In this age we say that the sun is in the Ram in the spring, from the same principle of condescension that we say that the sun turns round.

Hipparchus was the first among the Greeks who observed some change in the constellations with regard to the equinoxes, or rather who learnt it from the Egyptians. Philosophers ascribed this motion to the stars; for in those ages people were far from imagining such a revolution in the earth, which was supposed to be immovable in every respect. They therefore created a heaven in which they fixed the several stars, and gave this heaven a particular motion by which it was carried towards the east, whilst that all the stars seemed to perform their diurnal revolution from east to west. To this error they added a second of much greater consequence, by imagining that the pretended heaven of the fixed stars advanced one degree eastward every hundred years. In this manner they were no less mistaken in their astronomical calculation than in their system of natural philosophy. As for instance, an astronomer in that age would have said that the vernal equinox was in the time of such and such an observation, in such a sign, and in such a star. It has advanced two degrees of each since the time that observation was made to the present. Now two degrees are equivalent to two hundred years; consequently the astronomer who made that observation lived just so many years before me. It is certain that an astronomer who had argued in this manner would have mistook just fifty-four years; hence it is that the ancients, who were doubly deceived, made their great year of the world, that is, the revolution of the whole heavens, to consist of thirty-six thousand years. But the moderns are sensible that this imaginary revolution of the heaven of the stars is nothing else than the revolution of the poles of the earth, which is performed in twenty-five thousand nine hundred years. It may be proper to observe transiently in this place, that Sir Isaac, by determining the figure of the earth, has very happily explained the cause of this revolution.

All this being laid down, the only thing remaining to settle chronology is to see through what star the colure of the equinoxes passes, and where it intersects at this time the ecliptic in the spring; and to discover whether some ancient writer does not tell us in what point the ecliptic was intersected in his time, by the same colure of the equinoxes.

Clemens Alexandrinus informs us, that Chiron, who went with the Argonauts, observed the constellations at the time of that famous expedition, and fixed the vernal equinox to the middle of the Ram; the autumnal equinox to the middle of Libra; our summer solstice to the middle of Cancer, and our winter solstice to the middle of Capricorn.

A long time after the expedition of the Argonauts, and a year before the Peloponnesian war, Methon observed that the point of the summer solstice passed through the eighth degree of Cancer.

Now every sign of the zodiac contains thirty degrees. In Chiron's time, the solstice was arrived at the middle of the sign, that is to say to the fifteenth degree. A year before the Peloponnesian war it was at the eighth, and therefore it had retarded seven degrees. A degree is equivalent to seventy-two years; consequently, from the beginning of the Peloponnesian war to the expedition of the Argonauts, there is no more than an interval of seven times seventy-two years, which make five hundred and four years, and not seven hundred years, as the Greeks computed. Thus in comparing the position of the heavens at this time with their position in that age, we find that the expedition of the Argonauts ought to be placed about nine hundred years before Christ, and not about fourteen hundred; and consequently that the world is not so old by five hundred years as it was generally supposed to be. By this calculation all the eras are drawn nearer, and the several events are found to have happened later than is computed. I don't know whether this ingenious system will be favourably received; and whether these notions will prevail so far with the learned, as to prompt them to reform the chronology of the world. Perhaps these gentlemen would think it too great a condescension to allow one and the same man the glory of having improved natural philosophy, geometry, and history. This would be a kind of universal monarchy, with which the principle of self-love that is in man will scarce suffer him to indulge his fellow-creature; and, indeed, at the same time that some very great philosophers attacked Sir Isaac Newton's attractive principle, others fell upon his chronological system. Time, that should discover to which of these the victory is due, may perhaps only leave the dispute still more undetermined.

LETTER XVIII

ON TRAGEDY

THE English as well as the Spaniards were possessed of theatres at a time when the French had no more than moving, itinerant stages. Shakspeare, who was considered as the Corneille of the first-mentioned nation, was pretty nearly contemporary with Lope de Vega, and he created, as it were, the English theatre. Shakspeare boasted a strong fruitful genius. He was natural and sublime, but had not so much as a single spark of good taste, or knew one rule of the drama. I will now hazard a random, but, at the same time, true reflection, which is, that the great merit of this dramatic poet has been the ruin of the English stage. There are such beautiful, such noble, such dreadful scenes in this writer's monstrous farces, to which the name of tragedy is given, that they have always been exhibited with great success. Time, which alone gives reputation to writers, at last makes their very faults venerable. Most of the whimsical gigantic images of this poet, have, through length of time (it being a hundred and fifty years since they were first drawn) acquired a right of passing for sublime. Most of the modern dramatic writers have copied him; but the touches and descriptions which are applauded in Shakspeare, are hissed at in these writers; and you will easily believe that the veneration in which this author is held, increases in proportion to the contempt which is shown to the moderns. Dramatic writers don't consider that they should not imitate him; and the ill-success of Shakspeare's imitators produces no other effect, than to make him be considered as inimitable. You remember that in the tragedy of *Othello, Moor of Venice,* a most tender piece, a man strangles his wife on the stage; and that the poor woman, whilst she is strangling, cries aloud that she dies very unjustly. You know that in *Hamlet, Prince of Denmark,* two grave-diggers make a grave, and are all the time drinking, singing ballads, and making humorous reflections (natural indeed enough to persons of their profession) on the several skulls they throw up with their spades; but a circumstance which will surprise you is, that this ridiculous incident has been imitated. In the reign of King Charles II., which was that of politeness, and the Golden Age of the liberal arts; Otway, in his *Venice Preserved,* introduces Antonio the senator, and Naki, his courtesan, in the midst of the horrors of the Marquis of Bedemar's conspiracy. Antonio, the super-annuated senator plays, in his mistress's presence, all the apish tricks of a lewd, impotent debauchee, who is quite frantic and out of his senses. He mimics a bull and a dog, and bites his mistress's legs, who kicks and whips him. However, the players have struck these buffooneries (which indeed were calculated merely for the dregs of the people) out of Otway's tragedy; but they have still left in Shakspeare's *Julius Cæsar* the jokes of the Roman shoemakers and cobblers, who are intro-

duced in the same scene with Brutus and Cassius. You will undoubtedly complain, that those who have hitherto discoursed with
you on the English stage, and especially on the celebrated Shakspeare, have taken notice only of his errors; and that no one has
translated any of those strong, those forcible passages which atone
for all his faults. But to this I will answer, that nothing is easier
than to exhibit in prose all the silly impertinences which a poet may
have thrown out; but that it is a very difficult task to translate his
fine verses. All your junior academical sophs, who set up for censors
of the eminent writers, compile whole volumes; but methinks two
pages which display some of the beauties of great geniuses, are of
infinitely more value than all the idle rhapsodies of those com-
mentators; and I will join in opinion with all persons of good taste
in declaring, that greater advantage may be reaped from a dozen
verses of Homer or Virgil, than from all the critiques put together
which have been made on those two great poets.

I have ventured to translate some passages of the most celebrated
English poets, and shall now give you one from Shakspeare. Pardon
the blemishes of the translation for the sake of the original; and
remember always that when you see a version, you see merely a
faint print of a beautiful picture. I have made choice of part of the
celebrated soliloquy in *Hamlet,* which you may remember is as
follows:—

> "To be, or not to be? that is the question!
> Whether 't is nobler in the mind to suffer
> The slings and arrows of outrageous fortune,
> Or to take arms against a sea of troubles,
> And by opposing, end them? To die! to sleep!
> No more! and by a sleep to say we end
> The heart-ache, and the thousand natural shocks
> That flesh is heir to! 'T is a consummation
> Devoutly to be wished. To die! to sleep!
> To sleep; perchance to dream! Ay, there's the rub;
> For in that sleep of death, what dreams may come
> When we have shuffled off this mortal coil,
> Must give us pause. There 's the respect
> That makes calamity of so long life:
> For who would bear the whips and scorns of time,
> The oppressor's wrong, the poor man's contumely,

The pangs of despised love, the law's delay,
The insolence of office, and the spurns
That patient merit of the unworthy takes,
When he himself might his quietus make
With a bare bodkin. Who would fardels bear
To groan and sweat under a weary life,
But that the dread of something after death,
The undiscovered country, from whose bourn
No traveller returns, puzzles the will,
And makes us rather bear those ills we have,
Than fly to others that we know not of?
Thus conscience does make cowards of us all;
And thus the native hue of resolution
Is sicklied o'er with the pale cast of thought:
And enterprises of great weight and moment
With this regard their currents turn awry,
And lose the name of action—"

My version of it runs thus:—

"Demeure, il faut choisir et passer à l'instant
De la vie à la mort, ou de l'être au neant.
Dieux cruels, s'il en est, éclairez mon courage.
Faut-il vieillir courbé sous la main qui m'outrage,
Supporter, ou finir mon malheur et mon sort?
Qui suis je? Qui m'arrête! et qu'est-ce que la mort?
C'est la fin de nos maux, c'est mon unique asile
Après de longs transports, c'est un sommeil tranquile.
On s'endort, et tout meurt, mais un affreux reveil
Doit succeder peut etre aux douceurs du sommeil!
On nous menace, on dit que cette courte vie,
De tourmens éternels est aussi-tôt suivie.
O mort! moment fatal! affreuse eternité!
Tout cœur à ton seul nom se glace épouvanté.
Eh! qui pourroit sans toi supporter cette vie,
De nos prêtres menteurs benir l'hypocrisie;
D'une indigne maitresse encenser les erreurs,
Ramper sous un ministre, adorer ses hauteurs;
Et montrer les langueurs de son ame abattüe,
A des amis ingrats qui detournent la vüe?
La mort seroit trop douce en ces extrémitez,
Mais le scrupule parle, et nous crie, arrêtez;
Il defend à nos mains cet heureux homicide
Et d'un heros guerrier, fait un Chrétien timide," &c.

Do not imagine that I have translated Shakspeare in a servile manner. Woe to the writer who gives a literal version; who by rendering every word of his original, by that very means enervates the sense, and extinguishes all the fire of it. It is on such an occasion one may justly affirm, that the letter kills, but the Spirit quickens.

Here follows another passage copied from a celebrated tragic writer among the English. It is Dryden, a poet in the reign of Charles II.—a writer whose genius was too exuberant, and not accompanied with judgment enough. Had he written only a tenth part of the works he left behind him, his character would have been conspicuous in every part; but his great fault is his having endeavoured to be universal.

The passage in question is as follows:—

> "When I consider life, 't is all a cheat,
> Yet fooled by hope, men favour the deceit;
> Trust on and think, to-morrow will repay;
> To-morrow's falser than the former day;
> Lies more; and whilst it says we shall be blest
> With some new joy, cuts off what we possessed;
> Strange cozenage! none would live past years again,
> Yet all hope pleasure in what yet remain,
> And from the dregs of life think to receive
> What the first sprightly running could not give.
> I'm tired with waiting for his chymic gold,
> Which fools us young, and beggars us when old."

I shall now give you my translation:—

> "De desseins en regrets et d'erreurs en desirs
> Les mortels insensés promenent leur folie.
> Dans des malheurs presents, dans l'espoir des plaisirs
> Nous ne vivons jamais, nous attendons la vie.
> Demain, demain, dit-on, va combler tous nos vœus.
> Demain vient, et nous laisse encore plus malheureux.
> Quelle est l'erreur, helas! du soin qui nous dévore,
> Nul de nous ne voudroit recommencer son cours.
> De nos premiers momens nous maudissons l'aurore,
> Et de la nuit qui vient nous attendons encore,
> Ce qu'ont en vain promis les plus beaux de nos jours," &c.

It is in these detached passages that the English have hitherto excelled. Their dramatic pieces, most of which are barbarous and without decorum, order, or verisimilitude, dart such resplendent flashes through this gleam, as amaze and astonish. The style is too much inflated, too unnatural, too closely copied from the Hebrew writers, who abound so much with the Asiatic fustian. But then it must be also confessed that the stilts of the figurative style, on which the English tongue is lifted up, raises the genius at the same time very far aloft, though with an irregular pace. The first English writer who composed a regular tragedy, and infused a spirit of elegance through every part of it, was the illustrious Mr. Addison. His "Cato" is a masterpiece, both with regard to the diction and to the beauty and harmony of the numbers. The character of Cato is, in my opinion, vastly superior to that of Cornelia in the "Pompey" of Corneille, for Cato is great without anything like fustian, and Cornelia, who besides is not a necessary character, tends sometimes to bombast. Mr. Addison's Cato appears to me the greatest character that was ever brought upon any stage, but then the rest of them do not correspond to the dignity of it, and this dramatic piece, so excellently well writ, is disfigured by a dull love plot, which spreads a certain languor over the whole, that quite murders it.

The custom of introducing love at random and at any rate in the drama passed from Paris to London about 1660, with our ribbons and our perruques. The ladies who adorn the theatrical circle there, in like manner as in this city will suffer love only to be the theme of every conversation. The judicious Mr. Addison had the effeminate complaisance to soften the severity of his dramatic character, so as to adapt it to the manners of the age, and, from an endeavour to please, quite ruined a masterpiece in its kind. Since his time the drama is become more regular, the audience more difficult to be pleased, and writers more correct and less bold. I have seen some new pieces that were written with great regularity, but which, at the same time, were very flat and insipid. One would think that the English had been hitherto formed to produce irregular beauties only. The shining monsters of Shakspeare give infinite more delight than the judicious images of the moderns. Hitherto the poetical genius of the English resembles a tufted tree planted by the hand of Nature, that throws out a thousand branches at random, and spreads unequally, but with great vigour. It dies if you attempt to force its nature, and to lop and dress it in the same manner as the trees of the Garden of Marli.

LETTER XIX

ON COMEDY

I AM surprised that the judicious and ingenious Mr. de Muralt, who has published some letters on the English and French nations, should have confined himself, in treating of comedy, merely to censure Shadwell the comic writer. This author was had in pretty great contempt in Mr. de Muralt's time, and was not the poet of the polite part of the nation. His dramatic pieces, which pleased some time in acting, were despised by all persons of taste, and might be compared to many plays which I have seen in France, that drew crowds to the play-house, at the same time that they were intolerable to read; and of which it might be said, that the whole city of Paris exploded them, and yet all flocked to see them represented on the stage. Methinks Mr. de Muralt should have mentioned an excellent comic writer (living when he was in England), I mean Mr. Wycherley, who was a long time known publicly to be happy in the good graces of the most celebrated mistress of King Charles II. This gentleman, who passed his life among persons of the highest distinction, was perfectly well acquainted with their lives and their follies, and painted them with the strongest pencil, and in the truest colours. He has drawn a misanthrope or man-hater, in imitation of that of Molière. All Wycherley's strokes are stronger and bolder than those of our misanthrope, but then they are less delicate, and the rules of decorum are not so well observed in this play. The English writer has corrected the only defect that is in Molière's comedy, the thinness of the plot, which also is so disposed that the characters in it do not enough raise our concern. The English comedy affects us, and the contrivance of the plot is very ingenious, but at the same time it is too bold for the French manners. The fable is this:—A captain of a man-of-war, who is very brave, open-hearted, and inflamed with a spirit of contempt for all mankind, has a prudent, sincere friend, whom he yet is suspicious of, and a mistress that loves him with the utmost excess of passion. The captain so far from returning her love, will not even condescend to look upon her, but confides entirely in a false friend, who is the most worthless wretch living. At the same time he has given his heart to a creature, who is the greatest coquette and the most perfidious of her sex, and he is so credulous as to be confident she is a Penelope, and his false friend a Cato. He embarks on board his ship in order to go and fight the Dutch, having left all his money, his jewels, and everything he had in the world to this virtuous creature, whom at the same time he recommends to the care of his supposed faithful friend. Nevertheless the real man of honour, whom he suspects so unaccountably, goes on board the ship with him, and the mistress, on whom he would not bestow so much as one glance, disguises herself in the habit of a page, and is with him the whole voyage, without his once knowing that she is of a sex different from that she attempts to pass for, which, by the way, is not over natural.

The captain having blown up his own ship in an engagement, returns to England abandoned and undone, accompanied by his page and his friend, without knowing the friendship of the one or the tender passion of the other. Immediately he goes to the jewel among women, who he expected had preserved her fidelity to him and the treasure he had left in her hands. He meets with her indeed, but married to the honest knave in whom he had reposed so much confidence, and finds she had acted as treacherously with regard to the casket he had entrusted her with. The captain can scarce think it possible that a woman of virtue and honour can act so vile a part; but to convince him still more of the reality of it, this very worthy lady falls in love with the little page, and will force him to her embraces. But as it is requisite justice should be done, and that in a dramatic piece virtue ought to be rewarded and vice punished, it is at last found that the captain takes his page's place and lies with his faithless mistress, cuckolds his treacherous friend, thrusts his sword through his body, recovers his casket, and marries his page. You will observe that this play is also larded with a petulant, litigious old woman (a relation of the captain), who is the most comical character that was ever brought upon the stage.

Wycherley has also copied from Molière another play, of as singular and bold a cast, which is a kind of *Ecole des Femmes,* or, *School for Married Women.*

The principal character in this comedy is one Horner, a sly fortune hunter, and the terror of all the City husbands. This fellow, in order to play a surer game, causes a report to be spread, that in his last illness, the surgeons had found it necessary to have him made a eunuch. Upon his appearing in this noble character, all the husbands in town flocked to him with their wives, and now poor Horner is only puzzled about his choice. However, he gives the preference particularly to a little female peasant, a very harmless, innocent creature, who enjoys a fine flush of health, and cuckolds her husband with a simplicity that has infinitely more merit than the witty malice of the most experienced ladies. This play cannot indeed be called the school of good morals, but it is certainly the school of wit and true humour.

Sir John Vanbrugh has written several comedies, which are more humorous than those of Mr. Wycherley, but not so ingenious. Sir John was a man of pleasure, and likewise a poet and an architect. The general opinion is, that he is as sprightly in his writings as he is heavy in his buildings. It is he who raised the famous Castle of Blenheim, a ponderous and lasting monument of our unfortunate Battle of Hochstet. Were the apartments but as spacious as the walls are thick, this castle would be commodious enough. Some wag, in an epitaph he made on Sir John Vanbrugh, has these lines:—

> "Earth lie light on him, for he
> Laid many a heavy load on thee."

Sir John having taken a tour into France before the glorious war that broke out in 1701, was thrown into the Bastille, and detained there for some time, without being ever able to discover the motive which had prompted our ministry to indulge him with this mark of their distinction. He wrote a comedy during his confinement; and a circumstance which appears to me very extraordinary is, that we don't meet with so much as a single satirical stroke against the country in which he had been so injuriously treated.

The late Mr. Congreve raised the glory of comedy to a greater height than any English writer before or since his time. He wrote only a few plays, but they are all excellent in their kind. The laws of the drama are strictly observed in them; they abound with characters all which are shadowed with the utmost delicacy, and we don't meet with so much as one low or coarse jest. The language is everywhere that of men of honour, but their actions are those of knaves—a proof that he was perfectly well acquainted with human nature, and frequented what we call polite company. He was infirm and come to the verge of life when I knew him. Mr. Congreve had one defect, which was his entertaining too mean an idea of his first profession (that of a writer), though it was to this he owed his fame and fortune. He spoke of his works as of trifles that were beneath him; and hinted to me, in our first conversation, that I should visit him upon no other footing than that of a gentleman who led a life of plainness and simplicity. I answered, that had he been so unfortunate as to be a mere gentleman, I should never have come to see him; and I was very much disgusted at so unseasonable a piece of vanity.

Mr. Congreve's comedies are the most witty and regular, those of Sir John Vanbrugh most gay and humorous, and those of Mr. Wycherley have the greatest force and spirit. It may be proper to observe that these fine geniuses never spoke disadvantageously of Molière; and that none but the contemptible writers among the English have endeavoured to lessen the character of that great comic poet. Such Italian musicians as despise Lully are themselves persons of no character or ability; but a Buononcini esteems that great artist, and does justice to his merit.

The English have some other good comic writers living, such as Sir Richard Steele and Mr. Cibber, who is an excellent player, and also Poet Laureate—a title which, how ridiculous soever it may be thought, is yet worth a thousand crowns a year (besides some considerable privileges) to the person who enjoys it. Our illustrious Corneille had not so much.

To conclude. Don't desire me to descend to particulars with regard to these English comedies, which I am so fond of applauding; nor to give you a single smart saying or humorous stroke from Wycherley or Congreve. We don't laugh in reading a translation.

If you have a mind to understand the English comedy, the only way to do this will be for you to go to England, to spend three years in London, to make yourself master of the English tongue, and to frequent the playhouse every night. I receive but little pleasure from the perusal of Aristophanes and Plautus, and for this reason because I am neither a Greek nor a Roman. The delicacy of the humour, the allusion, the *à propos*—all these are lost to a foreigner.

But it is different with respect to tragedy, this treating only of exalted passions and heroical follies, which the antiquated errors of fable or history have made sacred. Œdipus, Electra, and such-like characters, may with as much propriety be treated of by the Spaniards, the English, or us, as by the Greeks. But true comedy is the speaking picture of the follies and ridiculous foibles of a nation; so that he only is able to judge of the painting who is perfectly acquainted with the people it represents.

Letter XX

ON SUCH OF THE NOBILITY AS CULTIVATE THE *BELLES LETTRES*

There once was a time in France when the polite arts were cultivated by persons of the highest rank in the state. The courtiers particularly were conversant in them, although indolence, a taste for trifles, and a passion for intrigue, were the divinities of the country. The Court methinks at this time seems to have given into a taste quite opposite to that of polite literature, but perhaps the mode of thinking may be revived in a little time. The French are of so flexible a disposition, may be moulded into such a variety of shapes, that the monarch needs but command and he is immediately obeyed. The English generally think, and learning is had in greater honour among them than in our country—an advantage that results naturally from the form of their government. There are about eight hundred persons in England who have a right to speak in public, and to support the interest of the kingdom and near five or six thousand may in their turns aspire to the same honour. The whole nation set themselves up as judges over these, and every man has the liberty of publishing his thoughts with regard to public affairs, which shows that all the people in general are indispensably obliged to cultivate their understandings. In England the governments of Greece and Rome are the subject of every conversation, so that every man is under a necessity of perusing such authors as treat of them, how disagreeable soever it may be to him; and this study leads naturally to that of polite literature. Mankind in general speak well in their respective professions. What is the reason why our magistrates, our lawyers, our physicians, and a great number of the clergy, are abler scholars, have a finer taste, and more wit, than persons of all other professions? The reason is, because their condition of life requires a cultivated and enlightened mind, in the same manner as a merchant is obliged to be acquainted with his traffic. Not long since an English nobleman, who was very young, came to see me at Paris on his return from Italy. He had written a poetical description of that country, which, for delicacy and politeness, may vie with anything we meet with in the Earl of Rochester, or in our Chaulieu, our Sarrasin, or Chapelle. The translation I have given of it is so inexpressive of the strength and delicate humour of the original, that I am obliged seriously to ask pardon of the author and of all who understand English. However, as this is the only method I have to make his lordship's verses known, I shall here present you with them in our tongue:—

"Qu'ay je donc vû dans l'Italie?
Orgueil, astuce, et pauvreté,
Grands complimens, peu de bonté
Et beaucoup de ceremonie

"L'extravagante comedie
Que souvent l'Inquisition
Veut qu'on nomme religion
Mais qu'ici nous nommons folie.

"La Nature en vain bienfaisante
Veut enricher ses lieux charmans,
Des prêtres la main desolante
Etouffe ses plus beaux présens.

"Les monsignors, soy disant Grands,
  Seuls dans leurs palais magnifiques
  Y sont d'illustres faineants,
  Sans argent, et sans domestiques.

"Pour les petits, sans liberté,
  Martyrs du joug qui les domine,
  Ils ont fait vœu de pauvreté,
  Priant Dieu par oisiveté
  Et toujours jeunant par famine.

"Ces beaux lieux du Pape benis
  Semblent habitez par les diables;
  Et les habitans miserables
  Sont damnes dans le Paradis."

LETTER XXI

ON THE EARL OF ROCHESTER AND MR. WALLER

The Earl of Rochester's name is universally known. Mr. de St. Evremont has made very frequent mention of him, but then he has represented this famous nobleman in no other light than as the man of pleasure, as one who was the idol of the fair; but, with regard to myself, I would willingly describe in him the man of genius, the great poet. Among other pieces which display the shining imagination his lordship only could boast, he wrote some satires on the same subjects as those our celebrated Boileau made choice of. I do not know any better method of improving the taste than to compare the productions of such great geniuses as have exercised their talent on the same subject. Boileau declaims as follows against human reason in his "Satire on Man":

"Cependant à le voir plein de vapeurs légeres,
  Soi-même se bercer de ses propres chimeres,
  Lui seul de la nature est la baze et l'appui,
  Et le dixieme ciel ne tourne que pour lui.
  De tous les animaux il est ici le maître;
  Qui pourroit le nier, poursuis tu? Moi peut-être
  Ce mâitre prétendu qui leur donne des loix,
  Ce roi des animaux, combien a-t'il de rois?"

"Yet, pleased with idle whimsies of his brain,
And puffed with pride, this haughty thing would fain
Be think himself the only stay and prop
That holds the mighty frame of Nature up.
The skies and stars his properties must seem,

* * * * * * * *

Of all the creatures he's the lord, he cries.

* * * * * * *

And who is there, say you, that dares deny
So owned a truth? That may be, sir, do I.

* * * * * * * *

This boasted monarch of the world who awes
The creatures here, and with his nod gives laws
This self-named king, who thus pretends to be
The lord of all, how many lords has he?"

OLDHAM, a little altered.

The Lord Rochester expresses himself, in his "Satire against Man," in pretty near the following manner. But I must first desire you always to remember that the versions I give you from the English poets are written with freedom and latitude, and that the restraint of our versification, and the delicacies of the French tongue, will not allow a translator to convey into it the licentious impetuosity and fire of the English numbers:—

"Cet esprit que je haïs, cet esprit plein d'erreur,
Ce n'est pas ma raison c'est la tienne, docteur
C'est la raison frivôle, inquiete, orgueilleuse
Des sages animaux, rivale dédaigneuse,
Qui croit entr'eux et l'Ange, occuper le milieu,
Et pense être ici bas l'image de son Dieu.
Vil atôme imparfait, qui croit, doute, dispute
Rampe, s'élève, tombe, et nie encore sa chûte,
Qui nous dit je suis libre, en nous montrant ses fers,
Et dont l'œil, trouble et faux, croit percer l'univers.
Allez, reverends fous, bienheureux fanatiques,
Compilez bien l'amas de vos riens scholastiques,
Pères de visions, et d'enigmes sacres,
Auteurs du labirinthe, où vous vous égarez.
Allez obscurement éclaircir vos mistères,
Et courez dans l'école adorer vos chimères.
Il est d'autres erreurs, il est de ces dévots

Condamné par eux mêmes à l'ennui du repos.
Ce mystique encloîtré, fier de son indolence
Tranquille, au sein de Dieu. Que peut il faire? Il pense.
Non, tu ne penses point, misérable, tu dors:
Inutile à la terre, et mis au rang des morts.
Ton esprit énervé croupit dans la molesse.
Reveille toi, sois homme, et sors de ton ivresse.
L'homme est né pour agir, et tu pretens penser?" &c.

The original runs thus:

"Hold mighty man, I cry all this we know,
And 'tis this very reason I despise,
This supernatural gift that makes a mite
Think he's the image of the Infinite;
Comparing his short life, void of all rest,
To the eternal and the ever blest.
This busy, puzzling stirrer up of doubt,
That frames deep mysteries, then finds them out,
Filling, with frantic crowds of thinking fools,
Those reverend bedlams, colleges, and schools;
Borne on whose wings each heavy sot can pierce
The limits of the boundless universe.
So charming ointments make an old witch fly,
And bear a crippled carcass through the sky.
'Tis this exalted power, whose business lies
In nonsense and impossibilities.
This made a whimsical philosopher
Before the spacious world his tub prefer;
And we have modern cloistered coxcombs, who
Retire to think, 'cause they have naught to do.
But thoughts are given for action's government,
Where action ceases, thought's impertinent."

Whether these ideas are true or false, it is certain they are expressed with an energy and fire which form the poet. I shall be very far from attempting to examine philosophically into these verses, to lay down the pencil, and take up the rule and compass on this occasion; my only design in this letter being to display the genius of the English poets, and therefore I shall continue in the same view.

The celebrated Mr. Waller has been very much talked of in France, and Mr. de la Fontaine, St. Evremont, and Bayle have written his eulogium, but still his name only is known. He had much the same reputation in London as Voiture had in Paris, and in my opinion deserved it better. Voiture was born in an age that was just emerging from barbarity; an age that was still rude and ignorant, the people of which aimed at wit, though they had not the least pretensions to it, and sought for points and conceits instead of sentiments. Bristol stones are more easily found than diamonds. Voiture, born with an easy and frivolous genius, was the first who shone in this aurora of French literature. Had he come into the world after those great geniuses who spread such a glory over the age of Louis XIV., he would either have been unknown, would have been despised, or would have corrected his style. Boileau applauded him, but it was in his first satires, at a time when the taste of that great poet was not yet formed. He was young, and in an age when persons form a judgment of men from their reputation, and not from their writings. Besides, Boileau was very partial both in his encomiums and his censures. He applauded Segrais, whose works nobody reads; he abused Quinault, whose poetical pieces every one has got by heart; and is wholly silent upon La Fontaine. Waller, though a better poet than Voiture, was not yet a finished poet. The graces breathe in such of Waller's works as are writ in a tender strain; but then they are languid through negligence, and often disfigured with false thoughts. The English had not in his time attained the art of correct writing. But his serious compositions exhibit a strength and vigour which could not have been expected from the softness and effeminacy of his other pieces. He wrote an elegy on Oliver Cromwell, which, with all its faults, is nevertheless looked upon as a masterpiece. To understand this copy of verses you are to know that the day Oliver died was remarkable for a great storm. His poem begins in this manner:—

> "Il n'est plus, s'en est fait, soumettons nous au sort,
> Le ciel a signalé ce jour par des tempêtes,
> Et la voix des tonnerres éclatant sur nos têtes
> Vient d'annoncer sa mort.

> "Par ses derniers soupirs il ébranle cet ile;
> Cet ile que son bras fit trembler tant de fois,
> Quand dans le cours de ses exploits,
> Il brisoit la téte des Rois,
> Et soumettoit un peuple à son joug seul docile.

"Mer tu t'en es troublé; O mer tes flots émus
Semblent dire en grondant aux plus lointains rivages
Que l'effroi de la terre et ton maitre n'est plus.

"Tel au ciel autrefois s'envola Romulus,
Tel il quitta la Terre, au milieu des orages,
Tel d'un peuple guerrier il reçut les homages;
Obéï dans sa vie, à sa mort adoré,
Son palais fut un Temple," &c.

"We must resign! heaven his great soul does claim
In storms as loud as his immortal fame;
His dying groans, his last breath shakes our isle,
And trees uncut fall for his funeral pile:
About his palace their broad roots are tost
Into the air; so Romulus was lost!
New Rome in such a tempest missed her king,
And from obeying fell to worshipping.
On Œta's top thus Hercules lay dead,
With ruined oaks and pines about him spread.
Nature herself took notice of his death,
And, sighing, swelled the sea with such a breath,
That to remotest shores the billows rolled,
Th' approaching fate of his great ruler told."

WALLER.

It was this eulogium that gave occasion to the reply (taken notice of in Bayle's Dictionary), which Waller made to King Charles II. This king, to whom Waller had a little before (as is usual with bards and monarchs) presented a copy of verses embroidered with praises, reproached the poet for not writing with so much energy and fire as when he had applauded the Usurper (meaning Oliver). "Sir," replied Waller to the king, "we poets succeed better in fiction than in truth." This answer was not so sincere as that which a Dutch Ambassador made, who, when the same monarch complained that his masters paid less regard to him than they had done to Cromwell: "Ah, sir!" says the Ambassador, "Oliver was quite another man ——." It is not my intent to give a commentary on Waller's character, nor on that of any other person; for I consider men after their death in no other light than as they were writers, and wholly disregard everything else. I shall only observe that Waller, though born in a Court, and to an estate of five or six thousand pounds sterling a year, was never so proud or so indolent as to lay aside the happy talent which Nature had indulged him. The Earls of Dorset and Roscommon, the two Dukes of Buckingham, the Lord Halifax, and so many other noblemen, did not think the reputation they obtained of very great poets and illustrious writers, any way derogatory to their quality. They are more glorious for their works than for their titles. These cultivated the polite arts with as much assiduity as though they had been their whole dependence. They also have made learning appear venerable in the eyes of the vulgar, who have need to be led in all things by the great; and who, nevertheless, fashion their manners less after those of the nobility (in England I mean) than in any other country in the world.

LETTER XXII

ON MR. POPE AND SOME OTHER FAMOUS POETS

I INTENDED to treat of Mr. Prior, one of the most amiable English poets, whom you saw Plenipotentiary and Envoy Extraordinary at Paris in 1712. I also designed to have given you some idea of the Lord Roscommon's and the Lord Dorset's muse; but I find that to do this I should be obliged to write a large volume, and that, after much pains and trouble, you would have but an imperfect idea of all those works. Poetry is a kind of music in which a man should have some knowledge before he pretends to judge of it. When I give you a translation of some passages from those foreign poets, I only prick down, and that imperfectly, their music; but then I cannot express the taste of their harmony.

There is one English poem especially which I should despair of ever making you understand, the title whereof is "Hudibras." The subject of it is the Civil War in the time of the grand rebellion, and the principles and practice of the Puritans are therein ridiculed. It is Don Quixote, it is our "Satire Menippée" blended together. I never found so much wit in one single book as in that, which at the same time is the most difficult to be translated. Who would believe that a work which paints in such lively and natural colours the

several foibles and follies of mankind, and where we meet with more
sentiments than words, should baffle the endeavours of the ablest
translator? But the reason of this is, almost every part of it alludes
to particular incidents. The clergy are there made the principal
object of ridicule, which is understood but by few among the laity.
To explain this a commentary would be requisite, and humour when
explained is no longer humour. Whoever sets up for a commentator
of smart sayings and repartees is himself a blockhead. This is the
reason why the works of the ingenious Dean Swift, who has been
called the English Rabelais, will never be well understood in France.
This gentleman has the honour (in common with Rabelais) of being
a priest, and, like him, laughs at everything; but, in my humble
opinion, the title of the English Rabelais which is given the dean is
highly derogatory to his genius. The former has interspersed his
unaccountably fantastic and unintelligible book with the most gay
strokes of humour; but which at the same time, has a greater proportion of impertinence. He has been vastly lavish of erudition, of smut,
and insipid raillery. An agreeable tale of two pages is purchased at
the expense of whole volumes of nonsense. There are but few
persons, and those of a grotesque taste, who pretend to understand
and to esteem this work; for, as to the rest of the nation, they laugh
at the pleasant and diverting touches which are found in Rabelais
and despise his book. He is looked upon as the prince of buffoons.
The readers are vexed to think that a man who was master of so
much wit should have made so wretched a use of it; he is an intoxi-
cated philosopher who never wrote but when he was in liquor.

Dean Swift is Rabelais in his senses, and frequently the politest
company. The former, indeed, is not so gay as the latter, but then
he possesses all the delicacy, the justness, the choice, the good taste, in
all which particulars our giggling rural Vicar Rabelais is wanting.
The poetical numbers of Dean Swift are of a singular and almost
inimitable taste; true humour, whether in prose or verse, seems to be
his peculiar talent; but whoever is desirous of understanding him
perfectly must visit the island in which he was born.

It will be much easier for you to form an idea of Mr. Pope's works.
He is, in my opinion, the most elegant, the most correct poet; and,
at the same time, the most harmonious (a circumstance which re-

dounds very much to the honour of this muse) that England ever
gave birth to. He has mellowed the harsh sounds of the English
trumpet to the soft accents of the flute. His compositions may be
easily translated, because they are vastly clear and perspicuous; besides, most of his subjects are general, and relative to all nations.

His "Essay on Criticism" will soon be known in France by the
translation which l'Abbé de Renel has made of it.

Here is an extract from his poem entitled the "Rape of the Lock,"
which I just now translated with the latitude I usually take on these
occasions; for, once again, nothing can be more ridiculous than to
translate a poet literally:—

> "Umbriel, à l'instant, vieil gnome rechigné,
> Va d'une aîle pesante et d'un air renfrogné
> Chercher en murmurant la caverne profonde,
> Où loin des doux raïons que répand l'œil du monde
> La Déesse aux Vapeurs a choisi son séjour,
> Les Tristes Aquilons y sifflent à l'entour,
> Et le souffle mal sain de leur aride haleine
> Y porte aux environs la fievre et la migraine.
> Sur un riche sofa derrière un paravent
> Loin des flambeaux, du bruit, des parleurs et du vent
> La quinteuse déesse incessamment repose,
> Le cœur gros de chagrin, sans en savoir la cause.
> N'aiant pensé jamais, l'esprit toujours troublé,
> L'œil chargé, le teint pâle, et l'hypocondre enflé.
> La médisante Envie, est assise auprès d'elle,
> Vieil spectre féminin, décrépite pucelle,
> Avec un air devot déchirant son prochain,
> Et chansonnant les Gens l'Evangile à la main.
> Sur un lit plein de fleurs negligemment panchée
> Une jeune beauté non loin d'elle est couchée,
> C'est l'Affectation qui grassaïe en parlant,
> Ecoute sans entendre, et lorgne en regardant.
> Qui rougit sans pudeur, et rit de tout sans joie,
> De cent maux différens prétend qu'elle est la proïe;
> Et pleine de santé sous le rouge et le fard,
> Se plaint avec molesse, et se pame avec art."

> "Umbriel, a dusky, melancholy sprite
> As ever sullied the fair face of light,
> Down to the central earth, his proper scene,

Repairs to search the gloomy cave of Spleen.
Swift on his sooty pinions flits the gnome,
And in a vapour reached the dismal dome.
No cheerful breeze this sullen region knows,
The dreaded east is all the wind that blows.
Here, in a grotto, sheltered close from air,
And screened in shades from day's detested glare,
She sighs for ever on her pensive bed,
Pain at her side, and Megrim at her head,
Two handmaids wait the throne. Alike in place,
But differing far in figure and in face,
Here stood Ill-nature, like an ancient maid,
Her wrinkled form in black and white arrayed;
With store of prayers for mornings, nights, and noons
Her hand is filled; her bosom with lampoons.
There Affectation, with a sickly mien,
Shows in her cheek the roses of eighteen,
Practised to lisp, and hang the head aside,
Faints into airs, and languishes with pride;
On the rich quilt sinks with becoming woe,
Wrapt in a gown, for sickness and for show."

This extract, in the original (not in the faint translation I have
given you of it), may be compared to the description of *La Molesse*
(softness or effeminacy), in Boileau's "Lutrin."

Methinks I now have given you specimens enough from the
English poets. I have made some transient mention of their philosophers, but as for good historians among them, I don't know of any;
and, indeed, a Frenchman was forced to write their history. Possibly
the English genius, which is either languid or impetuous, has not
yet acquired that unaffected eloquence, that plain but majestic air
which history requires. Possibly too, the spirit of party which exhibits objects in a dim and confused light may have sunk the credit
of their historians. One half of the nation is always at variance with
the other half. I have met with people who assured me that the
Duke of Marlborough was a coward, and that Mr. Pope was a fool;
just as some Jesuits in France declare Pascal to have been a man of
little or no genius, and some Jansenists affirm Father Bourdaloüe to
have been a mere babbler. The Jacobites consider Mary Queen of
Scots as a pious heroine, but those of an opposite party look upon her
as a prostitute, an adulteress, a murderer. Thus the English have

memorials of the several reigns, but no such thing as a history. There is, indeed, now living, one Mr. Gordon (the public are obliged to him for a translation of Tacitus), who is very capable of writing the history of his own country, but Rapin de Thoyras got the start of him. To conclude, in my opinion the English have not such good historians as the French, have no such thing as a real tragedy, have several delightful comedies, some wonderful passages in certain of their poems, and boast of philosophers that are worthy of instructing mankind. The English have reaped very great benefit from the writers of our nation, and therefore we ought (since they have not scrupled to be in our debt) to borrow from them. Both the English and we came after the Italians, who have been our instructors in all the arts, and whom we have surpassed in some. I cannot determine which of the three nations ought to be honoured with the palm; but happy the writer who could display their various merits.

LETTER XXIII

ON THE REGARD THAT OUGHT TO BE SHOWN TO MEN OF LETTERS

Neither the English nor any other people have foundations established in favour of the polite arts like those in France. There are Universities in most countries, but it is in France only that we meet with so beneficial an encouragement for astronomy and all parts of the mathematics, for physic, for researches into antiquity, for painting, sculpture, and architecture. Louis XIV. has immortalised his name by these several foundations, and this immortality did not cost him two hundred thousand livres a year.

I must confess that one of the things I very much wonder at is, that as the Parliament of Great Britain have promised a reward of £20,000 sterling to any person who may discover the longitude, they should never have once thought to imitate Louis XIV. in his munificence with regard to the arts and sciences.

Merit, indeed, meets in England with rewards of another kind, which redound more to the honour of the nation. The English have so great a veneration for exalted talents, that a man of merit in their country is always sure of making his fortune. Mr. Addison in France would have been elected a member of one of the academies, and, by the credit of some women, might have obtained a yearly pension of twelve hundred livres, or else might have been imprisoned in the Bastile, upon pretence that certain strokes in his tragedy of *Cato* had been discovered which glanced at the porter of some man in power. Mr. Addison was raised to the post of Secretary of State in England. Sir Isaac Newton was made Warden of the Royal Mint. Mr. Congreve had a considerable employment. Mr. Prior was Plenipotentiary. Dr. Swift is Dean of St. Patrick in Dublin, and is more revered in Ireland than the Primate himself. The religion which Mr. Pope professes excludes him, indeed, from preferments of every kind, but then it did not prevent his gaining two hundred thousand livres by his excellent translation of Homer. I myself saw a long time in France the author of *Rhadamistus* ready to perish for hunger. And the son of one of the greatest men our country ever gave birth to, and who was beginning to run the noble career which his father had set him, would have been reduced to the extremes of misery had he not been patronised by Monsieur Fagon.

But the circumstance which mostly encourages the arts in England is the great veneration which is paid them. The picture of the Prime Minister hangs over the chimney of his own closet, but I have seen that of Mr. Pope in twenty noblemen's houses. Sir Isaac Newton was revered in his lifetime, and had a due respect paid to him after his death; the greatest men in the nation disputing who should have the honour of holding up his pall. Go into Westminster Abbey, and you will find that what raises the admiration of the spectator is not the mausoleums of the English kings, but the monuments which the gratitude of the nation has erected to perpetuate the memory of those illustrious men who contributed to its glory. We view their statues in that abbey in the same manner as those of Sophocles, Plato, and other immortal personages were viewed in Athens; and I am persuaded that the bare sight of those glorious monuments has fired more than one breast, and been the occasion of their becoming great men.

The English have even been reproached with paying too extrava-gant honours to mere merit, and censured for interring the celebrated actress Mrs. Oldfield in Westminster Abbey, with almost the same pomp as Sir Isaac Newton. Some pretend that the English had paid her these great funeral honours, purposely to make us more strongly sensible of the barbarity and injustice which they object to in us, for having buried Mademoiselle Le Couvreur ignominiously in the fields.

But be assured from me, that the English were prompted by no other principle in burying Mrs. Oldfield in Westminster Abbey than their good sense. They are far from being so ridiculous as to brand with infamy an art which has immortalised a Euripides and a Sophocles; or to exclude from the body of their citizens a set of people whose business is to set off with the utmost grace of speech and action those pieces which the nation is proud of.

Under the reign of Charles I. and in the beginning of the civil wars raised by a number of rigid fanatics, who at last were the victims to it; a great many pieces were published against theatrical and other shows, which were attacked with the greater virulence because that monarch and his queen, daughter to Henry IV. of France, were passionately fond of them.

One Mr. Prynne, a man of most furiously scrupulous principles, who would have thought himself damned had he worn a cassock instead of a short cloak, and have been glad to see one-half of mankind cut the other to pieces for the glory of God, and the *Propaganda Fide;* took it into his head to write a most wretched satire against some pretty good comedies, which were exhibited very innocently every night before their majesties. He quoted the authority of the Rabbis, and some passages from St. Bonaventure, to prove that the Œdipus of Sophocles was the work of the evil spirit; that Terence was excommunicated *ipso facto;* and added, that doubtless Brutus, who was a very severe Jansenist, assassinated Julius Cæsar for no other reason but because he, who was Pontifex Maximus, presumed to write a tragedy the subject of which was Œdipus. Lastly, he declared that all who frequented the theatre were excommunicated, as they thereby renounced their baptism. This was casting the highest insult on the king and all the royal family; and as the English loved their prince at that time, they could not bear to hear a writer talk of excommunicating him, though they themselves afterwards cut his head off. Prynne was summoned to appear before the Star

Chamber; his wonderful book, from which Father Le Brun stole his, was sentenced to be burnt by the common hangman, and himself to lose his ears. His trial is now extant.

The Italians are far from attempting to cast a blemish on the opera, or to excommunicate Signor Senesino or Signora Cuzzoni. With regard to myself, I could presume to wish that the magistrates would suppress I know not what contemptible pieces written against the stage. For when the English and Italians hear that we brand with the greatest mark of infamy an art in which we excel; that we excommunicate persons who receive salaries from the king; that we condemn as impious a spectacle exhibited in convents and monasteries; that we dishonour sports in which Louis XIV. and Louis XV. performed as actors; that we give the title of the devil's works to pieces which are received by magistrates of the most severe character, and represented before a virtuous queen; when, I say, foreigners are told of this insolent conduct, this contempt for the royal authority, and this Gothic rusticity which some presume to call Christian severity, what an idea must they entertain of our nation? And how will it be possible for them to conceive, either that our laws give a sanction to an art which is declared infamous, or that some persons dare to stamp with infamy an art which receives a sanction from the laws, is rewarded by kings, cultivated and encouraged by the greatest men, and admired by whole nations? And that Father Le Brun's impertinent libel against the stage is seen in a bookseller's shop, standing the very next to the immortal labours of Racine, of Corneille, of Molière, &c.

Letter XXIV

ON THE ROYAL SOCIETY AND OTHER ACADEMIES

The English had an Academy of Sciences many years before us, but then it is not under such prudent regulations as ours, the only reason of which very possibly is, because it was founded before the Academy of Paris; for had it been founded after, it would very probably have adopted some of the sage laws of the former and improved upon others.

Two things, and those the most essential to man, are wanting in the Royal Society of London, I mean rewards and laws. A seat in the Academy at Paris is a small but secure fortune to a geometrician or a chemist; but this is so far from being the case at London, that the several members of the Royal Society are at a continual, though indeed small expense. Any man in England who declares himself a lover of the mathematics and natural philosophy, and expresses an inclination to be a member of the Royal Society, is immediately elected into it. But in France it is not enough that a man who aspires to the honour of being a member of the Academy, and of receiving the royal stipend, has a love for the sciences; he must at the same time be deeply skilled in them; and is obliged to dispute the seat with competitors who are so much the more formidable as they are fired by a principle of glory, by interest, by the difficulty itself, and by that inflexibility of mind which is generally found in those who devote themselves to that pertinacious study, the mathematics.

The Academy of Sciences is prudently confined to the study of Nature, and, indeed, this is a field spacious enough for fifty or three-score persons to range in. That of London mixes indiscriminately literature with physics; but methinks the founding an academy merely for the polite arts is more judicious, as it prevents confusion, and the joining, in some measure, of heterogeneals, such as a dissertation on the head-dresses of the Roman ladies with a hundred or more new curves.

As there is very little order and regularity in the Royal Society, and not the least encouragement; and that the Academy of Paris is on a quite different foot, it is no wonder that our transactions are drawn up in a more just and beautiful manner than those of the English. Soldiers who are under a regular discipline, and besides well paid, must necessarily at last perform more glorious achievements than others who are mere volunteers. It must indeed be confessed that the Royal Society boast their Newton, but then he did not owe his knowledge and discoveries to that body; so far from it, that the latter were intelligible to very few of his fellow members. A genius like that of Sir Isaac belonged to all the academies in the world, because all had a thousand things to learn of him.

The celebrated Dean Swift formed a design, in the latter end of the late Queen's reign, to found an academy for the English tongue upon the model of that of the French. This project was promoted by the late Earl of Oxford, Lord High Treasurer, and much more by the Lord Bolingbroke, Secretary of State, who had the happy talent of speaking without premeditation in the Parliament House with as much purity as Dean Swift wrote in his closet, and who would have been the ornament and protector of that academy. Those only would have been chosen members of it whose works will last as long as the English tongue, such as Dean Swift, Mr. Prior, whom we saw here invested with a public character, and whose fame in England is equal to that of La Fontaine in France; Mr. Pope, the English Boileau, Mr. Congreve, who may be called their Molière, and several other eminent persons whose names I have forgot; all these would have raised the glory of that body to a great height even in its infancy. But Queen Anne being snatched suddenly from the world, the Whigs were resolved to ruin the protectors of the intended academy, a circumstance that was of the most fatal consequence to polite literature. The members of this academy would have had a very great advantage over those who first formed that of the French, for Swift, Prior, Congreve, Dryden, Pope, Addison, &c. had fixed the English tongue by their writings; whereas Chapelain, Colletet, Cassaigne, Faret, Perrin, Cotin, our first academicians, were a disgrace to their country; and so much ridicule is now attached to their very names, that if an author of some genius in this age had the misfortune to be called Chapelain or Cotin, he would be under a necessity of changing his name.

One circumstance, to which the English Academy should especially have attended, is to have prescribed to themselves occupations of a quite different kind from those with which our academicians amuse themselves. A wit of this country asked me for the memoirs of the French Academy. I answered, they have no memoirs, but have printed threescore or fourscore volumes in quarto of compliments. The gentleman perused one or two of them, but without being able to understand the style in which they were written; though he understood all our good authors perfectly. "All," says he, "I see in these elegant discourses is, that the member elect having assured the audience that his predecessor was a great man, that Cardinal Richelieu was a very great man, that the Chancellor Seguier was a pretty great man, that Louis XIV. was a more than great man, the director answers in the very same strain, and adds, that the member elect may also be a sort of great man, and that himself, in quality of director, must also have some share in this greatness."

The cause why all these academical discourses have unhappily done so little honour to this body is evident enough. *Vitium est temporis potiùs quam hominis* (the fault is owing to the age rather than to particular persons). It grew up insensibly into a custom for every academician to repeat these eulogiums at his reception; it was laid down as a kind of law that the public should be indulged from time to time in the sullen satisfaction of yawning over these productions. If the reason should afterwards be sought, why the greatest geniuses who have been incorporated into that body have sometimes made the worst speeches, I answer, that it is wholly owing to a strong propension, the gentlemen in question had to shine, and to display a thread-bare, worn-out subject in a new and uncommon light. The necessity of saying something, the perplexity of having nothing to say, and a desire of being witty, are three circumstances which alone are capable of making even the greatest writer ridiculous. These gentlemen, not being able to strike out any new thoughts, hunted after a new play of words, and delivered themselves without thinking at all: in like manner as people who should seem to chew with great eagerness, and make as though they were eating, at the same time that they were just starved.

It is a law in the French Academy, to publish all those discourses by which only they are known, but they should rather make a law never to print any of them.

But the Academy of the *Belles Lettres* have a more prudent and more useful object, which is, to present the public with a collection of transactions that abound with curious researches and critiques. These transactions are already esteemed by foreigners; and it were only to be wished that some subjects in them had been more thoroughly examined, and that others had not been treated at all. As, for instance, we should have been very well satisfied, had they omitted I know not what dissertation on the prerogative of the right hand over the left; and some others, which, though not published under so ridiculous a title, are yet written on subjects that are almost as frivolous and silly.

The Academy of Sciences, in such of their researches as are of a more difficult kind and a more sensible use, embrace the knowledge of nature and the improvements of the arts. We may presume that such profound, such uninterrupted pursuits as these, such exact calculations, such refined discoveries, such extensive and exalted views, will, at last, produce something that may prove of advantage to the universe. Hitherto, as we have observed together, the most useful discoveries have been made in the most barbarous times. One would conclude that the business of the most enlightened ages and the most learned bodies, is, to argue and debate on things which were invented by ignorant people. We know exactly the angle which the sail of a ship is to make with the keel in order to make its sailing better; and yet Columbus discovered America without having the least idea of the property of this angle: however, I am far from inferring from hence that we are to confine ourselves merely to a blind practice, but happy it were, would naturalists and geometricians unite, as much as possible, the practice with the theory.

Strange, but so it is, that those things which reflect the greatest honour on the human mind are frequently of the least benefit to it! A man who understands the four fundamental rules of arithmetic, aided by a little good sense, shall amass prodigious wealth in trade, shall become a Sir Peter Delmé, a Sir Richard Hopkins, a Sir Gilbert Heathcote, whilst a poor algebraist spends his whole life in searching for astonishing properties and relations in numbers, which at the same time are of no manner of use, and will not acquaint him with the nature of exchanges. This is very nearly the case with most of the arts: there is a certain point beyond which all researches serve to no other purpose than merely to delight an inquisitive mind. Those ingenious and useless truths may be compared to stars which, by being placed at too great a distance, cannot afford us the least light.

With regard to the French Academy, how great a service would they do to literature, to the language, and the nation, if, instead of publishing a set of compliments annually, they would give us new editions of the valuable works written in the age of Louis XIV., purged from the several errors of diction which are crept into them. There are many of these errors in Corneille and Molière, but those in La Fontaine are very numerous. Such as could not be corrected might at least be pointed out. By this means, as all the Europeans read those works, they would teach them our language in its utmost purity—which, by that means, would be fixed to a lasting standard; and valuable French books being then printed at the King's expense, would prove one of the most glorious monuments the nation could boast. I have been told that Boileau formerly made this proposal, and that it has since been revived by a gentleman eminent for his genius, his fine sense, and just taste for criticism; but this thought has met with the fate of many other useful projects, of being applauded and neglected.

ON THE INEQUALITY AMONG MANKIND

BY

J. J. ROUSSEAU

INTRODUCTORY NOTE

Jean Jacques Rousseau was born at Geneva, June 28, 1712, the son of a watchmaker of French origin. His education was irregular, and though he tried many professions—including engraving, music, and teaching—he found it difficult to support himself in any of them. The discovery of his talent as a writer came with the winning of a prize offered by the Academy of Dijon for a discourse on the question, "Whether the progress of the sciences and of letters has tended to corrupt or to elevate morals." He argued so brilliantly that the tendency of civilization was degrading that he became at once famous. The discourse here printed on the causes of inequality among men was written in a similar competition.

He now concentrated his powers upon literature, producing two novels, "La Nouvelle Héloise," the forerunner and parent of endless sentimental and picturesque fictions; and "Émile, ou l'Education," a work which has had enormous influence on the theory and practise of pedagogy down to our own time and in which the Savoyard Vicar appears, who is used as the mouthpiece for Rousseau's own religious ideas. "Le Contrat Social" (1762) elaborated the doctrine of the discourse on inequality. Both historically and philosophically it is unsound; but it was the chief literary source of the enthusiasm for liberty, fraternity, and equality, which inspired the leaders of the French Revolution, and its effects passed far beyond France.

His most famous work, the "Confessions," was published after his death. This book is a mine of information as to his life, but it is far from trustworthy; and the picture it gives of the author's personality and conduct, though painted in such a way as to make it absorbingly interesting, is often unpleasing in the highest degree. But it is one of the great autobiographies of the world.

During Rousseau's later years he was the victim of the delusion of persecution; and although he was protected by a succession of good friends, he came to distrust and quarrel with each in turn. He died at Ermenonville, near Paris, July 2, 1778, the most widely influential French writer of his age.

The Savoyard Vicar and his "Profession of Faith" are introduced into "Émile" not, according to the author, because he wishes to exhibit his principles as those which should be taught, but to give an example of the way in which religious matters should be discussed with the young. Nevertheless, it is universally recognized that these opinions are Rousseau's own, and represent in short form his characteristic attitude toward religious belief. The Vicar himself is believed to combine the traits of two Savoyard priests whom Rousseau knew in his youth. The more important was the Abbé Gaime, whom he had known at Turin; the other, the Abbé Gâtier, who had taught him at Annecy.

QUESTION

PROPOSED BY THE

ACADEMY OF DIJON

What is the Origin of the Inequality Among Mankind; and whether such Inequality is authorized by the Law of Nature?

A DISCOURSE

UPON THE ORIGIN AND
THE FOUNDATION OF THE INEQUALITY AMONG
MANKIND

'TIS of man I am to speak; and the very question, in answer
to which I am to speak of him, sufficiently informs me
that I am going to speak to men; for to those alone, who are
not afraid of honouring truth, it belongs to propose discussions of
this kind. I shall therefore maintain with confidence the cause of
mankind before the sages, who invite me to stand up in its defence;
and I shall think myself happy, if I can but behave in a manner not
unworthy of my subject and of my judges.

I conceive two species of inequality among men; one which I call
natural, or physical inequality, because it is established by nature,
and consists in the difference of age, health, bodily strength, and the
qualities of the mind, or of the soul; the other which may be termed
moral, or political inequality, because it depends on a kind of convention, and is established, or at least authorized, by the common
consent of mankind. This species of inequality consists in the different privileges, which some men enjoy, to the prejudice of others,
such as that of being richer, more honoured, more powerful, and
even that of exacting obedience from them.

It were absurd to ask, what is the cause of natural inequality,
seeing the bare definition of natural inequality answers the question:
it would be more absurd still to enquire, if there might not be some
essential connection between the two species of inequality, as it would
be asking, in other words, if those who command are necessarily
better men than those who obey; and if strength of body or of mind,
wisdom or virtue are always to be found in individuals, in the same
proportion with power, or riches: a question, fit perhaps to be dis-

cussed by slaves in the hearing of their masters, but unbecoming free and reasonable beings in quest of truth.

What therefore is precisely the subject of this discourse? It is to point out, in the progress of things, that moment, when, right taking place of violence, nature became subject to law; to display that chain of surprising events, in consequence of which the strong submitted to serve the weak, and the people to purchase imaginary ease, at the expense of real happiness.

The philosophers, who have examined the foundations of society, have, every one of them, perceived the necessity of tracing it back to a state of nature, but not one of them has ever arrived there. Some of them have not scrupled to attribute to man in that state the ideas of justice and injustice, without troubling their heads to prove, that he really must have had such ideas, or even that such ideas were useful to him: others have spoken of the natural right of every man to keep what belongs to him, without letting us know what they meant by the word belong; others, without further ceremony ascribing to the strongest an authority over the weakest, have immediately struck out government, without thinking of the time requisite for men to form any notion of the things signified by the words authority and government. All of them, in fine, constantly harping on wants, avidity, oppression, desires and pride, have transferred to the state of nature ideas picked up in the bosom of society. In speaking of savages they described citizens. Nay, few of our own writers seem to have so much as doubted, that a state of nature did once actually exist; though it plainly appears by Sacred History, that even the first man, immediately furnished as he was by God himself with both instructions and precepts, never lived in that state, and that, if we give to the books of Moses that credit which every Christian philosopher ought to give to them, we must deny that, even before the deluge, such a state ever existed among men, unless they fell into it by some extraordinary event: a paradox very difficult to maintain, and altogether impossible to prove.

Let us begin therefore, by laying aside facts, for they do not affect the question. The researches, in which we may engage on this occasion, are not to be taken for historical truths, but merely as hypothetical and conditional reasonings, fitter to illustrate the nature of things, than to show their true origin, like those systems, which our naturalists daily make of the formation of the world. Religion commands us to believe, that men, having been drawn by God himself out of a state of nature, are unequal, because it is his pleasure they should be so; but religion does not forbid us to draw conjectures solely from the nature of man, considered in itself, and from that of the beings which surround him, concerning the fate of mankind, had they been left to themselves. This is then the question I am to answer, the question I propose to examine in the present discourse. As mankind in general have an interest in my subject, I shall endeavour to use a language suitable to all nations; or rather, forgetting the circumstances of time and place in order to think of nothing but the men I speak to, I shall suppose myself in the Lyceum of Athens, repeating the lessons of my masters before the Platos and the Xenocrates of that famous seat of philosophy as my judges, and in presence of the whole human species as my audience.

O man, whatever country you may belong to, whatever your opinions may be, attend to my words; you shall hear your history such as I think I have read it, not in books composed by those like you, for they are liars, but in the book of nature which never lies. All that I shall repeat after her, must be true, without any intermixture of falsehood, but where I may happen, without intending it, to introduce my own conceits. The times I am going to speak of are very remote. How much you are changed from what you once were! 'Tis in a manner the life of your species that I am going to write, from the qualities which you have received, and which your education and your habits could deprave, but could not destroy. There is, I am sensible, an age at which every individual of you would choose to stop; and you will look out for the age at which, had you your wish, your species had stopped. Uneasy at your present condition for reasons which threaten your unhappy posterity with still greater uneasiness, you will perhaps wish it were in your power to go back; and this sentiment ought to be considered, as the panegyric of your first parents, the condemnation of your contemporaries, and a source of terror to all those who may have the misfortune of succeeding you.

DISCOURSE

FIRST PART

HOWEVER important it may be, in order to form a proper judgment of the natural state of man, to consider him from his origin, and to examine him, as it were, in the first embryo of the species; I shall not attempt to trace his organization through its successive approaches to perfection: I shall not stop to examine in the animal system what he might have been in the beginning, to become at last what he actually is; I shall not inquire whether, as Aristotle thinks, his neglected nails were no better at first than crooked talons; whether his whole body was not, bear-like, thick covered with rough hair; and whether, walking upon all-fours, his eyes, directed to the earth, and confined to a horizon of a few paces extent, did not at once point out the nature and limits of his ideas. I could only form vague, and almost imaginary, conjectures on this subject. Comparative anatomy has not as yet been sufficiently improved; neither have the observations of natural philosophy been sufficiently ascertained, to establish upon such foundations the basis of a solid system. For this reason, without having recourse to the supernatural informations with which we have been favoured on this head, or paying any attention to the changes, that must have happened in the conformation of the interior and exterior parts of man's body, in proportion as he applied his members to new purposes, and took to new aliments, I shall suppose his conformation to have always been, what we now behold it; that he always walked on two feet, made the same use of his hands that we do of ours, extended his looks over the whole face of nature, and measured with his eyes the vast extent of the heavens.

If I strip this being, thus constituted, of all the supernatural gifts which he may have received, and of all the artificial faculties, which we could not have acquired but by slow degrees; if I consider him, in a word, such as he must have issued from the hands of nature;

I see an animal less strong than some, and less active than others, but, upon the whole, the most advantageously organized of any; I see him satisfying the calls of hunger under the first oak, and those of thirst at the first rivulet; I see him laying himself down to sleep at the foot of the same tree that afforded him his meal; and behold, this done, all his wants are completely supplied.

The earth left to its own natural fertility and covered with immense woods, that no hatchet ever disfigured, offers at every step food and shelter to every species of animals. Men, dispersed among them, observe and imitate their industry, and thus rise to the instinct of beasts; with this advantage, that, whereas every species of beasts is confined to one peculiar instinct, man, who perhaps has not any that particularly belongs to him, appropriates to himself those of all other animals, and lives equally upon most of the different aliments, which they only divide among themselves; a circumstance which qualifies him to find his subsistence, with more ease than any of them.

Men, accustomed from their infancy to the inclemency of the weather, and to the rigour of the different seasons; inured to fatigue, and obliged to defend, naked and without arms, their life and their prey against the other wild inhabitants of the forest, or at least to avoid their fury by flight, acquire a robust and almost unalterable habit of body; the children, bringing with them into the world the excellent constitution of their parents, and strengthening it by the same exercises that first produced it, attain by this means all the vigour that the human frame is capable of. Nature treats them exactly in the same manner that Sparta treated the children of her citizens; those who come well formed into the world she renders strong and robust, and destroys all the rest; differing in this respect from our societies, in which the state, by permitting children to become burdensome to their parents, murders them all without distinction, even in the wombs of their mothers.

The body being the only instrument that savage man is acquainted with, he employs it to different uses, of which ours, for want of practice, are incapable; and we may thank our industry for the loss of that strength and agility, which necessity obliges him to acquire. Had he a hatchet, would his hand so easily snap off from an oak so stout a branch? Had he a sling, would it dart a stone to so great a distance? Had he a ladder, would he run so nimbly up a tree? Had he a horse, would he with such swiftness shoot along the plain? Give civilized man but time to gather about him all his machines, and no doubt he will be an overmatch for the savage: but if you have a mind to see a contest still more unequal, place them naked and unarmed one opposite to the other; and you will soon discover the advantage there is in perpetually having all our forces at our disposal, in being constantly prepared against all events, and in always carrying ourselves, as it were, whole and entire about us.

Hobbes would have it that man is naturally void of fear, and always intent upon attacking and fighting. An illustrious philosopher thinks on the contrary, and Cumberland and Puffendorff likewise affirm it, that nothing is more fearful than man in a state of nature, that he is always in a tremble, and ready to fly at the first motion he perceives, at the first noise that strikes his ears. This, indeed, may be very true in regard to objects with which he is not acquainted; and I make no doubt of his being terrified at every new sight that presents itself, as often as he cannot distinguish the physical good and evil which he may expect from it, nor compare his forces with the dangers he has to encounter; circumstances that seldom occur in a state of nature, where all things proceed in so uniform a manner, and the face of the earth is not liable to those sudden and continual changes occasioned in it by the passions and inconstancies of collected bodies. But savage man living among other animals without any society or fixed habitation, and finding himself early under a necessity of measuring his strength with theirs, soon makes a comparison between both, and finding that he surpasses them more in address, than they surpass him in strength, he learns not to be any longer in dread of them. Turn out a bear or a wolf against a sturdy, active, resolute savage, (and this they all are,) provided with stones and a good stick; and you will soon find that the danger is at least equal on both sides, and that after several trials of this kind, wild beasts, who are not fond of attacking each other, will not be very fond of attacking man, whom they have found every whit as wild as themselves. As to animals who have really more strength than man has address, he is, in regard to them, what other weaker species are, who find means to subsist notwithstanding; he has even this great advantage over such weaker species, that being equally fleet with them, and finding on every tree an almost inviolable asylum, he is always at liberty to take it or leave it, as he likes best, and of course to fight or to fly, whichever is most agreeable to him. To this we may add that no animal naturally makes war upon man, except in the case of self-defence or extreme hunger; nor ever expresses against him any of these violent antipathies, which seem to indicate that some particular species are intended by nature for the food of others.

But there are other more formidable enemies, and against which man is not provided with the same means of defence; I mean natural infirmities, infancy, old age, and sickness of every kind, melancholy proofs of our weakness, whereof the two first are common to all animals, and the last chiefly attends man living in a state of society. It is even observable in regard to infancy, that the mother being able to carry her child about with her, wherever she goes, can perform the duty of a nurse with a great deal less trouble, than the females of many other animals, who are obliged to be constantly going and coming with no small labour and fatigue, one way to look out for their own subsistence, and another to suckle and feed their young ones. True it is that, if the woman happens to perish, her child is exposed to the greatest danger of perishing with her; but this danger is common to a hundred other species, whose young ones require a great deal of time to be able to provide for themselves; and if our infancy is longer than theirs, our life is longer likewise; so that, in this respect too, all things are in a manner equal; not but that there are other rules concerning the duration of the first age of life, and the number of the young of man and other animals, but they do not belong to my subject. With old men, who stir and perspire but little, the demand for food diminishes with their abilities to provide it; and as a savage life would exempt them from the gout and the rheumatism, and old age is of all ills that which human assistance is least capable of alleviating, they would at last go off, without its being perceived by others that they ceased to exist, and almost without perceiving it themselves.

In regard to sickness, I shall not repeat the vain and false declamations made use of to discredit medicine by most men, while they enjoy their health; I shall only ask if there are any solid observations from which we may conclude that in those countries where the healing art is most neglected, the mean duration of man's life is shorter than in those where it is most cultivated? And how is it possible this should be the case, if we inflict more diseases upon ourselves than medicine can supply us with remedies! The extreme inequalities in the manner of living of the several classes of mankind, the excess of idleness in some, and of labour in others, the facility of irritating and satisfying our sensuality and our appetites, the too exquisite and out of the way aliments of the rich, which fill them with fiery juices, and bring on indigestions, the unwholesome food of the poor, of which even, bad as it is, they very often fall short, and the want of which tempts them, every opportunity that offers, to eat greedily and overload their stomachs; watchings, excesses of every kind, immoderate transports of all the passions, fatigues, waste of spirits, in a word, the numberless pains and anxieties annexed to every condition, and which the mind of man is constantly a prey to; these are the fatal proofs that most of our ills are of our own making, and that we might have avoided them all by adhering to the simple, uniform and solitary way of life prescribed to us by nature. Allowing that nature intended we should always enjoy good health, I dare almost affirm that a state of reflection is a state against nature, and that the man who meditates is a depraved animal. We need only call to mind the good constitution of savages, of those at least whom we have not destroyed by our strong liquors; we need only reflect, that they are strangers to almost every disease, except those occasioned by wounds and old age, to be in a manner convinced that the history of human diseases might be easily composed by pursuing that of civil societies. Such at least was the opinion of Plato, who concluded from certain remedies made use of or approved by Podalyrus and Macaon at the Siege of Troy, that several disorders, which these remedies were found to bring on in his days, were not known among men at that remote period.

Man therefore, in a state of nature where there are so few sources of sickness, can have no great occasion for physic, and still less for physicians; neither is the human species more to be pitied in this respect, than any other species of animals. Ask those who make hunting their recreation or business, if in their excursions they meet with many sick or feeble animals. They meet with many carrying the marks of considerable wounds, that have been perfectly well healed and closed up; with many, whose bones formerly broken, and whose limbs almost torn off, have completely knit and united, without any other surgeon but time, any other regimen but their usual way of living, and whose cures were not the less perfect for their not having been tortured with incisions, poisoned with drugs, or worn out by diet and abstinence. In a word, however useful medicine well administered may be to us who live in a state of society, it is still past doubt, that if, on the one hand, the sick savage, destitute of help, has nothing to hope from nature, on the other, he has nothing to fear but from his disease; a circumstance, which often renders his situation preferable to ours.

Let us therefore beware of confounding savage man with the men, whom we daily see and converse with. Nature behaves towards all animals left to her care with a predilection, that seems to prove how jealous she is of that prerogative. The horse, the cat, the bull, nay the ass itself, have generally a higher stature, and always a more robust constitution, more vigour, more strength and courage in their forests than in our houses; they lose half these advantages by becoming domestic animals; it looks as if all our attention to treat them kindly, and to feed them well, served only to bastardize them. It is thus with man himself. In proportion as he becomes sociable and a slave to others, he becomes weak, fearful, mean-spirited, and his soft and effeminate way of living at once completes the enervation of his strength and of his courage. We may add, that there must be still a wider difference between man and man in a savage and domestic condition, than between beast and beast; for as men and beasts have been treated alike by nature, all the conveniences with which men indulge themselves more than they do the beasts tamed by them, are so many particular causes which make them degenerate more sensibly.

Nakedness therefore, the want of houses, and of all these unnecessaries, which we consider as so very necessary, are not such mighty evils in respect to these primitive men, and much less still any obstacle to their preservation. Their skins, it is true, are destitute of hair; but then they have no occasion for any such covering in warm climates; and in cold climates they soon learn to apply to that use those of the animals they have conquered; they have but two feet to run with, but they have two hands to defend themselves with, and provide for all their wants; it costs them perhaps a great deal of time and trouble to make their children walk, but the mothers carry them with ease; an advantage not granted to other species of animals, with whom the mother, when pursued, is obliged to abandon her young ones, or regulate her steps by theirs. In short, unless we admit those singular and fortuitous concurrences of circumstances, which I shall speak of hereafter, and which, it is very possible, may never have existed, it is evident, in every state of the question, that the man, who first made himself clothes and built himself a cabin, supplied himself with things which he did not much want, since he had lived without them till then; and why should he not have been able to support in his riper years, the same kind of life, which he had supported from his infancy?

Alone, idle, and always surrounded with danger, savage man must be fond of sleep, and sleep lightly like other animals, who think but little, and may, in a manner, be said to sleep all the time they do not think: self-preservation being almost his only concern, he must exercise those faculties most, which are most serviceable in attacking and in defending, whether to subdue his prey, or to prevent his becoming that of other animals: those organs, on the contrary, which softness and sensuality can alone improve, must remain in a state of rudeness, utterly incompatible with all manner of delicacy; and as his senses are divided on this point, his touch and his taste must be extremely coarse and blunt; his sight, his hearing, and his smelling equally subtle: such is the animal state in general, and accordingly if we may believe travellers, it is that of most savage nations. We must not therefore be surprised, that the Hottentots of the Cape of Good Hope, distinguish with their naked eyes ships on the ocean, at as great a distance as the Dutch can discern them with their glasses; nor that the savages of America should have tracked the Spaniards with their noses, to as great a degree of exactness, as the best dogs could have done; nor that all these barbarous nations support nakedness without pain, use such large quantities of Pimento to give their food a relish, and drink like water the strongest liquors of Europe.

As yet I have considered man merely in his physical capacity; let us now endeavour to examine him in a metaphysical and moral light.

I can discover nothing in any mere animal but an ingenious machine, to which nature has given senses to wind itself up, and guard, to a certain degree, against everything that might destroy or disorder it. I perceive the very same things in the human machine, with this difference, that nature alone operates in all the operations of the beast, whereas man, as a free agent, has a share in his. One chooses by instinct; the other by an act of liberty; for which reason the beast cannot deviate from the rules that have been prescribed to it, even in cases where such deviation might be useful, and man often deviates from the rules laid down for him to his prejudice. Thus a pigeon would starve near a dish of the best flesh-meat, and a cat on a heap of fruit or corn, though both might very well support life with the food which they thus disdain, did they but bethink themselves to make a trial of it: it is in this manner dissolute men run into excesses, which bring on fevers and death itself; because the mind depraves the senses, and when nature ceases to speak, the will still continues to dictate.

All animals must be allowed to have ideas, since all animals have senses; they even combine their ideas to a certain degree, and, in this respect, it is only the difference of such degree, that constitutes the difference between man and beast: some philosophers have even advanced, that there is a greater difference between some men and some others, than between some men and some beasts; it is not therefore so much the understanding that constitutes, among animals, the specifical distinction of man, as his quality of a free agent. Nature speaks to all animals, and beasts obey her voice. Man feels the same impression, but he at the same time perceives that he is free to resist or to acquiesce; and it is in the consciousness of this liberty, that the spirituality of his soul chiefly appears: for natural philosophy explains, in some measure, the mechanism of the senses and the formation of ideas; but in the power of willing, or rather of choosing, and in the consciousness of this power, nothing can be discovered but acts, that are purely spiritual, and cannot be accounted for by the laws of mechanics.

But though the difficulties, in which all these questions are involved, should leave some room to dispute on this difference between man and beast, there is another very specific quality that distinguishes them, and a quality which will admit of no dispute; this is the faculty of improvement; a faculty which, as circumstances offer, successively unfolds all the other faculties, and resides among us not only in the species, but in the individuals that compose it; whereas a beast is, at the end of some months, all he ever will be during the rest of his life; and his species, at the end of a thousand years, precisely what it was the first year of that long period. Why is man alone subject to dotage? Is it not, because he thus returns to his primitive condition? And because, while the beast, which has acquired nothing and has likewise nothing to lose, continues always in possession of his instinct, man, losing by old age, or by accident, all the acquisitions he had made in consequence of his perfectibility, thus falls back even lower than beasts themselves? It would be a melancholy necessity for us to be obliged to allow, that this distinctive and almost unlimited faculty is the source of all man's misfortunes; that it is this faculty, which, though by slow degrees, draws them out of their original condition, in which his days would slide away insensibly in peace and innocence; that it is this faculty, which, in a succession of ages, produces his discoveries and mistakes, his virtues and his vices, and, at long run, renders him both his own and nature's tyrant. It would be shocking to be obliged to commend, as a beneficent being, whoever he was that first suggested to the *Oronoco* Indians the use of those boards which they bind on the temples of their children, and which secure to them the enjoyment of some part at least of their natural imbecility and happiness.

Savage man, abandoned by nature to pure instinct, or rather indemnified for that which has perhaps been denied to him by faculties capable of immediately supplying the place of it, and of raising him afterwards a great deal higher, would therefore begin with functions that were merely animal: to see and to feel would be his first condition, which he would enjoy in common with other animals. To will and not to will, to wish and to fear, would be the first, and in a manner, the only operations of his soul, till new circumstances occasioned new developments.

Let moralists say what they will, the human understanding is greatly indebted to the passions, which, on their side, are likewise universally allowed to be greatly indebted to the human understanding. It is by the activity of our passions, that our reason improves: we covet knowledge merely because we covet enjoyment, and it is impossible to conceive why a man exempt from fears and desires should take the trouble to reason. The passions, in their turn, owe their origin to our wants, and their increase to our progress in science; for we cannot desire or fear anything, but in consequence of the ideas we have of it, or of the simple impulses of nature; and savage man, destitute of every species of knowledge, experiences no passions but those of this last kind; his desires never extend beyond his physical wants; he knows no goods but food, a female, and rest; he fears no evil but pain, and hunger; I say pain, and not death; for no animal, merely as such, will ever know what it is to die, and the knowledge of death, and of its terrors, is one of the first acquisitions made by man, in consequence of his deviating from the animal state.

I could easily, were it requisite, cite facts in support of this opinion, and show, that the progress of the mind has everywhere kept pace exactly with the wants, to which nature had left the inhabitants exposed, or to which circumstances had subjected them, and consequently to the passions, which inclined them to provide for these wants. I could exhibit in Egypt the arts starting up, and extending themselves with the inundations of the Nile; I could pursue them in their progress among the Greeks, where they were seen to bud forth, grow, and rise to the heavens, in the midst of the sands and rocks of Attica, without being able to take root on the fertile banks of the Eurotas; I would observe that, in general, the inhabitants of the north are more industrious than those of the south, because they can less do without industry; as if nature thus meant to make all things equal, by giving to the mind that fertility she has denied to the soil.

But exclusive of the uncertain testimonies of history, who does not perceive that everything seems to remove from savage man the temptation and the means of altering his condition? His imagination paints nothing to him; his heart asks nothing from him. His moderate wants are so easily supplied with what he everywhere finds ready to his hand, and he stands at such a distance from the degree of knowledge requisite to covet more, that he can neither have foresight nor curiosity. The spectacle of nature, by growing quite familiar to him, becomes at last equally indifferent. It is constantly the same order, constantly the same revolutions; he has not sense enough to feel surprise at the sight of the greatest wonders; and it is not in his mind we must look for that philosophy, which man must have to know how to observe once, what he has every day seen. His soul, which nothing disturbs, gives itself up entirely to the consciousness of its actual existence, without any thought of even the nearest futurity; and his projects, equally confined with his views, scarce extend to the end of the day. Such is, even at present, the degree of foresight in the Caribbean: he sells his cotton bed in the morning, and comes in the evening, with tears in his eyes, to buy it back, not having foreseen that he should want it again the next night.

The more we meditate on this subject, the wider does the distance between mere sensation and the most simple knowledge become in our eyes; and it is impossible to conceive how man, by his own powers alone, without the assistance of communication, and the spur of necessity, could have got over so great an interval. How many ages perhaps revolved, before men beheld any other fire but that of the heavens? How many different accidents must have concurred to make them acquainted with the most common uses of this element? How often have they let it go out, before they knew the art of reproducing it? And how often perhaps has not every one of these secrets perished with the discoverer? What shall we say of agriculture, an art which requires so much labour and foresight; which depends upon other arts; which, it is very evident, cannot be practised but in a society, if not a formed one, at least one of some standing, and which does not so much serve to draw aliments from the earth, for the earth would yield them without all that trouble, as to oblige her to produce those things, which we like best, preferably to others? But let us suppose that men had multiplied to such a degree, that the natural products of the earth no longer sufficed for their support; a supposition which, by the bye, would prove that this kind of life would be very advantageous to the human species; let us suppose that, without forge or anvil, the instruments of husbandry had dropped from the heavens into the hands of savages, that these men had got the better of that mortal aversion they all have for constant labour; that they had learned to foretell their wants at so great a distance of time; that they had guessed exactly how they were to break the earth, commit their seed to it, and plant trees; that they had found out the art of grinding their corn, and improving by fermentation the juice of their grapes; all operations which we must allow them to have learned from the gods, since we cannot conceive how they should make such discoveries of themselves; after all these fine presents, what man would be mad enough to cultivate a field, that may be robbed by the first comer, man or beast, who takes a fancy to the produce of it. And would any man consent to spend his day in labour and fatigue, when the rewards of his labour and fatigue became more and more precarious in proportion to his want of them? In a word, how could this situation engage men to cultivate the earth, as long as it was not parcelled out among them, that is, as long as a state of nature subsisted.

Though we should suppose savage man as well versed in the art of thinking, as philosophers make him; though we were, after them, to make him a philosopher himself, discovering of himself the sublimest truths, forming to himself, by the most abstract arguments, maxims of justice and reason drawn from the love of order in general, or from the known will of his Creator: in a word, though we were to suppose his mind as intelligent and enlightened, as it must, and is, in fact, found to be dull and stupid; what benefit would the species receive from all these metaphysical discoveries, which could not be communicated, but must perish with the individual who had made them? What progress could mankind make in the forests, scattered up and down among the other animals? And to what degree could men mutually improve and enlighten each other, when they had no fixed habitation, nor any need of each other's assistance; when the same persons scarcely met twice in their whole lives, and on meeting neither spoke to, or so much as knew each other?

Let us consider how many ideas we owe to the use of speech; how much grammar exercises, and facilitates the operations of the mind; let us, besides, reflect on the immense pains and time that the first invention of languages must have required: Let us add these reflections to the preceding; and then we may judge how many thousand ages must have been requisite to develop successively the operations, which the human mind is capable of producing.

I must now beg leave to stop one moment to consider the perplexities attending the origin of languages. I might here barely cite or repeat the researches made, in relation to this question, by the Abbé de Condillac, which all fully confirm my system, and perhaps even suggested to me the first idea of it. But, as the manner, in which the philosopher resolves the difficulties of his own starting, concerning the origin of arbitrary signs, shows that he supposes, what I doubt, namely a kind of society already established among the inventors of languages; I think it my duty, at the same time that I refer to his reflections, to give my own, in order to expose the same difficulties in a light suitable to my subject. The first that offers is how languages could become necessary; for as there was no correspondence between men, nor the least necessity for any, there is no conceiving the necessity of this invention, nor the possibility of it, if it was not indispensable. I might say, with many others, that languages are the fruit of the domestic intercourse between fathers, mothers, and children: but this, besides its not answering any difficulties, would be committing the same fault with those, who reasoning on the state of nature, transfer to it ideas collected in society, always consider families as living together under one roof, and their members as observing among themselves an union, equally intimate and permanent with that which we see exist in a civil state, where so many common interests conspire to unite them; whereas in this primitive state, as there were neither houses nor cabins, nor any kind of property, every one took up his lodging at random, and seldom continued above one night in the same place; males and females united without any premeditated design, as chance, occasion, or desire brought them together, nor had they any great occasion for language to make known their thoughts to each other. They parted with the same ease. The mother suckled her children, when just born, for her own sake; but afterwards out of love and affection to them, when habit and custom had made them dear to her; but they no sooner gained strength enough to run about in quest of food than they separated even from her of their own accord; and as they scarce had any other method of not losing each other, than that of remaining constantly in each other's sight, they soon came to such a pass of forgetfulness, as not even to know each other, when they happened to meet again. I must further observe that the child having all his wants to explain, and consequently more things to say to his mother, than the mother can have to say to him, it is he that must be at the chief expense of invention, and the language he makes use of must be in a great measure his own work; this makes the number of languages equal to that of the individuals who are to speak them; and this multiplicity of languages is further increased by their roving and vagabond kind of life, which allows no idiom time enough to acquire any consistency; for to say that the mother would have dictated to the child the words he must employ to ask her this thing and that, may well enough explain in what manner languages, already formed, are taught, but it does not show us in what manner they are first formed.

Let us suppose this first difficulty conquered: Let us for a moment consider ourselves at this side of the immense space, which must have separated the pure state of nature from that in which languages became necessary, and let us, after allowing such necessity, examine how languages could begin to be established. A new difficulty this, still more stubborn than the preceding; for if men stood in need of speech to learn to think, they must have stood in still greater need of the art of thinking to invent that of speaking; and though we could conceive how the sounds of the voice came to be taken for the conventional interpreters of our ideas we should not be the nearer knowing who could have been the interpreters of this convention for such ideas, as, in consequence of their not having any sensible objects, could not be made manifest by gesture or voice; so that we can scarce form any tolerable conjectures concerning the birth of this art of communicating our thoughts, and establishing a correspondence between minds: a sublime art which, though so remote from its origin, philosophers still behold at such a prodigious distance from its perfection, that I never met with one of them bold enough to affirm it would ever arrive there, though the revolutions necessarily produced by time were suspended in its favour; though prejudice could be banished from, or would be at least content to sit silent in the presence of our academies, and though these societies should consecrate themselves, entirely and during whole ages, to the study of this intricate object.

The first language of man, the most universal and most energetic of all languages, in short, the only language he had occasion for, before there was a necessity of persuading assembled multitudes, was the cry of nature. As this cry was never extorted but by a kind of instinct in the most urgent cases, to implore assistance in great danger, or relief in great sufferings, it was of little use in the common occurrences of life, where more moderate sentiments generally prevail. When the ideas of men began to extend and multiply, and a closer communication began to take place among them, they laboured to devise more numerous signs, and a more extensive language: they multiplied the inflections of the voice, and added to them gestures, which are, in their own nature, more expressive, and whose meaning depends less on any prior determination. They therefore expressed visible and movable objects by gestures and those which strike the ear, by imitative sounds: but as gestures scarcely indicate anything except objects that are actually present or can be easily described, and visible actions; as they are not of general use, since darkness or the interposition of an opaque medium renders them useless; and as besides they require attention rather than excite it: men at length bethought themselves of substituting for them the articulations of voice, which, without having the same relation to any determinate object, are, in quality of instituted signs, fitter to represent all our ideas; a substitution, which could only have been made by common consent, and in a manner pretty difficult to practise by men, whose rude organs were unimproved by exercise; a substitution, which is in itself more difficult to be conceived, since the motives to this unanimous agreement must have been somehow or another expressed, and speech therefore appears to have been exceedingly requisite to establish the use of speech.

We must allow that the words, first made use of by men, had in their minds a much more extensive signification, than those employed in languages of some standing, and that, considering how ignorant they were of the division of speech into its constituent parts; they at first gave every word the meaning of an entire proposition. When afterwards they began to perceive the difference between the subject and attribute, and between verb and noun, a distinction which required no mean effort of genius, the substantives for a time were only so many proper names, the infinitive was the only tense, and as to adjectives, great difficulties must have attended the development of the idea that represents them, since every adjective is an abstract word, and abstraction is an unnatural and very painful operation.

At first they gave every object a peculiar name, without any regard to its genus or species, things which these first institutors of language were in no condition to distinguish; and every individual presented itself solitary to their minds, as it stands in the table of nature. If they called one oak A, they called another oak B: so that their dictionary must have been more extensive in proportion as their knowledge of things was more confined. It could not but be a very difficult task to get rid of so diffuse and embarrassing a nomenclature; as in order to marshal the several beings under common and generic denominations, it was necessary to be first acquainted with their properties, and their differences; to be stocked with observations and definitions, that is to say, to understand natural history and metaphysics, advantages which the men of these times could not have enjoyed.

Besides, general ideas cannot be conveyed to the mind without the assistance of words, nor can the understanding seize them without the assistance of propositions. This is one of the reasons, why mere animals cannot form such ideas, nor ever acquire the perfectibility which depends on such an operation. When a monkey leaves without the least hesitation one nut for another, are we to think he has any general idea of that kind of fruit, and that he compares these two individual bodies with his archetype notion of them? No, certainly; but the sight of one of these nuts calls back to his memory the sensations which he has received from the other; and his eyes, modified after some certain manner, give notice to his palate of the modification it is in its turn going to receive. Every general idea is purely intellectual; let the imagination tamper ever so little with it, it immediately becomes a particular idea. Endeavour to represent to yourself the image of a tree in general, you never will be able to do it; in spite of all your efforts it will appear big or little, thin or tufted, of a bright or a deep colour; and were you master to see nothing in it, but what can be seen in every tree, such a picture would no longer resemble any tree. Beings perfectly abstract are perceivable in the same manner, or are only conceivable by the assistance of speech. The definition of a triangle can alone give you a just idea of that figure: the moment you form a triangle in your mind, it is this or that particular triangle and no other, and you cannot avoid giving breadth to its lines and colour to its area. We must therefore make use of propositions; we must therefore speak to have general ideas; for the moment the imagination stops, the mind must stop too, if not assisted by speech. If therefore the first inventors could give no names to any ideas but those they had already, it follows that the first substantives could never have been anything more than proper names.

But when by means, which I cannot conceive, our new grammarians began to extend their ideas, and generalize their words, the ignorance of the inventors must have confined this method to very narrow bounds; and as they had at first too much multiplied the names of individuals for want of being acquainted with the distinctions called genus and species, they afterwards made too few genera and species for want of having considered beings in all their differences; to push the divisions far enough, they must have had more knowledge and experience than we can allow them, and have made more researches and taken more pains, than we can suppose them willing to submit to. Now if, even at this present time, we every day discover new species, which had before escaped all our observations, how many species must have escaped the notice of men, who judged of things merely from their first appearances! As to the primitive classes and the most general notions, it were superfluous to add that these they must have likewise overlooked: how, for example, could they have thought of or understood the words, matter, spirit, substance, mode, figure, motion, since even our philosophers, who for so long a time have been constantly employing these terms, can themselves scarcely understand them, and since the ideas annexed to these words being purely metaphysical, no models of them could be found in nature?

I stop at these first advances, and beseech my judges to suspend their lecture a little, in order to consider, what a great way language has still to go, in regard to the invention of physical substantives alone, (though the easiest part of language to invent,) to be able to express all the sentiments of man, to assume an invariable form, to bear being spoken in public and to influence society: I earnestly entreat them to consider how much time and knowledge must have been requisite to find out numbers, abstract words, the aorists, and all the other tenses of verbs, the particles, and syntax, the method of connecting propositions and arguments, of forming all the logic of discourse. For my own part, I am so scared at the difficulties that multiply at every step, and so convinced of the almost demonstrated impossibility of languages owing their birth and establishment to means that were merely human, that I must leave to whoever may please to take it up, the task of discussing this difficult problem. "Which was the most necessary, society already formed to invent languages, or languages already invented to form society?"

But be the case of these origins ever so mysterious, we may at least infer from the little care which nature has taken to bring men together by mutual wants, and make the use of speech easy to them, how little she has done towards making them sociable, and how little she has contributed to anything which they themselves have done to become so. In fact, it is impossible to conceive, why, in this primitive state, one man should have more occasion for the assistance of another, than one monkey, or one wolf for that of another animal of the same species; or supposing that he had, what motive could induce another to assist him; or even, in this last case, how he, who wanted assistance, and he from whom it was wanted, could agree among themselves upon the conditions. Authors, I know, are continually telling us, that in this state man would have been a most miserable creature; and if it is true, as I fancy I have proved it, that he must have continued many ages without either the desire or the opportunity of emerging from such a state, this their assertion could only serve to justify a charge against nature, and not any against the being which nature had thus constituted; but, if I thoroughly understand this term miserable, it is a word, that either has no meaning, or signifies nothing, but a privation attended with pain, and a suffering state of body or soul; now I would fain know what kind of misery can be that of a free being, whose heart enjoys perfect peace, and body perfect health? And which is aptest to become insupportable to those who enjoy it, a civil or a natural life? In civil life we can scarcely meet a single person who does not complain of his existence; many even throw away as much of it as they can, and the united force of divine and human laws can hardly put bounds to this disorder. Was ever any free savage known to have been so much as tempted to complain of life, and lay violent hands on himself? Let us therefore judge with less pride on which side real misery is to be placed. Nothing, on the contrary, must have been so unhappy as savage man, dazzled by flashes of knowledge, racked by passions, and reasoning on a state different from that in which he saw himself placed. It was in consequence of a very wise Providence, that the faculties, which he potentially enjoyed, were not to develop themselves but in proportion as there offered occasions to exercise them, lest they should be superfluous or troublesome to him when he did not want them, or tardy and useless when he did. He had in his instinct alone everything requisite to live in a state of nature; in his cultivated reason he has barely what is necessary to live in a state of society.

It appears at first sight that, as there was no kind of moral relations between men in this state, nor any known duties, they could not be either good or bad, and had neither vices nor virtues, unless we take these words in a physical sense, and call vices, in the individual, the qualities which may prove detrimental to his own preservation, and virtues those which may contribute to it; in which case we should be obliged to consider him as most virtuous, who made least resistance against the simple impulses of nature. But without deviating from the usual meaning of these terms, it is proper to suspend the judgment we might form of such a situation, and be upon our guard against prejudice, till, the balance in hand, we have examined whether there are more virtues or vices among civilized men; or whether the improvement of their understanding is sufficient to compensate the damage which they mutually do to each other, in proportion as they become better informed of the services which they ought to do; or whether, upon the whole, they would not be much happier in a condition, where they had nothing to fear or to hope from each other, than in that where they had submitted to an universal subserviency, and have obliged themselves to depend for everything upon the good will of those, who do not think themselves obliged to give anything in return.

But above all things let us beware concluding with Hobbes, that man, as having no idea of goodness, must be naturally bad; that he is vicious because he does not know what virtue is; that he always refuses to do any service to those of his own species, because he believes that none is due to them; that, in virtue of that right which he justly claims to everything he wants, he foolishly looks upon himself as proprietor of the whole universe. Hobbes very plainly saw the flaws in all the modern definitions of natural right: but the consequences, which he draws from his own definition, show that it is, in the sense he understands it, equally exceptionable. This author, to argue from his own principles, should say that the state of nature, being that where the care of our own preservation interferes least with the preservation of others, was of course the most favourable to peace, and most suitable to mankind; whereas he advances the very reverse in consequence of his having injudiciously admitted, as objects of that care which savage man should take of his preservation, the satisfaction of numberless passions which are the work of society, and have rendered laws necessary. A bad man, says he, is a robust child. But this is not proving that savage man is a robust child; and though we were to grant that he was, what could this philosopher infer from such a concession? That if this man, when robust, depended on others as much as when feeble, there is no excess that he would not be guilty of. He would make nothing of striking his mother when she delayed ever so little to give him the breast; he would claw, and bite, and strangle without remorse the first of his younger brothers, that ever so accidentally jostled or otherwise disturbed him. But these are two contradictory suppositions in the state of nature, to be robust and dependent. Man is weak when dependent, and his own master before he grows robust. Hobbes did not consider that the same cause, which hinders savages from making use of their reason, as our jurisconsults pretend, hinders them at the same time from making an ill use of their faculties, as he himself pretends; so that we may say that savages are not bad, precisely because they don't know what it is to be good; for it is neither the development of the understanding, nor the curb of the law, but the calmness of their passions and their ignorance of vice that hinders them from doing ill: *tantus plus in illis proficit vitiorum ignorantia, quam in his cognito virtutis.* There is besides another principle that has escaped Hobbes, and which, having been given to man to moderate, on certain occasions, the blind and impetuous sallies of self-love, or the desire of self-preservation previous to the appearance of that passion, allays the ardour, with which he naturally pursues his private welfare, by an innate abhorrence to see beings suffer that resemble him. I shall not surely be contradicted, in granting to man the only natural virtue, which the most passionate detractor of human virtues could not deny him, I mean that of pity, a disposition suitable to creatures weak as we are, and liable to so many evils; a virtue so much the more universal, and withal useful to man, as it takes place in him of all manner of reflection; and so natural, that the beasts themselves sometimes give evident signs of it. Not to speak of the tenderness of mothers for their young; and of the dangers they face to screen them from danger; with what reluctance are horses known to trample upon living bodies; one animal never passes unmoved by the dead carcass of another animal of the same species: there are even some who bestow a kind of sepulture upon their dead fellows; and the mournful lowings of cattle, on their entering the slaughter-house, publish the impression made upon them by the horrible spectacle they are there struck with. It is with pleasure we see the author of the fable of the bees, forced to acknowledge man a compassionate and sensible being; and lay aside, in the example he offers to confirm it, his cold and subtle style, to place before us the pathetic picture of a man, who, with his hands tied up, is obliged to behold a beast of prey tear a child from the arms of his mother, and then with his teeth grind the tender limbs, and with his claws rend the throbbing entrails of the innocent victim. What horrible emotions must not such a spectator experience at the sight of an event which does not personally concern him? What anguish must he not suffer at his not being able to assist the fainting mother or the expiring infant?

Such is the pure motion of nature, anterior to all manner of reflection; such is the force of natural pity, which the most dissolute manners have as yet found it so difficult to extinguish, since we every day see, in our theatrical representation, those men sympathize with the unfortunate and weep at their sufferings, who, if in the tyrant's place, would aggravate the torments of their enemies. Mandeville was very sensible that men, in spite of all their morality, would never have been better than monsters, if nature had not given them pity to assist reason: but he did not perceive that from this quality alone flow all the social virtues, which he would dispute mankind the possession of. In fact, what is generosity, what clemency, what humanity, but pity applied to the weak, to the guilty, or to the human species in general? Even benevolence and friendship, if we judge right, will appear the effects of a constant pity, fixed upon a particular object: for to wish that a person may not suffer, what is it but to wish that he may be happy? Though it were true that commiseration is no more than a sentiment, which puts us in the place of him who suffers, a sentiment obscure but active in the savage, developed but dormant in civilized man, how could this notion affect the truth of what I advance, but to make it more evident. In fact, commiseration must be so much the more energetic, the more intimately the animal, that beholds any kind of distress, identifies himself with the animal that labours under it. Now it is evident that this identification must have been infinitely more perfect in the state of nature than in the state of reason. It is reason that engenders self-love, and reflection that strengthens it; it is reason that makes man shrink into himself; it is reason that makes him keep aloof from everything that can trouble or afflict him: it is philosophy that destroys his connections with other men; it is in consequence of her dictates that he mutters to himself at the sight of another in distress, You may perish for aught I care, nothing can hurt me. Nothing less than those evils, which threaten the whole species, can disturb the calm sleep of the philosopher, and force him from his bed. One man may with impunity murder another under his windows; he has nothing to do but clap his hands to his ears, argue a little with himself to hinder nature, that startles within him, from identifying him with the unhappy sufferer. Savage man wants this admirable talent; and for want of wisdom and reason, is always ready foolishly to obey the first whispers of humanity. In riots and street-brawls the populace flock together, the prudent man sneaks off. They are the dregs of the people, the poor basket and barrow-women, that part the combatants, and hinder gentle folks from cutting one another's throats.

It is therefore certain that pity is a natural sentiment, which, by moderating in every individual the activity of self-love, contributes to the mutual preservation of the whole species. It is this pity which hurries us without reflection to the assistance of those we see in distress; it is this pity which, in a state of nature, stands for laws, for manners, for virtue, with this advantage, that no one is tempted to disobey her sweet and gentle voice: it is this pity which will always hinder a robust savage from plundering a feeble child, or infirm old man, of the subsistence they have acquired with pain and difficulty, if he has but the least prospect of providing for himself by any other means: it is this pity which, instead of that sublime maxim of argumentative justice, Do to others as you would have others do to you, inspires all men with that other maxim of natural goodness a great deal less perfect, but perhaps more useful, Consult your own happiness with as little prejudice as you can to that of others. It is in a word, in this natural sentiment, rather than in fine-spun arguments, that we must look for the cause of that reluctance which every man would experience to do evil, even independently of the maxims of education. Though it may be the peculiar happiness of Socrates and other geniuses of his stamp, to reason themselves into virtue, the human species would long ago have ceased to exist, had it depended entirely for its preservation on the reasonings of the individuals that compose it.

With passions so tame, and so salutary a curb, men, rather wild than wicked, and more attentive to guard against mischief than to do any to other animals, were not exposed to any dangerous dissensions: As they kept up no manner of correspondence with each other, and were of course strangers to vanity, to respect, to esteem, to contempt; as they had no notion of what we call Meum and Tuum, nor any true idea of justice; as they considered any violence they were liable to, as an evil that could be easily repaired, and not as an injury that deserved punishment; and as they never so much as dreamed of revenge, unless perhaps mechanically and unpremeditatedly, as a dog who bites the stone that has been thrown at him; their disputes could seldom be attended with bloodshed, were they never occasioned by a more considerable stake than that of subsistence: but there is a more dangerous subject of contention, which I must not leave unnoticed.

Among the passions which ruffle the heart of man, there is one of a hot and impetuous nature, which renders the sexes necessary to each other; a terrible passion which despises all dangers, bears down all obstacles, and to which in its transports it seems proper to destroy the human species which it is destined to preserve. What must become of men abandoned to this lawless and brutal rage, without modesty, without shame, and every day disputing the objects of their passion at the expense of their blood?

We must in the first place allow that the more violent the passions, the more necessary are laws to restrain them: but besides that the disorders and the crimes, to which these passions daily give rise among us, sufficiently prove the insufficiency of laws for that purpose, we would do well to look back a little further and examine, if these evils did not spring up with the laws themselves; for at this rate, though the laws were capable of repressing these evils, it is the least that might be expected from them, seeing it is no more than stopping the progress of a mischief which they themselves have produced.

Let us begin by distinguishing between what is moral and what is physical in the passion called love. The physical part of it is that general desire which prompts the sexes to unite with each other; the moral part is that which determines that desire, and fixes it upon a particular object to the exclusion of all others, or at least gives it a greater degree of energy for this preferred object. Now it is easy to perceive that the moral part of love is a factitious sentiment, engendered by society, and cried up by the women with great care and address in order to establish their empire, and secure command to that sex which ought to obey. This sentiment, being founded on certain notions of beauty and merit which a savage is not capable of having, and upon comparisons which he is not capable of making, can scarcely exist in him: for as his mind was never in a condition to form abstract ideas of regularity and proportion, neither is his heart susceptible of sentiments of admiration and love, which, even without our perceiving it, are produced by our application of these ideas; he listens solely to the dispositions implanted in him by nature, and not to taste which he never was in a way of acquiring; and every woman answers his purpose.

Confined entirely to what is physical in love, and happy enough not to know these preferences which sharpen the appetite for it, at the same time that they increase the difficulty of satisfying such appetite, men, in a state of nature, must be subject to fewer and less violent fits of that passion, and of course there must be fewer and less violent disputes among them in consequence of it. The imagination which causes so many ravages among us, never speaks to the heart of savages, who peaceably wait for the impulses of nature, yield to these impulses without choice and with more pleasure than fury; and whose desires never outlive their necessity for the thing desired.

Nothing therefore can be more evident, than that it is society alone, which has added even to love itself as well as to all the other passions, that impetuous ardour, which so often renders it fatal to mankind; and it is so much the more ridiculous to represent savages constantly murdering each other to glut their brutality, as this opinion is diametrically opposite to experience, and the Caribbeans, the people in the world who have as yet deviated least from the state of nature, are to all intents and purposes the most peaceable in their amours, and the least subject to jealousy, though they live in a burning climate which seems always to add considerably to the activity of these passions.

As to the inductions which may be drawn, in respect to several species of animals, from the battles of the males, who in all seasons cover our poultry yards with blood, and in spring particularly cause our forests to ring again with the noise they make in disputing their females, we must begin by excluding all those species, where nature has evidently established, in the relative power of the sexes, relations different from those which exist among us: thus from the battle of cocks we can form no induction that will affect the human species. In the species, where the proportion is better observed, these battles must be owing entirely to the fewness of the females compared with the males, or, which is all one, to the exclusive intervals, during which the females constantly refuse the addresses of the males; for if the female admits the male but two months in the year, it is all the same as if the number of females were five-sixths less than what it is: now neither of these cases is applicable to the human species, where the number of females generally surpasses that of males, and where it has never been observed that, even among savages, the females had, like those of other animals, stated times of passion and indifference. Besides, among several of these animals the whole species takes fire all at once, and for some days nothing is to be seen among them but confusion, tumult, disorder and bloodshed; a state unknown to the human species where love is never periodical. We can not therefore conclude from the battles of certain animals for the possession of their females, that the same would be the case of man in a state of nature; and though we might, as these contests do not destroy the other species, there is at least equal room to think they would not be fatal to ours; nay it is very probable that they would cause fewer ravages than they do in society, especially in those countries where, morality being as yet held in some esteem, the jealousy of lovers, and the vengeance of husbands every day produce duels, murders and even worse crimes; where the duty of an eternal fidelity serves only to propagate adultery; and the very laws of continence and honour necessarily contribute to increase dissoluteness, and multiply abortions.

Let us conclude that savage man, wandering about in the forests, without industry, without speech, without any fixed residence, an equal stranger to war and every social connection, without standing in any shape in need of his fellows, as well as without any desire of hurting them, and perhaps even without ever distinguishing them individually one from the other, subject to few passions, and finding in himself all he wants, let us say, conclude that savage man thus circumstanced had no knowledge or sentiment but such as are proper to that condition, that he was alone sensible of his real necessities, took notice of nothing but what it was his interest to see, and that his understanding made as little progress as his vanity. If he happened to make any discovery, he could the less communicate it as he did not even know his children. The art perished with the inventor; there was neither education nor improvement; generations succeeded generations to no purpose; and as all constantly set out from the same point, whole centuries rolled on in the rudeness and barbarity of the first age; the species was grown old, while the individual still remained in a state of childhood.

If I have enlarged so much upon the supposition of this primitive condition, it is because I thought it my duty, considering what ancient errors and inveterate prejudices I have to extirpate, to dig to the very roots, and show in a true picture of the state of nature, how much even natural inequality falls short in this state of that reality and influence which our writers ascribe to it.

In fact, we may easily perceive that among the differences, which distinguish men, several pass for natural, which are merely the work of habit and the different kinds of life adopted by men living in a social way. Thus a robust or delicate constitution, and the strength and weakness which depend on it, are oftener produced by the hardy or effeminate manner in which a man has been brought up, than by the primitive constitution of his body. It is the same thus in regard to the forces of the mind; and education not only produces a difference between those minds which are cultivated and those which are not, but even increases that which is found among the first in proportion to their culture; for let a giant and a dwarf set out in the same path, the giant at every step will acquire a new advantage over the dwarf. Now, if we compare the prodigious variety in the education and manner of living of the different orders of men in a civil state, with the simplicity and uniformity that prevails in the animal and savage life, where all the individuals make use of the same aliments, live in the same manner, and do exactly the same things, we shall easily conceive how much the difference between man and man in the state of nature must be less than in the state of society, and how much every inequality of institution must increase the natural inequalities of the human species.

But though nature in the distribution of her gifts should really affect all the preferences that are ascribed to her, what advantage could the most favoured derive from her partiality, to the prejudice of others, in a state of things, which scarce admitted any kind of relation between her pupils? Of what service can beauty be, where there is no love? What will wit avail people who don't speak, or craft those who have no affairs to transact? Authors are constantly crying out, that the strongest would oppress the weakest; but let them explain what they mean by the word oppression. One man will rule with violence, another will groan under a constant subjection to all his caprices: this is indeed precisely what I observe among us, but I don't see how it can be said of savage men, into whose heads it would be a harder matter to drive even the meaning of the words domination and servitude. One man might, indeed, seize on the fruits which another had gathered, on the game which another had killed, on the cavern which another had occupied for shelter; but how is it possible he should ever exact obedience from him, and what chains of dependence can there be among men who possess nothing? If I am driven from one tree, I have nothing to do but look out for another; if one place is made uneasy to me, what can hinder me from taking up my quarters elsewhere? But suppose I should meet a man so much superior to me in strength, and withal so wicked, so lazy and so barbarous as to oblige me to provide for his subsistence while he remains idle; he must resolve not to take his eyes from me a single moment, to bind me fast before he can take the least nap, lest I should kill him or give him the slip during his sleep: that is to say, he must expose himself voluntarily to much greater troubles than what he seeks to avoid, than any he gives me. And after all, let him abate ever so little of his vigilance; let him at some sudden noise but turn his head another way; I am already buried in the forest, my fetters are broke, and he never sees me again.

But without insisting any longer upon these details, every one must see that, as the bonds of servitude are formed merely by the mutual dependence of men one upon another and the reciprocal necessities which unite them, it is impossible for one man to enslave another, without having first reduced him to a condition in which he can not live without the enslaver's assistance; a condition which, as it does not exist in a state of nature, must leave every man his own master, and render the law of the strongest altogether vain and useless.

Having proved that the inequality, which may subsist between man and man in a state of nature, is almost imperceivable, and that it has very little influence, I must now proceed to show its origin, and trace its progress, in the successive developments of the human mind. After having showed, that perfectibility, the social virtues, and the other faculties, which natural man had received *in potentia,* could never be developed of themselves, that for that purpose there was a necessity for the fortuitous concurrence of several foreign causes, which might never happen, and without which he must have eternally remained in his primitive condition; I must proceed to consider and bring together the different accidents which may have perfected the human understanding by debasing the species, render a being wicked by rendering him sociable, and from so remote a term bring man, at last, and the world, to the point in which we now see them.

I must own that, as the events I am about to describe might have happened many different ways, my choice of these I shall assign can be grounded on nothing but mere conjecture; but besides these conjectures becoming reasons, when they are not only the most probable that can be drawn from the nature of things, but the only means we can have of discovering truth, the consequences I mean to deduce from mine will not be merely conjectural, since, on the principles I have just established, it is impossible to form any other system, that would not supply me with the same results, and from which I might not draw the same conclusions.

This will authorize me to be the more concise in my reflections on the manner, in which the lapse of time makes amends for the little verisimilitude of events; on the surprising power of very trivial causes, when they act without intermission; on the impossibility there is on the one hand of destroying certain Hypotheses, if on the other we can not give them the degree of certainty which facts must be allowed to possess; on its being the business of history, when two facts are proposed, as real, to be connected by a chain of inter-mediate facts which are either unknown or considered as such, to furnish such facts as may actually connect them; and the business of philosophy, when history is silent, to point out similar facts which may answer the same purpose; in fine on the privilege of similitude, in regard to events, to reduce facts to a much smaller number of different classes than is generally imagined. It suffices me to offer these objects to the consideration of my judges; it suffices me to have conducted my inquiry in such a manner as to save common readers the trouble of considering them.

SECOND PART

THE first man, who, after enclosing a piece of ground, took it into his head to say, "This is mine," and found people simple enough to believe him, was the true founder of civil society. How many crimes, how many wars, how many murders, how many misfortunes and horrors, would that man have saved the human species, who pulling up the stakes or filling up the ditches should have cried to his fellows: Be sure not to listen to this imposter; you are lost, if you forget that the fruits of the earth belong equally to us all, and the earth itself to nobody! But it is highly probable that things were now come to such a pass, that they could not continue much longer in the same way; for as this idea of property depends on several prior ideas which could only spring up gradually one after another, it was not formed all at once in the human mind: men must have made great progress; they must have acquired a great stock of industry and knowledge, and transmitted and increased it from age to age before they could arrive at this last term of the state of nature. Let us therefore take up things a little higher, and collect into one point of view, and in their most natural order, this slow succession of events and mental improvements.

The first sentiment of man was that of his existence, his first care that of preserving it. The productions of the earth yielded him all the assistance he required; instinct prompted him to make use of them. Among the various appetites, which made him at different times experience different modes of existence, there was one that excited him to perpetuate his species; and this blind propensity, quite void of anything like pure love or affection, produced nothing but an act that was merely animal. The present heat once allayed, the sexes took no further notice of each other, and even the child ceased to have any tie in his mother, the moment he ceased to want her assistance.

Such was the condition of infant man; such was the life of an animal confined at first to pure sensations, and so far from harbouring any thought of forcing her gifts from nature, that he scarcely availed himself of those which she offered to him of her own accord. But difficulties soon arose, and there was a necessity for learning how to surmount them: the height of some trees, which prevented his reaching their fruits; the competition of other animals equally fond of the same fruits; the fierceness of many that even aimed at his life; these were so many circumstances, which obliged him to apply to bodily exercise. There was a necessity for becoming active, swift-footed, and sturdy in battle. The natural arms, which are stones and the branches of trees, soon offered themselves to his assistance. He learned to surmount the obstacles of nature, to contend in case of necessity with other animals, to dispute his subsistence even with other men, or indemnify himself for the loss of whatever he found himself obliged to part with to the strongest.

In proportion as the human species grew more numerous, and extended itself, its pains likewise multiplied and increased. The difference of soils, climates and seasons, might have forced men to observe some difference in their way of living. Bad harvests, long and severe winters, and scorching summers which parched up all the fruits of the earth, required extraordinary exertions of industry. On the sea shore, and the banks of rivers, they invented the line and the hook, and became fishermen and ichthyophagous. In the forests they made themselves bows and arrows, and became huntsmen and warriors. In the cold countries they covered themselves with the skins of the beasts they had killed; thunder, a volcano, or some happy accident made them acquainted with fire, a new resource against the rigours of winter: they discovered the method of preserving this element, then that of reproducing it, and lastly the way of preparing with it the flesh of animals, which heretofore they devoured raw from the carcass.

This reiterated application of various beings to himself, and to one another, must have naturally engendered in the mind of man the idea of certain relations. These relations, which we express by the words, great, little, strong, weak, swift, slow, fearful, bold, and the like, compared occasionally, and almost without thinking of it, produced in him some kind of reflection, or rather a mechanical prudence, which pointed out to him the precautions most essential to his preservation and safety.

The new lights resulting from this development increased his superiority over other animals, by making him sensible of it. He laid himself out to ensnare them; he played them a thousand tricks; and though several surpassed him in strength or in swiftness, he in time became the master of those that could be of any service to him, and a sore enemy to those that could do him any mischief. 'Tis thus, that the first look he gave into himself produced the first emotion of pride in him; 'tis thus that, at a time he scarce knew how to distinguish between the different ranks of existence, by attributing to his species the first rank among animals in general, he prepared himself at a distance to pretend to it as an individual among those of his own species in particular.

Though other men were not to him what they are to us, and he had scarce more intercourse with them than with other animals, they were not overlooked in his observations. The conformities, which in time he might discover between them, and between himself and his female, made him judge of those he did not perceive; and seeing that they all behaved as himself would have done in similar circumstances, he concluded that their manner of thinking and willing was quite conformable to his own; and this important truth, when once engraved deeply on his mind, made him follow, by a presentiment as sure as any logic, and withal much quicker, the best rules of conduct, which for the sake of his own safety and advantage it was proper he should observe towards them.

Instructed by experience that the love of happiness is the sole principle of all human actions, he found himself in a condition to distinguish the few cases, in which common interest might authorize him to build upon the assistance of his fellows, and those still fewer, in which a competition of interests might justly render it suspected. In the first case he united with them in the same flock, or at most by some kind of free association which obliged none of its members, and lasted no longer than the transitory necessity that had given birth to it. In the second case every one aimed at his own private advantage, either by open force if he found himself strong enough, or by cunning and address if he thought himself too weak to use violence.

Such was the manner in which men might have insensibly acquired some gross idea of their mutual engagements and the advantage of fulfilling them, but this only as far as their present and sensible interest required; for as to foresight they were utter strangers to it, and far from troubling their heads about a distant futurity, they scarce thought of the day following. Was a deer to be taken? Every one saw that to succeed he must faithfully stand to his post; but suppose a hare to have slipped by within reach of any one of them, it is not to be doubted but he pursued it without scruple, and when he had seized his prey never reproached himself with having made his companions miss theirs.

We may easily conceive that such an intercourse scarce required a more refined language than that of crows and monkeys, which flock together almost in the same manner. Inarticulate exclamations, a great many gestures, and some imitative sounds, must have been for a long time the universal language of mankind, and by joining to these in every country some articulate and conventional sounds, of which, as I have already hinted, it is not very easy to explain the institution, there arose particular languages, but rude, imperfect, and such nearly as are to be found at this day among several savage nations. My pen straightened by the rapidity of time, the abundance of things I have to say, and the almost insensible progress of the first improvements, flies like an arrow over numberless ages, for the slower the succession of events, the quicker I may allow myself to be in relating them.

At length, these first improvements enabled man to improve at a greater rate. Industry grew perfect in proportion as the mind became more enlightened. Men soon ceasing to fall asleep under the first tree, or take shelter in the first cavern, lit upon some hard and sharp kinds of stone resembling spades or hatchets, and employed them to dig the ground, cut down trees, and with the branches build huts, which they afterwards bethought themselves of plastering over with clay or dirt. This was the epoch of a first revolution, which produced the establishment and distinction of families, and which introduced a species of property, and along with it perhaps a thousand quarrels and battles. As the strongest however were probably the first to make themselves cabins, which they knew they were able to defend, we may conclude that the weak found it much shorter and safer to imitate than to attempt to dislodge them: and as to those, who were already provided with cabins, no one could have any great temptation to seize upon that of his neighbour, not so much because it did not belong to him, as because it could be of no service to him; and as besides to make himself master of it, he must expose himself to a very sharp conflict with the present occupiers.

The first developments of the heart were the effects of a new situation, which united husbands and wives, parents and children, under one roof; the habit of living together gave birth to the sweetest sentiments the human species is acquainted with, conjugal and paternal love. Every family became a little society, so much the more firmly united, as a mutual attachment and liberty were the only bonds of it; and it was now that the sexes, whose way of life had been hitherto the same, began to adopt different manners and customs. The women became more sedentary, and accustomed themselves to stay at home and look after the children, while the men rambled abroad in quest of subsistence for the whole family. The two sexes likewise by living a little more at their ease began to lose somewhat of their usual ferocity and sturdiness; but if on the one hand individuals became less able to engage separately with wild beasts, they on the other were more easily got together to make a common resistance against them.

In this new state of things, the simplicity and solitariness of man's life, the limitedness of his wants, and the instruments which he had invented to satisfy them, leaving him a great deal of leisure, he employed it to supply himself with several conveniences unknown to his ancestors; and this was the first yoke he inadvertently imposed upon himself, and the first source of mischief which he prepared for his children; for besides continuing in this manner to soften both body and mind, these conveniences having through use lost almost all their aptness to please, and even degenerated into real wants, the privation of them became far more intolerable than the possession of them had been agreeable; to lose them was a misfortune, to possess them no happiness.

Here we may a little better discover how the use of speech insensibly commences or improves in the bosom of every family, and may likewise from conjectures concerning the manner in which divers particular causes might have propagated language, and accelerated its progress by rendering it every day more and more necessary. Great inundations or earthquakes surrounded inhabited districts with water or precipices, portions of the continent were by revolutions of the globe torn off and split into islands. It is obvious that among men thus collected, and forced to live together, a common idiom must have started up much sooner, than among those who freely wandered through the forests of the main land. Thus it is very possible that the inhabitants of the islands formed in this manner, after their first essays in navigation, brought among us the use of speech; and it is very probable at least that society and languages commenced in islands and even acquired perfection there, before the inhabitants of the continent knew anything of either.

Everything now begins to wear a new aspect. Those who heretofore wandered through the woods, by taking to a more settled way of life, gradually flock together, coalesce into several separate bodies, and at length form in every country distinct nations, united in character and manners, not by any laws or regulations, but by an uniform manner of life, a sameness of provisions, and the common influence of the climate. A permanent neighborhood must at last infallibly create some connection between different families. The transitory commerce required by nature soon produced, among the youth of both sexes living in contiguous cabins, another kind of commerce, which besides being equally agreeable is rendered more durable by mutual intercourse. Men begin to consider different objects, and to make comparisons; they insensibly acquire ideas of merit and beauty, and these soon produce sentiments of preference. By seeing each other often they contract a habit, which makes it painful not to see each other always. Tender and agreeable sentiments steal into the soul, and are by the smallest opposition wound up into the most impetuous fury: Jealousy kindles with love; discord triumphs; and the gentlest of passions requires sacrifices of human blood to appease it.

In proportion as ideas and sentiments succeed each other, and the head and the heart exercise themselves, men continue to shake off their original wildness, and their connections become more intimate and extensive. They now begin to assemble round a great tree: singing and dancing, the genuine offspring of love and leisure, become the amusement or rather the occupation of the men and women, free from care, thus gathered together. Every one begins to survey the rest, and wishes to be surveyed himself; and public esteem acquires a value. He who sings or dances best; the handsomest, the strongest, the most dexterous, the most eloquent, comes to be the most respected: this was the first step towards inequality, and at the same time towards vice. From these first preferences there proceeded on one side vanity and contempt, on the other envy and shame; and the fermentation raised by these new leavens at length produced combinations fatal to happiness and innocence.

Men no sooner began to set a value upon each other, and know what esteem was, than each laid claim to it, and it was no longer safe for any man to refuse it to another. Hence the first duties of civility and politeness, even among savages; and hence every voluntary injury became an affront, as besides the mischief, which resulted from it as an injury, the party offended was sure to find in it a contempt for his person more intolerable than the mischief itself. It was thus that every man, punishing the contempt expressed for him by others in proportion to the value he set upon himself, the effects of revenge became terrible, and men learned to be sanguinary and cruel. Such precisely was the degree attained by most of the savage nations with whom we are acquainted. And it is for want of sufficiently distinguishing ideas, and observing at how great a distance these people were from the first state of nature, that so many authors have hastily concluded that man is naturally cruel, and requires a regular system of police to be reclaimed; whereas nothing can be more gentle than he in his primitive state, when placed by nature at an equal distance from the stupidity of brutes, and the pernicious good sense of civilized man; and equally confined by instinct and reason to the care of providing against the mischief which threatens him, he is withheld by natural compassion from doing any injury to others, so far from being ever so little prone even to return that which he has received. For according to the axiom of the wise Locke, Where there is no property, there can be no injury.

But we must take notice, that the society now formed and the relations now established among men required in them qualities different from those, which they derived from their primitive constitution; that as a sense of morality began to insinuate itself into human actions, and every man, before the enacting of laws, was the only judge and avenger of the injuries he had received, that goodness of heart suitable to the pure state of nature by no means suited infant society; that it was necessary punishments should become severer in the same proportion that the opportunities of offending became more frequent, and the dread of vengeance add strength to the too weak curb of the law. Thus, though men were become less patient, and natural compassion had already suffered some alteration, this period of the development of the human faculties, holding a just mean between the indolence of the primitive state, and the petulant activity of self-love, must have been the happiest and most durable epoch. The more we reflect on this state, the more convinced we shall be, that it was the least subject of any to revolutions, the best for man, and that nothing could have drawn him out of it but some fatal accident, which, for the public good, should never have happened. The example of the savages, most of whom have been found in this condition, seems to confirm that mankind was formed ever to remain in it, that this condition is the real youth of the world, and that all ulterior improvements have been so many steps, in appearance towards the perfection of individuals, but in fact towards the decrepitness of the species.

As long as men remained satisfied with their rustic cabins; as long as they confined themselves to the use of clothes made of the skins of other animals, and the use of thorns and fish-bones, in putting these skins together; as long as they continued to consider feathers and shells as sufficient ornaments, and to paint their bodies of different colours, to improve or ornament their bows and arrows, to form and scoop out with sharp-edged stones some little fishing boats, or clumsy instruments of music; in a word, as long as they undertook such works only as a single person could finish, and stuck to such arts as did not require the joint endeavours of several hands, they lived free, healthy, honest and happy, as much as their nature would admit, and continued to enjoy with each other all the pleasures of an independent intercourse; but from the moment one man began to stand in need of another's assistance; from the moment it appeared an advantage for one man to possess the quantity of provisions requisite for two, all equality vanished; property started up; labour became necessary; and boundless forests became smiling fields, which it was found necessary to water with human sweat, and in which slavery and misery were soon seen to sprout out and grow with the fruits of the earth.

Metallurgy and agriculture were the two arts whose invention produced this great revolution. With the poet, it is gold and silver, but with the philosopher it is iron and corn, which have civilized men, and ruined mankind. Accordingly both one and the other were unknown to the savages of America, who for that very reason have always continued savages; nay other nations seem to have continued in a state of barbarism, as long as they continued to exercise one only of these arts without the other; and perhaps one of the best reasons that can be assigned, why Europe has been, if not earlier, at least more constantly and better civilized than the other quarters of the world, is that she both abounds most in iron and is best qualified to produce corn.

It is a very difficult matter to tell how men came to know anything of iron, and the art of employing it: for we are not to suppose that they should of themselves think of digging it out of the mines, and preparing it for fusion, before they knew what could be the result of such a process. On the other hand, there is the less reason to attribute this discovery to any accidental fire, as mines are formed nowhere but in dry and barren places, and such as are bare of trees and plants, so that it looks as if nature had taken pains to keep from us so mischievous a secret. Nothing therefore remains but the extraordinary circumstance of some volcano, which, belching forth metallic substances ready fused, might have given the spectators a notion of imitating that operation of nature; and after all we must suppose them endued with an extraordinary stock of courage and foresight to undertake so painful a work, and have, at so great a distance, an eye to the advantages they might derive from it; qualities scarcely suitable but to heads more exercised, than those of such discoverers can be supposed to have been.

As to agriculture, the principles of it were known a long time before the practice of it took place, and it is hardly possible that men, constantly employed in drawing their subsistence from trees and plants, should not have early hit on the means employed by nature for the generation of vegetables; but in all probability it was very late before their industry took a turn that way, either because trees, which with their land and water game supplied them with sufficient food, did not require their attention; or because they did not know the use of corn; or because they had no instruments to cultivate it; or because they were destitute of foresight in regard to future necessities; or in fine, because they wanted means to hinder others from running away with the fruit of their labours. We may believe that on their becoming more industrious they began their agriculture by cultivating with sharp stones and pointed sticks a few pulse or roots about their cabins; and that it was a long time before they knew the method of preparing corn, and were provided with instruments necessary to raise it in large quantities; not to mention the necessity there is, in order to follow this occupation and sow lands, to consent to lose something at present to gain a great deal hereafter; a precaution very foreign to the turn of man's mind in a savage state, in which, as I have already taken notice, he can hardly foresee his wants from morning to night.

For this reason the invention of other arts must have been necessary to oblige mankind to apply to that of agriculture. As soon as men were wanted to fuse and forge iron, others were wanted to maintain them. The more hands were employed in manufactures, the fewer hands were left to provide subsistence for all, though the number of mouths to be supplied with food continued the same; and as some required commodities in exchange for their iron, the rest at last found out the method of making iron subservient to the multiplication of commodities. Hence on the one hand husbandry and agriculture, and on the other the art of working metals and of multiplying the uses of them.

To the tilling of the earth the distribution of it necessarily succeeded, and to property one acknowledged, the first rules of justice:

for to secure every man his own, every man must have something. Moreover, as men began to extend their views to futurity, and all found themselves in possession of more or less goods capable of being lost, every one in particular had reason to fear, lest reprisals should be made on him for any injury he might do to others. This origin is so much the more natural, as it is impossible to conceive how property can flow from any other source but industry; for what can a man add but his labour to things which he has not made, in order to acquire a property in them? 'Tis the labour of the hands alone, which giving the husbandman a title to the produce of the land he has tilled gives him a title to the land itself, at least till he has gathered in the fruits of it, and so on from year to year; and this enjoyment forming a continued possession is easily transformed into a property. The ancients, says Grotius, by giving to Ceres the epithet of Legislatrix, and to a festival celebrated in her honour the name of Thesmorphoria, insinuated that the distribution of lands produced a new kind of right; that is, the right of property different from that which results from the law of nature.

Things thus circumstanced might have remained equal, if men's talents had been equal, and if, for instance, the use of iron, and the consumption of commodities had always held an exact proportion to each other; but as this proportion had no support, it was soon broken. The man that had most strength performed most labour; the most dexterous turned his labour to best account; the most ingenious found out methods of lessening his labour; the husbandman required more iron, or the smith more corn, and while both worked equally, one earned a great deal by his labour, while the other could scarce live by his. It is thus that natural inequality insensibly unfolds itself with that arising from a variety of combinations, and that the difference among men, developed by the difference of their circumstances, becomes more sensible, more permanent in its effects, and begins to influence in the same proportion the condition of private persons.

Things once arrived at this period, it is an easy matter to imagine the rest. I shall not stop to describe the successive inventions of other arts, the progress of language, the trial and employments of talents, the inequality of fortunes, the use or abuse of riches, nor all the details which follow these, and which every one may easily supply. I shall just give a glance at mankind placed in this new order of things.

Behold then all our faculties developed; our memory and imagination at work, self-love interested; reason rendered active; and the mind almost arrived at the utmost bounds of that perfection it is capable of. Behold all our natural qualities put in motion; the rank and condition of every man established, not only as to the quantum of property and the power of serving or hurting others, but likewise as to genius, beauty, strength or address, merit or talents; and as these were the only qualities which could command respect, it was found necessary to have or at least to affect them. It was requisite for men to be thought what they really were not. To be and to appear became two very different things, and from this distinction sprang pomp and knavery, and all the vices which form their train. On the other hand, man, heretofore free and independent, was now in consequence of a multitude of new wants brought under subjection, as it were, to all nature, and especially to his fellows, whose slave in some sense he became even by becoming their master; if rich, he stood in need of their services, if poor, of their assistance; even mediocrity itself could not enable him to do without them. He must therefore have been continually at work to interest them in his happiness, and make them, if not really, at least apparently find their advantage in labouring for his: this rendered him sly and artful in his dealings with some, imperious and cruel in his dealings with others, and laid him under the necessity of using ill all those whom he stood in need of, as often as he could not awe them into a compliance with his will, and did not find it his interest to purchase it at the expense of real services. In fine, an insatiable ambition, the rage of raising their relative fortunes, not so much through real necessity, as to over-top others, inspire all men with a wicked inclination to injure each other, and with a secret jealousy so much the more dangerous, as to carry its point with the greater security, it often puts on the face of benevolence. In a word, sometimes nothing was to be seen but a contention of endeavours on the one hand, and an opposition of interests on the other, while a secret desire of thriving at the expense of others constantly prevailed. Such were the first

effects of property, and the inseparable attendants of infant inequality.

Riches, before the invention of signs to represent them, could
scarce consist in anything but lands and cattle, the only real goods
which men can possess. But when estates increased so much in
number and in extent as to take in whole countries and touch each
other, it became impossible for one man to aggrandise himself but
at the expense of some other; and the supernumerary inhabitants,
who were too weak or too indolent to make such acquisitions in their
turn, impoverished without losing anything, because while everything about them changed they alone remained the same, were
obliged to receive or force their subsistence from the hands of the
rich. And hence began to flow, according to the different characters
of each, domination and slavery, or violence and rapine. The rich
on their side scarce began to taste the pleasure of commanding,
when they preferred it to every other; and making use of their old
slaves to acquire new ones, they no longer thought of anything but
subduing and enslaving their neighbours; like those ravenous wolves,
who having once tasted human flesh, despise every other food, and
devour nothing but men for the future.

It is thus that the most powerful or the most wretched, respec-
tively considering their power and wretchedness as a kind of title to
the substance of others, even equivalent to that of property, the
equality once broken was followed by the most shocking disorders.
It is thus that the usurpations of the rich, the pillagings of the poor,
and the unbridled passions of all, by stifling the cries of natural
compassion, and the as yet feeble voice of justice, rendered man
avaricious, wicked and ambitious. There arose between the title of
the strongest, and that of the first occupier a perpetual conflict, which
always ended in battery and bloodshed. Infant society became a
scene of the most horrible warfare: Mankind thus debased and
harassed, and no longer able to retreat, or renounce the unhappy
acquisitions it had made; labouring, in short merely to its confusion by the abuse of those faculties, which in themselves do it so
much honour, brought itself to the very brink of ruin and destruction.

Attonitus novitate mali, divesque miserque,
Effugere optat opes; et quæ modò voverat, odit.

But it is impossible that men should not sooner or later have made reflections on so wretched a situation, and upon the calamities with which they were overwhelmed. The rich in particular must have soon perceived how much they suffered by a perpetual war, of which they alone supported all the expense, and in which, though all risked life, they alone risked any substance. Besides, whatever colour they might pretend to give their usurpations, they sufficiently saw that these usurpations were in the main founded upon false and precarious titles, and that what they had acquired by mere force, others could again by mere force wrest out of their hands, without leaving them the least room to complain of such a proceeding. Even those, who owed all their riches to their own industry, could scarce ground their acquisitions upon a better title. It availed them nothing to say, 'Twas I built this wall; I acquired this spot by my labour. Who traced it out for you, another might object, and what right have you to expect payment at our expense for doing that we did not oblige you to do? Don't you know that numbers of your brethren perish, or suffer grievously for want of what you possess more than suffices nature, and that you should have had the express and unanimous consent of mankind to appropriate to yourself of their common, more than was requisite for your private subsistence? Destitute of solid reasons to justify, and sufficient force to defend himself; crushing individuals with ease, but with equal ease crushed by numbers; one against all, and unable, on account of mutual jealousies, to unite with his equals against banditti united by the common hopes of pillage; the rich man, thus pressed by necessity, at last conceived the deepest project that ever entered the human mind: this was to employ in his favour the very forces that attacked him, to make allies of his enemies, to inspire them with other maxims, and make them adopt other institutions as favourable to his pretensions, as the law of nature was unfavourable to them.

With this view, after laying before his neighbours all the horrors of a situation, which armed them all one against another, which

rendered their possessions as burdensome as their wants were intolerable, and in which no one could expect any safety either in
poverty or riches, he easily invented specious arguments to bring
them over to his purpose. "Let us unite," said he, "to secure the
weak from oppression, restrain the ambitious, and secure to every
man the possession of what belongs to him: Let us form rules of
justice and peace, to which all may be obliged to conform, which
shall not except persons, but may in some sort make amends for
the caprice of fortune, by submitting alike the powerful and the
weak to the observance of mutual duties. In a word, instead of turning our forces against ourselves, let us collect them into a sovereign
power, which may govern us by wise laws, may protect and defend
all the members of the association, repel common enemies, and
maintain a perpetual concord and harmony among us."

Much fewer words of this kind were sufficient to draw in a parcel
of rustics, whom it was an easy matter to impose upon, who had
besides too many quarrels among themselves to live without arbiters,
and too much avarice and ambition to live long without masters.
All offered their necks to the yoke in hopes of securing their liberty;
for though they had sense enough to perceive the advantages of a
political constitution, they had not experience enough to see beforehand the dangers of it; those among them, who were best qualified
to foresee abuses, were precisely those who expected to benefit by
them; even the soberest judged it requisite to sacrifice one part of
their liberty to ensure the other, as a man, dangerously wounded in
any of his limbs, readily parts with it to save the rest of his body.

Such was, or must have been, had man been left to himself, the
origin of society and of the laws, which increased the fetters of
the weak, and the strength of the rich; irretrievably destroyed
natural liberty, fixed for ever the laws of property and inequality;
changed an artful usurpation into an irrevocable title; and for the
benefit of a few ambitious individuals subjected the rest of mankind
to perpetual labour, servitude, and misery. We may easily conceive
how the establishment of a single society rendered that of all the rest
absolutely necessary, and how, to make head against united forces,
it became necessary for the rest of mankind to unite in their turn.

Societies once formed in this manner, soon multiplied or spread to such a degree, as to cover the face of the earth; and not to leave a corner in the whole universe, where a man could throw off the yoke, and withdraw his head from under the often ill-conducted sword which he saw perpetually hanging over it. The civil law being thus become the common rule of citizens, the law of nature no longer obtained but among the different societies, in which, under the name of the law of nations, it was qualified by some tacit conventions to render commerce possible, and supply the place of natural compassion, which, losing by degrees all that influence over societies which it originally had over individuals, no longer exists but in some great souls, who consider themselves as citizens of the world, and forcing the imaginary barriers that separate people from people, after the example of the Sovereign Being from whom we all derive our existence, make the whole human race the object of their benevolence.

Political bodies, thus remaining in a state of nature among themselves, soon experienced the inconveniences which had obliged individuals to quit it; and this state became much more fatal to these great bodies, than it had been before to the individuals which now composed them. Hence those national wars, those battles, those murders, those reprisals, which make nature shudder and shock reason; hence all those horrible prejudices, which make it a virtue and an honour to shed human blood. The worthiest men learned to consider the cutting the throats of their fellows as a duty; at length men began to butcher each other by thousands without knowing for what; and more murders were committed in a single action, and more horrible disorders at the taking of a single town, than had been committed in the state of nature during ages together upon the whole face of the earth. Such are the first effects we may conceive to have arisen from the division of mankind into different societies. Let us return to their institution.

I know that several writers have assigned other origins of political society; as for instance, the conquests of the powerful, or the union of the weak; and it is no matter which of these causes we adopt in regard to what I am going to establish; that, however, which I have just laid down, seems to me the most natural, for the following reasons: First, because, in the first case, the right of conquest being in fact no right at all, it could not serve as a foundation for any other right, the conqueror and the conquered ever remaining with respect to each other in a state of war, unless the conquered, restored to the full possession of their liberty, should freely choose their conqueror for their chief. Till then, whatever capitulations might have been made between them, as these capitulations were founded upon violence, and of course *de facto* null and void, there could not have existed in this hypothesis either a true society, or a political body, or any other law but that of the strongest. Second, because these words strong and weak, are ambiguous in the second case; for during the interval between the establishment of the right of property or prior occupation and that of political government, the meaning of these terms is better expressed by the words poor and rich, as before the establishment of laws men in reality had no other means of reducing their equals, but by invading the property of these equals, or by parting with some of their own property to them. Third, because the poor having nothing but their liberty to lose, it would have been the height of madness in them to give up willingly the only blessing they had left without obtaining some consideration for it: whereas the rich being sensible, if I may say so, in every part of their possessions, it was much easier to do them mischief, and therefore more incumbent upon them to guard against it; and because, in fine, it is but reasonable to suppose, that a thing has been invented by him to whom it could be of service rather than by him to whom it must prove detrimental.

Government in its infancy had no regular and permanent form. For want of a sufficient fund of philosophy and experience, men could see no further than the present inconveniences, and never thought of providing remedies for future ones, but in proportion as they arose. In spite of all the labours of the wisest legislators, the political state still continued imperfect, because it was in a manner the work of chance; and, as the foundations of it were ill laid, time, though sufficient to discover its defects and suggest the remedies for them, could never mend its original vices. Men were continually repairing; whereas, to erect a good edifice, they should have begun as Lycurgus did at Sparta, by clearing the area, and removing the old materials. Society at first consisted merely of some general conventions which all the members bound themselves to observe, and for the performance of which the whole body became security to every individual. Experience was necessary to show the great weakness of such a constitution, and how easy it was for those, who infringed it, to escape the conviction or chastisement of faults, of which the public alone was to be both the witness and the judge; the laws could not fail of being eluded a thousand ways; inconveniences and disorders could not but multiply continually, till it was at last found necessary to think of committing to private persons the dangerous trust of public authority, and to magistrates the care of enforcing obedience to the people: for to say that chiefs were elected before confederacies were formed, and that the ministers of the laws existed before the laws themselves, is a supposition too ridiculous to deserve I should seriously refute it.

It would be equally unreasonable to imagine that men at first threw themselves into the arms of an absolute master, without any conditions or consideration on his side; and that the first means contrived by jealous and unconquered men for their common safety was to run hand over head into slavery. In fact, why did they give themselves superiors, if it was not to be defended by them against oppression, and protected in their lives, liberties, and properties, which are in a manner the constitutional elements of their being? Now in the relations between man and man, the worst that can happen to one man being to see himself at the discretion of another, would it not have been contrary to the dictates of good sense to begin by making over to a chief the only things for the preservation of which they stood in need of his assistance? What equivalent could he have offered them for so fine a privilege? And had he presumed to exact it on pretense of defending them, would he not have immediately received the answer in the apologue? What worse treatment can we expect from an enemy? It is therefore past dispute, and indeed a fundamental maxim of political law, that people gave themselves chiefs to defend their liberty and not be enslaved by them. If we have a prince, said Pliny to Trajan, it is in order that he may keep us from having a master.

Political writers argue in regard to the love of liberty with the same philosophy that philosophers do in regard to the state of nature; by the things they see they judge of things very different which they have never seen, and they attribute to men a natural inclination to slavery, on account of the patience with which the slaves within their notice carry the yoke; not reflecting that it is with liberty as with innocence and virtue, the value of which is not known but by those who possess them, though the relish for them is lost with the things themselves. I know the charms of your country, said Brasidas to a satrap who was comparing the life of the Spartans with that of the Persepolites; but you can not know the pleasures of mine.

As an unbroken courser erects his mane, paws the ground, and rages at the bare sight of the bit, while a trained horse patiently suffers both whip and spur, just so the barbarian will never reach his neck to the yoke which civilized man carries without murmuring but prefers the most stormy liberty to a calm subjection. It is not therefore by the servile disposition of enslaved nations that we must judge of the natural dispositions of man for or against slavery, but by the prodigies done by every free people to secure themselves from oppression. I know that the first are constantly crying up that peace and tranquillity they enjoy in their irons, and that *miserrimam servitutem pacem appellant:* but when I see the others sacrifice pleasures, peace, riches, power, and even life itself to the preservation of that single jewel so much slighted by those who have lost it; when I see free-born animals through a natural abhorrence of captivity dash their brains out against the bars of their prison; when I see multitudes of naked savages despise European pleasures, and brave hunger, fire and sword, and death itself to preserve their independency; I feel that it belongs not to slaves to argue concerning liberty.

As to paternal authority, from which several have derived absolute government and every other mode of society, it is sufficient, without having recourse to Locke and Sidney, to observe that nothing in the world differs more from the cruel spirit of despotism, than the gentleness of that authority, which looks more to the advantage of him who obeys than to the utility of him who commands; that by the law of nature the father continues master of his child no longer than the child stands in need of his assistance; that after that term they become equal, and that then the son, entirely independent of the father, owes him no obedience, but only respect. Gratitude is indeed a duty which we are bound to pay, but which benefactors can not exact. Instead of saying that civil society is derived from paternal authority, we should rather say that it is to the former that the latter owes its principal force: No one individual was acknowledged as the father of several other individuals, till they settled about him. The father's goods, which he can indeed dispose of as he pleases, are the ties which hold his children to their dependence upon him, and he may divide his substance among them in proportion as they shall have deserved his attention by a continual deference to his commands. Now the subjects of a despotic chief, far from having any such favour to expect from him, as both themselves and all they have are his property, or at least are considered by him as such, are obliged to receive as a favour what he relinquishes to them of their own property. He does them justice when he strips them; he treats them with mercy when he suffers them to live. By continuing in this manner to compare facts with right, we should discover as little solidity as truth in the voluntary establishment of tyranny; and it would be a hard matter to prove the validity of a contract which was binding only on one side, in which one of the parties should stake everything and the other nothing, and which could turn out to the prejudice of him alone who had bound himself.

This odious system is even, at this day, far from being that of wise and good monarchs, and especially of the kings of France, as may be seen by divers passages in their edicts, and particularly by that of a celebrated piece published in 1667 in the name and by the orders of Louis XIV. "Let it therefore not be said that the sovereign is not subject to the laws of his realm, since, that he is, is a maxim of the law of nations which flattery has sometimes attacked, but which good princes have always defended as the tutelary divinity of their realms. How much more reasonable is it to say with the sage Plato, that the perfect happiness of a state consists in the subjects obeying their prince, the prince obeying the laws, and the laws being equitable and always directed to the good of the public? I shall not stop to consider, if, liberty being the most noble faculty of man, it is not degrading one's nature, reducing one's self to the level of brutes, who are the slaves of instinct, and even offending the author of one's being, to renounce without reserve the most precious of his gifts, and submit to the commission of all the crimes he has forbid us, merely to gratify a mad or a cruel master; and if this sublime artist ought to be more irritated at seeing his work destroyed than at seeing it dishonoured. I shall only ask what right those, who were not afraid thus to degrade themselves, could have to subject their dependants to the same ignominy, and renounce, in the name of their posterity, blessings for which it is not indebted to their liberality, and without which life itself must appear a burthen to all those who are worthy to live.

Puffendorf says that, as we can transfer our property from one to another by contracts and conventions, we may likewise divest ourselves of our liberty in favour of other men. This, in my opinion, is a very poor way of arguing; for, in the first place, the property I cede to another becomes by such cession a thing quite foreign to me, and the abuse of which can no way affect me; but it concerns me greatly that my liberty is not abused, and I can not, without incurring the guilt of the crimes I may be forced to commit, expose myself to become the instrument of any. Besides, the right of property being of mere human convention and institution, every man may dispose as he pleases of what he possesses: But the case is otherwise with regard to the essential gifts of nature, such as life and liberty, which every man is permitted to enjoy, and of which it is doubtful at least whether any man has a right to divest himself: By giving up the one, we degrade our being; by giving up the other we annihilate it as much as it is our power to do so; and as no temporal enjoyments can indemnify us for the loss of either, it would be at once offending both nature and reason to renounce them for any consideration. But though we could transfer our liberty as we do our substance, the difference would be very great with regard to our children, who enjoy our substance but by a cession of our right; whereas liberty being a blessing, which as men they hold from nature, their parents have no right to strip them of it; so that as to establish slavery it was necessary to do violence to nature, so it was necessary to alter nature to perpetuate such a right; and the jurisconsults, who have gravely pronounced that the child of a slave comes a slave into the world, have in other words decided, that a man does not come a man into the world.

It therefore appears to me incontestably true, that not only governments did not begin by arbitrary power, which is but the corruption and extreme term of government, and at length brings it back to the law of the strongest, against which governments were at first the remedy, but even that, allowing they had commenced in this manner, such power being illegal in itself could never have served as a foundation to the rights of society, nor of course to the inequality of institution.

I shall not now enter upon the inquiries which still remain to be made into the nature of the fundamental pacts of every kind of government, but, following the common opinion, confine myself in this place to the establishment of the political body as a real contract between the multitude and the chiefs elected by it. A contract by which both parties oblige themselves to the observance of the laws that are therein stipulated, and form the bands of their union. The multitude having, on occasion of the social relations between them, concentered all their wills in one person, all the articles, in regard to which this will explains itself, become so many fundamental laws, which oblige without exception all the members of the state, and one of which laws regulates the choice and the power of the magistrates appointed to look to the execution of the rest. This power extends to everything that can maintain the constitution, but extends to nothing that can alter it. To this power are added honours, that may render the laws and the ministers of them respectable; and the persons of the ministers are distinguished by certain prerogatives, which may make them amends for the great fatigues inseparable from a good administration. The magistrate, on his side, obliges himself not to use the power with which he is intrusted but conformably to the intention of his constituents, to maintain every one of them in the peaceable possession of his property, and upon all occasions prefer the good of the public to his own private interest.

Before experience had demonstrated, or a thorough knowledge of the human heart had pointed out, the abuses inseparable from such a constitution, it must have appeared so much the more perfect, as those appointed to look to its preservation were themselves most concerned therein; for magistracy and its rights being built solely on the fundamental laws, as soon as these ceased to exist, the magistrates would cease to be lawful, the people would no longer be bound to obey them, and, as the essence of the state did not consist in the magistrates but in the laws, the members of it would immediately become entitled to their primitive and natural liberty.

A little reflection would afford us new arguments in confirmation of this truth, and the nature of the contract might alone convince us that it can not be irrevocable: for if there was no superior power capable of guaranteeing the fidelity of the contracting parties and of obliging them to fulfil their mutual engagements, they would remain sole judges in their own cause, and each of them would always have a right to renounce the contract, as soon as he discovered that the other had broke the conditions of it, or that these conditions ceased to suit his private convenience. Upon this principle, the right of abdication may probably be founded. Now, to consider as we do nothing but what is human in this institution, if the magistrate, who has all the power in his own hands, and who appropriates to himself all the advantages of the contract, has notwithstanding a right to divest himself of his authority; how much a better right must the people, who pay for all the faults of its chief, have to renounce their dependence upon him. But the shocking dissensions and disorders without number, which would be the necessary consequence of so dangerous a privilege, show more than anything else how much human governments stood in need of a more solid basis than that of mere reason, and how necessary it was for the public tranquillity, that the will of the Almighty should interpose to give to sovereign authority, a sacred and inviolable character, which should deprive subjects of the mischievous right to dispose of it to whom they pleased. If mankind had received no other advantages from religion, this alone would be sufficient to make them adopt and cherish it, since it is the means of saving more blood than fanaticism has been the cause of spilling. But to resume the thread of our hypothesis.

The various forms of government owe their origin to the various degrees of inequality between the members, at the time they first coalesced into a political body. Where a man happened to be eminent for power, for virtue, for riches, or for credit, he became sole magistrate, and the state assumed a monarchical form; if many of pretty equal eminence out-topped all the rest, they were jointly elected, and this election produced an aristocracy; those, between whose fortune or talents there happened to be no such disproportion, and who had deviated less from the state of nature, retained in common the supreme administration, and formed a democracy. Time demonstrated which of these forms suited mankind best. Some remained altogether subject to the laws; others soon bowed their necks to masters. The former laboured to preserve their liberty; the latter thought of nothing but invading that of their neighbours, jealous at seeing others enjoy a blessing which themselves had lost. In a word, riches and conquest fell to the share of the one, and virtue and happiness to that of the other.

In these various modes of government the offices at first were all elective; and when riches did not preponderate, the preference was given to merit, which gives a natural ascendant, and to age, which is the parent of deliberateness in council, and experience in execution. The ancients among the Hebrews, the Geronts of Sparta, the Senate of Rome, nay, the very etymology of our word seigneur, show how much gray hairs were formerly respected. The oftener the choice fell upon old men, the oftener it became necessary to repeat it, and the more the trouble of such repetitions became sensible; electioneering took place; factions arose; the parties contracted ill-blood; civil wars blazed forth; the lives of the citizens were sacrificed to the pretended happiness of the state; and things at last came to such a pass, as to be ready to relapse into their primitive confusion. The ambition of the principal men induced them to take advantage of these circumstances to perpetuate the hitherto temporary charges in their families; the people already inured to dependence, accustomed to ease and the conveniences of life, and too much enervated to break their fetters, consented to the increase of their slavery for the sake of securing their tranquillity; and it is thus that chiefs, become hereditary, contracted the habit of considering magistracies as a family estate, and themselves as proprietors of those communities, of which at first they were but mere officers; to call their fellow-citizens their slaves; to look upon them, like so many cows or sheep, as a part of their substance; and to style themselves the peers of Gods, and Kings of Kings.

By pursuing the progress of inequality in these different revolutions, we shall discover that the establishment of laws and of the right of property was the first term of it; the institution of magistrates the second; and the third and last the changing of legal into arbitrary power; so that the different states of rich and poor were authorized by the first epoch; those of powerful and weak by the second; and by the third those of master and slave, which formed the last degree of inequality, and the term in which all the rest at last end, till new revolutions entirely dissolve the government, or bring it back nearer to its legal constitution.

To conceive the necessity of this progress, we are not so much to consider the motives for the establishment of political bodies, as the forms these bodies assume in their administration; and the inconveniences with which they are essentially attended; for those vices, which render social institutions necessary, are the same which render the abuse of such institutions unavoidable; and as (Sparta alone excepted, whose laws chiefly regarded the education of children, and where Lycurgus established such manners and customs, as in a great measure made laws needless,) the laws, in general less strong than the passions, restrain men without changing them; it would be no hard matter to prove that every government, which carefully guarding against all alteration and corruption should scrupulously comply with the ends of its institution, was unnecessarily instituted; and that a country, where no one either eluded the laws, or made an ill use of magistracy, required neither laws nor magistrates.

Political distinctions are necessarily attended with civil distinctions. The inequality between the people and the chiefs increase so fast as to be soon felt by the private members, and appears among them in a thousand shapes according to their passions, their talents, and the circumstances of affairs. The magistrate can not usurp any illegal power without making himself creatures, with whom he must divide it. Besides, the citizens of a free state suffer themselves to be oppressed merely in proportion as, hurried on by a blind ambition, and looking rather below than above them, they come to love authority more than independence. When they submit to fetters, 'tis only to be the better able to fetter others in their turn. It is no easy matter to make him obey, who does not wish to command; and the most refined policy would find it impossible to subdue those men, who only desire to be independent; but inequality easily gains ground among base and ambitious souls, ever ready to run the risks of fortune, and almost indifferent whether they command or obey, as she proves either favourable or adverse to them. Thus then there must have been a time, when the eyes of the people were bewitched to such a degree, that their rulers needed only to have said to the most pitiful wretch, "Be great you and all your posterity," to make him immediately appear great in the eyes of every one as well as in his own; and his descendants took still more upon them, in proportion to their removes from him: the more distant and uncertain the cause, the greater the effect; the longer line of drones a family produced, the more illustrious it was reckoned.

Were this a proper place to enter into details, I could easily explain in what manner inequalities in point of credit and authority become unavoidable among private persons the moment that, united into one body, they are obliged to compare themselves one with another, and to note the differences which they find in the continual use every man must make of his neighbour. These differences are of several kinds; but riches, nobility or rank, power and personal merit, being in general the principal distinctions, by which men in society measure each other, I could prove that the harmony or conflict between these different forces is the surest indication of the good or bad original constitution of any state: I could make it appear that, as among these four kinds of inequality, personal qualities are the source of all the rest, riches is that in which they ultimately terminate, because, being the most immediately useful to the prosperity of individuals, and the most easy to communicate, they are made use of to purchase every other distinction. By this observation we are enabled to judge with tolerable exactness, how much any people has deviated from its primitive institution, and what steps it has still to make to the extreme term of corruption. I could show how much this universal desire of reputation, of honours, of preference, with which we are all devoured, exercises and compares our talents and our forces: how much it excites and multiplies our passions; and, by creating an universal competition, rivalship, or rather enmity among men, how many disappointments, successes, and catastrophes of every kind it daily causes among the innumerable pretenders whom it engages in the same career. I could show that it is to this itch of being spoken of, to this fury of distinguishing ourselves which seldom or never gives us a moment's respite, that we owe both the best and the worst things among us, our virtues and our vices, our sciences and our errors, our conquerors and our philosophers; that is to say, a great many bad things to a very few good ones. I could prove, in short, that if we behold a handful of rich and powerful men seated on the pinnacle of fortune and greatness, while the crowd grovel in obscurity and want, it is merely because the first, prize what they enjoy, but in the same degree that others want it, and that, without changing their condition, they would cease to be happy the minute the people ceased to be miserable.

But these details would alone furnish sufficient matter for a more considerable work, in which might be weighed the advantages and disadvantages of every species of government, relatively to the rights of man in a state of nature, and might likewise be unveiled all the different faces under which inequality has appeared to this day, and may hereafter appear to the end of time, according to the nature of these several governments, and the revolutions, time must unavoidably occasion in them. We should then see the multitude oppressed by domestic tyrants in consequence of those very precautions taken by them to guard against foreign masters. We should see oppression increase continually without its being ever possible for the oppressed to know where it would stop, nor what lawful means they had left to check its progress. We should see the rights of citizens, and the liberties of nations extinguished by slow degrees, and the groans, and protestations and appeals of the weak treated as seditious murmurings. We should see policy confine to a mercenary portion of the people the honour of defending the common cause. We should see imposts made necessary by such measures, the disheartened husbandman desert his field even in time of peace, and quit the plough to take up the sword. We should see fatal and whimsical rules laid down concerning the point of honour. We should see the champions of their country sooner or later become her enemies, and perpetually holding their poniards to the breasts of their fellow citizens. Nay, the time would come when they might be heard to say to the oppressor of their country:

Pectore si fratris gladium juguloque parentis
Condere me jubeas, gravidæque in viscera partu
Conjugis, in vitâ peragam tamen omnia dextrâ.

From the vast inequality of conditions and fortunes, from the great variety of passions and of talents, of useless arts, of pernicious arts, of frivolous sciences, would issue clouds of prejudices equally contrary to reason, to happiness, to virtue. We should see the chiefs foment everything that tends to weaken men formed into societies by dividing them; everything that, while it gives society an air of apparent harmony, sows in it the seeds of real division; everything that can inspire the different orders with mutual distrust and hatred by an opposition of their rights and interest, and of course strengthen that power which contains them all.

'Tis from the bosom of this disorder and these revolutions, that despotism gradually rearing up her hideous crest, and devouring in every part of the state all that still remained sound and untainted, would at last issue to trample upon the laws and the people, and establish herself upon the ruins of the republic. The times immediately preceding this last alteration would be times of calamity and trouble: but at last everything would be swallowed up by the monster; and the people would no longer have chiefs or laws, but only tyrants. At this fatal period all regard to virtue and manners would likewise disappear; for despotism, *cui ex honesto nulla est spes,* tolerates no other master, wherever it reigns; the moment it speaks, probity and duty lose all their influence, and the blindest obedience is the only virtue the miserable slaves have left them to practise.

This is the last term of inequality, the extreme point which closes the circle and meets that from which we set out. 'Tis here that all private men return to their primitive equality, because they are no longer of any account; and that, the subjects having no longer any law but that of their master, nor the master any other law but his passions, all notions of good and principles of justice again disappear. 'Tis here that everything returns to the sole law of the strongest, and of course to a new state of nature different from that with which we began, in as much as the first was the state of nature in its purity, and the last the consequence of excessive corruption. There is, in other respects, so little difference between these two states, and the contract of government is so much dissolved by despotism, that the despot is no longer master than he continues the strongest, and that, as soon as his slaves can expel him, they may do it without his having the least right to complain of their using him ill. The insurrection, which ends in the death or despotism of a sultan, is as juridical an act as any by which the day before he disposed of the lives and fortunes of his subjects. Force alone upheld him, force alone overturns him. Thus all things take place and succeed in their natural order; and whatever may be the upshot of these hasty and frequent revolutions, no one man has reason to complain of another's injustice, but only of his own indiscretion or bad fortune.

By thus discovering and following the lost and forgotten tracks, by which man from the natural must have arrived at the civil state; by restoring, with the intermediate positions which I have been just indicating, those which want of leisure obliges me to suppress, or which my imagination has not suggested, every attentive reader must unavoidably be struck at the immense space which separates these two states. 'Tis in this slow succession of things he may meet with the solution of an infinite number of problems in morality and politics, which philosophers are puzzled to solve. He will perceive that, the mankind of one age not being the mankind of another, the reason why Diogenes could not find a man was, that he sought among his cotemporaries the man of an earlier period: Cato, he will then see, fell with Rome and with liberty, because he did not suit the age in which he lived; and the greatest of men served only to astonish that world, which would have cheerfully obeyed him, had he come into it five hundred years earlier. In a word, he will find himself in a condition to understand how the soul and the passions of men by insensible alterations change as it were their nature; how it comes to pass, that at the long run our wants and our pleasures change objects; that, original man vanishing by degrees, society no longer

offers to our inspection but an assemblage of artificial men and
factitious passions, which are the work of all these new relations,
and have no foundation in nature. Reflection teaches us nothing on
that head, but what experience perfectly confirms. Savage man and
civilised man differ so much at bottom in point of inclinations and
passions, that what constitutes the supreme happiness of the one
would reduce the other to despair. The first sighs for nothing but
repose and liberty; he desires only to live, and to be exempt from
labour; nay, the ataraxy of the most confirmed Stoic falls short of his
consummate indifference for every other object. On the contrary,
the citizen always in motion, is perpetually sweating and toiling, and
racking his brains to find out occupations still more laborious: He
continues a drudge to his last minute; nay, he courts death to be able
to live, or renounces life to acquire immortality. He cringes to men
in power whom he hates, and to rich men whom he despises; he
sticks at nothing to have the honour of serving them; he is not
ashamed to value himself on his own weakness and the protection
they afford him; and proud of his chains, he speaks with disdain of
those who have not the honour of being the partner of his bondage.
What a spectacle must the painful and envied labours of an European
minister of state form in the eyes of a Caribbean! How many cruel
deaths would not this indolent savage prefer to such a horrid life,
which very often is not even sweetened by the pleasure of doing
good? But to see the drift of so many cares, his mind should first
have affixed some meaning to these words power and reputation; he
should be apprised that there are men who consider as something
the looks of the rest of mankind, who know how to be happy and
satisfied with themselves on the testimony of others sooner than upon
their own. In fact, the real source of all those differences, is that the
savage lives within himself, whereas the citizen, constantly beside
himself, knows only how to live in the opinion of others; insomuch
that it is, if I may say so, merely from their judgment that he derives
the consciousness of his own existence. It is foreign to my subject
to show how this disposition engenders so much indifference for
good and evil, notwithstanding so many and such fine discourses of
morality; how everything, being reduced to appearances, becomes
mere art and mummery; honour, friendship, virtue, and often vice

itself, which we at last learn the secret to boast of; how, in short, ever inquiring of others what we are, and never daring to question ourselves on so delicate a point, in the midst of so much philosophy, humanity, and politeness, and so many sublime maxims, we have nothing to show for ourselves but a deceitful and frivolous exterior, honour without virtue, reason without wisdom, and pleasure without happiness. It is sufficient that I have proved that this is not the original condition of man, and that it is merely the spirit of society, and the inequality which society engenders, that thus change and transform all our natural inclinations.

I have endeavoured to exhibit the origin and progress of inequality, the institution and abuse of political societies, as far as these things are capable of being deduced from the nature of man by the mere light of reason, and independently of those sacred maxims which give to the sovereign authority the sanction of divine right. It follows from this picture, that as there is scarce any inequality among men in a state of nature, all that which we now behold owes its force and its growth to the development of our faculties and the improvement of our understanding, and at last becomes permanent and lawful by the establishment of property and of laws. It likewise follows that moral inequality, authorised by any right that is merely positive, clashes with natural right, as often as it does not combine in the same proportion with physical inequality: a distinction which sufficiently determines, what we are able to think in that respect of that kind of inequality which obtains in all civilised nations, since it is evidently against the law of nature that infancy should command old age, folly conduct wisdom, and a handful of men should be ready to choke with superfluities, while the famished multitude want the commonest necessaries of life.

PROFESSION OF FAITH
OF A SAVOYARD VICAR

BY
J. J. ROUSSEAU

INTRODUCTION

About thirty years ago a young man, who had forsaken his own country and rambled into Italy, found himself reduced to a condition of great poverty and distress. He had been bred a Calvinist; but in consequence of his misconduct and of being unhappily a fugitive in a foreign country, without money or friends, he was induced to change his religion for the sake of subsistence. To this end he procured admittance into a *hospice* for catechumens, that is to say, a house established for the reception of proselytes. The instructions he here received concerning some controversial points excited doubts he had not before entertained, and first caused him to realize the evil of the step he had taken. He was taught strange dogmas, and was eye-witness to stranger manners; and to these he saw himself a destined victim. He now sought to make his escape, but was prevented and more closely confined. If he complained, he was punished for complaining; and, lying at the mercy of his tyrannical oppressors, found himself treated as criminal because he could not without reluctance submit to be so.

Let those who are sensible how much the first acts of violence and injustice irritate young and inexperienced minds, judge of the situation of this unfortunate youth. Swollen with indignation, the tears of rage burst from his eyes. He implored the assistance of heaven and earth in vain; he appealed to the whole world, but no one attended to his plea. His complaints could reach the ears only of a number of servile domestics,—slaves to the wretch by whom he was thus treated, or accomplices in the same crime,—who ridiculed his non-conformity and endeavored to secure his imitation. He would doubtless have been entirely ruined had it not been for the good offices of an honest ecclesiastic, who came to the hospital on some business, and with whom he found an opportunity for a private conference. The good priest was himself poor, and stood in need of every one's assistance; the oppressed proselyte, however, stood yet in greater need of him. The former did not hesitate, therefore, to favor his escape, even at the risk of making a powerful enemy.

Having escaped from vice only to return to indigence, this young adventurer struggled against his destiny without success. For a moment, indeed, he thought himself above it, and at the first prospect of good fortune, his former distresses and his protector were forgotten together.

He was soon punished, however, for his ingratitude, as his groundless hopes soon vanished. His youth stood in vain on his side; his romantic notions proving destructive to all his designs. Having neither capacity nor address to surmount the difficulties that fell in his way, and being a stranger to the virtues of moderation and the arts of knavery, he attempted so many things that he could bring none to perfection. Hence, having fallen into his former distress, and being not only in want of clothes and lodging, but even in danger of perishing with hunger, he recollected his former benefactor.

To him he returned, and was well received. The sight of the unhappy youth brought to the poor vicar's mind the remembrance of a good action;—a remembrance always grateful to an honest mind. This good priest was naturally humane and compassionate. His own misfortunes had taught him to feel for those of others, nor had prosperity hardened his heart. In a word, the maxims of true wisdom and conscious virtue had confirmed the kindness of his natural disposition. He cordially embraced the young wanderer, provided for him a lodging, and shared with him the slender means of his own subsistence. Nor was this all: he went still farther, freely giving him both instruction and consolation, and also endeavoring to teach him the difficult art of supporting adversity with patience. Could you believe, ye sons of prejudice! that a priest, and a priest in Italy too, could be capable of this?

This honest ecclesiastic was a poor Savoyard, who having in his younger days incurred the displeasure of his bishop, was obliged to pass the mountains in order to seek that provision which was denied him in his own country. He was neither deficient in literature nor understanding; his talents, therefore, joined with an engaging appearance, soon procured him a patron, who recommended him as tutor to a young man of quality. He preferred poverty, however, to dependence; and, being a stranger to the manners and behavior of the great, he remained but a short time in that situation. In quitting this service, however, he fortunately did not lose the esteem of his friend; and, as he behaved with great prudence and was universally beloved, he flattered himself that he shoud in time regain the good opinion of his bishop also, and be rewarded with some little benefice in the mountains, where he hoped to spend in tranquillity and peace the remainder of his days. This was the height of his ambition.

Interested by a natural affinity in favor of the young fugitive, he examined very carefully into his character and disposition. In this examination, he saw that his misfortunes had already debased his heart;—

that the shame and contempt to which he had been exposed had depressed his ambition, and that his disappointed pride, converted into indignation, had deduced, from the injustice and cruelty of mankind, the depravity of human nature and the emptiness of virtue. He had observed religion made use of as a mask to self-interest, and its worship as a cloak to hypocrisy. He had seen the terms heaven and hell prostituted in the subtility of vain disputes; the joys of the one and the pains of the other being annexed to a mere repetition of words. He had observed the sublime and primitive idea of the Divinity disfigured by the fantastical imaginations of men; and, finding that in order to believe in God it was necessary to give up that understanding he hath bestowed on us, he held in the same disdain as well the sacred object of our idle reveries as those idle reveries themselves. Without knowing anything of natural causes, or giving himself any trouble to investigate them, he remained in a condition of the most stupid ignorance, mixed with profound contempt for those who pretended to greater knowledge than his own.

A neglect of all religious duties leads to a neglect of all moral obligations. The heart of this young vagabond had already made a great progress from one toward the other. Not that he was constitutionally vicious; but misfortune and incredulity, having stifled by degrees the propensities of his natural disposition, were hurrying him on to ruin, adding to the manners of a beggar the principles of an atheist.

His ruin, however, though almost inevitable, was not absolutely completed. His education not having been neglected, he was not without knowledge. He had not yet exceeded that happy term of life, wherein the youthful blood serves to stimulate the mind without inflaming the passions, which were as yet unrelaxed and unexcited. A natural modesty and timidity of disposition had hitherto supplied the place of restraint, and prolonged the term of youthful innocence. The odious example of brutal depravity, and of vices without temptation, so far from animating his imagination, had mortified it. Disgust had long supplied the place of virtue in the preservation of his innocence, and to corrupt this required more powerful seductions.

The good priest saw the danger and the remedy. The difficulties that appeared in the application did not deter him from the attempt. He took a pleasure in the design, and resolved to complete it by restoring to virtue the victim he had snatched from infamy.

To this end he set out resolutely in the execution of his project. The merit of the motive increased his hopes, and inspired means worthy of his zeal. Whatever might be the success, he was sure that he should not throw away his labor:—we are always sure so far to succeed in well doing.

He began with striving to gain the confidence of the proselyte by conferring on him his favors disinterestedly,—by never importuning him with exhortations, and by descending always to a level with his ideas and manner of thinking. It must have been an affecting sight to see a grave divine become the comrade of a young libertine—to see virtue affect the air of licentiousness—in order to triumph the more certainly over it. Whenever the heedless youth made him the confidant of his follies, and unbosomed himself freely to his benefactor, the good priest listened attentively to his stories; and, without approving the evil, interested himself in the consequences. No ill-timed censure ever indiscreetly checked the pupil's communicative temper. The pleasure with which he thought himself heard increased that which he took in telling all his secrets. Thus he was induced to make a free and general confession without thinking he was confessing anything.

Having thus made himself master of the youth's sentiments and character, the priest was enabled to see clearly that, without being ignorant for his years, he had forgotten almost everything of importance for him to know, and that the state of meanness into which he had fallen had almost stifled in him the sense of good and evil. There is a degree of low stupidity which deprives the soul as it were of life; the voice of conscience is also but little heard by those who think of nothing but the means of subsistence. To rescue this unfortunate youth from the moral death that so nearly threatened him, he began, therefore, by awakening his self-love and exciting in him a due regard for himself. He represented to his imagination a more happy success, from the future employment of his talents; he inspired him with a generous ardor by a recital of the commendable actions of others, and by raising his admiration of those who performed them. In order to detach him insensibly from an idle and vagabond life, he employed him in copying books; and under pretence of having occasion for such extracts, cherished in him the noble sentiment of gratitude for his benefactor. By this method he also instructed him indirectly by the books he employed him to copy; and induced him to entertain so good an opinion of himself as to think he was not absolutely good for nothing, and to hold himself not quite so despicable in his own esteem as he had formerly done.

A trifling circumstance may serve to show the art which this benevolent instructor made use of to insensibly elevate the heart of his disciple, without appearing to think of giving him instruction. This good ecclesiastic was so well known and esteemed for his probity and discernment, that many persons chose rather to entrust him with the distribution of their alms than the richer clergy of the cities. Now it happened that receiving one day a sum of money in charge for the poor, the young man had the meanness to desire some of it, under that title, for himself. "No," replied his kind benefactor, "you and I are brethren; you belong to me, and I should not apply the charity entrusted with me to my own use." He then gave him the desired sum from his private funds. Lessons of this kind are hardly ever thrown away on young people, whose hearts are not entirely corrupted.

But I will continue to speak no longer in the third person, which is indeed a superfluous caution; as you, my dear countrymen, are very sensible that the unhappy fugitive I have been speaking of is myself. I believe that I am now so far removed from the irregularities of my youth as to dare to avow them, and think that the hand which extricated me from them is too well deserving of my gratitude for me not to do it honour even at the expense of a little shame.

The most striking circumstance of all was to observe in the retired life of my worthy master virtue without hypocrisy and humanity without weakness. His conversation was always honest and simple, and his conduct ever conformable to his discourse. I never found him troubling himself whether the persons he assisted went constantly to vespers—whether they went frequently to confession—or fasted on certain days of the week. Nor did I ever know him to impose on them any of those conditions without which a man might perish from want, and have no hope of relief from the devout.

Encouraged by these observations, so far was I from affecting in his presence the forward zeal of a new proselyte, that I took no pains to conceal my thoughts, nor did I ever remark his being scandalized at this freedom. Hence, I have sometimes said to myself, he certainly overlooks my indifference for the new mode of worship I have embraced, in consideration of the disregard which he sees I have for that in which I was educated; as he finds my indifference is not partial to either. But what could I think when I heard him sometimes approve dogmas contrary to those of the Romish church, and appear to hold its ceremonies in little esteem? I should have been apt to consider him a protestant in disguise, had I seen him less observant of those very ceremonies which he seemed to think of so little account; but knowing that he acquitted himself as punctually of his duties as a priest in private as in public, I knew not how to judge of these seeming contradictions. If we except the failing which first brought him into disgrace with his superior, and of which he was not altogether corrected, his life was exemplary, his manners irreproachable, and his conversation prudent and sensible. As I lived with him in the greatest intimacy, I learned every day to respect him more and more; and as he had entirely won my heart by so many acts of kindness, I waited with an impatient curiosity to know the principles on which a life and conduct so singular and uniform could be founded.

It was some time, however, before this curiosity was satisfied, as he endeavoured to cultivate those seeds of reason and goodness which he had endeavoured to instill, before he would disclose himself to his disciple. The greatest difficulty he met with was to eradicate from my heart a proud misanthropy, a certain rancorous hatred which I bore to the wealthy and fortunate, as if they were made so at my expense, and had usurped apparent happiness from what should have been my own. The idle vanity of youth, which is opposed to all constraint and humiliation, encouraged but too much my propensity to indulge this splenetic humor; whilst that self-love, which my mentor strove so earnestly to cherish, by increasing my pride, rendered mankind, in my opinion, still more detestable, and only added to my hatred of them the most egregious contempt.

Without directly attacking this pride, he yet strove to prevent it from degenerating into barbarity, and without diminishing my self-esteem, made me less disdainful of my neighbors. In withdrawing the gaudy veil of external appearances, and presenting to my view the real evils it concealed, he taught me to lament the failings of my fellow creatures, to sympathize with their miseries, and to pity instead of envying them. Moved to compassion for human frailties from a deep sense of his own, he saw mankind everywhere the victims of either their own vices or of the vices of others,—he saw the poor groan beneath the yoke of the rich, and the rich beneath the tyranny of their own idle habits and prejudices.

"Believe me," said he, "our mistaken notions of things are so far from hiding our misfortunes from our view, that they augment those evils by rendering trifles of importance, and making us sensible of a thousand wants which we should never have known but for our prejudices. Peace of mind consists in a contempt for everything that may disturb it. The man who gives himself the greatest concern about life is he who enjoys it least; and he who aspires the most earnestly after happiness is always the one who is the most miserable."

"Alas!" cried I, with all the bitterness of discontent, "what a deplorable picture do you present of human life! If we may indulge ourselves in nothing, to what purpose were we born? If we must despise even happiness itself, who is there that can know what it is to be happy?"

"I know," replied the good priest, in a tone and manner that struck me.

"You!" said I, "so little favored by fortune! so poor! exiled! persecuted! can you be happy? And if you are, what have you done to purchase happiness?"

"My dear child," he replied, embracing me, "I will willingly tell you. As you have freely confessed to me, I will do the same to you. I will disclose to you all the sentiments of my heart. You shall see me, if not such as I really am, at least such as I believe myself to be: and when you have heard my whole *Profession of Faith*—when you know fully the situation of my heart—you will know why I think myself happy; and, if you agree with me, what course you should pursue in order to become so likewise.

"But this profession is not to be made in a moment. It will require some time to disclose to you my thoughts on the situation of mankind and on the real value of human life. We will therefore take a suitable opportunity for a few hours' uninterrupted conversation on this subject."

As I expressed an earnest desire for such an opportunity, an appointment was made for the next morning. We rose at the break of day and prepared for the journey. Leaving the town, he led me to the top of a hill, at the foot of which ran the river Po, watering in its course the fertile vales. That immense chain of mountains, called the Alps, terminated the distant view. The rising sun cast its welcome rays over the gilded plains, and, by projecting the long shadows of the trees, the houses, and adjacent hills, formed the most beautiful scene ever mortal eye beheld. One might have been almost tempted to think that nature had at this moment displayed all its grandeur and beauty as a subject for our conversation. Here it was that, after contemplating for a short time the surrounding objects in silence, my teacher and benefactor confided to me with impressive earnestness the principles and faith which governed his life and conduct.

PROFESSION OF FAITH OF A
SAVOYARD VICAR

EXPECT from me neither learned declamations nor profound arguments. I am no great philosopher, and give myself but little trouble in regard to becoming such. Still I perceive sometimes the glimmering of good sense, and have always a regard for the truth. I will not enter into any disputation, or endeavor to refute you; but only lay down my own sentiments in simplicity of heart. Consult your own during this recital: this is all I require of you. If I am mistaken, it is undesignedly, which is sufficient to absolve me of all criminal error; and if I am right, reason, which is common to us both, shall decide. We are equally interested in listening to it, and why should not our views agree?

I was born a poor peasant, destined by my situation to the business of husbandry. It was thought, however, much more advisable for me to learn to get my bread by the profession of a priest, and means were found to give me a proper education. In this, most certainly, neither my parents nor I consulted what was really good, true, or useful for me to know; but only that I should learn what was necessary to my ordination. I learned, therefore, what was required of me to learn,—I said what was required of me to say—and, accordingly, was made a priest. It was not long, however, before I perceived too plainly that, in laying myself under an obligation to be no longer a man, I had engaged for more than I could possibly perform.

Some will tell us that conscience is founded merely on our prejudices, but I know from my own experience that its dictates constantly follow the order of nature, in contradiction to all human laws and institutions. We are in vain forbidden to do this thing or the other—we shall feel but little remorse for doing any thing to which a well-regulated natural instinct excites us, how strongly soever prohibited by reason. Nature, my dear youth, hath hitherto in this respect been silent in you. May you continue long in that happy state wherein her voice is the voice of innocence! Remember that you offend her more by anticipating her instructions than by refusing to hear them. In order to know when to listen to her without a crime, you should begin by learning to check her insinuations.

I had always a due respect for marriage as the first and most sacred institution of nature. Having given up my right to enter into such an engagement, I resolved, therefore, not to profane it: for, notwithstanding my manner of education, as I had always led a simple and uniform life, I had preserved all that clearness of understanding in which my first ideas were cultivated. The maxims of the world had not obscured my primitive notions, and my poverty kept me at a sufficient distance from those temptations that teach us the sophistry of vice.

The virtuous resolution I had formed, was, however, the very cause of my ruin, as my determination not to violate the rights of others, left my faults exposed to detection. To expiate the offence, I was suspended and banished; falling a sacrifice to my scruples rather than to my incontinence. From the reproaches made me on my disgrace, I found that the way to escape punishment for an offence is often by committing a greater.

A few instances of this kind go far with persons capable of reflection. Finding by sorrowful experience that the ideas I had formed of justice, honesty, and other moral obligations were contradicted in practice, I began to give up most of the opinions I had received, until at length the few which I retained being no longer sufficient to support themselves, I called in question the evidence on which they were established. Thus, knowing hardly what to think, I found myself at last reduced to your own situation of mind, with this difference only, that my unbelief being the later fruit of a maturer age, it was a work of greater difficulty to remove it.

I was in that state of doubt and uncertainty in which Descartes requires the mind to be involved, in order to enable it to investigate truth. This disposition of mind, however, is too disquieting to long continue, its duration being owing only to indolence or vice. My heart was not so corrupt as to seek fresh indulgence; and nothing preserves so well the habit of reflection as to be more content with ourselves than with our fortune.

I reflected, therefore, on the unhappy lot of mortals floating always on the ocean of human opinions, without compass or rudder—left to the mercy of their tempestuous passions, with no other guide than an inexperienced pilot, ignorant of his course, as well as from whence he came, and whither he is going. I often said to myself: I love the truth—I seek, yet cannot find it. Let any one show it to me and I will readily embrace it. Why doth it hide its charms from a heart formed to adore them?

I have frequently experienced at times much greater evils; and yet no part of my life was ever so constantly disagreeable to me as that interval of scruples and anxiety. Running perpetually from one doubt and uncertainty to another, all that I could deduce from my long and painful meditations was incertitude, obscurity, and contradiction; as well with regard to my existence as to my duty.

I cannot comprehend how any man can be sincerely a skeptic on principle. Such philosophers either do not exist, or they are certainly the most miserable of men. To be in doubt, about things which it is important for us to know, is a situation too perplexing for the human mind; it cannot long support such incertitude; but will, in spite of itself, determine one way or the other, rather deceiving itself than being content to believe nothing of the matter.

What added further to my perplexity was, that as the authority of the church in which I was educated was decisive, and tolerated not the slightest doubt, in rejecting one point, I thereby rejected in a manner all the others. The impossibility of admitting so many absurd decisions, threw doubt over those more reasonable. In being told I must believe all, I was prevented from believing anything, and I knew not what course to pursue.

In this situation I consulted the philosophers. I turned over their books, and examined their several opinions. I found them vain, dogmatical and dictatorial—even in their pretended skepticism. Ignorant of nothing, yet proving nothing; but ridiculing one another instead; and in this last particular only, in which they were all agreed, they seemed to be in the right. Affecting to triumph whenever they attacked their opponents, they lacked everything to make them capable of a vigorous defence. If you examine their reasons, you will find them calculated only to refute: If you number voices, every one is reduced to his own suffrage. They agree in nothing but in disputing, and to attend to these was certainly not the way to remove my uncertainty.

I conceived that the weakness of the human understanding was the first cause of the prodigious variety I found in their sentiments, and that pride was the second. We have no standard with which to measure this immense machine; we cannot calculate its various relations; we neither know the first cause nor the final effects; we are ignorant even of ourselves; we neither know our own nature nor principle of action; nay, we hardly know whether man be a simple or compound being. Impenetrable mysteries surround us on every side; they extend beyond the region of sense; we imagine ourselves possessed of understanding to penetrate them, and we have only imagination. Every one strikes out a way of his own across this imaginary world; but no one knows whether it will lead him to the point he aims at. We are yet desirous to penetrate, to know, every-thing. The only thing we know not is to contentedly remain ignorant of what it is impossible for us to know. We had much rather deter-mine at random, and believe the thing which is not, than to confess that none of us is capable of seeing the thing that is. Being ourselves but a small part of that great whole, whose limits surpass our most extensive views, and concerning which its creator leaves us to make our idle conjectures, we are vain enough to decide what that whole is in itself, and what we are in relation to it.

But were the philosophers in a situation to discover the truth, which of them would be interested in so doing? Each knows very well that his system is no better founded than the systems of others; he defends it, nevertheless, because it is his own. There is not one of them, who, really knowing truth from falsehood, would not pre-fer the latter, if of his own invention, to the former, discovered by any one else. Where is the philosopher who would not readily de-ceive mankind, to increase his own reputation? Where is he who secretly proposes any other object than that of distinguishing himself from the rest of mankind? Provided he raises himself above the vulgar, and carries away the prize of fame from his competitors, what doth he require more? The most essential point is to think differently from the rest of the world. Among believers he is an atheist, and among atheists he affects to be a believer.

The first fruit I gathered from these meditations was to learn to confine my enquiries to those things in which I was immediately interested;—to remain contented in a profound ignorance of the rest; and not to trouble myself so far as even to doubt about what it did not concern me to know.

I could further see that instead of clearing up any unnecessary doubts, the philosophers only contributed to multiply those which most tormented me, and that they resolved absolutely none. I therefore applied to another guide, and said to myself, let me consult my innate instructor, who will deceive me less than I may be deceived by others; or at least the errors I fall into will be my own, and I shall grow less depraved in the pursuit of my own illusions, than in giving myself up to the deceptions of others.

Taking a retrospect, then, of the several opinions which had successively prevailed with me from my infancy, I found that, although none of them were so evident as to produce immediate conviction, they had nevertheless different degrees of probability, and that my innate sense of truth and falsehood leaned more or less to each. On this first observation, proceeding to compare impartially and without prejudice these different opinions with each other, I found that the first and most common was also the most simple and most rational; and that it wanted nothing more to secure universal suffrage, than the circumstance of having been last proposed. Let us suppose that all our philosophers, ancient and modern, had exhausted all their whimsical systems of power, chance, fate, necessity, atoms, an animated world, sensitive matter, materialism, and of every other kind; and after them let us imagine the celebrated Dr. Clarke enlightening the world by displaying the being of beings—the supreme and sovereign disposer of all things. With what universal admiration,—with what unanimous applause would not the world receive this new system,—so great, so consolatory, so sublime,—so proper to elevate the soul, to lay the foundations of virtue,—and at the same time so striking, so enlightened, so simple,—and, as it appears to me, pregnant with less incomprehensibilities and absurdities than all other systems whatever! I reflected that unanswerable objections might be made to all, because the human understanding is incapable of resolving them, no proof therefore could be brought exclusively of any: but what difference is there in proofs! Ought not that system then, which explains everything, to be preferred, when attended with no greater difficulties than the rest?

The love of truth then comprises all my philosophy; and my method of research being the simple and easy rule of common sense, which dispenses with the vain subtilty of argumentation, I re-examined by this principle all the knowledge of which I was possessed, resolved to admit as evident everything to which I could not in the sincerity of my heart refuse to assent, to admit also as true all that seemed to have a necessary connection with it, and to leave everything else as uncertain, without either rejecting or admitting, being determined not to trouble myself about clearing up any point which did not tend to utility in practice.

But, after all, who am I? What right have I to judge of these things? And what is it that determines my conclusions? If, subject to the impressions I receive, these are formed in direct consequence of those impressions, I trouble myself to no purpose in these investigations. It is necessary, therefore, to examine myself, to know what instruments are made use of in such researches, and how far I may confide in their use.

In the first place, I know that I exist, and have senses whereby I am affected. This is a truth so striking that I am compelled to acquiesce in it. But have I properly a distinct sense of my existence, or do I only know it from my various sensations? This is my first doubt; which, at present, it is impossible for me to resolve: for, being continually affected by sensations, either directly from the objects or from the memory, how can I tell whether my self-consciousness be, or be not, something foreign to those sensations, and independent of them.

My sensations are all internal, as they make me sensible of my own existence; but the cause of them is external and independent, as they affect me without my consent, and do not depend on my will for their production or annihilation. I conceive very clearly, therefore, that the sensation which is internal, and its cause or object which is external, are not one and the same thing.

Thus I know that I not only exist, but that other beings exist as well as myself; to wit, the objects of my sensations; and though these objects should be nothing but ideas, it is very certain that these ideas are no part of myself.

Now, everything that I perceive out of myself, and which acts upon my senses, I call matter; and those portions of matter which I conceive are united in individual beings, I call bodies. Thus all the disputes between Idealists and Materialists signify nothing to me; their distinctions between the appearance and reality of bodies being chimerical.

Hence I have acquired as certain knowledge of the existence of the universe as of my own. I next reflect on the objects of my sensations; and, finding in myself the faculty of comparing them with each other, I perceive myself endowed with an active power with which I was before unacquainted.

To perceive is only to feel or be sensible of things; to compare them is to judge of their existence. To judge of things and to be sensible of them are very different. Things present themselves to our sensations as single and detached from each other, such as they barely exist in nature: but in our intellectual comparison of them they are removed, transported as it were, from place to place, disposed on and beside each other, to enable us to pronounce concerning their difference and similitude. The characteristic faculty of an intelligent, active being is, in my opinion, that of giving a sense to the word *exist*. In beings merely sensitive, I have searched in vain to discover the like force of intellect; nor can I conceive it to be in their nature. Such passive beings perceive every object singly or by itself; or if two objects present themselves, they are perceived as united into one. Such beings having no power to place one in competition with, beside, or upon the other, they cannot compare them, or judge of their separate existence.

To see two objects at once, is not to see their relations to each other, nor to judge of their difference; as to see many objects, though distinct from one another, is not to reckon their number. I may possibly have in my mind the ideas of a large stick and a small one, without comparing those ideas together, or judging that one is less than the other; as I may look at my hand without counting my fingers.[1] The comparative ideas of greater and less, as well as numerical ideas of one, two, etc., are certainly not sensations, although the understanding produces them only from our sensations.

It has been pretended that sensitive beings distinguish sensations one from the other, by the actual difference there is between those sensations: this, however, demands an explanation. When such sensations are different, a sensitive being is supposed to distinguish them by their difference; but when they are alike, they can then only distinguish them because they perceive one without the other; for, otherwise, how can two objects exactly alike be distinguished in a simultaneous sensation? Such objects must necessarily be blended together and taken for one and the same; particularly according to that system of philosophy in which it is pretended that the sensations, representative of extension, are not extended.

When two comparative sensations are perceived, they make both a joint and separate impression; but their relation to each other is not necessarily perceived in consequence of either. If the judgment we form of this relation were indeed a mere sensation, excited by the objects, we should never be deceived in it, for it can never be denied that I truly perceive what I feel.

How, therefore, can I be deceived in the relation between these two sticks, particularly, if they are not parallel? Why do I say, for instance, that the little one is a third part as long as the great one, when it is in reality only a fourth? Why is not the image, which is the sensation, conformable to its model, which is the object? It is because I am active when I judge, the operation which forms the comparison is defective, and my understanding, which judges of relations, mixes its errors with the truth of those sensations which are representative of objects.

Add to this the reflection, which I am certain you will think striking after duly weighing it, that if we were merely passive in the use of our senses, there would be no communication between them:

[1] M. de la Condamine tells of a people who knew how to reckon only as far as three. Yet these people must often have seen their fingers without ever having counted five.

so that it would be impossible for us to know that the body we touched with our hands and the object we saw with our eyes were one and the same. Either we should not be able to perceive external objects at all, or they would appear to exist as five perceptible substances of which we should have no method of ascertaining the identity.

Whatever name be given to that power of the mind which assembles and compares my sensations,—call it attention, meditation, reflection, or whatever you please,—certain it is that it exists in me, and not in the objects of those sensations. It is I alone who produce it, although it is displayed only in consequence of the impressions made on me by those objects. Without being so far master over myself as to perceive or not to perceive at pleasure, I am still more or less capable of making an examination into the objects perceived.

I am not, therefore, a mere sensitive and passive, but an active and intelligent being; and, whatever philosophers may pretend, lay claim to the honor of thinking. I know only that truth depends on the existence of things, and not on my understanding which judges of them; and that the less such judgment depends on me, the nearer I am certain of approaching the truth. Hence my rule of confiding more on sentiment than reason is confirmed by reason itself.

Being thus far assured of my own nature and capacity, I begin to consider the objects about me; regarding myself, with a kind of shuddering, as a creature thrown on the wide world of the universe, and as it were lost in an infinite variety of other beings, without knowing anything of what they are, either among themselves or with regard to me.

Everything that is perceptible to my senses is matter, and I deduce all the essential properties of matter from those sensible qualities, which cause it to be perceptible, and which are inseparable from it. I see it sometimes in motion and at other times at rest. This rest may be said to be only relative; but as we perceive degrees in motion, we can very clearly conceive one of the two extremes which is rest; and this we conceive so distinctly, that we are even induced to take that for absolute rest which is only relative. Now motion cannot be essential to matter, if matter can be conceived at rest. Hence I infer that neither motion nor rest are essential to it; but motion being an action, is clearly the effect of cause, of which rest is only the absence. When nothing acts on matter, it does not move; it is equally indifferent to motion and rest; its natural state, therefore, is to be at rest.

Again, I perceive in bodies two kinds of motion; that is a mechanical or communicated motion, and a spontaneous or voluntary one. In the first case, the moving cause is out of the body moved, and in the last, exists within it. I shall not hence conclude, however, that the motion of a watch, for example, is spontaneous; for if nothing should act upon it but the spring, that spring would not wind itself up again when once down. For the same reason, also, I should as little accede to the spontaneous motion of fluids, nor even to heat itself, the cause of their fluidity.

You will ask me if the motions of animals are spontaneous? I will freely answer, I cannot positively tell, but analogy speaks in the affirmative. You may ask me further, how I know there is such a thing as spontaneous motion? I answer, because I feel it. I *will* to move my arm, and, accordingly, it moves without the intervention of any other immediate cause. It is in vain to attempt to reason me out of this sentiment; it is more powerful than any rational evidence. You might as well attempt to convince me that I do not exist.

If the actions of men are not spontaneous, and there be no such spontaneous action in what passes on earth, we are only the more embarrassed to conceive what is the first cause of all motion. For my part I am so fully persuaded that the natural state of matter is a state of rest, and that it has in itself no principle of activity, that whenever I see a body in motion, I instantly conclude that it is either an animated body or that its motion is communicated to it. My understanding will by no means acquiesce in the notion that unorganized matter can move of itself, or be productive of any kind of action.

The visible universe, however, is composed of inanimate matter, which appears to have nothing in its composition of organization, or that sensation which is common to the parts of an animated body, as it is certain that we ourselves, being parts thereof, do not perceive our existence in the whole. The universe, also, is in motion; and its movements being all regular, uniform, and subjected to constant laws, nothing appears therein similar to that liberty which is remarkable in the spontaneous motion of men and animals. The world, therefore, is not a huge self-moving animal, but receives its motions from some foreign cause, which we do not perceive: but I am so strongly persuaded within myself of the existence of this cause, that it is impossible for me to observe the apparent diurnal revolution of the sun, without conceiving that some force must urge it forward; or if it is the earth itself that turns, I cannot but conceive that some hand must turn it.

If it be necessary to admit general laws that have no apparent relation to matter, from what fixed point must that enquiry set out? Those laws, being nothing real or substantial, have some prior foundation equally unknown and occult. Experience and observation have taught us the laws of motion; these laws, however, determine effects only without displaying their causes; and, therefore, are not sufficient to explain the system of the universe. Descartes could form a model of the heavens and earth with dice; but he could not give their motions to those dice, nor bring into play his centrifugal force without the assistance of a rotary motion. Newton discovered the law of attraction; but attraction alone would soon have reduced the universe into one solid mass: to this law, therefore, he found it necessary to add a projectile force, in order to account for the revolution of the heavenly bodies. Could Descartes tell us by what physical law his vortices were put and kept in motion? Could Newton produce the hand that first impelled the planets in the tangent of their respective orbits?

The first causes of motion do not exist in matter; bodies receive from and communicate motion to each other, but they cannot originally produce it. The more I observe the action and reaction of the powers of nature acting on each other, the more I am convinced that they are merely effects; and we must ever recur to some volition as the first cause: for to suppose there is a progression of causes to infinity, is to suppose there is no first cause at all. In a word, every motion that is not produced by some other, must be the effect of a spontaneous, voluntary act. Inanimate bodies have no action but motion; and there can be no real action without volition. Such is my first principle. I believe, therefore, that a *Will* gives motion to the universe, and animates all nature. This is my first article of faith.

In what manner volition is productive of physical and corporeal action I know not, but I experience within myself that it is productive of it. I *will* to act, and the action immediately follows; I *will* to move my body, and my body instantly moves; but, that an inanimate body lying at rest, should move itself, or produce motion, is incomprehensible and unprecedented. The *Will* also is known by its effects and not by its essence. I know it as the cause of motion; but to conceive matter producing motion, would be evidently to conceive an effect without a cause, or rather not to conceive any thing at all.

It is no more possible for me to conceive how the will moves the body, than how the sensations affect the soul. I even know not why one of these mysteries ever appeared more explicable than the other. For my own part, whether at the time I am active or passive, the means of union between the two substances appear to me absolutely incomprehensible. Is it not strange that the philosophers have thrown off this incomprehensibility, merely to confound the two substances together, as if operations so different could be better explained as the effects of one subject than of two.

The principle which I have here laid down, is undoubtedly something obscure; it is however intelligible, and contains nothing repugnant to reason or observation. Can we say as much of the doctrines of materialism? It is very certain that, if motion be essential to matter, it would be inseparable from it; it would be always the same in every portion of it, incommunicable, and incapable of increase or diminution; it would be impossible for us even to conceive matter at rest. Again, when I am told that motion is not indeed essential to matter, but necessary to its existence, I see through the attempt to impose on me by a form of words, which it would be more easy to refute, if more intelligible. For, whether the motion of matter arises from itself, and is therefore essential to it, or whether it is derived from some external cause, it is not further necessary to it than as the moving cause acting thereon: so that we still remain under the first difficulty.

General and abstract ideas form the source of our greatest errors. The jargon of metaphysics never discovered one truth; but it has filled philosophy with absurdities, of which we are ashamed as soon as they are stripped of their pompous expressions. Tell me truly, my friend, if any precise idea is conveyed to your understanding when you are told of a blind, unintelligent power being diffused throughout all nature? It is imagined that something is meant by those vague terms, Universal force and Necessary motion; and yet they convey no meaning. The idea of motion is nothing more than the idea of passing from one place to another, nor can there be any motion without some particular direction; for no individual being can move several ways at once. In what manner then is it that matter necessarily moves? Has all the matter of which bodies are composed a general and uniform motion, or has each atom a particular motion of its own? If we give assent to the first notion, the whole universe will appear to be one solid and indivisible mass; and according to the second, it should constitute a diffused and incoherent fluid, without a possibility that two atoms ever could be united. What can be the direction of this motion common to all matter? Is it in a right line upwards or downwards, to the right or to the left? Again, if every particle of matter has its particular direction, what can be the cause of all those directions and their variations? If every atom or particle of matter revolved only on its axis, none of them would change their place, and there would be no motion communicated; and even in this case it is necessary that such a revolving motion should be carried on one way. To ascribe to matter motion in the abstract, is to make use of terms without a meaning; and in giving it any determinate motion, we must of necessity suppose the cause that determines it. The more I multiply particular forces, the more new causes have I to explain, without ever finding one common agent that directs them. So far from being able to conceive any regularity or order in the fortuitous concourse of elements, I cannot even conceive the nature of their concurrence; and an universal chaos is more inconceivable than universal harmony. I easily comprehend that the mechanism of the world cannot be perfectly known to the human understanding, but whenever men undertake to explain it, they ought at least to speak in such a manner that others may understand them.

If from matter being put in motion I discover the existence of a *Will* as the first active cause, the subjugation of this matter to certain regular laws of motion displays also intelligence. This is my second article of faith. To act, to compare, to prefer, are the operations of an active, thinking being: such a being, therefore, exists. Do you proceed to ask me, where I discover its existence? I answer, not only in the revolutions of the celestial bodies; not only in myself; but in the flocks that feed on the plain, in the birds that fly in the air, in the stone that falls to the ground, and in the leaf that trembles in the wind.

I am enabled to judge of the physical order of things, although ignorant of their final cause; because to be able to form such a judgment it is sufficient for me to compare the several parts of the visible universe with each other, to study their mutual concurrence, their reciprocal relations, and to observe the general result of the whole. I am ignorant why the universe exists, but I am enabled nevertheless to see how it is modified. I cannot fail to perceive that intimate connection by which the several beings it is composed of afford each other mutual assistance. I resemble, in this respect, a man who sees the inside of a watch for the first time, and is captivated with the beauty of the work, although ignorant of its use. I know not, he may say, what this machine is good for, but I perceive that each part is made to fit some other. I admire the artist for every part of his performance, and am certain that all these wheels act thus in concert to some common end, which as yet I fail to comprehend.

But let us compare the partial and particular ends, the means whereby they are effected, and their constant relations of every kind; then let us appeal to our innate sense of conviction; and what man in his senses can refuse to acquiesce in such testimony? To what unprejudiced view does not the visible arrangement of the universe display the supreme intelligence of its author? How much sophistry does it not require to disavow the harmony of created beings, and that admirable order in which all the parts of the system concur to the preservation of each other? You may talk to me as much as you please of combinations and chances: what end will it answer to reduce me to silence, if you can persuade me into the truth of what you advance? and how will you divest me of that involuntary sentiment which continually contradicts you? If organized bodies are fortuitously combined in a thousand ways before they assume settled and constant forms; if at first they are formed stomachs without mouths, feet without heads, hands without arms, and imperfect organs of every kind, which have perished for want of the necessary faculties of self-preservation; how comes it that none of these imperfect essays have engaged our attention? Why hath nature at length confined herself to laws to which she was not at first subjected? I confess that I ought not to be surprised that any possible thing should happen, when the rarity of the event is compensated by the great odds that it did not happen. And yet if any one were to tell me that a number of printer's types, jumbled promiscuously together, had arranged themselves in the order of the letters composing the Æneid, I certainly should not deign to take one step to verify or disprove such a story. It may be said, I forget the number of chances: but pray how many must I suppose to render such a combination in any degree probable? I, who see only the one, must conclude that there is an infinite number against it, and that it is not the effect of chance. Add to this that the product of these combinations must be always of the same nature with the combined elements; hence life and organization never can result from a blind concourse of atoms, nor will the chemist, with all his art in compounds, ever find sensation and thought at the bottom of his crucible.

I have been frequently surprised and sometimes scandalized in the reading of Nieuwenteit. What a presumption was it to set down to make a book of those wonders of nature that display the wisdom of their author? Had his book been as big as the whole world, he would not have exhausted his subject; and no sooner do we enter into the minutiæ of things than the greatest wonder of all escapes us;—that is, the harmony and connection of the whole. The generation of living and organized bodies alone baffles all the efforts of the human understanding. That insurmountable barrier which nature hath placed between the various species of animals, that they might not be confounded with each other, makes her intentions sufficiently evident. Not contented only to establish order, she has taken effectual methods to prevent its being disturbed.

There is not a being in the universe which may not, in some respect, be regarded as the common center of all others, which are ranged around it in such a manner that they serve reciprocally as cause and effect to one another. The imagination is lost and the understanding confounded in such an infinite diversity of relations, of which, however, not one of them is either lost or confounded in the crowd. How absurd the attempt to deduce this wonderful harmony from the blind mechanism of a fortuitous jumble of atoms! Those who deny the unity of design, so manifest in the relation of all the parts of this grand system, may endeavor as much as they will to conceal their absurdities with abstract ideas, coördinations, general principles, and emblematical terms. Whatever they may advance, it is impossible for me to conceive that a system of beings can be so wisely regulated, without the existence of some intelligent cause which effects such regulation. It is not in my power to believe that passive inanimate matter could ever have produced living and sensible creatures,—that a blind fatality should be productive of intelligent beings,—or that a cause, incapable itself of thinking, should produce the faculty of thinking in its effects.

I believe, therefore, that the world is governed by a wise and powerful *Will*. I see it, or rather I feel it; and this is of importance for me to know. But is the world eternal, or is it created? Are things derived from one self-existent principle, or are there two or more, and what is their essence? Of all this I know nothing, nor do I see that it is necessary I should. In proportion as such knowledge may become interesting I will endeavor to acquire it: but further than this I give up all such idle disquisitions, which serve only to make me discontented with myself, which are useless in practice, and are above my understanding.

You will remember, however, that I am not dictating my sentiments to you, but only explaining what they are. Whether matter be eternal or only created, whether it have a passive principle or not, certain it is that the whole universe is one design, and sufficiently displays one intelligent agent: for I see no part of this system that is not under regulation, or that does not concur to one and the same end; viz. that of preserving the present and established order of things. That Being, whose will is his deed, whose principle of action is in himself,—that Being, in a word, whatever it be, that gives motion to all parts of the universe, and governs all things, I call GOD.

To this term I affix the ideas of intelligence, power, and will, which I have collected from the order of things; and to these I add that of goodness, which is a necessary consequence of their union. But I am not at all the wiser concerning the essence of the Being to which I give these attributes. He remains at an equal distance from my senses and my understanding. The more I think of him, the more I am confounded. I know of a certainty that he exists, and that his existence is independent of any of his creatures. I know also that my existence is dependent on his, and that every being I know is in the same situation as myself. I perceive the deity in all his works, I feel him within me, and behold him in every object around me: but I no sooner endeavor to contemplate what he is in himself,—I no sooner enquire where he is, and what is his substance, than he eludes the strongest efforts of my imagination; and my bewildered understanding is convinced of its own weakness.

For this reason I shall never take upon me to argue about the nature of God further than I am obliged to do by the relation he appears to stand in to myself. There is so great a temerity in such disquisitions that a wise man will never enter on them without trembling, and feeling fully assured of his incapacity to proceed far on so sublime a subject: for it is less injurious to entertain no ideas of the deity at all, than to harbor those which are unworthy and unjust.

After having discovered those of his attributes by which I am convinced of his existence, I return to myself and consider the place I occupy in that order of things, which is directed by him and subjected to my examination. Here I find my species stand incontestibly in the first rank; as man, by virtue of his will and the instruments he is possessed of to put it in execution, has a greater power over the bodies by which he is surrounded than they, by mere physical impulse, have over him. By virtue of his intelligence, I also find, he is the only created being here below that can take a general survey of the whole system. Is there one among them, except man, who knows how to observe all others?—to weigh, to calculate, to foresee their motions, their effects, and to join, if I may so express myself, the sentiment of a general existence to that of the individual? What is there so very ridiculous then in supposing every thing made for man, when he is the only created being who knows how to consider the relation in which all things stand to himself?

It is then true that man is lord of the creation,—that he is, at least, sovereign over the habitable earth; for it is certain that he not only subdues all other animals, and even disposes by his industry of the elements at his pleasure, but he alone of all terrestrial beings knows how to subject to his convenience, and even by contemplation to appropriate to his use, the very stars and planets he cannot approach. Let any one produce me an animal of another species who knows how to make use of fire, or hath faculties to admire the sun. What! am I able to observe, to know other beings and their relations,—am I capable of discovering what is order, beauty, virtue,—of contemplating the universe,—of elevating my ideas to the hand which governs the whole,—am I capable of loving what is good and doing it, and shall I compare myself to the brutes? Abject soul! it is your gloomy philosophy alone that renders you at all like them. Or, rather, it is vain you would debase yourself. Your own genius rises up against your principles;—your benevolent heart gives the lie to your absurd doctrines,—and even the abuse of your faculties demonstrates their excellence in spite of yourself.

For my part, who have no system to maintain, who am only a simple, honest man, attached to no party, unambitious of being the founder of any sect, and contented with the situation in which God hath placed me, I see nothing in the world, except the deity, better than my own species; and were I left to choose my place in the order of created beings, I see none that I could prefer to that of man.

This reflection, however, is less vain than affecting; for my state is not the effect of choice, and could not be due to the merit of a being that did not before exist. Can I behold myself, nevertheless thus distinguished, without thinking myself happy in occupying so honorable a post; or without blessing the hand that placed me here? From the first view I thus took of myself, my heart began to glow with a sense of gratitude towards the author of our being; and hence arose my first idea of the worship due to a beneficent deity. I adore the supreme power, and melt into tenderness at his goodness. I have no need to be taught artificial forms of worship; the dictates of nature are sufficient. Is it not a natural consequence of self-love to honor those who protect us, and to love such as do us good?

But when I come afterwards to take a view of the particular rank and relation in which I stand, as an individual, among the fellow-creatures of my species; to consider the different ranks of society and the persons by whom they are filled; what a scene is presented to me! Where is that order and regularity before observed? The scenes of nature present to my view the most perfect harmony and proportion: those of mankind nothing but confusion and disorder. The physical elements of things act in concert with each other; the moral world alone is a chaos of discord. Mere animals are happy; but man, their lord and sovereign, is miserable! Where, Supreme Wisdom! are thy laws? Is it thus, O Providence! thou governest the world? What is become of thy power, thou Supreme Beneficence! when I behold evil thus prevailing upon the earth?

Would you believe, my good friend, that from such gloomy reflections and apparent contradictions, I should form to myself more sublime ideas of the soul than ever resulted from my former researches? In meditating on the nature of man, I conceived that I discovered two distinct principles; the one raising him to the study of eternal truth, the love of justice and moral beauty—bearing him aloft to the regions of the intellectual world, the contemplation of which yields the truest delight to the philosopher; the other debasing him even below himself, subjecting him to the slavery of sense, the tyranny of the passions, and exciting these to counteract every noble and generous sentiment inspired by the former. When I perceived myself hurried away by two such contrary powers, I naturally concluded that man is not one simple and individual substance. I will, and I will not; I perceive myself at once free, and a slave; I see what is good, I admire it, and yet I do the evil: I am active when I listen to my reason, and passive when hurried away by my passions; while my greatest uneasiness is to find, when fallen under temptations, that I had the power of resisting them.

Attend, young man, with confidence to what I say; you will find I shall never deceive you. If conscience be the offspring of our prejudices, I am doubtless in the wrong, and moral virtue is not to be demonstrated; but if self-love, which makes us prefer ourselves to every thing else, be natural to man, and if nevertheless an innate sense of justice be found in his heart, let those who imagine him to be a simple uncompounded being reconcile these contradictions, and I will give up my opinion and acknowledge him to be one substance.

You will please to observe that by the word substance I here mean, in general, a being possessed of some primitive quality, abstracted from all particular or secondary modifications. Now, if all known primitive qualities may be united in one and the same being, we have no need to admit of more than one substance; but if some of these qualities are incompatible with, and necessarily exclusive of each other, we must admit of the existence of as many different substances as there are such incompatible qualities. You will do well to reflect on this subject. For my part, notwithstanding what Mr. Locke hath said on this head, I need only to know that matter is extended and divisible, to be assured that it cannot think; and when a philosopher comes and tells me that trees and rocks have thought and perception, he may, perhaps, embarrass me with the subtlety of his arguments, but I cannot help regarding him as a disingenuous sophist, who had rather attribute sentiment to stocks and stones than acknowledge men to have a soul.

Let us suppose that a man, born deaf, should deny the reality of sounds, because his ears were never sensible of them. To convince him of his error, I place a violin before his eyes; and, by playing on another, concealed from him, give a vibration to the strings of the former. This motion, I tell him, is effected by sound.

"Not at all," says he; "the cause of the vibration of the string, is in the string itself: it is a common quality in all bodies so to vibrate."

"Show me then," I reply, "the same vibration in other bodies; or at least, the cause of it in this string."

"I cannot," the deaf man may reply, "but wherefore must I, because I do not conceive how this string vibrates, attribute the cause to your pretended sounds, of which I cannot entertain the least idea? This would be to attempt an explanation of one obscurity by another still greater. Either make your sounds perceptible to me, or I shall continue to doubt their existence."

The more I reflect on our capacity of thinking, and the nature of the human understanding, the greater is the resemblance I find between the arguments of our materialists and that of such a deaf man. They are, in effect, equally deaf to that internal voice which, nevertheless, calls to them so loud and emphatically. A mere machine is evidently incapable of thinking, it has neither motion nor figure productive of reflection: whereas in man there exists something perpetually prone to expand, and to burst the fetters by which it is confined. Space itself affords not bounds to the human mind: the whole universe is not extensive enough for man; his sentiments, his desires, his anxieties, and even his pride, take rise from a principle different from that body within which he perceives himself confined.

No material being can be self-active, and I perceive that I am so. It is in vain to dispute with me so clear a point. My own sentiment carries with it a stronger conviction than any reason which can ever be brought against it. I have a body on which other bodies act, and which acts reciprocally upon them. This reciprocal action is indubitable; but my will is independent of my senses. I can either consent to, or resist their impressions. I am either vanquished or victor, and perceive clearly within myself when I act according to my will, and when I submit to be governed by my passions. I have always the power to will, though not the force to execute it. When I give myself up to any temptation, I act from the impulse of external objects. When I reproach myself for my weakness in so doing, I listen only to the dictates of my will. I am a slave in my vices, and free in my repentance. The sentiment of my liberty is effaced only by my depravation, and when I prevent the voice of the soul from being heard in opposition to the laws of the body.

All the knowledge I have of volition, is deduced from a sense of my own; and, of the understanding, my knowledge is no greater. When I am asked what is the cause that determines my will, I ask in my turn, what is the cause that determines my judgment? for it is clear that these two causes make but one; and if we conceive that man is active in forming his judgment of things—that his understanding is only a power of comparing and judging, we shall see that his liberty is only a similar power, or one derived from this—he chooses the good as he judges of the true, and for the same reason as he deduces a false judgment, he makes a bad choice. What then is the cause that determines his will? It is his judgment. And what is the cause that determines his judgment? It is his intelligent faculty,—his power of judging. The determining cause lies in himself. If we proceed beyond this point, I know nothing of the matter.

Not that I can suppose myself at liberty not to will my own good, or to will my own evil: but my liberty consists in this very circumstance, that I am incapable to will any thing but what is useful to me, or at least what appears so, without any foreign object interfering in my determination. Does it follow from hence that I am not my own master because I am incapable of assuming another being, or of divesting myself of what is essential to my existence?

The principle of all action lies in the will of a free being. We can go no farther in search of its source. It is not the word liberty that has no signification; it is that of necessity. To suppose any act or effect, which is not derived from an active principle, is indeed to suppose effects without a cause. Either there is no first impulse, or every first impulse can have no prior cause; nor can there be any such thing as will without liberty. Man is, therefore, a free agent, and as such animated by an immaterial substance. This is my third article of faith. From these three first you may easily deduce all the rest, without my continuing to number them.

If man be an active and free being, he acts of himself. None of his spontaneous actions, therefore, enter into the general system of Providence, nor can be imputed to it. Providence doth not contrive the evil, which is the consequence of man's abusing the liberty his creator gave him; it only doth not prevent it, either because the evil which so impotent a being is capable of doing is beneath its notice, or because it cannot prevent it without laying a restraint upon his liberty, and causing a greater evil by debasing his nature. Providence hath left man at liberty, not that he should do evil, but good, by choice. It hath capacitated him to make such choice, in making a proper use of the faculties it hath bestowed on him. His powers, however, are at the same time so limited and confined, that the use he makes of his liberty is not of importance enough to disturb the general order of the universe. The evil done by man falls upon his own head, without making any change in the system of the world,— without hindering the human species from being preserved in spite of themselves. To complain, therefore, that God doth not prevent man from doing evil is, in fact, to complain that he hath given a superior excellence to human nature,—that he hath ennobled our actions by annexing to them the merit of virtue.

The highest enjoyment is that of being contented with ourselves. It is in order to deserve this contentment that we are placed here on earth and endowed with liberty,—that we are tempted by our passions, and restrained by conscience. What could Omnipotence itself do more in our favor? Could it have established a contradiction in our nature, or have allotted a reward for well-doing to a being incapable of doing ill? Is it necessary, in order to prevent man from being wicked, to reduce all his faculties to a simple instinct and make him a mere brute? No! never can I reproach the Deity for having given me a soul made in his own image, that I might be free, good, and happy like himself.

It is the abuse of our faculties which makes us wicked and miserable. Our cares, our anxieties, our griefs, are all owing to ourselves. Moral evil is incontestibly our own work, and physical evil would in fact be nothing, did not our vices render us sensible of it. Is it not for our preservation that nature makes us sensible of our wants? Is not pain of body an indication that the machine is out of order, and a caution for us to provide a remedy? And as to death, do not the wicked render both our lives and their own miserable? Who can be desirous of living here forever? Death is a remedy for all the evils we inflict on ourselves. Nature will not let us suffer perpetually. To how few evils are men subject who live in primeval simplicity! They hardly know any disease, and are irritated by scarcely any passions. They neither foresee death, nor suffer by the apprehensions of it. When it approaches, their miseries render it desirable, and it is to them no evil. If we could be contented with being what we are, we should have no inducement to lament our fate; but we inflict on ourselves a thousand real evils in seeking after an imaginary happiness. Those who are impatient under trifling inconveniences, must expect to suffer much greater. In our endeavors to reëstablish by medicines a constitution impaired by irregularities, we always add to the evil we feel, the greater one which we fear. Our apprehensions of death anticipate its horrors and hasten its approach. The faster we endeavor to fly, the swifter it pursues us. Thus we are terrified as long as we live, and die murmuring against nature on account of those evils which we bring on ourselves by doing outrage to her laws.

Enquire no longer then, who is the author of evil. Behold him in yourself. There exists no other evil in nature than what you either do or suffer, and you are equally the author of both. A general evil could exist only in disorder, but in the system of nature I see an established order, which is never disturbed. Particular evil exists only in the sentiment of the suffering being; and this sentiment is not given to man by nature, but is of his own acquisition. Pain and sorrow have but little hold on those who, unaccustomed to reflection, have neither memory nor foresight. Take away our fatal improvements—take away our errors and our vices—take away, in short, every thing that is the work of man, and all that remains is good.

Where every thing is good, nothing can be unjust, justice being inseparable from goodness. Now goodness is the necessary effect of infinite power and self-love essential to every being conscious of its existence. An omnipotent Being extends its existence also, if I may so express myself, with that of its creatures. Production and preservation follow from the constant exertion of its power: it does not act on non-existence. God is not the God of the dead, but of the living. He cannot be mischievous or wicked without hurting himself. A being capable of doing every thing cannot *will* to do any thing but what is good. He who is infinitely good, therefore, because he is infinitely powerful, must also be supremely just, otherwise he would be inconsistent with himself. For that love of order which produces it we call goodness, and that love of order which preserves it is called justice.

God, it is said, owes nothing to his creatures. For my part, I believe he owes them every thing he promised them when he gave them being. Now what is less than to promise them a blessing, if he gives them an idea of it, and has so constituted them as to feel the want of it? The more I look into myself, the more plainly I read these words written in my soul: *Be just and thou wilt be happy.* I see not the truth of this, however, in the present state of things, wherein the wicked triumph and the just are trampled on and oppressed. What indignation, hence, arises within us to find that our hopes are frustrated! Conscience itself rises up and complains of its maker. It cries out to him, lamenting, *thou hast deceived me!*

"I have deceived thee! rash man? Who hath told thee so? Is thy soul annihilated? Dost thou cease to exist? Oh, Brutus! stain not a life of glory in the end. Leave not thy honor and thy hopes with thy body in the fields of Philippi. Wherefore dost thou say, virtue is a shadow, when thou wilt yet enjoy the reward of thine own? Dost thou imagine thou art going to die? No! thou art going to live! and then will I make good every promise I have made to thee."

One would be apt to think, from the murmurs of impatient mortals, that God owed them a recompense before they had deserved it; and that he was obliged to reward their virtue beforehand. No; let us first be virtuous, and rest assured we shall sooner or later be happy. Let us not require the prize before we have won the victory, nor demand the price of our labor before the work be finished. "It is not in the lists," says Plutarch, "that the victors at our games are crowned, but after the contests are over."

If the soul be immaterial, it may survive the body, and if so, Providence is justified. Had I no other proof of the immateriality of the soul, than the oppression of the just and the triumph of the wicked in this world, this alone would prevent my having the least doubt of it. So shocking a discord amidst the general harmony of things, would make me naturally look out for the cause. I should say to myself, we do not cease to exist with this life,—every thing reassumes its order after death. I should, indeed, be embarrassed to tell where man was to be found, when all his perceptible properties were destroyed. At present, however, there appears to me no difficulty in this point, as I acknowledge the existence of two different substances. It is very plain that during my corporeal life, as I perceive nothing but by means of my senses, whatever is not submitted to their cognizance must escape me. When the union of the body and the soul is broken, I conceive that the one may be dissolved, and the other preserved entire. Why should the dissolution of the one necessarily bring on that of the other? On the contrary, being so different in their natures, their state of union is a state of violence, and when it is broken they both return to their natural situation. The active and living substance regains all the force it had employed in giving motion to the passive and dead substance to which it had been united. Alas! my failings make me but too sensible that man is but half alive in this life, and that the life of the soul commences at the death of the body.

But what is that life? Is the soul immortal in its own nature? My limited comprehension is incapable of conceiving any thing that is unlimited. Whatever we call infinite is beyond my conception. What can I deny or affirm?—what arguments can I employ on a subject I cannot conceive? I believe that the soul survives the body so long as is necessary to justify Providence in the good order of things; but who knows that this will be forever? I can readily conceive how material bodies wear away and are destroyed by the separation of their parts, but I cannot conceive a like dissolution of a thinking being; and hence, as I cannot imagine how it can die, I presume it cannot die at all. This presumption, also, being consolatory and not unreasonable, why should I be fearful to indulge it?

I feel that I have a soul: I know it both from thought and senti-ment: I know that it exists, without knowing its essence: I cannot reason, therefore, on ideas which I have not. One thing, indeed, I know very well, which is, that the identity of my being can be pre-served only by the memory, and that to be in fact the same person, I must remember to have previously existed. Now I cannot recollect, after my death, what I was during life, without also recollecting my perceptions, and consequently my actions: and I doubt not but this remembrance will one day constitute the happiness of the just and the torment of the wicked. Here below, the violence of our passions absorbs the innate sentiment of right and wrong, and stifles remorse. The mortification and obloquy which virtue often suffers in the world, may prevent our being sensible of its charms. But when, de-livered from the delusions of sense, we shall enjoy the contemplation of the Supreme Being, and those eternal truths of which he is the source;—when the beauty of the natural order of things shall strike all the faculties of the soul, and when we shall be employed solely in comparing what we have really done with what we ought to have done, then will the voice of conscience reassume its tone and strength; then will that pure delight, which arises from a consciousness of virtue, and the bitter regret of having debased ourselves by vice, determine the lot which is severally prepared for us. Ask me not, my good friend, if there may not be some other causes of future happiness and misery. I confess I am ignorant. These, however, which I conceive, are sufficient to console me under the inconveniencies of this life, and give me hopes of another. I do not pretend to say that the virtuous will receive any peculiar rewards; for what other advantage can a being, excellent in its own nature, expect than to exist in a manner agreeable to the excellence of its constitution? I dare affirm, nevertheless, that they will be happy: because their Creator, the author of all justice, having given them sensibility, cannot have made them to be miserable; and as they have not abused their liberty on earth, they have not perverted the design of their creation by their own fault: yet, as they have suffered evils in this life, they will certainly be indemnified in another. This opinion is not so much founded on the merits of a man, as on the notion of that goodness which appears to me inseparable from the divine nature. I only suppose the order of things strictly maintained, and that the Deity is ever consistent with himself.

It would be to as little purpose to ask me whether the torments of the wicked will be eternal. On this subject I am entirely ignorant, and have not the vain curiosity to perplex myself with such useless disquisitions. Indeed, why should I interest myself to discover their ultimate fate and destiny? I can never believe, however, that they will be condemned to everlasting torments.

If supreme justice avenges itself on the wicked, it avenges itself on them here below. It is you and your errors, ye nations! that are its ministers of vengeance. It employs the evils you bring on each other, to punish the crimes for which you deserve them. It is in the insatiable hearts of mankind,—corroding with envy, avarice, and ambition,—that their avenging passions punish them for their vices, amidst all the false appearances of prosperity. Where is the necessity of seeking a hell in another life, when it is to be found even in this,—in the hearts of the wicked.

Where our momentary necessities or senseless desires have an end, there ought our passions and our vices to end also. Of what perversity can pure spirits be susceptible? As they stand in need of nothing, to what end should they be vicious? If destitute of our grosser senses, can they be desirous of any thing but good? Doth not their happiness consist principally in contemplation, and is it possible that those who cease to be wicked should be eternally miserable?

This is what I am inclined to believe on this head, without giving myself the trouble to determine positively concerning the matter.

O righteous and merciful being! whatever be thy decrees, I acknowledge their rectitude. If thou punishest the wicked, my weak reason is dumb before thy justice. But if the remorse of those unfortunate wretches is to have an end,—if the same fate is one day to attend us all,—my soul exults in thy praise. Is not the wicked man, after all, my brother? How often have I been tempted to resemble him in partaking of his vices. O! may he be delivered from his misery; may he cast off, also, that malignity which accompanies it; may he be ever as happy as myself; so far from exciting my jealousy, his happiness will only add to my own.

It is thus by contemplating God in his works, and studying him in those attributes which it imports me to know, that I learn by degrees to extend that imperfect and confined idea I had at first formed of the Supreme Being. But, if this idea becomes thus more grand and noble, it is proportionably less adapted to the weakness of the human understanding. In proportion as my mind approaches eternal light, its brightness dazzles and confounds me; so that I am forced to give up all those mean and earthly images which assist my imagination. God is no longer a corporeal and perceptible being: the supreme Intelligence which governs the world, is no longer the world itself; but in vain I endeavour to elevate my thoughts to a conception of his essence. When I reflect that it is he who gives life and activity to that living and active substance which moves and governs animated bodies,—when I am told that my soul is a spiritual being, and that God is also a spirit, I am incensed at this debasement of the divine essence, as if God and my soul were of the same nature, as if God was not the only absolute, the only truly active being,—perceiving, thinking and willing of himself,—from whom his creatures derive thought, activity, will, liberty, and existence. We are free only because it is his will that we should be so; his inexplicable substance being, with respect to our souls, such as our souls are in regard to our bodies. I know nothing of his having created matter, bodies, spirits, or the world. The idea of creation confounds me and surpasses my conception, though I believe as much of it as I am able to conceive. But I know that God hath formed the universe and all that exists, in the most consummate order. He is doubtless eternal, but I am incapacitated to conceive an idea of eternity. Why then should I amuse myself with words? All that I conceive is, that he existed before all things, that he exists with them, and will exist after them, if they should ever have an end. That a being, whose essence is inconceivable, should give existence to other beings, is at best obscure and incomprehensible to our ideas; but that something and nothing should be reciprocally converted into each other is a palpable contradiction, a most manifest absurdity.

God is intelligent; but in what manner? Man is intelligent by the act of reasoning, but the supreme intelligence lies under no necessity to reason. He requires neither premises nor consequences; nor even the simple form of a proposition. His knowledge is purely intuitive. He beholds equally what is and will be. All truths are to him as one idea, as all places are but one point, and all times one moment. Human power acts by the use of means, the divine power in and of itself. God is powerful because he is willing, his will constituting his power. God is good. Nothing is more manifest than this truth. Goodness in man, however, consists in a love to his fellow-creatures, and the goodness of God in a love of order; for it is on such order that the connexion and preservation of all things depend. Again, God is just. This I am fully convinced of, as justice is the natural consequence of goodness. The injustice of men is their own work, not his; and that moral disorder, which in the judgment of some philosophers makes against the system of providence, is in mine the strongest argument for it. Justice in man, indeed, is to render every one his due: but the justice of God requires at the hands of every one an account of the talents with which he has entrusted them.

In the discovery by the force of reason, however, of those divine attributes of which I have no absolute idea, I only affirm what I do not clearly comprehend; which is in effect to affirm nothing. I may say, it is true that, God is this or that; I may be sensible of it and fully convinced within myself, but I may yet be unable to conceive how, or in what manner he is so.

In short, the greater efforts I make to contemplate his infinite essence, the less I am able to conceive it. But I am certain that he is, and that is sufficient. The more he surpasses my conceptions, the more I adore him. I humble myself before him, and say:

"Being of beings! I am, because thou art. To meditate continually on thee is to elevate my thoughts to the fountain of existence. The most meritorious use of my reason is to be annihilated before thee. It is the delight of my soul, to feel my weak faculties overcome by the splendor of thy greatness."

After having thus deduced this most important truth, from the impressions of perceptible objects and that innate principle which leads me to judge of natural causes from experience, it remains for me to inquire what maxims I ought to draw therefrom for my conduct in life,—what rules I ought to prescribe to myself, in order to fulfill my destiny on earth agreeably to the design of him who placed me here. To pursue my own method, I deduce these rules, not from the sublime principles of philosophy, but find them written in indelible characters on my heart. I have only to consult myself concerning what I ought to do. All that I feel to be right, is right: whatever I feel to be wrong, is wrong. Conscience is the ablest of all casuists, and it is only when we are trafficking with her, that we have recourse to the subtilties of logical ratiocination. The chief of our concerns is that of ourselves; yet how often have we not been told by the monitor within, that to pursue our own interest at the expense of others would be to do wrong! We imagine, thus, that we are sometimes obeying the impulse of nature, and we are all the while resisting it. In listening to the voice of our senses we turn a deaf ear to the dictates of our hearts,—the active being obeys,—the passive being commands. Conscience is the voice of the soul,—the passions are the voice of the body. Is it surprising that these two voices should sometimes contradict each other, or can it be doubted, when they do, which ought to be obeyed? Reason deceives us but too often, and has given us a right to distrust her conclusions; but conscience never deceives us. She is to the soul what instinct[2] is to the body,—

---

[2] Modern philosophy, which affects to admit of nothing but what it can explain, hath nevertheless very unadvisedly admitted of that obscure faculty, called instinct, which appears to direct animals to the purposes of their being, without any acquisition of knowledge. Instinct, according to one of our greatest philosophers, is a habit destitute of reflection, but acquired by reflecting. Thus from the manner in which he explains its progress, we are led to conclude that children reflect more than grown persons; a paradox singular enough to require some examination. Without entering, however,

she is man's truest and safest guide. Whoever puts himself under the conduct of this guide pursues the direct path of nature, and need not fear to be misled. This point is very important, (pursued my benefactor, perceiving I was going to interrupt him), permit me to detain you a little longer in order to clear it up.

All the morality of our actions lies in the judgments we ourselves form of them. If virtue be any thing real, it ought to be the same in our hearts as in our actions; and one of the first rewards of virtue is to be conscious of our putting it in practice. If moral goodness be agreeable to our nature, a man cannot be sound of mind or perfectly constituted, unless he be good. On the contrary, if it be not so and man is naturally wicked, he cannot become good without a corruption of his nature; goodness being contrary to his constitution. Formed for the destruction of his fellow-creatures, as the wolf is to devour its prey, an humane and compassionate man would be as depraved an animal as a meek and lamb-like wolf, while virtue only would leave behind it the stings of remorse.

Let us examine ourselves, my young friend, all partiality apart, and see which way our inclinations tend. Which is most agreeable to us, to contemplate the happiness or the miseries of others? Which is the most pleasing for us to do, and leaves the most agreeable reflection after it, an act of benevolence or of cruelty? For whom are we the most deeply interested at our theatres? Do you take a pleasure in acts of villainy? or do you shed tears at seeing the authors of

---

into the discussion of it at present, I would only ask what name I am to give to that eagerness which my dog shows to pursue a mole, for instance, which he does not eat when he has caught it;—to that patience with which he stands watching for them whole hours, and to that expertness with which he makes them a prey the moment they reach the surface of the earth; and that in order only to kill them, without ever having been trained to mole hunting, or having been taught that moles were beneath the spot? I would ask further, as more important, why the first time I threaten the same dog, he throws himself down with his back to the ground and his feet raised in a suppliant attitude, the most proper of all others to excite my compassion; an attitude in which he would not long remain if I were so obdurate as to beat him lying in such a posture? Is it possible that a young puppy can have already acquired moral ideas? Can he have any notion of clemency and generosity? What experience can encourage him to hope he shall appease me, by giving himself up to my mercy? Almost all dogs do nearly the same thing in the same circumstances, nor do I advance any thing here of which every one may not convince himself. Let the philosophers, who reject so disdainfully the term instinct, explain this fact merely by the operation of our senses, and the knowledge thereby acquired; let them explain it, I say, in a manner satisfactory to any person of common sense, and I have no more to say in favor of instinct.

them brought to condign punishment? It has been said that every thing is indifferent to us in which we are not interested: the contrary, however, is certain; as the soothing endearments of friendship and humanity console us under affliction; and even in our pleasures we should be too solitary, too miserable, if we had nobody to partake them with us. If there be nothing moral in the heart of man, whence arise those transports of admiration and esteem we entertain for heroic actions and great minds? What has this virtuous enthusiasm to do with our private interest? Wherefore do I rather wish to be an expiring Cato, than a triumphant Cæsar? Deprive our hearts of a natural affection for the sublime and beautiful, and you deprive us of all the pleasures of life. The man whose meaner passions have stifled in his narrow soul such delightful sentiments,—he who by dint of concentrating all his affections within himself hath arrived at the pitch of having no regard for any one else, is no longer capable of such transports. His frozen heart never flutters with joy; no sympathetic tenderness brings the tears into his eyes; he is incapable of enjoyment. The unhappy wretch is void of sensibility: he is already dead.

But how great soever may be the number of the wicked, there are but few of these cadaverous souls—but few persons so insensible, if their own interest be set aside, to what is just and good. Iniquity never pleases unless we profit by it: in every other case it is natural for us to desire the protection of the innocent. When we see, for instance, in the street or on the highway, an act of injustice or violence committed, an emotion of resentment and indignation immediately rises in the heart, and incites us to stand up in defence of the injured and oppressed: but a more powerful consideration restrains us, and the laws deprive individuals of the right of taking upon themselves to avenge insulted innocence. On the contrary, if we happen to be witnesses to any act of compassion or generosity, with what admiration, with what esteem are we instantly inspired! Who is there that doth not, on such an occasion, say to himself, would that I had done as much! It is certainly of very little consequence to us whether a man was good or bad who lived two thousand years ago; and yet we are as much affected in this respect by the relations we meet with in ancient history, as if the transactions recorded had happened in our own times. Of what hurt is the wickedness of a Catiline to me? Am I afraid of falling a victim to his villainy? Wherefore, then, do I look upon him with the same horror as if he were my contemporary? We hate the wicked not only because their vices are hurtful, but also because they are wicked. We are not only desirous of happiness for ourselves, but also for the happiness of others; and when that happiness doth not diminish ours, it necessarily increases it. In a word, we cannot help sympathizing with the unfortunate, and always suffer when we are witnesses to their misery. The most perverse natures cannot be altogether divested of this sympathy; though it frequently causes them to act in contradiction to themselves. The robber who strips the passenger on the highway, will frequently distribute his spoils to cover the nakedness of the poor, and the most barbarous assassin may be induced humanely to support a man falling into a fit.

We hear daily of the cries of remorse for secret crimes, and frequently see remarkable instances of conscience bringing these crimes to light. Alas! who is a total stranger to this importunate voice? We speak of it from experience, and would be glad to silence so disagreeable a monitor. But let us be obedient to nature. We know that her government is very mild and gracious, and that nothing is more agreeable than the testimony of a good conscience, which ever follows our observance of her laws. The wicked man is afraid of, and shuns himself. He turns his eyes on every side in search of objects to amuse him. Without an opportunity for satire and raillery he would be always sad. His only pleasure lies in mockery and insult. On the contrary, the serenity of the just is internal. His smiles are not those of malignity but of joy. The source of them is found in himself, and he is as cheerful when alone as in the midst of an assembly. He derives not contentment from those who approach him, but communicates it to them.

Cast your eye over the several nations of the world: take a retrospective view of their various histories. Amidst all the many inhuman and absurd forms of worship,—amidst all that prodigious diversity of manners and characters,—you will everywhere find the same ideas of justice and honesty,—the same notions of good and evil. Ancient paganism adopted the most abominable deities, which it would have punished on earth as infamous criminals—deities that presented no other picture of supreme happiness than the commission of crimes, and the gratification of their passions. But vice, armed even with sacred authority, descended in vain on earth. Moral instinct influenced the human heart to rebel against it. Even in celebrating the debaucheries of Jupiter, the world admired and respected the continence of *Xenocrates*. The chaste Lucretia adored the impudent Venus. The intrepid Roman sacrificed to Fear. They invoked the god Jupiter who disabled his father Saturn, and yet they died without murmuring by the hand of their own. The most contemptible divinities were adored by the noblest of men. The voice of nature, more powerful than that of the gods, made itself respected on earth, and seemed to have banished vice to heaven.

There evidently exists, then, in the soul of man, an innate principle of justice and goodness, by which, in spite of our own maxims, we approve or condemn the actions of ourselves and others. To this principle it is that I give the appellation of conscience.

At this word, however, I hear the clamor of our pretentious philosophers, who all exclaim about the mistakes of infancy and the prejudices of education. There is nothing, they say, in the human mind but what is instilled by experience; nor can we judge of anything but from the ideas we have acquired. Nay, they go farther, and venture to reject the universal sense of all nations; seeking some obscure example known only to themselves, to controvert this striking uniformity in the judgment of mankind: as if all the natural inclinations of the race were annihilated by the depravation of one people, and as if when monsters appeared the species itself were extinct. But what end did it serve to the skeptical Montaigne, to take so much trouble to discover in an obscure corner of the world a custom opposed to the common notions of justice? What end did it answer for him to place that confidence in the most suspicious travellers which he refused to the most celebrated writers? Should a few whimsical and uncertain customs, founded on local motives unknown to us, invalidate a general induction drawn from the united concurrence of all nations, contradicting each other in every other point and agreeing only in this? You pique yourself, Montaigne, on being ingenuous and sincere. Give us a proof, if it be in the power of a philosopher, of your frankness and veracity. Tell me if there be any country upon earth in which it is deemed a crime to be sincere, compassionate, beneficent, and generous,—in which an honest man is despicable, and knavery held in esteem?

It is pretended that every one contributes to the public good for his own interest; but whence comes it that the virtuous man contributes to it to his prejudice? Can a man lay down his life for his own interest? It is certain all our actions are influenced by a view to our own good; but unless we take moral good into the account, none but the actions of the wicked can ever be explained by motives of private interest. We imagine, indeed, that no more will be attempted; as that would be too abominable a kind of philosophy, by which we should be puzzled to account for virtuous actions; or could extricate ourselves out of the difficulty only by attributing them to base designs and sinister views;—by debasing a Socrates and calumniating a Regulus. If ever such doctrines should take rise among us, the voice of nature as well as of reason would check their growth and leave not even one of those who inculcate them the simple excuse of being sincere.

It is not my design here to enter into such metaphysical investigations, as surpass both your capacity and mine, and which in fact are useless. I have already told you I would not talk philosophy to you, but only assist you to consult your own heart. Were all the philosophers in Europe to prove me in the wrong, yet if you were sensible I was in the right, I should desire nothing more.

To this end you need only to distinguish between our acquired ideas and our natural sentiments, for we are sensible before we are intelligent; and as we do not learn to desire our own good and to avoid what is evil, but possess this desire immediately from nature, so the love of virtue and hatred of vice are as natural as the love of ourselves. The operations of conscience are not intellectual, but sentimental; for though all our ideas are acquired from without, the sentiments which estimate them arise from within; and it is by these alone that we know the agreement or disagreement which exists between us and those things which we ought to seek or shun.

To exist is, with us, to be sensible. Our sensibility is incontestably prior to our intelligence, and we were possessed of sentiment before we formed ideas. Whatever was the cause of our being, it hath provided for our preservation in furnishing us with sentiments agreeable to our constitution, nor can it possibly be denied that these at least are innate.

These sentiments are, in the individual,—the love of himself, aversion to pain, dread of death, and the desire of happiness. But if, as it cannot be doubted, man is by nature a social being, or at least formed to become such, his sociability absolutely requires that he should be furnished with other innate sentiments relative to his species; for to consider only the physical wants of men, it would certainly be better for them to be dispersed than assembled.

Now it is from this moral system,—formed by its duplicate relation to himself and his fellow creatures, that the impulse of conscience arises. To know what is virtuous is not to love virtue. Man has no innate knowledge of virtue; but no sooner is it made known to him by reason, than conscience induces him to love and admire it. This is the innate sentiment I mean.

I cannot think it impossible therefore to explain, from natural consequences, the immediate principle of conscience independent of reason; and, though it were impossible, it is not at all necessary; since those who reject this principle (admitted, however, and acknowledged in general by all mankind) do not prove its non-existence, but content themselves with affirming it only. When we affirm that it doth exist, we stand at least on as good a footing as they, and have besides that internal testimony for us,—the voice of conscience deposing in behalf of itself. If the first glimmerings of the understanding dazzle our sight, and make objects appear at first obscure or confused, let us wait but a little while till our eyes recover themselves and gather strength, and we shall presently see, by the light of reason, those same objects to be such as nature first presented them: or rather, let us be more simple and less vain; let us confine ourselves to the sentiments we first discovered, as it is to these our well-regulated studies must always recur.

O Conscience! Conscience! thou divine instinct, thou certain guide of an ignorant and confined, though intelligent and free being;—thou infallible judge of good and evil, who makest man to resemble the Deity. In thee consist the excellence of our nature and the morality of our actions. Without thee I perceive nothing in myself that should elevate me above the brutes, except the melancholy privilege of wandering from error to error by the assistance of an ill-regulated understanding and undisciplined reason.

Thank heaven, we are delivered from this formidable apparatus of philosophy. We can be men without being sages. Without spending our days in the study of morality, we possess at a cheaper rate a more certain guide through the immense and perplexing labyrinth of human opinions. It is not enough, however, that such a guide exists,—it is necessary to know and follow her. If she speaks to all hearts, it may be said, how comes it that so few understand her? It is, alas! because she speaks to us in the language of nature, which every thing conspires to make us forget. Conscience is timid,—she loves peace and retirement. The world and its noises terrify her. The prejudices she has been compelled to give rise to are her most cruel enemies, before whom she is silent or avoids their presence. Their louder voice entirely overpowers her's, and prevents her being heard. Fanaticism counterfeits her nature, and dictates in her name the greatest of crimes. Thus, from being often rejected, she at length ceases to speak to us, and answers not our inquiries after being long held in contempt; it also costs us as much trouble to recall, as it did at first to banish her from our bosoms.

How often in my researches have I found myself fatigued from my indifference! How often hath uneasiness and disgust, poisoning my meditations, rendered them insupportable! My insensible heart was susceptible only of a luke-warm and languishing zeal for truth. I said to myself, why should I take the trouble to seek after things that have no existence? Virtue is a mere chimera, nor is there any thing desirable but the pleasures of sense. When a man hath once lost a taste for the pleasures of the mind, how difficult to recover it! How much more difficult it also is for one to acquire such a taste who never possessed it! If there be in the world a man so miserable as never in his life to have done an action the remembrance of which must make him satisfied with himself, that man must be ever incapable of such a taste; and for want of being able to perceive that goodness which is conformable to his nature, must of necessity remain wicked as he is, and eternally miserable. But can you believe there exists on earth a human creature so depraved as never to have given up his heart to the inclination of doing good? The temptation is so natural and seductive, that it is impossible always to resist it, and the remembrance of the pleasure it hath once given us is sufficient to commend it to us ever afterwards. Unhappily, this propensity is at first difficult to gratify. There are a thousand reasons for our not complying with the dictates of our hearts. The false prudence of the world confines our good inclinations to ourselves, and all our fortitude is necessary to cast off the yoke. To take a pleasure in virtue is the reward of having been virtuous, nor is this prize to be obtained till it be merited.

Nothing is more amiable than virtue, but we must possess it, in order to find it such. When we court at first its embraces, it assumes, like Proteus in the fable, a thousand terrifying forms, and displays at last its own only to those who are tenacious of their hold.

Wavering perpetually between my natural sentiments, tending to the general good of mankind, and my reason, confining everything to my own, I should have remained all my life in this continual dilemma, doing evil yet loving good, in constant contradiction with myself, had not new knowledge enlightened my heart; had not the truth, which determined my opinions, directed also my conduct and rendered me consistent.

It is in vain to attempt the establishment of virtue on the foundation of reason alone. What solidity is there in such a base? Virtue, it is said, is the love of order; but can or ought this love of order to prevail over that of my own happiness? Let there be given me a clear and sufficient reason for my giving it the preference. This pretended principle is at the bottom only a mere play upon words; as I may as well say that vice also consists in the love of order taken in a different sense. There is some kind of moral order in every thing that has sentiment and intelligence. The difference is that a good being regulates himself according to the general order of things, and a wicked being regulates things agreeably to his own private interest: the latter makes himself the centre of all things, and the former measures his radius and disposes himself in the circumference. Here he is arranged, with respect to the common centre, as God, and with respect to all concentric circles, as his fellow creatures.

If there be no God, the wicked man only reasons right—the good man is a mere fool.

O my child! may you be one day sensible how great a weight we are relieved from, when, having exhausted the vanity of human opinions and tasted of the bitterness of the passions, we see ourselves at last so near the path to wisdom,—the reward of our good actions, and the source of that happiness we had despaired of obtaining.

Every duty prescribed by the laws of nature, though almost effaced from my heart by the injustice of mankind, again revived at the name of that eternal justice which imposed them, and was a witness to my discharge of them. I see in myself nothing more than the work and instrument of a superior being desirous of and doing good, desirous also of effecting mine by the concurrence of my will to his own, and by my making a right use of my liberty. I acquiesce in the regularity and order he hath established, being certain of enjoying one day or other that order in myself, and of finding my happiness therein: for what can afford greater felicity than to perceive one's self making a part of a system where every thing is constructed aright? On every occasion of pain or sorrow I support them with patience, reflecting that they are transitory and that they are derived from a body that is detached from myself. If I do a good action in secret, I know that it is nevertheless seen, and make the consideration of another life the rule of my conduct in this. If I am ever dealt with unjustly I say to myself, that just Being, who governs all things, knows how to indemnify me. My corporeal necessities and the miseries inseparable from this mortal life, make the apprehensions of death more supportable. I have hence so many chains the less to break when I am obliged to quit this mortal scene.

For what reason my soul is thus subjected to the organs of sense and chained to a body which lays it under so much restraint, I know not, nor presume to enter into the decrees of the Almighty. But I may, without temerity, form a modest conjecture or two on this subject. I reflect that, if the mind of man had remained perfectly free and pure, what merit could he have pretended to in admiring and pursuing that order which he saw already established, and which he would lie under no temptation to disturb? It is true he would have been happy, but he could not have attained that most sublime degree of felicity—the glory of virtue and the testimony of a good conscience. We should in such a case have been no better than the angels, and without doubt a virtuous man will be one day much superior. Being united on earth to a mortal body by ties not less powerful than incomprehensible, the preservation of that body becomes the great concern of the soul, and makes its present apparent interests contrary to the general order of things, which it is nevertheless capable of seeing and admiring. It is in this situation that by making a good use of his liberty, it becomes at once his merit and his reward; and that he prepares for himself eternal happiness in combating his earthly passions, and preserving the primitive purity of his will.

But even supposing that in our present state of depravity our primitive propensities were such as they ought to be, yet if all our vices are derived from ourselves, why do we complain that we are subjected by them? Why do we impute to the Creator those evils which we bring on ourselves, and those enemies we arm against our own happiness? Ah! let us not spoil the man of nature, and he will always be virtuous without constraint, and happy without remorse. The criminals who pretend they are compelled to sin, are as false as they are wicked. Is it possible for them not to see that the weakness they complain of is their own work; that their first depravation was owing to their own will; that by their willfully yielding at first to temptations, they at length find them irresistible? It is true they now cannot help their being weak and wicked; but it is their fault that they at first became so. How easily might men preserve the mastery over themselves and their passions even during life if, before their vicious habits are acquired, when the faculties of the mind are just beginning to be displayed, they should employ themselves on those objects which it is necessary for them to know in order to judge of those which are unknown; if they were sincerely desirous of acquiring knowledge, not with a view of making a parade in the eyes of others, but in order to render themselves wise, good, and happy in the practice of their natural duties! This study appears difficult because we only apply to it after being already corrupted by vice, and made slaves to our passions. We place our judgment and esteem on objects before we arrive at the knowledge of good and evil, and then referring every thing to that false standard, we hold nothing in its due estimation.

The heart, at a certain age, while it is yet free, eager, restless, and anxious for happiness, is ever seeking it with an impatient and uncertain curiosity; when deceived by the senses, it fixes on the shadow of it, and imagines it to be found where it doth not exist. This illusion hath prevailed too long with me. I discovered it, alas! too late; and have not been able entirely to remove it: no, it will remain with me as long as this mortal body, which gave rise to it. It may prove as seductive, however, as it will, it can no longer deceive me. I know it for what it is, and even while I am misled by it, despise it. So far from esteeming it an object of happiness, I see it is an obstacle to it. Hence I long for that moment when I shall shake off this incumbrance of body and be myself, without inconsistency or participation with matter, and shall depend on myself only to be happy. In the mean time I make myself happy in this life, because I hold the evils of life as trifling in themselves; as almost foreign to my being; and conceive at the same time that all the real good which may thence be deduced depends on myself.

To anticipate as much as possible that desirable state of happiness, power and liberty, I exercise my mind in sublime contemplations. I meditate on the order of the universe, not indeed with a view to explain it by vain systems, but to admire it perpetually and to adore its all-wise Creator, whose features I trace in his workmanship. With him I am thus enabled to converse, and to exert my faculties in the contemplation of his divine essence. I am affected by his beneficence, I praise him for his mercies, but never so far forget myself as to pray. For what should I ask of him? That he should for my sake pervert the order of things, and work miracles in my favor? Shall I, who ought to love and admire above all things that order which is established by his wisdom and maintained by his providence, desire that such order should be broken for me? No! such a rash petition would rather merit punishment than acceptance. Nor can I pray to him for the power of acting aright: for why should I petition for what he hath already given me? Hath he not given me conscience to love virtue, reason to know what it is, and liberty to make it my choice? If I do evil, I have no excuse: I do it because I will. To desire him to change my will, is to require that of him which he requires of me. This would be to desire him to do my work, while I receive the reward. Not to be content with my situation in the order of things, is to desire to be no longer a man;—it is to wish that things were otherwise constituted than they are,—to wish for evil and disorder. No, thou source of justice and truth, God! merciful and just! placing my confidence in thee, the chief desire of my heart is that thy will be done. By rendering my will conformable to thine, I act as thou dost,—I acquiesce in thy goodness, and conceive myself already a partaker of that supreme felicity which is its reward.

The only thing which, under a just diffidence of myself, I request of him, or rather expect from his justice, is that he will correct my errors when I go astray. To be sincere, however, I do not think my judgment infallible: such of my opinions as seem to be the best founded may, nevertheless, be false; for what man hath not his opinions, and how few are there who agree in every thing? It is to no purpose that the illusions by which I am misled arise from myself; it is he alone who can dissipate them. I have done every thing in my power to arrive at truth; but its source is elevated beyond my reach. If my faculties fail me, in what am I culpable? Is it not then necessary for truth to stoop to my capacity?

The good priest spoke with much earnestness: he was deeply moved, and I was also greatly affected. I imagined myself attending to the divine Orpheus singing his hymns and teaching mankind the worship of the gods. A number of objections, however, to what he had said, suggested themselves; though I did not urge one, as they were less solid than perplexing; and though not convinced, I was nevertheless persuaded he was in the right. In proportion as he spoke to me from the conviction of his own conscience, mine confirmed me in the truth of what he said.

The sentiments you have been delivering, said I to him, appear newer to me in what you confess yourself ignorant of, than in what you profess to believe. I see in the latter a resemblance to that theism or natural religion which Christians affect to confound with atheism and impiety, though in fact diametrically opposite. In the present condition of my mind I find it difficult to adopt precisely your opinions and to be as wise as you. To be at least as sincere, however, I will consult my own conscience on these points. It is that internal sentiment which, according to your example, ought to be my monitor; and you have yourself taught me that, after having imposed silence on it for a long time, it is not to be awakened again in a moment. I will treasure up your discourse in my heart and meditate thereon. If I am as much convinced as you are, after I have duly weighed it, I will trust you as my apostle and will be your proselyte till death. Go on, however, to instruct me. You have only informed me of half I ought to know. Give me your thoughts on revelation, the scriptures, and those mysterious doctrines concerning which I have been in the dark from my infancy, without being able to conceive or believe them, and yet not knowing how to either admit or reject them.

Yes, my dear child, (said he), I will proceed to tell you what I think further. I meant not to open my heart to you by halves: but the desire which you express to be informed in these particulars, was necessary to authorize me to be totally without reserve. I have hitherto told you nothing but what I thought might be useful to you, and in the truth of which I am most firmly persuaded. The examination which I am now going to make is very different; presenting to my view nothing but perplexity, mysteriousness, and obscurity. I enter on it, therefore, with distrust and uncertainty. I almost tremble to determine about any thing, and shall, therefore, rather inform you of my doubts than of my opinions. Were your own sentiments more confirmed, I should hesitate to acquaint you with mine; but in your present skeptical situation, you will be a gainer by thinking as I do. Let my discourse, however, carry with it no greater authority than that of reason, for I frankly confess myself ignorant as to whether I am in the right or wrong. It is difficult, indeed, in all discussions, not to assume sometimes an affirmative tone; but remember that all my affirmations, in treating these matters, are only so many rational doubts. I leave you to investigate the truth of them. On my part, I can only promise to be sincere.

You will find that my exposition treats of nothing more than natural religion. It is very strange that we should stand in need of any other! By what means can I find out such necessity? In what respect can I be culpable for serving God agreeably to the dictates of the understanding he hath given me, and the sentiments he hath implanted in my heart? What purity of morals, what system of faith useful to man, or honorable to his Creator, can I deduce from any positive doctrines, that I cannot deduce equally as well from a good use of my natural faculties? Let any one show me what can be added, either for the glory of God, the good of society, or my own advantage, to the obligations we are laid under by nature. Let him show me what virtue can be produced from any new worship, which is not also the consequence of mine. The most sublime ideas of the Deity are inculcated by reason alone. Take a view of the works of nature, listen to the voice within, and then tell me what God hath omitted to say to your sight, your conscience, your understanding? Where are the men who can tell us more of him than he thus tells us of himself? Their revelations only debase the Deity, in ascribing to him human passions. So far from giving us enlightened notions of the Supreme Being, their particular tenets, in my opinion, give us the most obscure and confused ideas. To the inconceivable mysteries by which the Deity is hid from our view, they add the most absurd contradictions. They serve to make man proud, persecuting, and cruel. Instead of establishing peace on earth, they bring fire and sword. I ask myself what good purpose all this contention serves, without being able to resolve the question. Artificial religion presents to my view only the wickedness and miseries of mankind.

I am told, indeed, that revelation is necessary to teach mankind the manner in which God should be served. As a proof of this, they bring the diversity of whimsical modes of worship which prevail in the world; and that without remarking that this very diversity arises from the practice of adopting revelations. Ever since men have taken it into their heads to make the Deity speak, every people make him speak in their own way, and say what they like best. Had they listened only to what the Deity hath said to their hearts, there would have been but one religion on earth.

It is necessary that the worship of God should be uniform; I would have it so: but is this a point so very important that the whole apparatus of divine power was necessary to establish it? Let us not confound the ceremonials of religion with religion itself. The worship of God demands that of the heart; and this, when it is sincere, is ever uniform. Men must entertain very ridiculous notions of the Deity, indeed, if they imagine he can interest himself in the gown or cassock of a priest,—in the order of words he pronounces, or in the gestures and genuflexions he makes at the altar. Alas! my friend, where is the use of kneeling? Stand as upright as you may, you will always be near enough to the earth. God requires to be worshipped in spirit and in truth. This is a duty incumbent on men of all religions and countries. With regard to exterior forms, if their uniformity be expedient for the sake of peace and good order, it is merely an affair of government; the administration of which surely requires not the aid of revelation.

I did not set out at first with these reflections. Hurried on by the prejudices of education, and by that dangerous self-conceit which ever elates mankind above their sphere, as I could not raise my feeble conceptions to the Supreme Being, I foolishly endeavored to debase him to my ideas. Thus I connected relations infinitely distant from each other, comparing the incomprehensible nature of the deity with my own. I require still further a more immediate communication with the Divinity, and more particular instructions concerning his will. Not content with reducing God to a similitude with man, I wanted to be further distinguished by his favor, and to enjoy supernatural lights. I longed for an exclusive and peculiar privilege of adoration, and that God should have revealed to me what he had kept secret from others, or that others should not understand his revelations so well as myself.

Looking on the point at which I had arrived,—at that whence all believers set out in order to reach an enlightened mode of worship, I regarded natural religion only as the elements of all religion. I took a survey of that variety of sects which are scattered over the face of the earth, and who mutually accuse each other of falsehood and error. I asked which of them was right?

Every one of them in their turn answered *theirs*. I and my partisans only think truly; all the rest are mistaken.

But, how do you know that your sect is in the right?

Because God hath declared so.

And who tells you that God hath so declared!

My spiritual guide, who knows it well. My pastor tells me to believe so and so, and accordingly I believe it; he assures me that every one who says to the contrary speaks falsely; and, therefore, I listen to nobody who controverts his doctrine.[3]

How, thought I, is not the truth every where the same? Is it possible that what is true with one person can be false with another? If the method taken by him who is in the right, and by him who is in the wrong, be the same, what merit or demerit hath the one more than the other? Their choice is the effect of accident, and to impute it to them is unjust:—it is to reward or punish them for being born in this or that country. To say that the Deity can judge us in this manner is the highest impeachment of his justice.

Now, either all religions are good and agreeable to God, or if there be one which he hath dictated to man, and will punish him for rejecting, he hath certainly distinguished it by manifest signs and tokens as the only true one. These signs are common to all times and places, and are equally obvious to all mankind—to the young and old, the learned and ignorant, to Europeans, Indians, Africans, and Savages.

If there be only one religion in the world that can prevent our suffering eternal damnation, and there be on any part of the earth a single mortal who is sincere, and is not convinced by its evidence, the God of that religion must be the most iniquitous and cruel of tyrants. Would we seek the truth therefore in sincerity, we must lay no stress on the place or circumstance of our birth, nor on the authority of fathers and teachers; but appeal to the dictates of reason and conscience concerning every thing that is taught us in our youth. It is to no purpose to bid me subject my reason to the truth of things of which it is incapable of judging. The man who

[3] All of them, says a certain wise and good priest, pretend that they derive their doctrines not from men, nor from any created being, but from God. But to say truth, without flattery or disguise, there is nothing in such pretentions: however they may talk, they owe their religion to human means. Witness the manner in which they first adopt it. The nation, country and place where they are born and bred determine it. Are we not circumcised or baptized,—made Jews, Turks, or Christians before we are men? Our religion is not the effect of choice; witness our lives and manners so little accordant to it; witness how we act contrary to the tenets of it on the most trifling occasions.—*Charron, on Wisdom.*

would impose on me a falsehood, may bid me do the same. It is necessary, therefore, I should employ my reason even to know when it ought to submit.

All the theology I am myself capable of acquiring, by taking a prospect of the universe and by the proper use of my faculties, is confined to what I have here laid down. To know more, we must have recourse to extraordinary means. These means cannot depend on the authority of men: for as all men are of the same species as myself, whatever another can by natural means come to the knowledge of, I can do the same; and another man is as liable to be deceived as I am. When I believe, therefore, what he says, it is not because he says it, but because he proves it. The testimony of mankind, therefore, is really that of my reason, and adds nothing to the natural means God hath given me for the discovery of the truth.

What then can even the apostle of truth have to tell me, of which I am not still to judge?

But God himself hath spoken; listen to the voice of revelation.

That, indeed, is another thing. God hath spoken! This is saying a great deal: but to whom hath he spoken?

He hath spoken to man.

How comes it then that I heard nothing of it?

He hath appointed others to teach you his word.

I understand you. There are certain men who are to tell me what God hath said. I had much rather have heard it from himself. This, had he so pleased, he could easily have done; and I should then have run no risk of deception. Will it be said I am secured from that by his manifesting the mission of his messengers by miracles? Where are those miracles to be seen? Are they related only in books? Pray, who wrote those books?

Men.

Who were witnesses to these miracles?

Men.

Always human testimony! It is always men who tell me what other men have told them. What a number of those are constantly between me and the Deity! We are always reduced to the necessity of examining, comparing, and verifying such evidence. O! that

God had deigned to have saved me all this anxiety! Should I in that case have served him with a less willing heart?

Consider, my friend, in what a terrible discussion I am already engaged; what immense erudition I stand in need of to recur back to the earliest antiquity—to examine, to weigh, to confront prophecies, revelations, facts, with all the monuments of faith that have made their appearance in all the countries of the world; to ascertain their time, place, authors, and occasions. How great the critical sagacity which is requisite to enable me to distinguish between pieces that are suppositious, and those which are authentic; to compare objections with their replies, translations with their originals; to judge of the impartiality of witnesses, of their good sense, of their capacity; to know if nothing be suppressed or added to their testimony, if nothing be changed, transposed, or falsified; to obviate the contradictions that remain, to judge what weight we ought to ascribe to the silence of our opponents in regard to facts alleged against them; to discover whether such allegations were known to them; whether they did not disdain them too much to make any reply; whether books were common enough for ours to reach them; or, if we were honest enough to let them have free circulation among us, and to leave their strongest objections in full force.

Again, supposing that all these monuments of faith are acknowledged to be incontestable, we must proceed to examine the proofs of the mission of their authors. It would be necessary for us to be perfectly acquainted with the laws of chance and the doctrine of probabilities, to judge correctly what prediction could not be accomplished without a miracle; to know the genius of the original languages, in order to distinguish what is predictive in these languages and what is only figurative. It would be requisite for us to know what facts are agreeable to the established order of nature, and what are not so; to be able to say how far an artful man may not fascinate the eyes of the simple, and even astonish the most enlightened spectators; to know of what kind a miracle should be, and the authenticity it ought to bear, not only to claim our belief, but to make it criminal to doubt it; to compare the proofs of false and true miracles, and discover the certain means of distinguishing them; and after all to tell why the Deity should choose, in order to confirm the truth of his word, to make use of means which in their turn require confirmation, as if he took delight in playing upon the credulity of mankind, and had purposely avoided the direct means to persuade them.

Suppose that the divine majesty hath really condescended to make man the organ of promulgating its sacred will, is it reasonable, is it just, to require all mankind to obey the voice of such a minister, without his making himself known to be such? Where is the equity or propriety in furnishing him, for universal credentials, with only a few particular tokens displayed before a handful of obscure persons, and of which all the rest of mankind know nothing but by hearsay? In every country in the world, if we should believe all the prodigies to be true which the common people and the ignorant affirm to have seen, every sect would be in the right; there would be more miraculous events than natural ones; and the greatest miracle of all would be to find that no miracles had happened where fanaticism had been persecuted.

The Supreme Being is best displayed by the fixed and unalterable order of nature. If there should happen many exceptions to such general laws, I should no longer know what to think; and for my part, I must confess I believe too much in God to believe in so many miracles so little worthy of him.

What if a man should come and harangue us in the following manner:

"I come, ye mortals, to announce to you the will of the most high. Acknowledge in my voice that of him who sent me. I command the sun to move backwards, the stars to change their places, the mountains to disappear, the waves to remain fixed on high, and the earth to wear a different aspect."

Who would not, at the sight of such miracles, immediately attribute them to the author of nature?

Nature is not obedient to impostors. Their miracles are always performed in the highways, in the fields, or in apartments where they are displayed before a small number of spectators, previously disposed to believe every thing they see.

Who is there that will venture to decide how many eye-witnesses are necessary to render a miracle worthy of credit? If the miracles, intended to prove the truth of your doctrine, stand themselves in need of proof, of what use are they? Their performance might as well have been omitted.

The most important examination after all remains to be made into the truth of the doctrines delivered; for as those who say that God is pleased to work these miracles, pretend that the devil sometimes imitates them, we are no nearer a decision than before, though such miracles should be ever so well attested. As the magicians of Pharaoh worked the same miracles, even in the presence of Moses, as he himself performed by the express command of God, why might not they, in his absence, from the same proofs, pretend to the same authority? Thus after proving the truth of the doctrine by the miracle, you are reduced to the necessity of proving the truth of the miracle by that of the doctrine,[4] lest the works of the devil should be mistaken for those of the Lord. What think you of this alternative?

The doctrines coming from God, ought to bear the sacred characters of the divinity; and should not only clear up those confused ideas which unenlightened reason excites in the mind, but should also furnish us with a system of religion and morals agreeable to those attributes by which only we form a conception of his essence. If then they teach us any absurdities, if they inspire us with the sentiments of aversion for our fellow-creatures and fear for ourselves; if they describe the Deity as a vindictive, partial, jealous and angry being; as a God of war and of battles, always ready to thunder and destroy; always threatening slaughter and revenge, and even boasting

[4] This is expressly mentioned in many places in Scripture, particularly in Deuteronomy, chap. xiii., where it is said that, if a prophet, teaching the worship of strange Gods, confirm his discourse by signs and wonders, and what he foretells really comes to pass, so far from paying any regard to his mission, the people should stone him to death. When the Pagans, therefore, put the Apostles to death, for preaching up to them the worship of a strange God, proving their divine mission by prophesies and miracles, I see not what could be objected to them, which they might not with equal justice have retorted upon us. Now, what is to be done in this case? There is but one step to be taken, to recur to reason and leave miracles to themselves: better indeed had it been never to have had recourse to them, nor to have perplexed good sense with such a number of subtle distinctions. What! do I talk of subtle distinctions in Christianity? If there are such, our Saviour was in the wrong surely to promise the Kingdom of Heaven to the weak and simple! How came he to begin his fine discourse on the Mount, with blessing the poor in spirit, if it requires so much ingenuity to comprehend and believe his doctrines? When you prove that I ought to subject my reason to his dictates, it is very well; but to prove that, you must render them intelligible to my understanding; you must adapt your arguments to the poverty of my genius, or I shall not acknowledge you to be the true disciple of your Master, or think that it is his doctrines which you would inculcate.

of punishing the innocent, my heart cannot be incited to love so terrible a Deity, and I shall take care how I give up my natural religion to embrace such doctrines.

I should say to the advocates and professors of such a religion:

"Your God is not mine! A Being who began his dispensations with partiality, selecting one people and proscribing the rest of mankind, is not the common father of the human race; a Being who destines to eternal punishment the greater part of his creatures, is not that good and merciful God who is pointed out by my reason."

With regard to articles of faith, my reason tells me they should be clear, perspicuous, and evident. If natural religion be insufficient, it is owing to the obscurity in which it necessarily leaves those sublime truths it professes to teach. It is the business of revelation to exhibit them to the mind in a more clear and sensible manner; to adapt them to our understanding, and to enable us to conceive, in order that we may be capable of believing them. True faith is assured and confirmed by the understanding. The best of all religions is undoubtedly the clearest. That which is clouded with mysteries and contradictions, the worship that is to be taught me by preaching, teaches me by that very circumstance to distrust it. The God whom I adore is not a God of darkness; he hath not given me an understanding to forbid me the use of it. To bid me give up my reason, is to insult the author of it. The minister of truth doth not tyrannize over my understanding,—he enlightens it.

We have set aside all human authority, and without it, I cannot see how one man can convince another by preaching to him an unreasonable doctrine. Let us suppose two persons engaged in a dispute on this head, and see how they will express themselves in the language generally made use of on such occasions.

Dogmatist.—Your reason tells you that the whole is greater than a part, but I tell you from God, that a part is greater than the whole.

Rationalist.—And who are you, that dare to tell me God contradicts himself? In whom shall I rather believe; in him who instructs me in the knowledge of eternal truths by means of reason, or in you who in his name would impose on me the greatest absurdities?

Dogmatist.—In me, for my instructions are more positive, and I will prove to you incontestably that he hath sent me.

Rationalist.—How! will you prove that God hath sent you to depose against himself? What sort of proofs can you bring to convince me it is more certain that God speaks by your mouth, than by the understanding he hath given me?

Dogmatist.—The understanding he hath given you! Ridiculous and contemptible man! You talk as if you were the first infidel who was ever misled by an understanding depraved by sin.

Rationalist.—Nor may you, man of God! be the first knave whose impudence hath been the only proof he could give of his divine mission.

Dogmatist.—How! can Philosophers be thus abusive?

Rationalist.—Sometimes, when Saints set them the example.

Dogmatist.—Oh! but I am authorized to abuse you. I speak on the part of God Almighty.

Rationalist.—It would not be improper, however, to produce your credentials before you assume your privileges.

Dogmatist.—My credentials are sufficiently authenticated. Both heaven and earth are witnesses in my favor. Attend, I pray you, to my arguments.

Rationalist.—Arguments! why, you surely do not pretend to any! To tell me that my reason is fallacious, is to refute whatever it may say in your favor. Whoever refuses to abide by the dictates of reason, ought to be able to convince without making use of it. For, supposing that in the course of your arguments you should convince me, how shall I know whether it be not through the fallacy of reason depraved by sin, that I acquiesce in what you affirm? Besides, what proof, what demonstration, can you ever employ more evident than the axiom which destroys it? It is fully as credible that a just syllogism should be false, as that a part is greater than the whole.

Dogmatist.—What a difference! My proofs admit of no reply; they are of a supernatural kind.

Rationalist.—Supernatural! What is the meaning of that term? I do not understand it.

Dogmatist.—Contraventions of the order of nature; prophecies, miracles, and prodigies of every kind.

Rationalist.—Prodigies and miracles! I have never seen any of these things.

Dogmatist.—No matter; others have seen them for you. We can bring clouds of witnesses—the testimony of whole nations—

Rationalist.—The testimony of whole nations! Is that a proof of the supernatural kind?

Dogmatist.—No! But when it is unanimous it is incontestable.

Rationalist.—There is nothing more incontestable than the dictates of reason, nor can the testimony of all mankind prove the truth of an absurdity. Let us see some of your supernatural truths then, as the attestation of men is not so.

Dogmatist.—Infidel wretch! It is plain that the grace of God doth not speak to thy understanding.

Rationalist.—Whose fault is that? Not mine; for, according to you, it is necessary to be enlightened by grace to know how to ask for it. Begin then, and speak to me in its stead.

Dogmatist.—Is not this what I am doing? But you will not hear. What do you say to prophecies?

Rationalist.—As to prophecies; I say, in the first place, I have heard as few of them as I have seen miracles; and in the second, I say that no prophecy bears any weight with me.

Dogmatist.—Thou disciple of Satan! And why have prophecies no weight with you?

Rationalist.—Because, to give them such weight requires three things, the concurrence of which is impossible. These are, that I should in the first place be a witness to the delivery of the prophecy; next, that I should be witness also to the event; lastly, that it should be clearly demonstrated to me that such event could not have occurred by accident. For, though a prophecy were as precise, clear, and determinate as an axiom of geometry, yet as the perspicuity of a prediction made at random does not render the accomplishment of it impossible, that accomplishment when it happens proves nothing in fact concerning the fore-knowledge of him who predicted it. You see, therefore, to what your pretended supernatural proofs, your miracles, and your prophecies reduce us:—to the folly of believing them all on the credit of others, and of submitting the authority of God speaking to our reason, to that of man. If those eternal truths, of which my understanding forms the strongest conception, can possibly be false, I can have no hope of ever arriving at certitude; and so far from being capable of being assured that you speak to me from God, I cannot even be assured of his existence.

You see, my child, how many difficulties must be removed before our disputants can agree; nor are these all. Among so many different religions, each of which proscribes and excludes the other, one only can be true; if, indeed, there be such a one among them all. Now, to discover which this is, it is not enough to examine that one; it is necessary to examine them all, as we should not, on any occasion whatever, condemn without a hearing. It is necessary to compare objections with proofs, and to know what each objects to in the others, as well as what the others have to say in their defence. The more clearly any sentiment or opinion appears demonstrated, the more narrowly it behooves us to inquire, what are the reasons which prevent its opponents from subscribing to it?

We must be very simple indeed, to think that an attention to the theologists of our own party sufficient to instruct us in what our adversaries have to offer. Where shall we find divines, of any persuasion, perfectly candid and honest? Do they not all begin to weaken the arguments of their opponents before they proceed to refute them? Each is the oracle of his party, and makes a great figure among his own partisans, with such proofs as would expose him to ridicule among those of a different persuasion.

Are you desirous of gaining information from books? What a fund of erudition will not this require! How many languages must you learn! How many libraries must you turn over! And who is to direct you in the choice of the books? There are hardly to be found in any one country the best books on the contrary side of the question, and still less is it to be expected that we should find books on all sides. The writings of the adverse and absent party, were they found also, would be very easily refuted. The absent are always in the wrong; and the most weak and insufficient arguments laid down with a confident assurance, easily efface the most sensible and valid, when exposed with contempt. Add to all this, that nothing is more fallacious than books, nor exhibit less faithfully the sentiments of their writers. The judgment which you formed, for instance, of the Roman Catholic religion, from the treatise of Bossuet, was very different from that which you acquired by residing among us. You have seen that the doctrines we maintain in our controversies with the Protestants, are not those which are taught the common people; and that Bossuet's book by no means resembles the instructions delivered from the pulpit.

To form a proper judgment of any religion, we are not to deduce its tenets from the books of its professors; we must go and learn it among the people. Each sect have their peculiar traditions,—their customs, prejudices, and modes of acceptation, which constitute the peculiar mode of their faith. This should all be taken into consideration when we form a judgment of their religion.

How many considerable nations are there who print no books of their own, and read none of ours? How are they to judge of our opinions, or we of theirs? We laugh at them—they despise us; and though our travellers have turned them into ridicule, they need only to travel among us, to ridicule us in their turn. In what country are there not to be found men of sense and sincerity, friends of humanity, who require only to know truth, in order to embrace it? And yet every one imagines that truth is confined to his own particular system, and thinks that the religion of all other nations in the world is absurd. These foreign modes, therefore, cannot be in reality so very absurd as they appear, or the apparent reasonableness of ours is less real.

We have three principal religions in Europe. One admits only of one revelation, another of two, and the third of three. Each holds the other in detestation, anathematizes its possessors, accuses them of ignorance, obstinacy, and falsehood. What impartial person will presume to decide between them, without having first examined their proofs and heard their reasons? That which admits only of one revelation is the most ancient and seems the least disputable; that which admits of three is the most modern and seems to be the most consistent; that which admits of two and rejects the third, may possibly be the best, but it hath certainly every prepossession against it—its inconsistency stares one full in the face.

In all these three revelations, the sacred books are written in languages unknown to the people who believe in them. The Jews no longer understand Hebrew; the Christians neither Greek nor Hebrew; the Turks and Persians understand no Arabic, and even the modern Arabs themselves speak not the language of Mahomet. Is not this a very simple manner of instructing mankind, by talking to them always in a language which they do not comprehend? But these books, it will be said, are translated; a most unsatisfactory answer, indeed! Who can assure me that they are translated faithfully, or that it is even possible they should be so? Who can give me a sufficient reason why God, when he hath a mind to speak to mankind, should stand in need of an interpreter?

I can never conceive that what every man is indispensably obliged to know can be shut up in these books; or that he who is incapacitated to understand them, or the persons who explain them, will be punished for involuntary ignorance. But we are always plaguing ourselves with books. What a frenzy! Because Europe is full of books, the Europeans conceive them to be indispensable, without reflecting that three-fourths of the world know nothing at all about them. Are not all books written by men? How greatly, therefore, must man have stood in need of them, to instruct him in his duty, and by what means did he come to the knowledge of such duties, before books were written? Either he must have acquired such knowledge of himself, or it must have been totally dispensed with.

We, Roman Catholics, make a great noise about the authority of the church: but what do we gain by it, if it requires as many proofs to establish this authority as other sects also require to establish their doctrines? The church determines that the church has a right to determine. Is not this a special proof of its authority? And yet, depart from this, and we enter into endless discussions.

Do you know many Christians who have taken the pains to examine carefully into what the Jews have alleged against us? If there are a few who know something of them, it is from what they have met with in the writings of Christians: a very strange manner indeed of instructing themselves in the arguments of their opponents! But what can be done? If any one should dare to publish among us such books as openly espouse the cause of Judaism, we should punish the author, the editor, and the bookseller.[5] This policy is very convenient, and very sure to make us always in the right. We can refute at pleasure those who are afraid to speak.

Those among us, also, who have an opportunity to converse with the Jews, have but little advantage. These unhappy people know that they are at our mercy. The tyranny we exercise over them, renders them justly timid and reserved. They know how far cruelty and injustice are compatible with Christian charity. What, therefore, can they venture to say to us, without running the risk of incurring the charge of blasphemy? Avarice inspires us with zeal, and they are too rich not to be ever in the wrong. The most sensible and learned among them are the most circumspect and reserved. We make a convert, perhaps, of some wretched hireling, to calumniate his sect; we set a parcel of pitiful brokers disputing, who give up the point merely to gratify us; but while we triumph over the ignorance or meanness of such wretched opponents, the learned among them smile in contemptuous silence at our folly. But do you think that in places where they might write and speak securely, we should have so much the advantage of them? Among the doctors of the Sorbonne, it is as clear as daylight, that the predictions concerning the Messiah relate to Jesus Christ. Among the Rabbins at Amsterdam, it is just as evident that they have no relation whatever to him. I shall never believe that I have acquired a sufficient acquaintance with the arguments of the Jews, till they compose a free and independent State, and have their schools and universities, where they may talk and dispute with freedom and impunity. Till then we can never really know what arguments they have to offer.

At Constantinople, the Turks make known their reasons, and we dare not publish ours. There it is our turn to submit. If the Turks require us to pay to Mahomet, in whom we do not believe, the

[5] Among a thousand known instances, the following stands in no need of comment: the Catholic divines of the sixteenth century having condemned all the Jewish books without exception to be burnt, a learned and illustrious theologue, who was consulted on that occasion, had very nearly involved himself in ruin by being simply of the opinion that such of them might be preserved as did not relate to Christianity, or treated of matters foreign to religion.

same respect which we require the Jews to pay to Jesus Christ, in whom they believe as little, can the Turks be in the wrong and we in the right? On what principle of equity can we resolve that question in our own favor?

Two-thirds of mankind are neither Jews, Christians, nor Mahometans. How many millions of men, therefore, must there be who never heard of Moses, of Jesus Christ, or of Mahomet? Will this be denied? Will it be said that our missionaries are dispersed over the face of the whole earth? This, indeed, is easily affirmed; but are there any of them in the interior parts of Africa, where no European hath ever yet penetrated? Do they travel through the inland parts of Tartary, or follow on horseback the wandering hordes, whom no stranger ever approaches, and who, so far from having heard of the Pope, hardly know any thing of their own Grand Lama? Do our missionaries traverse the immense continent of America, where there are whole nations still ignorant that the people of another world have set foot on theirs? Are there any missionaries in Japan, from whence their ill-behavior hath banished them forever, and where the fame of their predecessors is transmitted to succeeding generations as that of artful knaves, who, under cover of a religious zeal, wanted to make themselves gradually masters of the empire? Do they penetrate into the harems of the Asiatic princes, to preach the gospel to millions of wretched slaves? What will become of these secluded women for want of a missionary to preach to them this gospel? Must every one of them go to hell for being a recluse?

But were it true that the gospel is preached in every part of the earth, the difficulty is not removed. On the eve preceding the arrival of the first missionary in any country, some one person of that country expired without hearing the glad tidings. Now what must we do with this one person? If there be but a single individual in the whole universe, to whom the gospel of Christ is not made known, the objection which presents itself on account of this one person, is as cogent as if it included a fourth part of the human race.

Again, supposing that the ministers of the gospel are actually present and preaching in those distant nations, how can they reasonably hope to be believed on their own word, and expect that their hearers will not scrupulously require a confirmation of what is taught? Might not any one of them very reasonably say to these preachers:

"You tell me of a God who was born and put to death nearly two thousand years ago, in another portion of the world, and in I know not what obscure town; assuring me that all those who do not believe in this mysterious tale are damned.

"These are things too strange to be readily credited on the sole authority of a man who is himself a perfect stranger.

"Why hath your God brought those events to pass, of which he requires me to be instructed, at so great a distance? Is it a crime to be ignorant of what passes at the antipodes? Is it possible for me to divine that there existed in the other hemisphere a people called Jews, and a city called Jerusalem? I might as well be required to know what happens in the moon.

"You are come, you say, to inform me; but why did you not come soon enough to inform my father, or why do you damn that innocent man because he knew nothing of the matter? Must he be eternally punished for your delay; he who was so just, so benevolent, and so desirous of knowing the truth?

"Be honest, and suppose yourself in my place. Do you think that I can believe, upon your testimony alone, all these incredible things you tell me, or that I can reconcile so much injustice with the character of that just God, whom you pretend to make known?

"Let me first, I pray you, go and see this distant country where so many miracles have happened that are totally unknown here. Let me go and be well informed why the inhabitants of that Jerusalem you speak of presumed to treat God like a thief or a murderer.

"They did not, you will say, acknowledge his divinity. How then can I, who never have heard of him but from you?

"You add, that they were punished, dispersed, and led into captivity;—not one of them ever approaching their former city.

"Assuredly, they deserved all this: but its present inhabitants,— what say they of the unbelief and *Deicide* of their predecessors? Do they not deny it, and acknowledge the divinity of the sacred personage just as little as did its ancient inhabitants?

"What! in the same city in which your God was put to death,

neither the ancient nor present inhabitants acknowledge his divinity! And yet you would have me believe it, who was born nearly two thousand years after the event, and two thousand leagues distant from the place!

"Do you not see that, before I can give credit to this book, which you call sacred and of which I comprehend nothing, I ought to be informed from others as to when and by whom it was written; how it hath been preserved and transmitted to you; what is said of it in the country where it originated; and what are the reasons of those who reject it, although they know as well as you every thing of which you have informed me? You must perceive, therefore, the necessity I am under of going first to Europe, then to Asia, and lastly into Palestine to investigate and examine this subject for myself, and that I must be an absolute idiot to even listen to you before I have completed this investigation."

Such a discourse as this appears to me not only very reasonable, but I affirm that every sensible man ought under such circumstances to speak in the same manner, and to send a missionary about his business, who should be in haste to instruct and baptize him before he had sufficiently verified the proofs of his mission.

Now, I maintain that there is no revelation against which the same objections might not be made, and that with even greater force than against Christianity. Hence it follows that if there be in the world but one true religion, and if every one is obliged to adopt it under pain of damnation, it is necessary to spend our lives in the study of all religions,—to visit the countries where they have been established, and examine and compare them with each other. No man is exempted from the principal duty of his species, and no one hath a right to confide in the judgment of another. The artisan who lives only by his industry, the husbandman who cannot read, the timid and delicate virgin, the feeble valetudinarian, all must, without exception, study, meditate, dispute, and travel the world over in search of truth. There would no longer be any settled inhabitants in a country, the face of the earth being covered with pilgrims going from place to place, at great trouble and expense, to verify, examine, and compare the several different systems and modes of worship to be met with in different countries.

We must in such a case bid adieu to the arts and sciences, to trade, and to all the civil occupations of life. Every other study must give place to that of religion; while the man who should enjoy the greatest share of health and strength, and make the best use of his time and reason for the longest term of years allotted to human life, would, in his extreme old age, be still perplexed and undecided; and it would be indeed wonderful if, after all his researches, he should be able to learn before his death what religion he ought to have believed and practiced during his life.

Do you endeavor to mitigate the severity of this method, and place as little confidence as possible in the authority of your fellow men? In so doing, however, you place in them the greatest confidence: for if the son of a Christian does right in adopting, without a scrupulous and impartial examination, the religion of his father, how can the son of a Turk do wrong in adopting in the same manner the religion of Mahomet?

I defy all the persecutors in the world to answer this question in a manner satisfactory to any person of common sense. Nay, some of them, when hard pressed by such arguments, will sooner admit that God is unjust, and visits the sins of the fathers upon the children, than give up their cruel and persecuting principles. Others, indeed, strive to elude the force of these reasons by civilly sending an angel to instruct those who, under absolute ignorance, lived, nevertheless, good moral lives. A very pretty device, truly, is that of the angel! Not contented with subjecting us to this angelic hierarchy, they would reduce even the Deity himself to the necessity of employing it.

See, my son, to what absurdities we are led by pride, and the spirit of persecution,—by being puffed up with our own vanity, and conceiving that we possess a greater share of reason than the rest of mankind.

I call to witness that God of peace whom I adore, and whom I would make known to you, that my researches have been always sincere; but seeing that they were and always must be unsuccessful, and that I was launched out into a boundless ocean of perplexity, I returned the way I came, and confined my creed within the limits of my first notions. I could never believe that God required me, under pain of eternal damnation, to be so very learned; and, there-fore, I shut up all my books.

The book of nature lies open to every eye. It is from this sublime and wonderful volume that I learn to serve and adore its Divine Author. No person is excusable for neglecting to read this book, as it is written in an universal language, intelligible to all mankind.

Had I been born on a desert island, or had never seen a human creature beside myself; had I never been informed of what had formerly happened in a certain corner of the world; I might yet have learned, by the exercise and cultivation of my reason, and by the proper use of those faculties God hath given me, to know and to love him. I might hence have learned to love and admire his power and goodness, and to have properly discharged my duty here on earth. What can the knowledge of the learned teach me more?

With regard to revelation: could I reason better or were I better informed, I might be made sensible perhaps of its truth and of its utility to those who are so happy as to believe it. But if there are some proofs in its favor which I cannot invalidate, there appear also to me many objections against it which I cannot resolve. There are so many reasons both for and against its authority that, not knowing what to conclude, I neither admit nor reject it. I reject only the obligation of submitting to it, because this pretended obligation is incompatible with the justice of God, and that, so far from its removing the obstacles to salvation, it raises those which are in-surmountable by the greater part of mankind. Except in this article, therefore, I remain respectfully in doubt concerning the Scriptures. I have not the presumption to think myself infallible. More able persons may possibly determine in cases that to me appear undeterminable. I reason for myself, not for them. I neither censure nor imitate them. Their judgment may possibly be better than mine, but am I to blame that it is not mine?

I will confess to you further, that the majesty of the Scriptures strikes me with admiration, as the purity of the gospel hath its influence on my heart. Peruse the works of our philosophers, en-riched with all their pomp of diction: how mean, how contemptible are they, compared with the Scriptures! Is it possible that a book at once so simple and sublime should be merely the work of man? Is it possible that the sacred personage, whose history it contains, should be himself a mere man? Do we find that he assumed the tone of an enthusiast or ambitious sectary? What purity, what sweetness in his manners! What an affecting gracefulness in his delivery! What sublimity in his maxims! What profound wisdom in his discourses! What presence of mind, what subtilty, what truth in his replies! How great the command over his passions! Where is the man, where the philosopher who could so live and so die, without weakness and without ostentation? When Plato described an imaginary good man[6] loaded with all the shame of guilt, yet meriting the highest reward of virtue, he describes exactly the character of Jesus. The resemblance was so striking that all the fathers perceived it. What prepossession, what blindness must it be to compare the son of Sophroniscus to the son of Mary? What an infinite disproportion is there between them! Socrates, dying without pain or ignominy, easily supported his character to the last; and if his death, however easy, had not crowned his life, it might have been doubted whether Socrates, with all his wisdom, was any thing more than a vain sophist. He invented, it is said, the theory of morals. Others, however, had already put them in practice; he had only to say what they had done, and reduce their examples to precepts. Aristides had been just, before Socrates defined justice. Leonidas gave up his life for his country before Socrates declared patriotism to be a duty. The Spartans were a sober people before Socrates recommended sobriety. Before he had even defined virtue, Greece abounded in virtuous men. But where could Jesus learn, among his compatriots, that pure and sublime morality of which he only hath given us both precept and example?[7] The greatest wisdom was made known amidst the most bigoted fanaticism; and the simplicity of the most heroic virtues did honor to the vilest people on the earth. The death of Socrates, peaceably philosophizing with his friends, appears the most agreeable form that could be desired;—that of Jesus, expiring in the midst of agonizing pains, abused, insulted, cursed by a whole nation, is the most horrible that could be feared. Socrates, in receiving the cup of poison, blessed indeed the weeping executioner who admin-

[6] De Rep. dial. 1.

[7] See in his discourse on the Mount the parallel he makes between the morality of Moses and his own. Matthew v. 21, &c.

istered it; but Jesus, in the midst of excruciating tortures, prayed for his merciless tormentors. Yes, if the life and death of Socrates are those of a sage, the life and death of Jesus are those of a God.

Shall we suppose the evangelic history a mere fiction? Indeed, my friend, it bears not the marks of fiction. On the contrary, the history of Socrates, which nobody presumes to doubt, is not so well attested as that of Jesus Christ. Such a supposition, in fact, only shifts the difficulty without removing it. It is more inconceivable that a number of persons should agree to write such a history than that one only should furnish the subject of it. The Jewish authors were incapable of the diction, and were strangers to the morality contained in the gospel,—the marks of whose truth are so striking and inimitable, that the inventor would be a more astonishing character than the hero. And yet, with all this, the same gospel abounds with incredible relations, with circumstances repugnant to reason, and which it is impossible for a man of sense either to conceive of or to admit. What is to be done amidst all these contradictions? Be modest and circumspect. Regard in silence what cannot be either disproved or comprehended, and humble thyself before the Supreme Being who alone knoweth the truth.

Such is the involuntary skepticism in which I remain. This skepticism, however, is not painful to me, because it extends not to any essential point of practice; and as my mind is firmly settled regarding the principles of my duty, I serve God in the sincerity of my heart. In the mean time, I seek not to know any thing more than what relates to my moral conduct; and as to those dogmas which have no influence over the behavior, and about which so many persons give themselves so much trouble, I am not at all solicitous. I look upon the various particular religions as so many salutary institutions, prescribing in different countries an uniform manner of public worship; and which may all have their respective reasons, peculiar to the climate, government, or laws of the people adopting them, or some other motive which renders the one preferable to the other according to the circumstance of time and place. I believe all that are established to be good when God is served in sincerity of heart. This service is all that is essential. He rejects not the homage of the sincere, under whatsoever form they present it. Being called to the service of the church, I comply, therefore, with a scrupulous exactness, to all the forms it prescribes in my duty, and should reproach myself for the least wilful neglect of them. After having lain under a long prohibition I obtained, through the interest of M. de Mellerade, a permission to re-assume the functions of the priesthood, to procure me a livelihood. I had been accustomed formerly to say mass with all that levity and carelessness with which we perform the most serious and important offices after having very often repeated them. Since I entertained my new principles, however, I celebrate it with greater veneration:—penetrated by reflecting on the majesty of the Supreme Being, and the insufficiency of the human mind that is so little able to form conceptions relative to its author, I consider that I offer up the prayers of a people under a prescribed form of worship, and therefore carefully observe all its rites. I recite carefully; and strive not to omit the least word or ceremony. Before going to communicate, I first recollect myself, in order to do it with all those dispositions that the church and the importance of the sacrament require. I endeavor on this occasion to silence the voice of reason before the Supreme Intelligence. I say to myself: who art thou, to presume to set bounds to omnipotence? I reverently pronounce the sacramental words, and annex to them all the faith that depends on me. Whatever, therefore, be the truth with regard to that inconceivable mystery, I am not fearful of being charged at the day of judgment with profaning it in my heart.

Honored with the ministerial office, though of the lowest rank, I will never do or say any thing that may make me unworthy to fulfill its sacred functions. I will always inculcate virtue, exhort my auditors to pursue it, and as far as it is in my power, set them an example. It does not depend on me to make their religion amiable, nor to confine the articles of their faith to what is necessary for all to believe: but God forbid that I should ever preach up the cruel tenets of persecution,—that I should even induce them to hate their neighbors, or to consign others to damnation.[8] Were I, indeed,

---

[8] The duty of adopting and respecting the religion of our country does not extend to such tenets as are contrary to moral virtue; such as that of persecution. It is this horrible dogma which arms mankind inhumanly against each other, and renders them destructive to the human race. The distinction between political and theological toleration is puerile and ridiculous, as they are inseparable, so that one cannot be admitted without the other.

in a superior station, this reserve might incur censure; but I am too insignificant to have much to fear, and I can never fall lower than I am. But whatever may happen, I shall never blaspheme Divine Justice, nor lie against the Spirit of Truth.

I have long been ambitious of the honor of being a pastor. I am indeed still ambitious, though I have no longer any hopes of it. There is no character in the world, my good friend, which appears to me so desirable as that of a pastor. A good pastor is a minister of goodness, as a good magistrate is a minister of justice. A pastor can have no temptation to evil; and though he may not always have it in his power to do good himself, he is really doing his duty when soliciting it of others, and very often obtains it when he learns to make himself truly worthy of respect.

O that I enjoyed but some little benefice among the poor people in our mountains! How happy should I then feel! for I cannot but think that I should make my parishioners happy! I should never, indeed, make them rich, but I should cheerfully partake of their poverty. I would raise them above meanness and contempt,—more insupportable than indigence itself. I would induce them to love concord, and to cherish that equality which often banishes poverty, and always renders it more supportable. When they should see that I was no richer than themselves, and yet lived content, they would learn to console themselves under their lot, and to live contented also.

In the instructions I should give them, I should be less directed by the sense of the church than by that of the gospel; whose tenets are more simple, and whose morals are more sublime;—that teaches few religious forms and many deeds of charity.

Before I should teach them their duty, I should always endeavor to practice it myself, in order to let them see that I really thought as I spoke.

Had I any Protestants in my neighborhood, or in my parish, I would make no distinction between them and my own flock, in every thing that regarded acts of Christian charity. I would endeavor to make them all love and regard each other as brethren—tolerating all religions, and peacefully enjoying their own.

Thus, my young friend, have I given you with my own lips a recital of my creed, such as the Supreme Being reads it in my heart. You are the first person to whom I have made this *Profession of Faith;* and you are the only one, probably, to whom I shall ever make it. * * * *

If I were more positive in myself, I should have assumed a more positive and dogmatic air; but I am a man ignorant and subject to error. I have opened to you my heart without reserve. What I have thought certain, I have given you as such. My doubts I have declared as doubts; my opinions as opinions; and I have honestly given you my reasons for both. What can I do more? It remains now for you to judge. Be sincere with yourself. Whether men love or hate, admire or despise you, is of but little moment. Speak only what is true, do only what is right; for, after all, the object of greatest importance is to faithfully discharge our duty. Adopt only those of my sentiments which you believe are true, and reject all the others; and whatever religion you may ultimately embrace, remember that its real duties are independent of human institutions—that no religion upon earth can dispense with the sacred obligations of morality—that an upright heart is the temple of the Divinity—and that, in every country and in every sect, to love God above all things, and thy neighbor as thyself, is the substance and summary of the law—the end and aim of religious duty.

OF MAN,
BEING THE FIRST PART OF LEVIATHAN

BY

THOMAS HOBBES

INTRODUCTORY NOTE

THOMAS HOBBES was born at Westport, now part of Malmesbury, in Wiltshire, England, April 5, 1588. His father was a clergyman of the Church of England, and he was educated at Magdalen Hall, Oxford, whence he graduated in 1608. From this time till 1640 he was, with a short break, a member of the household of the Earls of Devonshire, acting as tutor and secretary, and traveling on several occasions on the Continent as companion to the second and later to the third Earl. He made the acquaintance of many of the leading philosophers and scientists of the Continent, including Descartes, Gassendi, and Galileo. He is also reported to have acted for a time as amanuensis to Bacon.

On the meeting of the Long Parliament, Hobbes fled to Paris, afraid of what might happen to him on account of opinions expressed in certain philosophical treatises which had been circulated in manuscript. While abroad he published his "De Cive," containing the political theories later embodied in his "Leviathan." In 1646 he was appointed mathematical tutor to the future king, Charles II; but after the publication of the "Leviathan" in 1651, he was excluded from the court, and returned to England.

The rest of Hobbes's life was spent largely in controversy, in which— especially in mathematical matters—he had by no means always the best of the argument. He lived in fear of prosecution for heresy, but was saved by the protection of the king. He died December 4, 1679.

Hobbes's writings produced much commotion in his own day, but his opponents were more conspicuous than his disciples. Yet he exerted a notable influence on such thinkers as Spinoza, Leibniz, Diderot, and Rousseau; and the utilitarian movement led to a revival of interest in his philosophy in the nineteenth century. He was a fearless if one-sided thinker, and he presented his views in a style of great vigor and clearness. "A great partizan by nature," says his most recent critic, "Hobbes became by the sheer force of his fierce, concentrated intellect a master builder in philosophy. . . . He hated error, and therefore, to confute it, he shouldered his way into the very sanctuary of truth."

INTRODUCTION

NATURE, the art whereby God hath made and governs the world, is by the 'art,' of man, as in many other things, so in this also imitated, that it can make an artificial animal. For seeing life is but a motion of limbs, the beginning whereof is in some principal part within; why may we not say, that all 'automata' (engines that move themselves by springs and wheels as doth a watch) have an artificial life? For what is the 'heart' but a 'spring'; and the 'nerves' but so many 'strings'; and the 'joints' but so many 'wheels,' giving motion to the whole body, such as was intended by the artificer? 'Art' goes yet further, imitating that rational and most excellent work of nature, 'man.' For by art is created that great 'Leviathan' called a 'Commonwealth' or 'State,' in Latin *civitas,* which is but an artificial man, though of greater stature and strength than the natural, for whose protection and defence it was intended; and in which the 'sovereignty' is an artificial 'soul,' as giving life and motion to the whole body; the 'magistrates' and other 'officers' of judicature and execution, artificial 'joints'; 'reward' and 'punishment,' by which fastened to the seat of the sovereignty every joint and member is moved to perform his duty, are the 'nerves,' that do the same in the body natural; the 'wealth' and 'riches' of all the particular members are the 'strength'; *salus populi,* the 'people's safety,' its 'business'; 'counsellors,' by whom all things needful for it to know are suggested unto it, are the 'memory'; 'equity' and 'laws,' an artificial 'reason' and 'will'; 'concord,' 'health'; 'sedition,' 'sickness'; and 'civil war,' 'death.' Lastly, the 'pacts' and 'covenants,' by which the parts of this body politic were at first made, set together, and united, resemble that 'fiat,' or the 'let us make man,' pronounced by God in the creation.

To describe the nature of this artificial man, I will consider:

First, the 'matter' thereof, and the 'artificer,' both which is 'man.'

Secondly, 'how,' and by what 'covenants' it is made; what are the 'rights' and just 'power' or 'authority' of a 'sovereign,' and what it is that 'preserveth' or 'dissolveth' it.

Thirdly, what is a 'Christian commonwealth.'

Lastly, what is the 'kingdom of darkness.'

Concerning the first, there is a saying much usurped of late that 'wisdom' is acquired, not by reading of 'books' but of 'men.' Consequently whereunto, those persons that for the most part can give no other proof of being wise take great delight to show what they think they have read in men, by uncharitable censures of one another behind their backs. But there is another saying not of late understood, by which they might learn truly to read one another, if they would take the pains; that is, *nosce teipsum,* 'read thyself': which was not meant, as it is now used, to countenance, either the barbarous state of men in power towards their inferiors, or to encourage men of low degree to a saucy behaviour towards their betters; but to teach us that for the similitude of the thoughts and passions of one man to the thoughts and passions of another, whosoever looketh into himself and considereth what he doth, when he does 'think,' 'opine,' 'reason,' 'hope,' 'fear,' etc., and upon what grounds; he shall thereby read and know what are the thoughts and passions of all other men upon the like occasions. I say the similitude of 'passions,' which are the same in all men, 'desire,' 'fear,' 'hope,' etc.; not the similitude of the 'objects' of the passions, which are the things 'desired,' 'feared,' 'hoped,' etc.: for these the constitution individual, and particular education, do so vary, and they are so easy to be kept from our knowledge, that the characters of man's heart, blotted and confounded as they are with dissembling, lying, counterfeiting, and erroneous doctrines, are legible only to Him that searcheth hearts. And though by men's actions we do discover their design sometimes, yet to do it without comparing them with our own, and distinguishing all circumstances, by which the case may come to be altered, is to decipher without a key, and be for the most part deceived, by too much trust or by too much diffidence; as he that reads is himself a good or evil man.

But let one man read another by his actions never so perfectly, it serves him only with his acquaintance, which are but few. He that is to govern a whole nation must read in himself, not this or that particular man, but mankind: which, though it be hard to do, harder than to learn any language or science, yet, when I shall have set down my own reading orderly and perspicuously, the pains left another will be only to consider if he also find not the same in himself. For this kind of doctrine admitteth no other demonstration.

OF MAN,

BEING THE FIRST PART OF LEVIATHAN

CHAPTER I

OF SENSE

CONCERNING the thoughts of man, I will consider them first singly, and afterwards in train, or dependence upon one another. Singly, they are every one a 'representation' or 'appearance' of some quality, or other accident of a body without us, which is commonly called an 'object.' Which object worketh on the eyes, ears, and other parts of a man's body, and, by diversity of working, produceth diversity of appearances.

The original of them all is that which we call 'sense,' for there is no conception in a man's mind which hath not at first, totally or by parts, been begotten upon the organs of sense. The rest are derived from that original.

To know the natural cause of sense is not very necessary to the business now in hand; and I have elsewhere written of the same at large. Nevertheless, to fill each part of my present method I will briefly deliver the same in this place.

The cause of sense is the external body, or object, which presseth the organ proper to each sense, either immediately, as in the taste and touch, or mediately, as in seeing, hearing, and smelling; which pressure, by the mediation of the nerves and other strings and membranes of the body continued inwards to the brain and heart, causeth there a resistance, or counter-pressure, or endeavour of the heart to deliver itself, which endeavour, because 'outward,' seemeth to be some matter without. And this 'seeming' or 'fancy' is that which men call 'sense' and consisteth, as to the eye, in a 'light' or 'colour figured'; to the ear, in a 'sound'; to the nostril, in an 'odour'; to the tongue and palate, in a 'savour'; and to the rest of the body, in 'heat,' 'cold,' 'hardness,' 'softness,' and such other qualities as we discern by 'feeling.' All which qualities, called 'sensible' are in the object that causeth them but so many several motions of the matter, by which it presseth our organs diversely. Neither in us that are pressed are they anything else but divers motions; for motion produceth nothing but motion. But their appearance to us is fancy, the same waking that dreaming. And as pressing, rubbing, or striking the eye, makes us fancy a light, and pressing the ear produceth a din, so do the bodies also we see or hear produce the same by their strong, though unobserved, action. For if those colours and sounds were in the bodies, or objects that cause them, they could not be severed from them, as by glasses, and in echoes by reflection, we see they are, where we know the thing we see is in one place, the appearance in another. And though at some certain distance the real and very object seem invested with the fancy it begets in us, yet still the object is one thing, the image or fancy is another. So that sense in all cases is nothing else but original fancy, caused, as I have said, by the pressure, that is by the motion, of external things upon our eyes, ears, and other organs thereunto ordained.

But the philosophy schools through all the universities of Christendom, grounded upon certain texts of Aristotle, teach another doctrine, and say, for the cause of 'vision,' that the thing seen sendeth forth on every side a 'visible species,' in English, a 'visible show,' 'apparition,' or 'aspect,' or 'a being seen'; the receiving whereof into the eye is 'seeing.' And for the cause of 'hearing,' that the thing heard sendeth forth an 'audible species,' that is an 'audible aspect,' or 'audible being seen,' which entering at the ear maketh 'hearing.' Nay, for the cause of 'understanding' also, they say the thing understood sendeth forth an 'intelligible species,' that is, an 'intelligible being seen,' which, coming into the understanding, makes us understand. I say not this as disproving the use of universities; but, because I am to speak hereafter of their office in a commonwealth, I must let you see on all occasions by the way what things would be amended in them, amongst which the frequency of insignificant speech is one.

CHAPTER II

Of Imagination

THAT when a thing lies still, unless somewhat else stir it, it will lie still for ever, is a truth that no man doubts of. But that when a thing is in motion, it will eternally be in motion, unless somewhat else stay it, though the reason be the same, namely that nothing can change itself, is not so easily assented to. For men measure not only other men but all other things, by themselves; and, because they find themselves subject after motion to pain and lassitude, think everything else grows weary of motion, and seeks repose of its own accord; little considering whether it be not some other motion wherein that desire of rest they find in themselves consisteth. From hence it is that the schools say heavy bodies fall downwards out of an appetite to rest, and to conserve their nature in that place which is most proper for them; ascribing appetite and knowledge of what is good for their conservation, which is more than man has, to things inanimate, absurdly.

When a body is once in motion, it moveth, unless something else hinder it, eternally; and whatsoever hindereth it cannot in an instant, but in time and by degrees, quite extinguish it; and, as we see in the water though the wind cease the waves give not over rolling for a long time after: so also it happeneth in that motion which is made in the internal parts of a man, then, when he sees, dreams, etc. For, after the object is removed, or the eye shut, we still retain an image of the thing seen, though more obscure than when we see it. And this is it the Latins call 'imagination,' from the image made in seeing; and apply the same, though improperly, to all the other senses. But the Greeks call it 'fancy,' which signifies 'appearance,' and is as proper to one sense as to another. 'Imagination,' therefore, is nothing but 'decaying sense,' and is found in men, and many other living creatures, as well sleeping as waking.

The decay of sense in men waking is not the decay of the motion made in sense, but an obscuring of it in such manner as the light of the sun obscureth the light of the stars, which stars do no less exercise their virtue, by which they are visible, in the day than in the night. But because amongst many strokes which our eyes, ears, and other organs, receive from external bodies, the predominant only is sensible; therefore, the light of the sun being predominant, we are not affected with the action of the stars. And any object being removed from our eyes, though the impression it made in us remain, yet other objects more present succeeding and working on us, the imagination of the past is obscured, and made weak, as the voice of a man is in the noise of the day. From whence it followeth that the longer the time is, after the sight or sense of any object, the weaker is the imagination. For the continual change of man's body destroys in time the parts which in sense were moved; so that distance of time, and of place, hath one and the same effect in us. For as at a great distance of place that which we look at appears dim and without distinction of the smaller parts, and as voices grow weak and inarticulate, so also after great distance of time our imagination of the past is weak; and we lose, for example, of cities we have seen many particular streets, and of actions many particular circumstances. This 'decaying sense,' when we would express the thing itself, I mean 'fancy' itself, we call 'imagination,' as I said before; but when we would express the decay, and signify that the sense is fading, old, and past, it is called 'memory.' So that imagination and memory are but one thing, which for divers considerations hath divers names.

'Much memory, or memory of many things, is called experience.' Again, imagination being only of those things which have been formerly perceived by sense, either all at once or by parts at several times, the former, which is the imagining the whole object as it was presented to the sense, is 'simple' imagination, as when one imagineth a man, or horse, which he hath seen before. The other is 'compounded,' as when, from the sight of a man at one time, and of a horse at another, we conceive in our mind a Centaur. So when a man compoundeth the image of his own person with the image of the actions of another man, as when a man images himself a Hercules or an Alexander, which happeneth often to them that are much taken with reading of romances, it is a compound imagination, and properly but a fiction of the mind. There be also other imaginations that rise in men, though waking, from the great impression made in sense; as, from gazing upon the sun, the impression leaves an image of the sun before our eyes a long time after; and, from being long and vehemently attent upon geometrical figures, a man shall in the dark, though awake, have the images of lines and angles before his eyes; which kind of fancy hath no particular name, as being a thing that doth not commonly fall into men's discourse.

The imaginations of them that sleep are those we call 'dreams.' And these also, as also all other imaginations, have been before, either totally or by parcels, in the sense. And, because in sense, the brain and nerves, which are the necessary organs of sense, are so benumbed in sleep as not easily to be moved by the action of external objects, there can happen in sleep no imagination, and therefore no dream, but what proceeds from the agitation of the inward parts of man's body; which inward parts, for the connection they have with the brain and other organs, when they be distempered, do keep the same in motion; whereby the imaginations there formerly made, appear as if a man were waking; saving that the organs of sense being now benumbed, so as there is no new object which can master and obscure them with a more vigorous impression, a dream must needs be more clear in this silence of sense than our waking thoughts. And hence it cometh to pass that it is a hard matter, and by many thought impossible, to distinguish exactly between sense and dreaming. For my part, when I consider that in dreams I do not often nor constantly think of the same persons, places, objects, and actions, that I do waking, nor remember so long a train of coherent thoughts, dreaming, as at other times, and because waking I often observe the absurdity of dreams, but never dream of the absurdities of my waking thoughts, I am well satisfied, that, being awake, I know I dream not, though when I dream I think myself awake.

And, seeing dreams are caused by the distemper of some of the inward parts of the body, divers distempers must needs cause different dreams. And hence it is that lying cold breedeth dreams of fear, and raiseth the thought and image of some fearful object, the motion from the brain to the inner parts and from the inner parts to the brain being reciprocal; and that, as anger causeth heat in some parts of the body when we are awake, so when we sleep the overheating of the same parts causeth anger, and raiseth up in the brain the imagination of an enemy. In the same manner, as natural kindness, when we are awake, causeth desire, and desire makes heat in certain other parts of the body; so also too much heat in those parts, while we sleep, raiseth in the brain an imagination of some kindness shown. In sum, our dreams are the reverse of our waking imaginations, the motion when we are awake beginning at one end, and when we dream at another.

The most difficult discerning of a man's dream from his waking thoughts is, then, when by some accident we observe not that we have slept: which is easy to happen to a man full of fearful thoughts, and whose conscience is much troubled, and that sleepeth without the circumstances of going to bed or putting off his clothes, as one that noddeth in a chair. For he that taketh pains, and industriously lays himself to sleep, in case any uncouth and exorbitant fancy come unto him, cannot easily think it other than a dream. We read of Marcus Brutus (one that had his life given him by Julius Cæsar, and was also his favorite, and notwithstanding murdered him) how at Philippi, the night before he gave battle to Augustus Cæsar, he saw a fearful apparition, which is commonly related by historians as a vision; but, considering the circumstances, one may easily judge to have been but a short dream. For, sitting in his tent, pensive and troubled with the horror of his rash act, it was not hard for him, slumbering in the cold, to dream of that which most affrighted him; which fear, as by degrees it made him wake, so also it must needs make the apparition by degrees to vanish; and, having no assurance that he slept, he could have no cause to think it a dream or anything but a vision. And this is no very rare accident; for even they that be perfectly awake, if they be timorous and superstitious, possessed with fearful tales, and alone in the dark, are subject to the like fancies, and believe they see spirits and dead men's ghosts walking in churchyards; whereas it is either their fancy only, or else the knavery of such persons as make use of such superstitious fear to pass disguised in the night to places they would not be known to haunt.

From this ignorance of how to distinguish dreams and other strong fancies from vision and sense, did arise the greatest part of the religion of the Gentiles in time past that worshipped satyrs, fawns, nymphs, and the like; and now-a-days the opinion that rude people have of fairies, ghosts, and goblins, and of the power of witches. For as for witches, I think not that their witchcraft is any real power; but yet that they are justly punished for the false belief they have that they can do such mischief, joined with their purpose to do it if they can; their trade being nearer to a new religion than to a craft or science. And for fairies and walking ghosts, the opinion of them has, I think, been on purpose either taught, or not confuted, to keep in credit the use of exorcism, of crosses, of holy water, and other such inventions of ghostly men. Nevertheless there is no doubt but God can make unnatural apparitions; but that He does it so often as men need to fear such things more than they fear the stay or change of the course of nature, which He also can stay and change, is no point of Christian faith. But evil men, under pretext that God can do anything, are so bold as to say anything when it serves their turn, though they think it untrue; it is the part of a wise man to believe them no farther than right reason makes that which they say appear credible. If this superstitious fear of spirits were taken away, and with it prognostics from dreams, false prophecies, and many other things depending thereon, by which crafty ambitious persons abuse the simple people, men would be much more fitted than they are for civil obedience.

And this ought to be the work of the schools; but they rather nourish such doctrine. For, not knowing what imagination or the senses are, what they receive they teach; some saying that imaginations rise of themselves and have no cause; others that they rise most commonly from the will, and that good thoughts are blown (inspired) into a man by God, and evil thoughts by the devil; or that good thoughts are poured (infused) into a man by God, and evil ones by the devil. Some say the senses receive the species of things, and deliver them to the common sense, and the common sense delivers them over to the fancy, and the fancy to the memory, and the memory to the judgment, like handling of things from one to another, with many words making nothing understood.

The imagination that is raised in man, or any other creature indued with the faculty of imagining, by words or other voluntary signs, is that we generally call 'understanding,' and is common to man and beast. For a dog by custom will understand the call or the rating of his master; and so will many other beasts. That understanding which is peculiar to man is the understanding not only his will but his conceptions and thoughts, by the sequel and contexture of the names of things into affirmations, negations, and other forms of speech; and of this kind of understanding I shall speak hereafter.

CHAPTER III

OF THE CONSEQUENCE OR TRAIN OF IMAGINATIONS

BY 'consequence,' or 'train,' of thoughts I understand that succession of one thought to another which is called, to distinguish it from discourse in words, 'mental discourse.'

When a man thinketh on anything whatever, his next thought after is not altogether so casual as it seems to be. Not every thought to every thought succeeds indifferently. But as we have no imagination whereof we have not formerly had sense, in whole or in parts, so we have no transition from one imagination to another whereof we never had the like before in our senses. The reason whereof is this. All fancies are motions within us, relics of those made in the sense, and those motions that immediately succeeded one another in the sense continue also together after sense: in so much as the former coming again to take place, and be predominant, the latter followeth, by coherence of the matter moved, in such manner as water upon a plane table is drawn which way any one part of it is guided by the finger. But because in sense to one and the same thing perceived, sometimes one thing sometimes another, succeedeth, it comes to pass in time that in the imagining of anything there is no certainty what we shall imagine next: only this is certain, it shall be something that succeeded the same before, at one time or another.

This train of thoughts, or mental discourse, is of two sorts. The first is 'unguided,' 'without design,' and inconstant; wherein there is no passionate thought, to govern and direct those that follow, to itself, as the end and scope of some desire or other passion: in which case the thoughts are said to wander, and seem impertinent one to another as in a dream. Such are commonly the thoughts of men that are not only without company but also without care of anything; though even then their thoughts are as busy as at other times, but without harmony; as the sound which a lute out of tune would yield to any man, or in tune to one that could not play. And yet in this wild ranging of the mind a man may oft-times perceive the way of it, and the dependence of one thought upon another. For in a discourse of our present civil war, what could seem more impertinent than to ask, as one did, what was the value of a Roman penny. Yet the coherence to me was manifest enough. For the thought of the war introduced the thought of the delivering up the king to his enemies; the thought of that brought in the thought of the delivering up of Christ; and that again the thought of the thirty pence, which was the price of that treason; and thence easily followed that malicious question; and all this in a moment of time—for thought is quick.

The second is more constant; as being 'regulated' by some desire and design. For the impression made by such things as we desire, or fear, is strong and permanent, or, if it cease for a time, of quick return: so strong it is sometimes as to hinder and break our sleep. From desire ariseth the thought of some means we have seen produce the like of that which we aim at; and from the thought of that, the thought of means to that mean; and so continually till we come to some beginning within our own power. And because the end, by the greatness of the impression, comes often to mind, in case our thoughts begin to wander, they are quickly again reduced into the way: which observed by one of the Seven Wise Men, made him give men this precept, which is now worn out, *Respice finem,* that is to say, in all your actions look often upon what you would have as the thing that directs all your thoughts in the way to attain it.

The train of regulated thoughts is of two kinds; one, when of an effect imagined we seek the causes or means that produce it; and this is common to man and beast. The other is when imagining anything whatsoever we seek all the possible effects that can by it be produced, that is to say, we imagine what we can do with it when we have it. Of which I have not at any time seen any sign but in man only; for this is a curiosity hardly incident to the nature of any living creature that has no other passion but sensual, such as are hunger, thirst, lust, and anger. In sum, the discourse of the mind, when it is governed by design, is nothing but 'seeking,' or the faculty of invention, which the Latins called *sagacitas,* and *solertia;* a hunting out of the causes, of some effect, present or past; or of the effects, of some present or past cause. Sometimes a man seeks what he hath lost; and from that place and time wherein he misses it his mind runs back, from place to place, and time to time, to find where and when he had it, that is to say, to find some certain and limited time and place in which to begin a method of seeking. Again, from thence his thoughts run over the same places and times to find what action or other occasion might make him lose it. This we call 'remembrance,' or calling to mind: the Latins call it *reminiscentia,* as it were a 're-conning' of our former actions.

Sometimes a man knows a place determinate, within the compass whereof he is to seek; and then his thoughts run over all the parts thereof, in the same manner as one would sweep a room to find a jewel, or as a spaniel ranges the field till he find a scent, or as a man should run over the alphabet to start a rhyme.

Sometimes a man desires to know the event of an action; and then he thinketh of some like action past, and the events thereof one after another, supposing like events will follow like actions. As he that foresees what will become of a criminal re-cons what he has seen follow on the like crime before, having this order of thoughts, the crime, the officer, the prison, the judge, and the gallows. Which kind of thoughts is called 'foresight,' and 'prudence,' or 'providence,' and sometimes 'wisdom,' though such conjecture, through the difficulty of observing all circumstances, be very fallacious. But this is certain: by how much one man has more experience of things past than another, by so much also he is more prudent, and his expectations the seldomer fail him. The 'present' only has a being in nature; things 'past' have a being in the memory only, but things 'to come' have no being at all, the 'future' being but a fiction of the mind, applying the sequels of actions past to the actions that are present; which with most certainty is done by him that has most experience, but not with certainty enough. And though it be called prudence, when the event answereth our expectation, yet, in its own nature, it is but presumption. For the foresight of things to come, which is providence, belongs only to him by whose will they are to come. From him only, and supernaturally, proceeds prophecy. The best prophet naturally is the best guesser; and the best guesser he that is most versed and studied in the matters he guesses at, for he hath most 'signs' to guess by.

A 'sign' is the event antecedent of the consequent; and, contrarily, the consequent of the antecedent, when the like consequences have been observed before; and the oftener they have been observed, the less uncertain is the sign. And therefore he that has most experience in any kind of business has most signs whereby to guess at the future time, and consequently is the most prudent; and so much more prudent than he that is new in that kind of business as not to be equalled by any advantage of natural and extemporary wit; though perhaps many young men think the contrary.

Nevertheless it is not prudence that distinguisheth man from beast. There be beasts that at a year old observe more, and pursue that which is for their good more prudently than a child can do at ten.

As prudence is a 'presumption' of the 'future' contracted from the 'experience' of time 'past,' so there is a presumption of things past taken from other things, not future, but past also. For he that hath seen by what courses and degrees a flourishing state hath first come into civil war, and then to ruin, upon the sight of the ruins of any other state will guess the like war and the like courses have been there also. But this conjecture has the same uncertainty almost with the conjecture of the future, both being grounded only upon experience.

There is no other act of man's mind that I can remember naturally planted in him, so as to need no other thing to the exercise of it but to be born a man, and live with the use of his five senses. Those other faculties of which I shall speak by and by, and which seem proper to man only, are acquired and increased by study and industry, and of most men learned by instruction and discipline; and proceed all from the invention of words and speech. For besides sense, and thoughts, and the train of thoughts, the mind of man has no other motion, though by the help of speech and method the same faculties may be improved to such a height as to distinguish men from all other living creatures.

Whatsoever we imagine is 'finite.' Therefore there is no idea or conception of any thing we call 'infinite.' No man can have in his mind an image of infinite magnitude, nor conceive infinite swiftness, infinite time, or infinite force, or infinite power. When we say anything is infinite, we signify only that we are not able to conceive the ends and bounds of the things named; having no conception of the thing, but of our own inability. And therefore the name of God is used, not to make us conceive Him, for He is incomprehensible, and His greatness and power are unconceivable; but that we may honour Him. Also because, whatsoever, as I said before, we conceive, has been perceived first by sense, either all at once or by parts; a man can have no thought representing anything not subject to sense. No man therefore can conceive anything but he must conceive it in some place, and indued with some determinate magnitude, and which may be divided into parts; nor that anything is all in this place and all in another place at the same time; nor that two or more things can be in one and the same place at once: for none of these things ever have or can be incident to sense, but are absurd speeches, taken upon credit, without any signification at all, from deceived philosophers, and deceived or deceiving schoolmen.

CHAPTER IV

Of Speech

THE invention of 'printing,' though ingenious compared with the invention of 'letters,' is no great matter. But who was the first that found the use of letters is not known. He that first brought them into Greece men say was Cadmus, the son of Agenor, king of Phœnicia. A profitable invention for continuing the memory of time past and the conjunction of mankind, dispersed into so many and distant regions of the earth; and withal difficult, as proceeding from a watchful observation of the divers motions of the tongue, palate, lips, and other organs of speech, whereby to make as many differences of characters, to remember them. But the most noble and profitable invention of all other was that of 'speech' consisting of 'names' or 'appellations,' and their connection; whereby men register their thoughts, recall them when they are past, and also declare them one to another for mutual utility and conversation; without which there had been amongst men neither commonwealth, nor society, nor contract, nor peace, no more than amongst lions, bears, and wolves. The first author of 'speech' was God Himself, that instructed Adam how to name such creatures as He presented to his sight; for the Scripture goeth no further in this matter. But this was sufficient to direct him to add more names, as the experience and use of the creatures should give him occasion, and to join them in such manner by degrees as to make himself understood; and so, by succession of time, so much language might be gotten as he had found use for; though not so copious, as an orator or philosopher has need of: for I do not find anything in the Scripture out of which, directly or by consequence, can be gathered that Adam was taught the names of all figures, numbers, measures, colours, sounds, fancies, relations—much less the names of words and speech, as 'general,' 'special,' 'affirmative,' 'negative,' 'interrogative,' 'optative,' 'infinitive,' all which are useful, and, least of all, of 'entity,' 'intentionality,' 'quiddity,' and other insignificant words of the school.

But all this language gotten, and augmented by Adam and his posterity was again lost at the Tower of Babel, when by the hand of God every man was stricken for his rebellion with an oblivion of his former language. And being hereby forced to disperse themselves into several parts of the world, it must needs be that the diversity of tongues that now is proceeded by degrees from them in such manner as need, the mother of all inventions, taught them; and in tract of time grew everywhere more copious.

The general use of speech is to transfer our mental discourse into verbal, or the train of our thoughts into a train of words, and that for two commodities, whereof one is the registering of the consequences of our thoughts, which, being apt to slip out of our memory and put us to a new labour, may again be recalled by such words as they were marked by. So that the first use of names is to serve for 'marks,' or 'notes,' of remembrance. Another is, when many use the same words to signify by their connection and order one to another what they conceive or think of each matter; and also what they desire, fear, or have any other passion for. And for this use they are called 'signs.' Special uses of speech are these:

first, to register what by cogitation we find to be the cause of anything, present or past; and what we find things present or past may produce, or effect; which, in sum, is acquiring of arts. Secondly, to show to others that knowledge which we have attained, which is to counsel and teach one another. Thirdly, to make known to others our wills and purposes, that we may have the mutual help of one another. Fourthly, to please and delight ourselves and others by playing with our words, for pleasure or ornament, innocently.

To these uses there are also four correspondent abuses. First, when men register their thoughts wrong, by the inconstancy of the signification of their words; by which they register for their conceptions that which they never conceived, and so deceive themselves. Secondly, when they use words metaphorically, that is, in other sense than that they are ordained for; and thereby deceive others. Thirdly, when by words, they declare that to be their will which is not. Fourthly, when they use them to grieve one another; for seeing Nature hath armed living creatures, some with teeth, some with horns, and some with hands, to grieve an enemy, it is but an abuse of speech to grieve him with the tongue, unless it be one whom we are obliged to govern; and then it is not to grieve, but to correct and amend.

The manner how speech serveth to the remembrance of the consequence of causes and effects consisteth in the imposing of 'names,' and the 'connection' of them.

Of names, some are 'proper,' and singular to one only thing, as 'Peter,' 'John,' 'this man,' 'this tree'; and some are 'common' to many things, 'man,' 'horse,' 'tree'—every of which, though but one name, is nevertheless the name of divers particular things; in respect of all which together it is called an 'universal,' there being nothing in the world universal but names; for the things named are every one of them individual and singular.

One universal name is imposed on many things, for their similitude in some quality or other accident; and whereas a proper name bringeth to mind one thing only, universals recall any one of those many.

And, of names universal, some are of more, and some of less extent, the larger comprehending the less large; and some again of equal extent, comprehending each other reciprocally. As, for example, the name 'body' is of larger signification than the word 'man,' and comprehendeth it; and the names 'man' and 'rational' are of equal extent, comprehending mutually one another. But here we must take notice that by a name is not always understood, as in grammar, one only word; but sometimes, by circumlocution, many words together. For all these words, 'he that in his actions observeth the laws of his country' make but one name, equivalent to this one word 'just.'

By this imposition of names, some of larger, some of stricter signification, we turn the reckoning of the consequences of things imagined in the mind into a reckoning of the consequences of appellations. For example: a man that hath no use of speech at all, such as is born and remains perfectly deaf and dumb, if he set before his eyes a triangle and by it two right angles, such as are the corners of a square figure, he may by meditation compare and find that the three angles of that triangle are equal to those two right angles that stand by it. But if another triangle be shown him, different in shape from the former, he cannot know without a new labour whether the three angles of that also be equal to the same. But he that hath the use of words, when he observes that such equality was consequent not to the length of the sides nor to any other particular thing in his triangle, but only to this, that the sides were straight, and the angles three, and that that was all for which he named it a triangle, will boldly conclude universally that such equality of angles is in all triangles whatsoever, and register his invention in these general terms, 'every triangle hath its three angles equal to two right angles.' And thus the consequence found in one particular comes to be registered and remembered as a universal rule, and discharges our mental reckoning of time and place, and delivers us from all labour of the mind saving the first; and makes that which was found true 'here' and 'now' to be true in 'all times' and 'places.'

But the use of words in registering our thoughts is in nothing so evident as in numbering. A natural fool that could never learn by heart the order of numeral words, as 'one,' 'two,' and 'three,' may observe every stroke of the clock, and nod to it, or say 'one,'

'one,' 'one,' but can never know what hour it strikes. And it seems there was a time when those names of number were not in use, and men were fain to apply their fingers of one or both hands to those things they desired to keep account of; and that thence it proceeded that now our numeral words are but ten in any nation, and in some but five; and then they begin again. And he that can tell ten, if he recite them out of order, will lose himself and not know when he has done. Much less will he be able to add, and subtract, and perform all other operations of arithmetic. So that without words there is no possibility of reckoning of numbers; much less of magnitudes, of swiftness, of force, and other things, the reckonings whereof are necessary to the being, or well-being of mankind.

When two names are joined together into a consequence, or affirmation as thus, 'a man is a living creature,' or thus, 'if he be a man, he is a living creature,' if the latter name, 'living creature,' signify all that the former name, 'man,' signifieth, then the affirmation, or consequence, is 'true'; otherwise 'false.' For 'true' and 'false' are attributes of speech, not of things. And where speech is not, there is neither 'truth' nor 'falsehood': 'error' there may be, as when we expect that which shall not be, or suspect what has not been; but in neither case can a man be charged with untruth.

Seeing then that truth consisteth in the right ordering of names in our affirmations, a man that seeketh precise truth had need to remember what every name he uses stands for, and to place it accordingly, or else he will find himself entangled in words, as a bird in lime twigs—the more he struggles the more belimed. And therefore in geometry, which is the only science that it hath pleased God hitherto to bestow on mankind, men begin at settling the significations of their words; which settling of significations they call 'definitions,' and place them in the beginning of their reckoning.

By this it appears how necessary it is for any man that aspires to true knowledge to examine the definitions of former authors; and either to correct them, where they are negligently set down, or to make them himself. For the errors of definitions multiply themselves according as the reckoning proceeds, and lead men into absurdities which at last they see, but cannot avoid without reckoning anew from the beginning, in which lies the foundation of their errors. From whence it happens that they which trust to books do as they that cast up many little sums into a greater, without considering whether those little sums were rightly cast up or not; and at last, finding the error visible and not mistrusting their first grounds, know not which way to clear themselves, but spend time in fluttering over their books, as birds that, entering by the chimney and finding themselves enclosed in a chamber, flutter at the false light of a glass window for want of wit to consider which way they came in. So that in the right definition of names lies the first use of speech, which is the acquisition of science; and in wrong, or no definitions, lies the first abuse; from which proceed all false and senseless tenets: which make those men that take their instruction from the authority of books and not from their own meditation to be as much below the condition of ignorant men as men endued with true science are above it. For between true science and erroneous doctrines ignorance is in the middle. Natural sense and imagination are not subject to absurdity. Nature itself cannot err; and as men abound in copiousness of language, so they become more wise, or more mad, than ordinary. Nor is it possible without letters for any man to become either excellently wise, or, unless his memory be hurt by disease or ill constitution of organs, excellently foolish. For words are wise men's counters—they do but reckon by them; but they are the money of fools, that value them by the authority of an Aristotle, a Cicero, or a Thomas or any other doctor whatsoever, if but a man.

'Subject to names' is whatsoever can enter into or be considered in an account, and be added one to another to make a sum, or subtracted one from another and leave a remainder. The Latins called accounts of money *rationes,* and accounting *ratiocinatio;* and that which we in bills or books of account call 'items' they call *nomina,* that is 'names,' and thence it seems to proceed that they extended the word *ratio* to the faculty of reckoning in all other things. The Greeks have but one word, λόγος, for both 'speech' and 'reason'; not that they thought there was no speech without reason, but no reasoning without speech; and the act of reasoning they called 'syllogism,' which signifieth summing up of the consequences of one saying to another. And because the same thing may enter into account for divers accidents, their names are, to show that diversity, diversely wrested and diversified. This diversity of names may be reduced to four general heads.

First, a thing may enter into account for 'matter' or 'body,' as 'living,' 'sensible,' 'rational,' 'hot,' 'cold,' 'moved,' 'quiet'; with all which names the word 'matter' or 'body' is understood; all such being names of matter.

Secondly, it may enter into account, or be considered, for some accident or quality which we conceive to be in it; as for 'being moved,' for 'being so long,' for 'being hot,' etc.; and then, of the name of the thing itself, by a little change or wresting we make a name for that accident which we consider; and for 'living' put into the account 'life,' for 'moved' 'motion,' for 'hot' 'heat,' for 'long' 'length,' and the like; and all such names are the names of the accidents and properties by which one matter and body is distinguished from another. These are called 'names abstract,' because severed not from matter but from the account of matter.

Thirdly, we bring into account the properties of our own bodies, whereby we make such distinction; as, when anything is seen by us, we reckon not the thing itself but the sight, the colour, the idea of it in the fancy; and when anything is heard, we reckon it not, but the hearing or sound only, which is our fancy or conception of it by the ear; and such are names of fancies.

Fourthly, we bring into account, consider, and give names, to 'names' themselves, and to 'speeches,' for 'general,' 'universal,' 'special,' 'equivocal,' are names of names. And 'affirmation,' 'interrogation,' 'commandment,' 'narration,' 'syllogism,' 'sermon,' 'oration,' and many other such, are names of speeches. And this is all the variety of names 'positive,' which are put to mark somewhat which is in Nature, or may be feigned by the mind of man, as bodies that are or may be conceived to be; or of bodies, the properties that are or may be feigned to be; or words and speech.

There be also other names, called 'negative,' which are notes to signify that a word is not the name of the thing in question; as these words 'nothing,' 'no man,' 'infinite,' 'indocible,' 'three want four,' and the like; which are nevertheless of use in reckoning, or in correcting of reckoning, and call to mind our past cogitations, though they be not names of anything, because they make us refuse to admit of names not rightly used.

All other names are but insignificant sounds; and those of two sorts. One when they are new, and yet their meaning not explained by definition; whereof there have been abundance coined by school-men, and puzzled philosophers.

Another, when men make a name of two names, whose significations are contradictory and inconsistent; as this name, an 'incorporeal body,' or, which is all one, an 'incorporeal substance,' and a great number more. For, whensoever any affirmation is false, the two names of which it is composed put together and made one signify nothing at all. For example, if it be a false affirmation to say 'a quadrangle is round,' the word 'round quadrangle' signifies nothing, but is a mere sound. So likewise, if it be false to say that virtue can be poured, or blown up and down, the words 'inpoured virtue,' 'inblown virtue,' are as absurd and insignificant as a 'round quadrangle.' And therefore you shall hardly meet with a senseless and insignificant word that is not made up of some Latin or Greek names. A Frenchman seldom hears our Saviour called by the name of *parole,* but by the name of *verbe* often; yet *verbe* and *parole* differ no more but that one is Latin, the other French.

When a man, upon the hearing of any speech, hath those thoughts which the words of that speech and their connection were ordained and constituted to signify, then he is said to understand it, 'understanding' being nothing else but conception caused by speech. And therefore, if speech be peculiar to man, as for aught I know it is, then is understanding peculiar to him also. And therefore of absurd and false affirmations, in case they be universal, there can be no understanding; though many think they understand, then, when they do but repeat the words softly, or con them in their mind.

What kinds of speeches signify the appetites, aversions, and passions of man's mind, and of their use and abuse, I shall speak when I have spoken of the passions.

The names of such things as affect us, that is, which please and displease us, because all men be not alike affected with the same thing nor the same man at all times, are in the common discourses of men of 'inconstant' signification. For seeing all names are imposed to signify our conceptions, and all our affections are but conceptions, when we conceive the same things differently we can hardly avoid different naming of them. For though the nature of that we conceive be the same, yet the diversity of our reception of it, in respect of different constitutions of body and prejudices of opinion, gives everything a tincture of our different passions. And therefore in reasoning a man must take heed of words, which, besides the signification of what we imagine of their nature, have a signification also of the nature, disposition, and interest of the speaker; such as are the names of virtues and vices; for one man calleth 'wisdom' what another calleth 'fear,' and one 'cruelty' what another 'justice'; one 'prodigality' what another 'magnanimity'; and one 'gravity' what another 'stupidity,' etc. And therefore such names can never be true grounds of any ratiocination. No more can metaphors and tropes of speech; but these are less dangerous, because they profess their inconstancy, which the other do not.

CHAPTER V

OF REASON AND SCIENCE

WHEN a man 'reasoneth' he does nothing else but conceive a sum total, from 'addition' of parcels, or conceive a remainder, from 'subtraction' of one sum from another; which, if it be done by words, is conceiving of the consequence of the names of all the parts, to the name of the whole; or from the names of the whole and one part, to the name of the other part. And, though in some things, as in numbers, besides adding and subtracting men name other operations, as 'multiplying' and 'dividing,' yet they are the same; for multiplication is but adding together of things equal; and division but subtracting of one thing, as often as we can. These operations are not incident to numbers only, but to all manner of things that can be added together, and taken one out of another. For as arithmeticians teach to add and subtract in 'numbers,' so the geometricians teach the same in 'lines,' 'figures,' solid and superficial, 'angles,' 'proportions,' 'times,' degrees of 'swiftness,' 'force,' 'power' and the like; the logicians teach the same in 'consequences of words,' adding together two 'names' to make an 'affirmation,' and two 'affirmations' to make a 'syllogism'; and 'many syllogisms' to make a 'demonstration'; and from the 'sum,' or 'conclusion,' of a 'syllogism' they subtract one 'proposition' to find the other. Writers of politics add together 'pactions' to find men's 'duties,' and lawyers 'laws' and 'facts,' to find what is 'right' and 'wrong' in the actions of private men. In sum, in what matter soever there is place for 'addition' and 'subtraction' there also is place for 'reason,' and where these have no place, there 'reason' has nothing at all to do.

Out of all which we may define, that is to say determine, what that is which is meant by this word 'reason,' when we reckon it amongst the faculties of the mind. For 'reason' in this sense is nothing but 'reckoning,' that is adding and subtracting, of the consequences of general names agreed upon for the 'marking' and 'signifying' of our thoughts; I say 'marking' them when we reckon by ourselves, and 'signifying' when we demonstrate or approve our reckonings to other men.

And, as in arithmetic, unpractised men must, and professors themselves may often, err, and cast up false; so also in any other subject of reasoning the ablest, most attentive, and most practised men may deceive themselves, and infer false conclusions; not but that reason itself is always right reason, as well as arithmetic is a certain and infallible art; but no one man's reason, nor the reason of any one number of men, makes the certainty; no more than an account is therefore well cast up, because a great many men have unanimously approved it. And therefore, as when there is a controversy in an account the parties must by their own accord set up for right reason the reason of some arbitrator, or judge, to whose sentence they will both stand, or their controversy must either come to blows, or be undecided, for want of a right reason constituted by Nature; so is it also in all debates of what kind soever. And when men that think themselves wiser than all others clamour and demand right reason for judge, yet seek no more but that things should be determined by no other men's reason but their own, it is as intolerable in the society of men as it is in play after trump is turned, to use for trump on every occasion that suit whereof they have most in their hand. For they do nothing else that will have every of their passions, as it comes to bear sway in them, to be taken for right reason, and that in their own controversies, bewraying their want of right reason, by the claim they lay to it.

The use and end of reason is not the finding of the sum and truth of one or a few consequences remote from the first definitions and settled significations of names, but to begin at these, and proceed from one consequence to another. For there can be no certainty of the last conclusion without a certainty of all those affirmations and negations on which it was grounded and inferred. As when a master of a family in taking an account casteth up the sums of all the bills of expense into one sum, and, not regarding how each bill is summed up by those that give them in account nor what it is he pays for, he advantages himself no more than if he allowed the account in gross, trusting to every of the accountants' skill and honesty; so also, in reasoning of all other things, he that takes up conclusions on the trust of authors and doth not fetch them from the first items in every reckoning, which are the significations of names settled by definitions, loses his labour, and does not know anything, but only believeth.

When a man reckons without the use of words, which may be done in particular things, as when upon the sight of any one thing we conjecture what was likely to have preceded or is likely to follow upon it, if that which he thought likely to follow follows not, or that which he thought likely to have preceded it hath not preceded it, this is called 'error,' to which even the most prudent men are subject. But when we reason in words of general signification, and fall upon a general inference which is false, though it be commonly called 'error,' it is indeed an 'absurdity,' or senseless speech. For error is but a deception, in presuming that somewhat is past or to come, of which, though it were not past or not to come, yet there was no impossibility discoverable. But when we make a general assertion, unless it be a true one, the possibility of it is inconceivable. And words whereby we conceive nothing but the sound are those we call 'absurd,' 'insignificant,' and 'nonsense.' And therefore if a man should talk to me of a 'round quadrangle,' or 'accidents of bread in cheese,' or 'immaterial substances,' or of 'a free subject,' 'a free will,' or any 'free' but free from being hindered by opposition, I should not say he were in an error, but that his words were without meaning, that is to say absurd.

I have said before, in the second chapter, that a man did excel all other animals in this faculty that when he conceived anything whatsoever he was apt to inquire the consequences of it, and what effects he could do with it. And now I add this other degree of the same excellence, that he can by words reduce the consequences he finds to general rules, called 'theorems,' or 'aphorisms,' that is, he can reason, or reckon, not only in number, but in all other things whereof one may be added unto, or subtracted from another.

But this privilege is allayed by another, and that is, by the privilege of absurdity; to which no living creature is subject, but man only. And of men, those are of all most subject to it that profess philosophy. For it is most true that Cicero saith of them somewhere that there can be nothing so absurd but may be found in the books of philosophers. And the reason is manifest. For there is not one of them that begins his ratiocination from the definitions or explications of the names they are to use, which is a method that hath been used only in geometry, whose conclusions have thereby been made indisputable.

I. The first cause of absurd conclusions I ascribe to the want of method, in that they begin not their ratiocination from definitions, that is, from settled significations of their words; as if they could cast account without knowing the value of the numeral words 'one,' 'two,' and 'three.'

And whereas all bodies enter into account upon divers considerations, which I have mentioned in the precedent chapter, these considerations being diversely named, divers absurdities proceed from the confusion, and unfit connexion of their names into assertions. And therefore:

II. The second cause of absurd assertions I ascribe to the giving of names of 'bodies' to 'accidents,' or of 'accidents' to 'bodies,' as they do that say 'faith is infused' or 'inspired,' when nothing can be 'poured' or 'breathed' into anything but body; and that 'extension' is 'body,' that 'phantasms' are 'spirits,' etc.

III. The third I ascribe to the giving of the names of the 'accidents' of 'bodies without us' to the 'accidents' of our 'own bodies,' as they do that say 'the colour is in the body,' and 'the sound is in the air,' etc.

IV. The fourth to the giving of the names of 'bodies' to 'names' or 'speeches,' as they do that say that 'there be things universal,' that 'a living creature is genus,' or 'a general thing,' etc.

V. The fifth to the giving of the names of 'accidents' to 'names' and 'speeches,' as they do that say, 'the nature of a thing is its definition,' 'a man's command is his will,' and the like.

VI. The sixth to the use of metaphors, tropes, and other rhetorical figures, instead of words proper. For though it be lawful to say, for example, in common speech, 'the way goeth, or leadeth hither or thither,' 'the proverb says this or that,' whereas ways cannot go, nor proverbs speak; yet in reckoning and seeking of truth such speeches are not to be admitted.

VII. The seventh to names that signify nothing, but are taken up and learned by rote from the schools, as 'hypostatical,' transubstantiate,' 'consubstantiate,' 'eternal-now,' and the like canting of schoolmen.

To him that can avoid these things it is not easy to fall into any absurdity, unless it be by the length of an account, wherein he may perhaps forget what went before. For all men by nature reason alike, and well, when they have good principles. For who is so stupid as both to mistake in geometry and also to persist in it, when another detects his error to him?

By this it appears that reason is not, as sense and memory, born with us, nor gotten by experience only, as prudence is; but attained by industry, first in apt imposing of names, and secondly by getting a good and orderly method in proceeding from the elements, which are names, to assertions made by connection of one of them to another, and so to syllogisms, which are the connections of one assertion to another, till we come to a knowledge of all the consequences of names appertaining to the subject in hand; and that is it men call 'science.' And whereas sense and memory are but knowledge of fact, which is a thing past and irrevocable, 'science' is the knowledge of consequences, and dependence of one fact upon another, by which, out of that we can presently do, we know how to do something else when we will, or the like another time; because when we see how anything comes about, upon what causes, and by what manner, when the like causes come into our power, we see how to make it produce the like effects.

Children therefore are not endued with reason at all, till they have attained the use of speech; but are called reasonable creatures, for the possibility apparent of having the use of reason in time to come. And the most part of men, though they have the use of reasoning a little way, as in numbering to some degree, yet it serves them to little use in common life, in which they govern themselves, some better, some worse according to their differences of experience, quickness of memory, and inclinations to several ends; but specially according to good or evil fortune, and the errors of one another. For as for 'science,' or certain rules of their actions, they are so far from it that they know not what it is. Geometry they have thought conjuring; but for other sciences, they who have not been taught the beginnings and some progress in them, that they may see how they be acquired and generated, are in this point like children that, having no thought of generation, are made believe by the women that their brothers and sisters are not born but found in the garden.

But yet they that have no 'science' are in better and nobler condition, with their natural prudence, than men, that by mis-reasoning, or by trusting them that reason wrong, fall upon false and absurd general rules. For ignorance of causes and of rules does not set men so far out of their way as relying on false rules, and taking for causes of what they aspire to those that are not so, but rather causes of the contrary.

To conclude, the light of human minds is perspicuous words, but by exact definitions first snuffed and purged from ambiguity; 'reason' is the 'pace,' increase of 'science' the 'way,' and the benefit of mankind the 'end.' And, on the contrary, metaphors, and senseless and ambiguous words, are like *ignes fatui;* and reasoning upon them is wandering amongst innumerable absurdities; and their end contention and sedition, or contempt.

As much experience is 'prudence,' so is much science 'sapience.' For though we usually have one name of wisdom for them both, yet the Latins did always distinguish between *prudentia* and *sapientia,* ascribing the former to experience, the latter to science. But, to make their difference appear more clearly, let us suppose one man endued with an excellent natural use and dexterity in handling his arms, and another to have added to that dexterity an acquired science of where he can offend or be offended by his adversary in every possible posture or guard: the ability of the former would be to the ability of the latter as prudence to sapience, both useful, but the latter infallible. But they that, trusting only to the authority of books, follow the blind blindly are like him that, trusting to the false rules of a master of fence, ventures presumptuously upon an adversary that either kills or disgraces him.

The signs of science are, some certain and infallible, some, uncertain. Certain, when he that pretendeth the science of anything can teach the same, that is to say, demonstrate the truth thereof perspicuously to another; uncertain, when only some particular events answer to his pretence, and upon many occasions prove so as he says they must. Signs of prudence are all uncertain, because to observe by experience, and remember all circumstances that may alter the success, is impossible. But in any business whereof a man has not infallible science to proceed by, to forsake his own natural judgment, and be guided by general sentences read in authors and subject to many exceptions, is a sign of folly, and generally scorned by the name of pedantry. And even of those men themselves that in councils of the commonwealth love to show their reading of politics and history, very few do it in their domestic affairs, where their particular interest is concerned, having prudence enough for their private affairs; but in public they study more the reputation of their own wit than the success of another's business.

CHAPTER VI

Of the Interior Beginnings of Voluntary Motions, Commonly Called the Passions; and the Speeches by Which They Are Expressed

There be in animals two sorts of 'motions' peculiar to them: one called 'vital,' begun in generation, and continued without interruption through their whole life, such as are the 'course' of the 'blood,' the 'pulse,' the 'breathing,' the 'concoction, nutrition, excretion,' etc., to which motions there needs no help of imagination: the other is 'animal motion,' otherwise called 'voluntary motion,' as to 'go,' to 'speak,' to 'move' any of our limbs in such manner as is first fancied in our minds. That sense is motion in the organs and interior parts of man's body, caused by the action of the things we see, hear, etc.; and that fancy is but the relics of the same motion, remaining after sense, has been already said in the first and second chapters. And, because 'going,' 'speaking,' and the like voluntary motions, depend always upon a precedent thought of 'whither,' 'which way,' and 'what,' it is evident that the imagination is the first internal beginning of all voluntary motion. And, although unstudied men do not conceive any motion at all to be there where the thing moved is invisible, or the space it is moved in is, for the shortness of it, insensible; yet that doth not hinder but that such motions are. For, let a space be never so little, that which is moved over a greater space, whereof that little one is part, must first be moved over that. These small beginnings of motion within the body of man, before they appear in walking, speaking, striking, and other visible actions, are commonly called 'endeavour.'

This endeavour, when it is toward something which causes it, is called 'appetite,' or 'desire,' the latter being the general name, and the other oftentimes restrained to signify the desire of food, namely 'hunger' and 'thirst.' And, when the endeavour is fromward something, it is generally called 'aversion.' These words, 'appetite' and 'aversion,' we have from the Latins; and they both of them signify the motions, one of approaching, the other of retiring. So also do the Greek words for the same, which are ὁρμὴ and ἀφορμὴ. For Nature itself does often press upon men those truths which afterwards, when they look for somewhat beyond Nature, they stumble at. For the schools find in mere appetite to go, or move, no actual motion at all; but, because some motion they must acknowledge, they call it metaphorical motion, which is but an absurd speech; for though words may be called metaphorical, bodies and motions cannot.

That which men desire they are also said to 'love'; and to 'hate' those things for which they have aversion. So that desire and love are the same thing, save that by desire we always signify the absence of the object, by love most commonly the presence of the same. So also by aversion we signify the absence, and by hate, the presence of the object.

Of appetites and aversions, some are born with men, as appetite of food, appetite of excretion, and exoneration, which may also and more properly be called aversions from somewhat they feel in their bodies; and some other appetites, not many. The rest, which are appetites of particular things, proceed from experience and trial of their effects upon themselves or other men. For of things we know not at all, or believe not to be, we can have no further desire than to taste and try. But aversion we have for things not only which we know have hurt us, but also that we do not know whether they will hurt us or not.

Those things which we neither desire nor hate we are said to 'contemn,' 'contempt' being nothing else but an immobility or contumacy of the heart in resisting the action of certain things, and proceeding from that the heart is already moved otherwise by other more potent objects, or from want of experience of them.

And, because the constitution of a man's body is in continual mutation, it is impossible that all the same things should always cause in him the same appetites and aversions: much less can all men consent in the desire of almost any one and the same object.

But whatsoever is the object of any man's appetite or desire, that is it which he for his part calleth 'good'; and the object of his hate and aversion, 'evil'; and of his contempt 'vile' and 'inconsiderable.' For these words of good, evil, and contemptible, are ever used with relation to the person that useth them, there being nothing simply and absolutely so; nor any common rule of good and evil, to be taken from the nature of the objects themselves; but from the person of the man, where there is no commonwealth, or, in a commonwealth, from the person that representeth it; or from an arbitrator or judge, whom men disagreeing shall by consent set up, and make his sentence the rule thereof.

The Latin tongue has two words whose significations approach to those of good and evil, but are not precisely the same; and those are *pulchrum* and *turpe*. Whereof the former signifies that which by some apparent signs promiseth good; and the latter that which promiseth evil. But in our tongue we have not so general names to express them by. But for *pulchrum* we say in some things 'fair,' in others, 'beautiful,' or 'handsome,' or 'gallant,' or 'honourable,' or 'comely,' or 'amiable'; and for *turpe,* 'foul,' 'deformed,' 'ugly,' 'base,' 'nauseous,' and the like, as the subject shall require; all which words, in their proper places, signify nothing else but the 'mien,' or countenance, that promiseth good and evil. So that of good there be three kinds: good in the promise, that is *pulchrum;* good in effect, as the end desired, which is called *jucundum,* 'delightful'; and good as the means which is called *utile,* 'profitable'; and as many of evil: for 'evil' in promise is that they call *turpe;* evil in effect, and end is *molestum,* 'unpleasant,' 'troublesome'; and evil in the means, *inutile,* 'unprofitable,' 'hurtful.'

As, in sense, that which is really within us is, as I have said before, only motion caused by the action of external objects but in appearance—to the sight, light and colour; to the ear, sound; to the nostril, odour, etc.; so, when the action of the same object is continued from the eyes, ears, and other organs to the heart, the real effect there is nothing but motion or endeavour which consisteth in appetite, or aversion, to or from the object moving. But the apparence, or sense of that motion, is that we either call 'delight' or 'trouble of mind.'

This motion, which is called appetite, and for the apparence of it 'delight' and 'pleasure,' seemeth to be a corroboration of vital motion, and a help thereunto; and therefore such things as caused delight were not improperly called *jucunda,* (*a juvando,*) from helping or fortifying; and the contrary *molesta,* 'offensive,' from hindering and troubling the motion vital.

'Pleasure,' therefore, or 'delight,' is the apparence or sense of good; and 'molestation,' or 'displeasure,' the apparence or sense of evil. And consequently all appetite, desire, and love, is accompanied with some delight more or less; and all hatred and aversion with more or less displeasure and offence.

Of pleasures or delights some arise from the sense of an object present; and those may be called 'pleasures of sense,' the word 'sensual,' as it is used by those only that condemn them, having no place till there be laws. Of this kind are all onerations and exonerations of the body, as also all that is pleasant in the 'sight,' 'hearing,' 'smell,' 'taste,' or 'touch.' Others arise from the expectation that proceeds from foresight of the end or consequence of things, whether those things in the sense please or displease. And these are 'pleasures of the mind' of him that draweth those consequences, and are generally called 'joy.' In the like manner, displeasures are some in the sense, and called 'pain'; others in the expectation of consequences, and are called 'grief.'

These simple passions called 'appetite,' 'desire,' 'love,' 'aversion,' 'hate,' 'joy,' and 'grief,' have their names for divers considerations diversified. As first, when they one succeed another, they are diversely called from the opinion men have of the likelihood of attaining what they desire. Secondly, from the object loved or hated. Thirdly, from the consideration of many of them together. Fourthly, from the alteration or succession itself.

For 'appetite' with an opinion of attaining is called 'hope.'

The same without such opinion, 'despair.'

'Aversion' with opinion of 'hurt' from the object 'fear.'

The same with hope of avoiding that hurt by resistance, 'courage.'

Sudden 'courage,' 'anger.'

Constant 'hope,' 'confidence' of ourselves.

Constant 'despair,' 'diffidence' of ourselves.

'Anger' for great hurt done to another, when we conceive the same to be done by injury, 'indignation.'

'Desire' of good to another, 'benevolence,' 'good will,' 'charity.' If to man generally, 'good-nature.'

'Desire' of riches, 'covetousness,' a name used always in signification of blame, because men contending for them are displeased with one another attaining them, though the desire in itself be to be blamed, or allowed, according to the means by which those riches are sought.

'Desire' of office, or precedence, 'ambition,' a name used also in the worse sense, for the reason before mentioned.

'Desire' of things that conduce but a little to our ends, and fear of things that are but of little hindrance, 'pusillanimity.'

'Contempt' of little helps and hindrances, 'magnanimity.'

'Magnanimity' in danger of death or wounds, 'valour,' 'fortitude.'

'Magnanimity' in the use of riches, 'liberality.'

'Pusillanimity' in the same, 'wretchedness,' 'miserableness,' or 'parsimony,' as it is liked or disliked.

'Love' of persons for society, 'kindness.'

'Love' of persons for pleasing the sense only, 'natural lust.'

'Love' of the same, acquired from rumination, that is imagination of pleasure past, 'luxury.'

'Love' of one singularly, with desire to be singularly beloved, 'the passion of love.' The same, with fear that the love is not mutual, 'jealousy.'

'Desire,' by doing hurt to another, to make him condemn some fact of his own, 'revengefulness.'

'Desire' to know why and how, 'curiosity,' such as is in no living creature but 'man,' so that man is distinguished not only by his reason but also by this singular passion from other 'animals,' in whom the appetite of food, and other pleasures of sense, by predominance take away the care of knowing causes, which is a lust of the mind, that by a perseverance of delight in the continual and indefatigable generation of knowledge exceedeth the short vehemence of any carnal pleasure.

'Fear' of power invisible, feigned by the mind or imagined from tales publicly allowed, 'religion,' not allowed, 'superstition.' And when the power imagined is truly such as we imagine, 'true religion.'

'Fear,' without the apprehension of why or what, 'panic terror,' called so from the fables that make Pan the author of them, whereas in truth there is always in him that so feareth, first some apprehension of the cause, though the rest run away by example, every one supposing his fellow to know why. And therefore this passion happens to none but in a throng or multitude of people.

'Joy' from apprehension of novelty 'admiration,' proper to man, because it excites the appetite of knowing the cause.

'Joy,' arising from imagination of a man's own power and ability is that exultation of the mind which is called 'glorying,' which, if grounded upon the experience of his own former actions, is the same as 'confidence,' but if grounded on the flattery of others or only supposed by himself for delight in the consequences of it, is called 'vain-glory,' which name is properly given, because a well-grounded 'confidence' begetteth attempt, whereas the supposing of power does not, and is therefore rightly called 'vain.'

'Grief' from opinion of want of power is called 'dejection of mind.'

The 'vain-glory' which consisteth in the feigning or supposing of abilities in ourselves which we know are not is most incident to young men, and nourished by the histories or fictions of gallant persons, and is corrected oftentimes by age and employment.

'Sudden glory' is the passion which maketh those 'grimaces' called 'laughter'; and is caused either by some sudden act of their own that pleaseth them, or by the apprehension of some deformed thing in another by comparison whereof they suddenly applaud themselves. And it is incident most to them that are conscious of the fewest abilities in themselves; who are forced to keep themselves in their own favour by observing the imperfections of other men. And therefore much laughter at the defects of others is a sign of pusillanimity. For of great minds one of the proper works is to help and free others from scorn and compare themselves only with the most able.

On the contrary, 'sudden dejection' is the passion that causeth 'weeping,' and is caused by such accidents as suddenly take away some vehement hope or some prop of their power; and they are most subject to it that rely principally on helps external, such as are women and children. Therefore some weep for the loss of friends, others for their unkindness, others for the sudden stop made to their thoughts of revenge by reconciliation. But in all cases, both laughter and weeping, are sudden motions, custom taking them both away. For no man laughs at old jests, or weeps for an old calamity.

'Grief' for the discovery of some defect of ability is 'shame,' or the passion that discovereth itself in 'blushing,' and consisteth in the apprehension of something dishonourable; and in young men is a sign of the love of good reputation, and commendable: in old men it is a sign of the same; but, because it comes too late, not commendable.

The 'contempt' of good reputation is called 'impudence.'

'Grief' for the calamity of another is 'pity,' and ariseth from the imagination that the like calamity may befall himself; and there-

fore is called also 'compassion,' and in the phrase of this present
time a 'fellow-feeling'; and therefore for calamity arriving from
great wickedness the best men have the least pity; and for the same
calamity those have least pity that think themselves least obnoxious
to the same.

'Contempt,' or little sense of the calamity of others, is that which
men call 'cruelty,' proceeding from security of their own fortune.
For, that any man should take pleasure in other men's great harms
without other end of his own, I do not conceive it possible.

'Grief' for the success of a competitor in wealth, honour, or other
good, if it be joined with endeavour to enforce our own abilities to
equal or exceed him, is called 'emulation'; but joined with endeavour
to supplant or hinder a competitor, 'envy.'

When in the mind of man, appetites and aversions, hopes and fears,
concerning one and the same thing, arise alternately, and divers
good and evil consequences of the doing or omitting the thing propounded, come successively into our thoughts, so that sometimes we
have an appetite to it, sometimes an aversion from it, sometimes
hope to be able to do it, sometimes despair or fear to attempt it, the
whole sum of desires, aversions, hopes, and fears, continued till the
thing be either done or thought impossible, is that we call 'deliberation.'

Therefore of things past there is no 'deliberation,' because manifestly impossible to be changed; nor of things known to be impossible, or thought so, because men know, or think, such deliberation
vain. But of things impossible which we think possible we may deliberate; not knowing it is in vain. And it is called 'deliberation,'
because it is a putting an end to the 'liberty' we had of doing or
omitting according to our own appetite or aversion.

This alternate succession of appetites, aversions, hopes, and fears,
is no less in other living creatures than in man; and therefore beasts
also deliberate.

Every 'deliberation' is then said to 'end' when that whereof they
deliberate is either done or thought impossible; because till then we
retain the liberty of doing or omitting, according to our appetite or
aversion.

In 'deliberation,' the last appetite, or aversion, immediately adhering to the action, or to the omission thereof, is that we call the 'will'; the act, not the faculty, of 'willing.' And beasts that have 'deliberation' must necessarily also have 'will.' The definition of the 'will' given commonly by the schools, that it is a 'rational appetite,' is not good. For if it were, then could there be no voluntary act against reason. For a 'voluntary act' is that which proceedeth from the 'will' and no other. But if instead of a rational appetite we shall say an appetite resulting from a precedent deliberation, then the definition is the same that I have given here. Will, therefore, is the last appetite in deliberating. And, though we say in common discourse a man had a will once to do a thing, that nevertheless he forbore to do, yet that is properly but an inclination, which makes no action voluntary; because the action depends not of it, but of the last inclination or appetite. For if the intervenient appetites make any action voluntary, then by the same reason all intervenient aversions should make the same action involuntary; and so one and the same action should be both voluntary and involuntary.

By this it is manifest that not only actions that have their beginning from covetousness, ambition, lust, or other appetites to the thing propounded, but also those that have their beginning from aversion, or fear of those consequences that follow the omission, are 'voluntary actions.'

The forms of speech by which the passions are expressed are partly the same, and partly different from those by which we express our thoughts. And, first, generally all passions may be expressed 'indicatively,' as 'I love,' 'I fear,' 'I joy,' 'I deliberate,' 'I will,' 'I command,' but some of them have particular expressions by themselves, which nevertheless are not affirmations, unless it be when they serve to make other inferences besides that of the passion they proceed from. Deliberation is expressed 'subjunctively,' which is a speech proper to signify suppositions, with their consequences: as, 'if this be done, then this will follow,' and differs not from the language of reasoning, save that reasoning is in general words; but deliberation for the most part is of particulars. The language of desire, and aversion, is 'imperative,' as 'do this,' 'forbear that,' which when the party is obliged to do, or forbear, is 'command'; otherwise 'prayer,' or else 'counsel.' The language of vain-glory, of indignation,

pity and revengefulness, 'optative,' but of the desire to know there is
a peculiar expression, called 'interrogative,' as 'what is it'? 'when shall
it'? 'how is it done'? and 'why so'? Other language of the passions
I find none; for cursing, swearing, reviling, and the like, do not
signify as speech, but as the actions of a tongue accustomed.

These forms of speech, I say, are expressions, or voluntary significations of our passions; but certain signs they be not, because they
may be used arbitrarily, whether they that use them have such
passions or not. The best signs of passions present are either in the
countenance, motions of the body, actions, and ends, or aims, which
we otherwise know the man to have.

And because in deliberation the appetites and aversions are raised
by foresight of the good and evil consequences, and sequels of the
action whereof we deliberate, the good or evil effect thereof dependeth on the foresight of a long chain of consequences of which
very seldom any man is able to see to the end. But for so far as a
man seeth, if the good in those consequences be greater than the
evil, the whole chain is that which writers call 'apparent' or 'seeming
good.' And, contrarily, when the evil exceedeth the good, the whole
is 'apparent' or 'seeming evil,' so that he who hath by experience,
or reason, the greatest and surest prospect of consequences, deliberates
best himself, and is able, when he will, to give the best counsel unto
others.

'Continual success' in obtaining those things which a man from
time to time desireth, that is to say continual prospering, is that
men call 'felicity'—I mean the felicity of this life. For there is no
such thing as perpetual tranquility of mind while we live here, because life itself is but motion, and can never be without desire, nor
without fear, no more than without sense. What kind of felicity
God hath ordained to them that devoutly honour Him a man shall
no sooner know than enjoy, being joys that now are as incomprehensible as the word of schoolmen 'beatifical vision' is unintelligible.

The form of speech whereby men signify their opinion of the
goodness of anything is 'praise.' That whereby they signify the
power and greatness of anything is 'magnifying.' And that whereby
they signify the opinion they have of a man's felicity is by the

Greeks called μακαρισμός for which we have no name in our tongue. And thus much is sufficient for the present purpose, to have been said of the 'passions.'

CHAPTER VII

OF THE ENDS, OR RESOLUTIONS OF DISCOURSE

OF all 'discourse,' governed by desire of knowledge there is at last an 'end,' either by attaining or by giving over. And in the chain of discourse, wheresoever it be interrupted, there is an end for that time.

If the discourse be merely mental, it consisteth of thoughts that the thing will be, and will not be; or that it has been, and has not been, alternately. So that wheresoever you break off the chain of a man's discourse, you leave him in a presumption of 'it will be,' or 'it will not be,' or 'it has been,' or 'has not been.' All which is 'opinion.' And that which is alternate appetite in deliberating concerning good and evil, the same is alternate opinion in the enquiry of the truth of 'past' and 'future.' And as the last appetite in deliberation is called the 'will,' so the last opinion in search of the truth of past and future is called the 'judgment' or 'resolute' and 'final sentence' of him that 'discourseth.' And as the whole chain of appetites alternate, in the question of good or bad, is called 'deliberation,' so the whole chain of opinions alternate, in the question of true or false, is called 'doubt.'

No discourse whatsoever can end in absolute knowledge of fact, past or to come. For, as for the knowledge of fact, it is originally sense; and ever after, memory. And for the knowledge of consequence, which I have said before is called science, it is not absolute, but conditional. No man can know by discourse that this or that is, has been, or will be—which is to know absolutely; but only that if this be, that is; if this has been, that has been, if this shall be, that shall be—which is to know conditionally and that not the consequence of one thing to another, but of one name of a thing to another name of the same thing.

And therefore, when the discourse is put into speech, and begins with the definitions of words, and proceeds by connection of the same into general affirmations, and of these again into syllogisms, the end or last sum is called the conclusion, and the thought of the mind by it signified is that conditional knowledge or knowledge of the consequence of words, which is commonly called 'science.' But if the first ground of such discourse be not definitions, or if the definitions be not rightly joined together into syllogisms, then the end or conclusion is again 'opinion' namely of the truth of somewhat said, though sometimes in absurd and senseless words, without possibility of being understood. When two or more men know of one and the same fact, they are said to be 'conscious,' of it one to another; which is as much as to know it together. And because such are fittest witnesses of the facts of one another or of a third, it was, and ever will be, reputed a very evil act for any man to speak against his 'conscience,' or to corrupt or force another so to do: insomuch that the plea of conscience has been always hearkened unto very diligently in all times. Afterwards men made use of the same word metaphorically, for the knowledge of their own secret facts and secret thoughts; and therefore it is rhetorically said that the conscience is a thousand witnesses. And, last of all, men vehemently in love with their own opinions, though never so absurd, and obstinately bent to maintain them, gave those their opinions also that reverenced name of conscience, as if they would have it seem unlawful to change or speak against them, and so pretend to know they are true, when they know at most but that they think so.

When a man's discourse beginneth not at definitions, it beginneth either at some other contemplation of his own, and then it is still called opinion; or it beginneth at some saying of another, of whose ability to know the truth and of whose honesty in not deceiving he doubteth not; and then the discourse is not so much concerning the thing as the person; and the resolution is called 'belief,' and 'faith'—'faith' in the man, 'belief' both of the man and of the truth of what he says. So that in belief are two opinions; one of the saying of the man, the other of his virtue. To 'have faith in' or 'trust to' or 'believe a man' signify the same thing, namely, an opinion of the veracity of the man; but to 'believe what is said' signifieth only an opinion of the truth of the saying. But we are to observe that this phrase, 'I believe in,' as also the Latin *credo in,* and the Greek πιστεύω ἔις are never used but in the writings of divines. Instead of them in other writings are put 'I believe him,' 'I trust him,' 'I have faith in him,' 'I rely on him,' and in Latin *credo illi, fido illi;* and in Greek πιστεύω ἀυτῷ; and that this singularity of the ecclesiastic use of the word hath raised many disputes about the right object of the Christian faith.

But by 'believing in,' as it is in the creed, is meant, not trust in the person, but confession and acknowledgment of the doctrine. For not only Christians but all manner of men do so believe in God as to hold all for truth they hear Him say, whether they understand it or not; which is all the faith and trust can possibly be had in any person whatsoever; but they do not all believe the doctrine of the creed.

From whence we may infer that, when we believe any saying whatsoever it be to be true, from arguments taken not from the thing itself, or from the principles of natural reason, but from the authority and good opinion we have of him that hath said it, then is the speaker, or person we believe in or trust in, and whose word we take, the object of our faith, and the honour done in believing is done to him only. And consequently when we believe that the Scriptures are the word of God, having no immediate revelation from God Himself, our belief, faith, and trust, is in the Church, whose word we take and acquiesce therein. And they that believe that which a prophet relates unto them in the name of God take the word of the prophet, do honour to him, and in him trust and believe, touching the truth of what he relateth, whether he be a true or a false prophet. And so it is also with all other history. For if I should not believe all that is written by historians of the glorious acts of Alexander or Cæsar, I do not think the ghost of Alexander or Cæsar had any just cause to be offended, or anybody else but the historian. If Livy say the gods made once a cow speak, and we believe it not, we distrust not God therein, but Livy. So that it is evident, that whatsoever we believe, upon no other reason than what is drawn from authority of men only, and their writings, whether they be sent from God or not, is faith in men only.

CHAPTER VIII

OF THE VIRTUES COMMONLY CALLED INTELLECTUAL, AND THEIR CONTRARY DEFECTS

VIRTUE generally, in all sorts of subjects, is somewhat that is valued for eminence, and consisteth in comparison. For, if all things were equal in all men, nothing would be prized. And by 'virtues intellectual' are always understood such abilities of the mind as men praise, value, and desire should be in themselves, and go commonly under the name of a 'good wit,' though the same word 'wit' be used also to distinguish one certain ability from the rest.

These 'virtues' are of two sorts, 'natural' and 'acquired.' By natural I mean not that which a man hath from his birth; for that is nothing else but sense, wherein men differ so little one from another and from brute beasts as it is not to be reckoned amongst virtues. But I mean that 'wit' which is gotten by use only and experience; without method, culture, or instruction. This 'natural wit' consisteth principally in two things, 'celerity of imagining,' that is, swift succession of one thought to another, and steady direction to some approved end. On the contrary, a slow imagination maketh that defect or fault of the mind which is commonly called 'dulness,' 'stupidity,' and sometimes by other names that signify slowness of motion or difficulty to be moved.

And this difference of quickness is caused by the difference of men's passions, that love and dislike, some one thing, some another; and therefore some men's thoughts run one way, some another; and are held to and observe differently the things that pass through their imagination. And whereas in this succession of men's thoughts there is nothing to observe in the things they think on, but either in what they be 'like one another,' or in what they be 'unlike,' or 'what they serve for,' or 'how they serve to such a purpose;' those that observe their similitudes, in case they be such as are but rarely observed by others, are said to have a 'good wit,' by which in this occasion is meant a 'good fancy.' But they that observe their differences and dissimilitudes, which is called 'distinguishing' and 'discerning' and 'judging' between thing and thing, in case such discerning be not easy, are said to have a 'good judgment;' and, particularly in matter of conversation and business, wherein times, places, and persons, are to be discerned, this virtue is called 'discretion.' The former, that is, fancy, without the help of judgment, is not commended as a virtue; but the latter, which is judgment and discretion, is commended for itself, without the help of fancy. Besides the discretion of times, places, and persons, necessary to a good fancy, there is required also an often application of his thoughts to their end, that is to say, to some use to be made of them. This done, he that hath this virtue will be easily fitted with similitudes that will please not only by illustrations of his discourse, and adorning it with new and apt metaphors, but also by the rarity of their invention. But without steadiness and direction to some end a great fancy is one kind of madness; such as they have that, entering into any discourse, are snatched from their purpose by everything that comes in their thought, into so many and so long digressions and parentheses that they utterly lose themselves—which kind of folly I know no particular name for, but the cause of it is sometimes want of experience, whereby that seemeth to a man new and rare which doth not so to others, sometimes pusillanimity, by which that seems great to him which other men think a trifle; and whatsoever is new or great, and therefore thought fit to be told, withdraws a man by degrees from the intended way of his discourse.

In a good poem, whether it be 'epic' or 'dramatic,' as also in 'sonnets,' 'epigrams,' and other pieces, both judgment and fancy are required; but the fancy must be more eminent, because they please for the extravagancy, but ought not to displease by indiscretion.

In a good history the judgment must be eminent, because the goodness consisteth in the method, in the truth, and in the choice of the actions that are most profitable to be known. Fancy has no place but only in adorning the style.

In orations of praise, and in invectives, the fancy is predominant, because the design is not truth, but to honour or dishonour, which is done by noble or by vile comparisons. The judgment does but suggest what circumstances make an action laudable or culpable.

In hortatives and pleadings, as truth or disguise serveth best to the design in hand, so is the judgment or the fancy most required.

In demonstration, in counsel, and all rigorous search of truth, judgment does all, except sometimes the understanding have need to be opened by some apt similitude, and then there is so much use of fancy. But for metaphors, they are in this case utterly excluded. For seeing they openly profess deceit: to admit them into counsel or reasoning were manifest folly.

And in any discourse whatsoever, if the defect of discretion be apparent, how extravagant soever the fancy be, the whole discourse will be taken for a sign of want of wit; and so will it never when the discretion is manifest, though the fancy be never so ordinary.

The secret thoughts of a man run over all things, holy, profane, clean, obscene, grave, and light, without shame or blame; which verbal discourse cannot do farther than the judgment shall approve of the time, place, and persons. An anatomist or a physician may speak or write his judgment of unclean things, because it is not to please but profit; but for another man to write his extravagant and pleasant fancies of the same is as if a man, from being tumbled into the dirt, should come and present himself before good company. And it is the want of discretion that makes the difference. Again, in professed remissness of mind, and familiar company, a man may play with the sounds and equivocal significations of words, and that many times with encounters of extraordinary fancy; but in a sermon, or in public, or before persons unknown, or whom we ought to reverence, there is no jingling of words that will not be accounted folly; and the difference is only in the want of discretion. So that, where wit is wanting, it is not fancy that is wanting but discretion. Judgment therefore without fancy is wit, but fancy without judgment, not.

When the thoughts of a man that has a design in hand, running over a multitude of things, observes how they conduce to that design or what design they may conduce unto, if his observations be such as are not easy or usual, this wit of his is called 'prudence,' and depends on much experience and memory of the like things and their consequences heretofore. In which there is not much difference of men as there is in their fancies and judgments, because the experience of men equal in age is not much unequal as to the quantity, but lies in different occasions, every one having his private designs. To govern well a family and a kingdom are not different degrees of prudence, but different sorts of business; no more than to draw a picture in little, or as great or greater than the life, are different degrees of art. A plain husbandman is more prudent in affairs of his own house than a privy-councillor in the affairs of another man.

To prudence, if you add the use of unjust or dishonest means, such as usually are prompted to men by fear or want, you have that crooked wisdom which is called 'craft,' which is a sign of pusillanimity. For magnanimity is contempt of unjust or dishonest helps. And that which the Latins call *versutia,* translated into English 'shifting,' and is a putting off of a present danger or incommodity by engaging into a greater, as when a man robs one to pay another, is but a short-sighted craft, called *versutia,* from *versura,* which signifies taking money at usury for the present payment of interest.

As for 'acquired wit,' I mean acquired by method and instruction, there is none but reason, which is grounded on the right use of speech, and produceth the sciences. But of reason and science I have already spoken, in the fifth and sixth chapters.

The causes of this difference of wits are in the passions; and the difference of passions proceedeth partly from the different constitution of the body, and partly from different education. For if the difference proceeded from the temper of the brain and the organs of sense, either exterior or interior, there would be no less difference of men in their sight, hearing, or other senses, than in their fancies and discretions. It proceeds therefore from the passions, which are different not only from the difference of men's complexions, but also from their difference of customs and education.

The passions that most of all cause the difference of wit are principally the more or less desire of power, of riches, of knowledge, and of honour. All which may be reduced to the first, that is, desire of power. For riches, knowledge, and honour, are but several sorts of power.

And, therefore, a man who has no great passion for any of these things, but is, as men term it, indifferent, though he may be so far a good man as to be free from giving offence, yet he cannot possibly have either a great fancy or much judgment. For the thoughts are to the desires as scouts and spies, to range abroad and find the way of the things desired, all steadiness of the mind's motion, and all quickness of the same, proceeding from thence; for as to have no desire is to be dead, so to have weak passions is dulness; and to have passions indifferently for everything, 'giddiness' and 'distraction'; and to have stronger and more vehement passions for anything than is ordinarily seen in others is that which men call 'madness.'

Whereof there be almost as many kinds as of the passions themselves. Sometimes the extraordinary and extravagant passion proceedeth from the evil constitution of the organs of the body, or harm done them; and sometimes the hurt and indisposition of the organs is caused by the vehemence or long continuance of the passion. But in both cases the madness is of one and the same nature.

The passion whose violence, or continuance, maketh madness is either great 'vain-glory,' which is commonly called 'pride' and 'self-conceit,' or great 'dejection' of mind.

Pride subjecteth a man to anger, the excess whereof is the madness called 'rage' and 'fury.' And thus it comes to pass that excessive desire of revenge, when it becomes habitual, hurteth the organs, and becomes rage; that excessive love, with jealousy, becomes also rage; excessive opinion of a man's own self, for divine inspiration, for wisdom, learning, form and the like, becomes distraction and giddiness; the same, joined with envy, rage; vehement opinion of the truth of anything contradicted by others, rage.

Dejection subjects a man to causeless fears; which is a madness; commonly called 'melancholy,' apparent also in divers manners, as in haunting of solitudes and graves, in superstitious behaviour, and in fearing, some one some another particular thing. In sum, all passions that produce strange and unusual behaviour are called by the general name of madness. But of the several kinds of madness he that would take the pains might enrol a legion. And if the excesses be madness, there is no doubt but the passions themselves, when they tend to evil, are degrees of the same.

For example, though the effect of folly in them that are possessed of an opinion of being inspired be not visible always in one man by any very extravagant action that proceedeth from such passion, yet, when many of them conspire together, the rage of the whole multitude is visible enough. For what argument of madness can there be greater than to clamour, strike, and throw stones at our best friends? Yet this is somewhat less than such a multitude will do. For they will clamour, fight against, and destroy, those by whom all their lifetime before they have been protected and secured from injury. And if this be madness in the multitude, it is the same in every particular man. For, as in the midst of the sea though a man perceive no sound of that part of the water next him, yet he is well assured that part contributes as much to the roaring of the sea as any other part of the same quantity, so also, though we perceive no great unquietness in one or two men, yet we may be well assured that their singular passions are parts of the seditious roaring of a troubled nation. And if there were nothing else that bewrayed their madness, yet that very arrogating such inspiration to themselves is argument enough. If some man in Bedlam should entertain you with sober discourse, and you desire in taking leave, to know what he were, that you might another time requite his civility, and he should tell you he were God the Father, I think you need expect no extravagant action or argument of his madness.

This opinion of inspiration, called commonly private spirit, begins very often from some lucky finding of an error generally held by others; and not knowing, or not remembering, by what conduct of reason they came to so singular a truth (as they think it, though it be many times an untruth they light on) they presently admire themselves, as being in the special grace of God Almighty, who hath revealed the same to them supernaturally by His Spirit.

Again, that madness is nothing else but too much appearing passion may be gathered out of the effects of wine, which are the same with those of the evil disposition of the organs. For the variety of behaviour in men that have drunk too much is the same with that of madmen: some of them raging, others loving, others laughing, all extravagantly, but according to their several domineering passions; for the effect of the wine does but remove dissimulation and take from them the sight of the deformity of their passions. For I believe the most sober men, when they walk alone without care and employment of the mind, would be unwilling the vanity and extravagance of their thoughts at that time should be publicly seen; which is a confession that passions unguided are for the most part mere madness.

The opinions of the world, both in ancient and later ages, concerning the cause of madness have been two. Some deriving them from the passions; some from demons, or spirits, either good or bad, which they thought might enter into a man, possess him, and move his organs in such strange and uncouth manner as madmen use to do. The former sort, therefore, called such men madmen; but the latter called them sometimes 'demoniacs,' that is, possessed with spirits; sometimes *energumeni,* that is, agitated or moved with spirits; and now in Italy they are called not only *pazzi,* madmen, but also *spiritati,* men possessed.

There was once a great conflux of people in Abdera, a city of the Greeks, at the acting of the tragedy of *Andromeda* upon an extreme hot day; whereupon a great many of the spectators falling into fevers had this accident from the heat and from the tragedy together, that they did nothing but pronounce iambics, with the names of Perseus and Andromeda; which, together with the fever, was cured by the coming on of winter; and this madness was thought to proceed from the passion imprinted by the tragedy. Likewise there reigned a fit of madness in another Grecian city, which seized only the young maidens, and caused many of them to hang themselves. This was by most then thought an act of the devil. But one that suspected that contempt of life in them might proceed from some passion of the mind, and supposing that they did not contemn also their honour, gave counsel to the magistrates to strip such as so hanged themselves, and let them hang out naked. This, the story says, cured that madness. But, on the other side, the same Grecians did often ascribe madness to the operation of Eumenides, or Furies; and sometimes of Ceres, Phœbus, and other gods; so much did men attribute to phantasms as to think them aërial living bodies, and generally to call them spirits. And as the Romans in this held the same opinion with the Greeks, so also did the Jews, for they called madmen prophets, or, according as they thought the spirits good or bad, demoniacs; and some of them called both prophets and demoniacs madmen; and some called the same man both demoniac and madman. But for the Gentiles it is no wonder, because diseases and health, vices and virtues, and many natural accidents, were with them termed and worshipped as demons. So that a man was to understand by demon as well sometimes an ague as a devil. But for the Jews to have such opinion is somewhat strange. For neither Moses nor Abraham pretended to prophesy by possession of a spirit; but from the voice of God, or by a vision or dream; nor is there anything in his law, moral or ceremonial, by which they were taught there was any such enthusiasm or any possession. When God is said (*Numb.* xi. 25) to take from the spirit that was in Moses, and give to the seventy elders, the Spirit of God (taking it for the substance of God) is not divided. The Scriptures by the Spirit of God in man mean a man's spirit, inclined to godliness. And where it is said (*Exod.* xxviii. 3) 'whom I have filled with the spirit of wisdom to make garments for Aaron' is not meant a spirit put into them that can make garments, but the wisdom of their own spirits in that kind of work. In the like sense, the spirit of man, when it produceth unclean actions, is ordinarily called an unclean spirit, and so other spirits, though not always, yet as often as the virtue or vice so styled is extraordinary and eminent. Neither did the other prophets of the Old Testament pretend enthusiasm, or that God spake in them, but to them, by voice, vision, or dream; and the 'burthen of the Lord' was not possession, but command. How then could the Jews fall into this opinion of possession? I can imagine no reason but that which is common to all men, namely the want of curiosity to search natural causes, and their placing felicity in the acquisition of the gross pleasures of the senses and the things that most immediately conduce thereto. For they that see any strange and unusual ability or defect in a man's mind, unless they see withal from what cause it may probably proceed, can hardly think it natural; and, if not natural, they must needs think it supernatural; and then what can it be but that either God or the devil is in him? And hence it came to pass, when our Saviour (*Mark* iii, 21) was compassed about with the multitude, those of the house doubted He was mad, and went out to hold Him; but the Scribes said He had Beelzebub, and that was it by which He cast out devils; as if the greater madman had awed the lesser; and that (*John* x, 20) some said 'He hath a devil, and is mad,' whereas others holding Him for a prophet said 'these are not the words of one that hath a devil.' So in the Old Testament he that came to anoint Jehu (2 *Kings* ix, 11) was a prophet; but some of the company asked Jehu 'what came that madman for'? So that in sum it is manifest that whosoever behaved himself in extraordinary manner was thought by the Jews to be possessed either with a good or evil spirit, except by the Sadducees, who erred so far on the other hand as not to believe there were at all any spirits, which is very near to direct atheism; and thereby perhaps the more provoked others to term such men demoniacs rather than madmen.

But why then does our Saviour proceed in the curing of them, as if they were possessed, and not as if they were mad? To which I can give no other kind of answer but that which is given to those that urge the Scripture in like manner against the opinion of the motion of the earth. The Scripture was written to show unto men the kingdom of God, and to prepare their minds to become his obedient subjects, leaving the world, and the philosophy thereof to the disputation of men, for the exercising of their natural reason. Whether the earth's or sun's motion make the day and night, or whether the exorbitant action of men proceed from passion or from the devil, so we worship him not, it is all one, as to our obedience and subjection to God Almighty; which is the thing for which the Scripture was written. As for that our Saviour speaketh to the disease as to a person, it is the usual phrase of all that cure by words only, as Christ did and enchanters pretend to do, whether they speak to a devil or not. For is not Christ also said (*Matt.* viii, 26) to have rebuked the winds? Is not He said also (*Luke* iv, 39) to rebuke a fever? Yet this does not argue that a fever is a devil. And whereas many of the devils are said to confess Christ, it is not necessary to interpret those places otherwise than that those madmen confessed Him. And whereas our Saviour (*Matt.* xii, 43) speaketh of an unclean spirit, that having gone out of a man wandereth through dry places, seeking rest and finding none, and returning into the same man with seven other spirits worse than himself, it is manifestly a parable alluding to a man that after a little endeavour to quit his lusts is vanquished by the strength of them, and becomes seven times worse than he was. So that I see nothing at all in the Scripture that requireth a belief that demoniacs were any other thing but madmen.

There is yet another fault in the discourses of some men, which may also be numbered amongst the sorts of madness, namely that abuse of words, whereof I have spoken before in the fifth chapter, by the name of absurdity. And that is when men speak such words as, put together, have in them no signification at all, but are fallen upon by some, through misunderstanding of the words they have received and repeat by rote, by others from intention to deceive by obscurity. And this is incident to none but those that converse in questions of matters incomprehensible, as the schoolmen, or in questions of abstruse philosophy. The common sort of men seldom speak insignificantly, and are therefore by those other egregious persons counted idiots. But, to be assured their words are without anything correspondent to them in the mind, there would need some examples, which if any man require, let him take a schoolman in his hands and see if he can translate any one chapter concerning any difficult point, as the Trinity, the Deity, the nature of Christ, transubstantiation, free-will, etc., into any of the modern tongues, so as to make the same intelligible, or into any tolerable Latin, such as they were acquainted withal, that lived when the Latin tongue was vulgar. What is the meaning of these words: 'The first cause does not necessarily inflow anything into the second, by force of the essential subordination of the second causes, by which it may help it to work?' They are the translation of the title of the sixth chapter of Suarez, first book, *Of the Concourse, Motion, and Help of God*. When men write whole volumes of such stuff, are they not mad, or intend to make others so? And particularly in the question of transubstantiation, where, after certain words spoken, they that say the white*ness,* round*ness,* magni*tude,* quali*ty,* corruptibili*ty,* all which are incorporeal, etc., go out of the wafer into the body of our blessed Saviour, do they not make those 'nesses,' 'tudes,' and 'ties' to be so many spirits possessing his body? For by spirits they mean always things that, being incorporeal, are nevertheless movable from one place to another. So that this kind of absurdity may rightly be numbered amongst the many sorts of madness, and all the time that guided by clear thoughts of their worldly lust they forbear disputing or writing thus, but lucid intervals. And thus much of the virtues and defects intellectual.

CHAPTER IX

OF THE SEVERAL SUBJECTS OF KNOWLEDGE

THERE are of 'knowledge' two kinds, whereof one is 'knowledge of fact,' the other 'knowledge of the consequence of one affirmation to another.' The former is nothing else but sense and memory, and is 'absolute knowledge,' as when we see a fact doing or remember it done; and this is the knowledge required in a witness. The latter is called 'science,' and is 'conditional,' as when we know that 'if the figure shown be a circle, then any straight line through the centre shall divide it into two equal parts.' And this is the knowledge required in a philosopher, that is to say of him that pretends to reasoning.

The register of 'knowledge of fact' is called 'history,' whereof there be two sorts: one called 'natural history,' which is the history of such facts or effects of Nature as have no dependence on man's 'will,' such as are the histories of 'metals,' 'plants,' 'animals,' 'regions,' and the like. The other is 'civil history,' which is the history of the voluntary actions of men in commonwealths.

The registers of science are such 'books,' as contain the 'demonstrations' of consequences of one affirmation to another, and are commonly called 'books of philosophy,' whereof the sorts are many, according to the diversity of the matter, and may be divided in such manner as I have divided them in the following table (pp. 360–361).

CHAPTER X

OF POWER, WORTH, DIGNITY, HONOUR, AND WORTHINESS

THE 'power of a man,' to take it universally, is his present means, to obtain some future apparent good; and is either 'original' or 'instrumental.'

'Natural power' is the eminence of the faculties of body or mind,

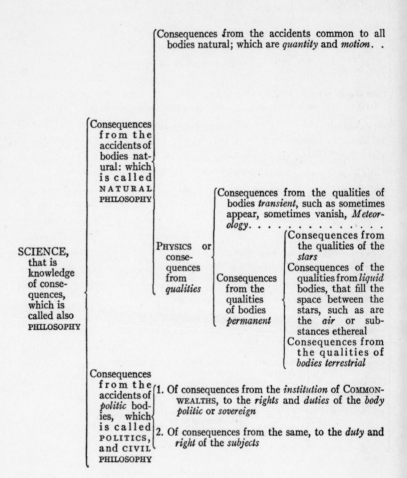

SCIENCE, that is knowledge of consequences, which is called also PHILOSOPHY

Consequences from the accidents of bodies natural: which is called NATURAL PHILOSOPHY

Consequences from the accidents common to all bodies natural; which are *quantity* and *motion*. .

PHYSICS or consequences from *qualities*

Consequences from the qualities of bodies *transient*, such as sometimes appear, sometimes vanish, *Meteorology*. . . . .

Consequences from the qualities of bodies *permanent*

Consequences from the qualities of the *stars*

Consequences of the qualities from *liquid* bodies, that fill the space between the stars, such as are the *air* or substances ethereal

Consequences from the qualities of *bodies terrestrial*

Consequences from the accidents of *politic* bodies, which is called POLITICS, and CIVIL PHILOSOPHY

1. Of consequences from the *institution* of COMMONWEALTHS, to the *rights* and *duties* of the *body politic* or *sovereign*

2. Of consequences from the same, to the *duty* and *right* of the *subjects*

Consequences from quantity, and motion *indeterminate*, which, being the principles or first foundation of philosophy, is called *Philosophia Prima* . . . . **PHILOSOPHIA PRIMA**

Consequences from motion and quantity *determined*	Consequences from quanti-ty, and mo-tion deter-mined	By Figure	**GEOMETRY**
		Mathematics	
		By Number	**ARITHMETIC**
	Consequences from the mo-tion, and quantity of bodies in *special*	Consequences from the mo-tion and quantity of the greater parts of the world, as the *earth* and stars	*Cosmography* {**ASTRONOMY** **GEOGRAPHY**}
		Consequences from the mo-tion of spe-cial kinds, and figures of body	*Mechanics* Doctrine of *weight* {**Science of ENGINEERS** **ARCHITECTURE** **NAVIGATION**}

. . . . **METEOROLOGY**

Consequences from the *light* of the stars. Out of this, and the motion of the sun, is made the science of . . . . } **SCIOGRAPHY**

Consequences from the *influences* of the stars . . . . **ASTROLOGY**

Consequences from the parts of the earth that are *without sense*	Consequences from the qualities of *minerals*, as *stones, metals*, etc.	
	Consequences from the qualities of *vegetables*	
Consequences from the qualities of *animals*	Consequences from the qualities of *animals in general*	Consequences from *vision* — **OPTICS**
		Consequences from *sounds* — **MUSIC**
		Consequences from the rest of the *senses*
	Consequences from the qualities of *men in special*	Consequences from the *passions* of men . . . . . . } **ETHICS**
		Consequences from *speech* {In *magnifying, vilifying*, etc. — **POETRY**; In *persuading* — **RHETORIC**; In *reasoning* — **LOGIC**; In *contracting* — The *Science* of **JUST and UNJUST**}

as extraordinary strength, form, prudence, arts, eloquence, liberality, nobility. 'Instrumental' are those powers which, acquired by these or by fortune are means and instruments to acquire more, as riches, reputation, friends, and the secret working of God, which men call good luck. For the nature of power is in this point like to fame, increasing as it proceeds; or like the motion of heavy bodies, which the further they go make still the more haste.

The greatest of human powers is that which is compounded of the powers of most men, united by consent, in one person, natural or civil, that has the use of all their powers depending on his will such as is the power of a commonwealth. Or depending on the wills of each particular, such as is the power of a faction or of divers factions leagued. Therefore to have servants is power; to have friends is power; for they are strengths united.

Also riches joined with liberality is power, because it procureth friends and servants; without liberality, not so; because in this case they defend not, but expose men to envy, as a prey.

Reputation of power is power, because it draweth with it the adherence of those that need protection.

So is reputation of love of a man's country, called popularity, for the same reason.

Also, what quality soever maketh a man beloved or feared of many, or the reputation of such quality, is power, because it is a means to have the assistance and service of many.

Good success is power, because it maketh reputation of wisdom or good fortune, which makes men either fear him or rely on him.

Affability of men already in power is increase of power, because it gaineth love.

Reputation of prudence in the conduct of peace or war is power, because to prudent men we commit the government of ourselves more willingly than to others.

Nobility is power, not in all places but only in those commonwealths where it has privileges, for in such privileges consisteth their power.

Eloquence is power, because it is seeming prudence.

Form is power, because, being a promise of good, it recommendeth men to the favour of women and strangers.

The sciences are small power, because not eminent and therefore not acknowledged in any man; nor are at all, but in a few, and in them but of a few things. For science is of that nature as none can understand it to be but such as in a good measure have attained it.

Arts of public use, as fortification, making of engines, and other instruments of war, because they confer to defence and victory, are power; and though the true mother of them be science, namely the mathematics, yet, because they are brought into the light by the hand of the artificer, they be esteemed, the midwife passing with the vulgar for the mother, as his issue.

The 'value,' or 'worth,' of a man is, as of all other things, his price; that is to say, so much as would be given for the use of his power; and therefore is not absolute, but a thing dependent on the need and judgment of another. An able conductor of soldiers is of great price in time of war present, or imminent; but in peace not so. A learned and uncorrupt judge is much worth in time of peace, but not so much in war. And, as in other things so in men, not the seller but the buyer determines the price. For let a man, as most men do, rate themselves [himself] at the highest value they [he] can, yet their [his] true value is no more than it is esteemed by others.

The manifestation of the value we set on one another is that which is commonly called honouring and dishonouring. To value a man at a high rate is to 'honour' him; at a low rate, 'to dishonour' him. But high and low, in this case, is to be understood by comparison to the rate that each man setteth on himself.

The public worth of a man, which is the value set on him by the commonwealth, is that which men commonly call 'dignity.' And this value of him by the commonwealth is understood by offices of command, judicature, public employment, or by names and titles introduced for distinction of such value.

To pray to another for aid of any kind is 'to honour,' because a sign we have an opinion he has power to help; and the more difficult the aid is, the more is the honour.

To obey is to honour, because no man obeys them whom they think have no power to help or hurt them. And consequently to disobey is to 'dishonour.'

To give great gifts to a man is to honour him, because it is buying of protection and acknowledging of power. To give little gifts is to dishonour, because it is but alms and signifies an opinion of the need of small helps.

To be sedulous in promoting another's good, also to flatter is to honour, as a sign we seek his protection or aid. To neglect is to dishonour.

To give way or place to another in any commodity is to honour, being a confession of greater power. To arrogate is to dishonour.

To show any sign of love or fear of another is to honour, for both to love and to fear is to value. To contemn, or less to love or fear than he expects, is to dishonour, for it is undervaluing.

To praise, magnify, or call happy, is to honour, because nothing but goodness, power, and felicity, is valued. To revile, mock, or pity, is to dishonour.

To speak to another with consideration, to appear before him with decency, and humility, is to honour him, as signs of fear to offend. To speak to him rashly, to do anything before him obscenely, slovenly, impudently, is to dishonour.

To believe, to trust, to rely on another, is to honour him, a sign of opinion of his virtue and power. To distrust, or not believe, is to dishonour.

To hearken to a man's counsel or discourse, of what kind soever, is to honour, as a sign we think him wise, or eloquent, or witty. To sleep, or go forth, or talk the while, is to dishonour.

To do those things to another which he takes for signs of honour, or which the law or custom makes so, is to honour, because in approving the honour done by others he acknowledgeth the power which others acknowledge. To refuse to do them is to dishonour.

To agree with in opinion is to honour, as being a sign of approving his judgment and wisdom. To dissent is dishonour, and an upbraiding of error, and, if the dissent be in many things, of folly.

To imitate is to honour, for it is vehemently to approve. To imitate one's enemy, is to dishonour.

To honour those another honours is to honour him, as a sign of approbation of his judgment. To honour his enemies is to dishonour him.

To employ in counsel or in actions of difficulty is to honour, as a sign of opinion of his wisdom or other power. To deny employment in the same cases to those that seek it is to dishonour.

All these ways of honouring are natural, and as well within as without commonwealths. But in commonwealths, where he or they that have the supreme authority can make whatsoever they please to stand for signs of honour, there be other honours.

A sovereign doth honour a subject with whatsoever title, or office, or employment, or action, that he himself will have taken for a sign of his will to honour him.

The King of Persia honoured Mordecai when he appointed he should be conducted through the streets in the king's garment upon one of the king's horses, with a crown on his head and a prince before him, proclaiming 'Thus shall it be done to him that the king will honour.' And yet another king of Persia, or the same another time, to one that demanded for some great service to wear one of the king's robes, gave him leave so to do; but with this addition, that he should wear it as the king's fool; and then it was dishonour. So that of civil honour the fountain is in the person of the commonwealth, and dependeth on the will of the sovereign; and is therefore temporary, and called 'civil honour,' such as magistracy, offices, titles, and, in some places, coats and scutcheons painted; and men honour such as have them, as having so many signs of favour in the commonwealth: which favour is power.

'Honourable' is whatsoever possession, action, or quality, is an argument and sign of power.

And therefore to be honoured, loved, or feared of many, is honourable, as arguments of power. To be honoured of few or none, 'dishonourable.'

Dominion and victory is honourable, because acquired by power; and servitude, for need or fear, is dishonourable.

Good fortune, if lasting, honourable, as a sign of the favour of God. Ill fortune and losses dishonourable. Riches are honourable, for they are power. Poverty, dishonourable. Magnanimity, liberality, hope, courage, confidence, are honourable, for they proceed from the conscience of power. Pusillanimity, parsimony, fear, diffidence, are dishonourable.

Timely resolution, or determination of what a man is to do, is honourable, as being the contempt of small difficulties and dangers. And irresolution, dishonourable, as a sign of too much valuing of little impediments and little advantages; for when a man has weighed things as long as the time permits, and resolves not, the difference of weight is but little, and therefore, if he resolve not, he over-values little things, which is pusillanimity.

All actions and speeches that proceed, or seem to proceed, from much experience, science, discretion, or wit, are honourable, for all these are powers. Actions or words that proceed from error, ignorance, or folly, dishonourable.

Gravity, as far forth as it seems to proceed from a mind employed on something else, is honourable, because employment is a sign of power. But, if it seem to proceed from a purpose to appear grave, it is dishonourable. For the gravity of the former is like the steadiness of a ship laden with merchandise, but of the latter like the steadiness of a ship ballasted with sand and other trash.

To be conspicuous, that is to say to be known, for wealth, office, great actions, or any eminent good, is honourable, as a sign of the power for which he is conspicuous. On the contrary, obscurity is dishonourable.

To be descended from conspicuous parents is honourable, because they the more easily attain the aids and friends of their ancestors. On the contrary, to be descended from obscure parentage is dishonourable.

Actions proceeding from equity joined with loss are honourable, as signs of magnanimity; for magnanimity is a sign of power. On the contrary, craft, shifting, neglect of equity, is dishonourable.

Covetousness of great riches, and ambition of great honours are honourable, as signs of power to obtain them. Covetousness and ambition of little gains or preferments is dishonourable.

Nor does it alter the case of honour whether an action, so it be great and difficult and consequently a sign of much power, be just or unjust; for honour consisteth only in the opinion of power. Therefore the ancient heathen did not think they dishonoured, but greatly honoured, the gods when they introduced them in their poems committing rapes, thefts, and other great but unjust or unclean acts;

insomuch as nothing is so much celebrated in Jupiter as his adulteries; nor in Mercury as his frauds and thefts: of whose praises, in a hymn of Homer, the greatest is this, that, being born in the morning, he had invented music at noon, and before night stolen away the cattle of Apollo from his herdsmen.

Also amongst men, till there were constituted great commonwealths, it was thought no dishonour to be a pirate or a highway thief, but rather a lawful trade, not only amongst the Greeks but also amongst all other nations as is manifest by the histories of ancient time. And at this day, in this part of the world, private duels are and always will be honourable, though unlawful, till such time as there shall be honour ordained for them that refuse, and ignominy for them that make the challenge. For duels also are many times effects of courage, and the ground of courage is always strength or skill, which are power; though for the most part they be effects of rash speaking and of the fear of dishonour, in one or both the combatants, who, engaged by rashness, are driven into the lists to avoid disgrace.

Scutcheons and coats of arms hereditary, where they have any eminent privileges, are honourable; otherwise not: for their power consisteth either in such privileges, or in riches, or some such thing as is equally honoured in other men. This kind of honour, commonly called gentry, hath been derived from the ancient Germans. For there never was any such thing known where the German customs were unknown. Nor is it now anywhere in use where the Germans have not inhabited. The ancient Greek commanders, when they went to war, had their shields painted with such devices as they pleased; insomuch that an unpainted buckler was a sign of poverty and of a common soldier; but they transmitted not the inheritance of them. The Romans transmitted the marks of their families: but they were the images, not the devices, of their ancestors. Amongst the people of Asia, Africa, and America, there is not, nor was ever, any such thing. The Germans only had that custom; from whom it has been derived into England, France, Spain, and Italy, when in great numbers they either aided the Romans or made their own conquests in these western parts of the world.

For Germany, being anciently, as all other countries in their beginnings, divided amongst an infinite number of little lords, or masters of families, that continually had wars one with another, those masters, or lords, principally to the end they might when they were covered with arms be known by their followers, and partly for ornament, both painted their armour or their scutcheon or coat with the picture of some beast or other thing, and also put some eminent and visible mark upon the crest of their helmets. And this ornament both of the arms and crest descended by inheritance to their children; to the eldest pure, and to the rest with some note of diversity, such as the old master, that is to say in Dutch, the *Here-alt,* thought fit. But when many such families, joined together, made a greater monarchy, this duty of the Here-alt to distinguish scutcheons was made a private office apart. And the issue of these lords is the great and ancient gentry, which for the most part bear living creatures, noted for courage and rapine; or castles, battlements, belts, weapons, bars, palisadoes, and other notes of war; nothing being then in honour but virtue military. Afterwards not only kings but popular commonwealths gave divers manners of scutcheons to such as went forth to the war, or returned from it, for encouragement or recompense to their service. All which, by an observing reader, may be found in such ancient histories, Greek and Latin, as make mention of the German nation and manners in their times.

Titles of 'honour,' such as are duke, count, marquis, and baron, are honourable, as signifying the value set upon them by the sovereign power of the commonwealth; which titles were in old time titles of office and command, derived some from the Romans, some from the Germans and French: dukes, in Latin *duces,* being generals in war; counts, *comites,* such as bear the general company out of friendship and were left to govern and defend places conquered and pacified; marquises, *marchiones,* were counts that governed the marches or bounds of the empire. Which titles of duke, count, and marquis, came into the empire about the time of Constantine the Great, from the customs of the German *militia.* But baron seems to have been a title of the Gauls, and signifies a great man, such as were the king's or prince's men, whom they employed in war about their persons, and seems to be derived from *vir,* to 'ber,' and 'bar,' that signified the same in the language of the Gauls, that *vir* in Latin, and thence to 'bero' and 'baro' so that such men were called 'berones,' and after 'barones,' and in Spanish, 'varones.' But he that would know more particularly the original of titles of honour may find it, as I have done this, in Mr. Selden's most excellent treatise of that subject. In process of time these offices of honour, by occasion of trouble and for reasons of good and peaceable government, were turned into mere titles, serving for the most part to distinguish the precedence, place, and order of subjects in the commonwealths; and men were made dukes, counts, marquises and barons, of places wherein they had neither possession nor command; and other titles also were devised to the same end.

'Worthiness' is a thing different from the worth or value of a man, and also from his merit, or desert, and consisteth in a particular power or ability for that whereof he is said to be worthy: which particular ability is usually named 'fitness,' or 'aptitude.'

For he is worthiest to be a commander, to be a judge, or to have any other charge, that is best fitted with the qualities required to the well discharging of it; and worthiest of riches that has the qualities most requisite for the well using of them: any of which qualities being absent, one may nevertheless be a worthy man, and valuable for something else. Again, a man may be worthy of riches, office, and employment, and nevertheless can plead no right to have it before another; and therefore cannot be said to merit or deserve it. For merit presupposeth a right and that the thing deserved is due by promise; of which I shall say more hereafter, when I shall speak of contracts.

CHAPTER XI

OF THE DIFFERENCE OF MANNERS

By manners I mean not here decency of behaviour, as how one man should salute another, or how a man should wash his mouth, or pick his teeth before company, and such other points of the 'small morals'; but those qualities of mankind that concern their living together in peace and unity. To which end we are to consider that the felicity of this life consisteth not in the repose of a mind satisfied. For there is no such *finis ultimus* (utmost aim), nor *summum bonum* (greatest good), as is spoken of in the books of the old moral philosophers. Nor can a man any more live whose desires are at an end than he whose senses and imaginations are at a stand. Felicity is a continual progress of the desire from one object to another, the attaining of the former being still but the way to the latter. The cause whereof is that the object of man's desire is not to enjoy once only and for one instant of time, but to assure for ever the way of his future desire. And therefore the voluntary actions and inclinations of all men tend not only to the procuring, but also to the assuring, of a contented life, and differ only in the way; which ariseth partly from the diversity of passions in divers men, and partly from the difference of the knowledge or opinion each one has of the causes which produce the effect desired.

So that in the first place I put for a general inclination of all mankind a perpetual and restless desire of power after power, that ceaseth only in death. And the cause of this is not always that a man hopes for a more intensive delight than he has already attained to, or that he cannot be content with a moderate power; but because he cannot assure the power and means to live well which he hath present, without the acquisition of more. And from hence it is that kings, whose power is greatest, turn their endeavours to the assuring it at home by laws, or abroad by wars; and, when that is done, there succeedeth a new desire, in some of fame from new conquest, in others of ease and sensual pleasure, in others of admiration or being flattered for excellence in some art or other ability of the mind.

Competition of riches, honour, command, or other power, inclineth to contention, enmity, and war; because the way of one competitor, to the attaining of his desire, is to kill, subdue, supplant, or repel the other. Particularly, competition of praise inclineth to a reverence of antiquity. For men contend with the living, not with the dead, to these ascribing more than due, that they may obscure the glory of the other.

Desire of ease, and sensual delight, disposeth men to obey a common power, because by such desires a man doth abandon the protection that might be hoped for from his own industry and labour. Fear of death, and wounds, disposeth to the same, and for the same reason. On the contrary, needy men, and hardy, not contented with their present condition, as also all men that are ambitious of military command, are inclined to continue the cause of war, and to stir up trouble and sedition, for there is no honour military but by war, nor any such hope to mend an ill game as by causing a new shuffle.

Desire of knowledge, and arts of peace, inclineth men to obey a common power; for such desire, containeth a desire of leisure, and consequently protection from some other power than their own.

Desire of praise disposeth to laudable actions, such as please them whose judgment they value; for, of those men whom we contemn, we contemn also the praises. Desire of fame after death does the same. And though after death there be no sense of the praise given us on earth, as being joys that are either swallowed up in the unspeakable joys of Heaven or extinguished in the extreme torments of hell, yet is not such fame vain; because men have a present delight therein, from the foresight of it, and of the benefit that may redound thereby to their posterity, which, though they now see not, yet they imagine; and anything that is pleasure in the sense, the same also is pleasure in the imagination.

To have received from one to whom we think ourselves equal greater benefits than there is hope to requite disposeth to counterfeit love, but really secret hatred; and puts a man into the estate of a desperate debtor that, in declining the sight of his creditor, tacitly wishes him there where he might never see him more. For benefits oblige, and obligation is thraldom, and unrequitable obligation perpetual thraldom, which is to one's equal, hateful. But to have received benefits from one whom we acknowledge for superior inclines to love; because the obligation is no new depression: and cheerful acceptation, which men call 'gratitude,' is such an honour done to the obliger as is taken generally for retribution. Also to receive benefits, though from an equal or inferior, as long as there is hope of requital, disposeth to love; for, in the intention of the receiver, the obligation is of aid and service mutual, from whence proceedeth an emulation of who shall exceed in benefiting, the most noble and profitable contention possible, wherein the victor is pleased with his victory, and the other revenged by confessing it.

To have done more hurt to a man than he can or is willing to expiate inclineth the doer to hate the sufferer. For he must expect revenge or forgiveness, both which are hateful.

Fear of oppression disposeth a man to anticipate or to seek aid by society; for there is no other way by which a man can secure his life and liberty.

Men that distrust their own subtilty are, in tumult and sedition, better disposed for victory than they that suppose themselves wise or crafty. For these love to consult the other, fearing to be circumvented, to strike, first. And in sedition, men being always in the precincts of battle, to hold together and use all advantages of force is a better stratagem than any that can proceed from subtilty of wit.

Vain-glorious men, such as without being conscious to themselves of great sufficiency delight in supposing themselves gallant men, are inclined only to ostentation, but not to attempt; because, when danger or difficulty appears, they look for nothing but to have their insufficiency discovered.

Vain-glorious men, such as estimate their sufficiency by the flattery of other men or the fortune of some precedent action, without assured ground of hope from the true knowledge of themselves, are inclined to rash engaging, and in the approach of danger or difficulty to retire if they can; because, not seeing the way of safety, they will rather hazard their honour, which may be salved with an excuse, than their lives, for which no salve is sufficient.

Men that have a strong opinion of their own wisdom in matter of government are disposed to ambition. Because without public employment in council or magistracy the honour of the wisdom is lost. And therefore eloquent speakers are inclined to ambition, for eloquence seemeth wisdom, both to themselves and others.

Pusillanimity disposeth men to irresolution, and consequently to lose the occasions and fittest opportunities of action. For after men have been in deliberation till the time of action approach, if it be not then manifest what is best to be done, it is a sign the difference of motives, the one way and the other, are not great: therefore not to resolve then is to lose the occasion by weighing of trifles, which is pusillanimity.

Frugality, though in poor men a virtue, maketh a man unapt to achieve such actions as require the strength of many men at once; for it weakeneth their endeavour, which is to be nourished and kept in vigour by reward.

Eloquence, with flattery disposeth men to confide in them that have it; because the former is seeming wisdom, the latter seeming kindness. Add to them military reputation, and it disposeth men to adhere and subject themselves to those men that have them. The two former having given them caution against danger from him, the latter gives them caution against danger from others.

Want of science, that is, ignorance of causes, disposeth, or rather constraineth, a man to rely on the advice and authority of others. For all men whom the truth concerns, if they rely not on their own, must rely on the opinion of some other whom they think wiser than themselves and see not why he should deceive them.

Ignorance of the signification of words, which is want of understanding, disposeth men to take on trust not only the truth they know not, but also the errors, and which is more, the nonsense of them they trust; for neither error nor nonsense can, without a perfect understanding of words, be detected.

From the same it proceedeth that men give different names to one and the same thing, from the difference of their own passions: as they that approve a private opinion call it opinion, but they that mislike it, heresy: and yet heresy signifies no more than private opinion, but has only a greater tincture of choler.

From the same also it proceedeth that men cannot distinguish, without study and great understanding, between one action of many men and many actions of one multitude; as for example, between the one action of all the senators of Rome in killing Catiline, and the many actions of a number of senators in killing Cæsar; and therefore are disposed to take for the action of the people that which is a multitude of actions done by a multitude of men, led perhaps by the persuasion of one.

Ignorance of the causes and original constitution of right, equity, law, and justice, disposeth a man to make custom and example the rule of his actions; in such manner as to think that unjust which it hath been the custom to punish, and that just of the impunity and approbation whereof they can produce an example, or, as the lawyers which only use this false measure of justice barbarously call it, a precedent; like little children, that have no other rule of good and evil manners but the correction they receive from their parents and masters; save that children are constant to their rule, whereas men are not so; because, grown strong and stubborn, they appeal from custom to reason, and from reason to custom, as it serves their turn; receding from custom when their interest requires it, and setting themselves against reason as oft as reason is against them; which is the cause that the doctrine of right and wrong is perpetually disputed, both by the pen and the sword; whereas the doctrine of lines and figures is not so, because men care not in that subject what be truth, as a thing that crosses no man's ambition, profit, or lust. For I doubt not but, if it had been a thing contrary to any man's right of dominion, or to the interest of men that have dominion, 'that the three angles of a triangle should be equal to two angles of a square,' that doctrine should have been, if not disputed, yet by the burning of all books of geometry, suppressed, as far as he whom it concerned was able.

Ignorance of remote causes disposeth men to attribute all events to the causes immediate and instrumental, for these are all the causes they perceive. And hence it comes to pass that in all places men that are grieved with payments to the public, discharge their anger upon the publicans, that is to say farmers, collectors, and other officers of the public revenue, and adhere to such as find fault with the public government; and thereby, when they have engaged themselves beyond hope of justification, fall also upon the supreme authority, for fear of punishment or shame of receiving pardon.

Ignorance of natural causes disposeth a man to credulity, so as to believe many times impossibilities; for such know nothing to the contrary but that they may be true, being unable to detect the impossibility. And credulity, because men like to be hearkened unto in company, disposeth them to lying, so that ignorance itself without malice is able to make a man both to believe lies and tell them, and sometimes also to invent them.

Anxiety for the future time disposeth men to inquire into the causes of things; because the knowledge of them maketh men the better able to order the present to their best advantage.

Curiosity, or love of the knowledge of causes, draws a man from the consideration of the effect to seek the cause, and, again, the cause of that cause; till of necessity he must come to this thought at last that there is some cause whereof there is no former cause, but is eternal; which is it men call God. So that it is impossible to make any profound inquiry into natural causes without being inclined thereby to believe there is one God eternal; though they cannot have any idea of Him in their mind answerable to His nature. For as a man that is born blind, hearing men talk of warming themselves by the fire and being brought to warm himself by the same, may easily conceive and assure himself, there is somewhat there, which men call 'fire' and is the cause of the heat he feels, but cannot imagine what it is like, nor have an idea of it in his mind such as they have that see it, so also by the visible things of this world, and their admirable order, a man may conceive there is a cause of them, which men call God, and yet not have an idea or image of Him in his mind.

And they that make little or no inquiry into the natural causes of things, yet, from the fear that proceeds from the ignorance itself of what it is that hath the power to do them much good or harm, are inclined to suppose and feign unto themselves several kinds of powers invisible, and to stand in awe of their own imaginations, and in time of distress to invoke them, as also in the time of an expected good success to give them thanks, making the creatures of their own fancy their gods. By which means it hath come to pass that, from the innumerable variety of fancy, men have created in the world innumerable sorts of gods. And this fear of things invisible is the natural seed of that which every one in himself calleth religion, and in them that worship or fear that power otherwise than they do, superstition.

And this seed of religion, having been observed by many, some of those that have observed it have been inclined thereby to nourish, dress, and form it into laws; and to add to it of their own invention any opinion of the causes of future events by which they thought they should be best able to govern others, and make unto themselves the greatest use of their powers.

CHAPTER XII

Of Religion

SEEING there are no signs nor fruit of 'religion' but in man only, there is no cause to doubt but that the seed of 'religion' is also only in man; and consisteth in some peculiar quality or at least in some eminent degree thereof not to be found in other living creatures.

And, first, it is peculiar to the nature of man to be inquisitive into the causes of the events they see, some more, some less; but all men so much as to be curious in the search of the causes of their own good and evil fortune.

Secondly, upon the sight of anything that hath a beginning, to think also it had a cause which determined the same to begin, then when it did, rather than sooner or later.

Thirdly, whereas there is no other felicity of beasts but the enjoying of their quotidian food, ease, and lusts, as having little or no foresight of the time to come, for want of observation and memory of the order, consequence, and dependence of the things they see, man observeth how one event hath been produced by another, and remembereth in them antecedence and consequence; and, when he cannot assure himself of the true causes of things (for the causes of good and evil fortune for the most part are invisible), he supposes causes of them, either such as his own fancy suggesteth, or trusteth the authority of other men, such as he thinks to be his friends and wiser than himself.

The two first make anxiety. For, being assured that there be causes of all things that have arrived hitherto or shall arrive hereafter, it is impossible for a man, who continually endeavoureth to secure himself against the evil he fears and procure the good he desireth, not to be in a perpetual solicitude of the time to come; so that every man, especially those that are over-provident, are in a state like to that of Prometheus. For as Prometheus, which interpreted is 'the prudent man,' was bound to the hill Caucasus, a place of large prospect, where an eagle feeding on his liver devoured in the day as much as was repaired in the night, so that man, which looks too far before him in the care of future time, hath his heart all the day long gnawed on by fear of death, poverty, or other calamity, and has no repose nor pause of his anxiety but in sleep.

This perpetual fear, always accompanying mankind in the ignorance of causes, as it were in the dark, must needs have for object something. And therefore, when there is nothing to be seen, there is nothing to accuse, either of their good or evil fortune, but some 'power' or agent 'invisible' in which sense perhaps it was that some of the old poets said that the gods were at first created by human fear; which spoken of the gods, that is to say of the many gods of the Gentiles, is very true. But the acknowledging of one God, eternal, infinite, and omnipotent, may more easily be derived, from the desire men have to know the causes of natural bodies and their several virtues and operations, than from the fear of what was to befall them in time to come. For he that from any effect he seeth come to pass should reason to the next and immediate cause thereof, and from thence to the cause of that cause, and plunge himself profoundly in the pursuit of causes, shall at last come to this, that there must be, as even the heathen philosophers confessed, one first mover, that is, a first and an eternal cause of all things, which is that which men mean by the name of God, and all this without thought of their fortune; the solicitude whereof both inclines to fear and hinders them from the search of the causes of other things, and thereby gives occasion of feigning of as many gods as there be men that feign them.

And, for the matter or substance of the invisible agents so fancied, they could not by natural cogitation fall upon any other conceit, but that it was the same with that of the soul of man; and that the soul of man was of the same substance with that which appeareth in a dream to one that sleepeth, or in a looking-glass to one that is awake; which, men not knowing that such apparitions are nothing else but creatures of the fancy, think to be real and external substances, and therefore call them ghosts; as the Latins called them *imagines* and *umbræ,* and thought them spirits, that is thin aërial bodies, and those invisible agents which they feared, to be like them, save that they appear and vanish when they please. But the opinion that such spirits were incorporeal, or immaterial, could never enter into the mind of any man by nature, because, though men may put together words of contradictory signification, as 'spirit' and 'incorporeal,' yet they can never have the imagination of anything answering to them; and therefore men that by their own meditation arrive to the acknowledgment of one infinite, omnipotent, and eternal God chose rather to confess He is incomprehensible and above their understanding than to define His nature by 'spirit incorporeal,' and then confess their definition to be unintelligible; or, if they give Him such a title, it is not 'dogmatically' with intention to make the divine nature understood, but 'piously,' to honour Him with attributes of significations as remote as they can from the grossness of bodies visible.

Then for the way by which they think these invisible agents wrought their effects, that is to say, what immediate causes they used in bringing things to pass, men that know not what it is that we call 'causing,' that is almost all men, have no other rule to guess by but by observing and remembering what they have seen to precede the like effect at some other time or times before, without seeing between the antecedent and subsequent event any dependence or connection at all; and therefore from the like things past they expect the like things to come, and hope for good or evil luck, superstitiously, from things that have no part at all in the causing of it: as the Athenians did for their war at Lepanto, demand another Phormio; the Pompeian faction for their war in Africa, another Scipio; and others have done in divers other occasions since. In like manner they attribute their fortune to a stander-by, to a lucky or unlucky place, to words spoken, especially if the name God be amongst them, as charming and conjuring, the liturgy of witches; inasmuch as to believe they have power to turn a stone into bread, bread into a man, or anything into anything.

Thirdly, for the worship which naturally men exhibit to powers invisible, it can be no other but such expressions of their reverence, as they would use towards men; gifts, petitions, thanks, submission of body, considerate addresses, sober behaviour, premeditated words, swearing, that is assuring one another of their promises by invoking them. Beyond that, reason suggesteth nothing, but leaves them either to rest there, or, for further ceremonies, to rely on those they believe to be wiser than themselves.

Lastly, concerning how these invisible powers declare to men the things which shall hereafter come to pass, especially concerning their good or evil fortune in general or good or ill-success in any particular undertaking, men are naturally at a stand, save that, using to conjecture of the time to come by the time past, they are very apt not only to take casual things, after one or two encounters, for prognostics of the like encounter ever after, but also to believe the like prognostics from other men of whom they have once conceived a good opinion.

And, in these four things, opinion of ghosts, ignorance of second causes, devotion towards what men fear, and taking of things casual for prognostics, consisteth the natural seed of 'religion,' which, by reason of the different fancies, judgments, and passions of several men, hath grown up into ceremonies so different that those which are used by one man are for the most part ridiculous to another.

. For these seeds have received culture from two sorts of men. One sort have been they that have nourished and ordered them according to their own invention. The other have done it by God's commandment and direction; but both sorts have done it with a purpose to make those men that relied on them the more apt to obedience, laws, peace, charity, and civil society. So that the religion of the former sort is a part of human politics, and teacheth part of the duty which earthly kings require of their subjects. And the religion of the latter sort is divine politics, and containeth precepts to those that have yielded themselves subjects in the kingdom of God. Of the former sort were all the founders of commonwealths and the lawgivers of the Gentiles; of the latter sort, were Abraham, Moses, and our blessed Saviour, by whom have been derived unto us the laws of the kingdom of God.

And, for that part of religion which consisteth in opinions concerning the nature of powers invisible, there is almost nothing that has a name that has not been esteemed amongst the Gentiles, in one place or another, a god or devil, or by their poets feigned to be inanimated, inhabited, or possessed, by some spirit or other.

The unformed matter of the world was a god by the name of Chaos.

The heaven, the ocean, the planets, the fire, the earth, the winds, were so many gods.

Men, women, a bird, a crocodile, a calf, a dog, a snake, an onion, a leek, were deified. Besides that, they filled almost all places with spirits called 'demons': the plains with Pan and Panises or Satyrs, the woods with Fauns and Nymphs, the sea with Tritons and other Nymphs, every river and fountain with a ghost of his name and with Nymphs, every house with its 'Lares' or familiars, every man with his 'Genius,' hell with ghosts and spiritual officers, as Charon, Cerberus, and the Furies, and in the night-time, all places with 'larvæ,' 'lemures,' ghosts of men deceased and a whole kingdom of fairies and bugbears. They have also ascribed divinity, and built temples to mere accidents and qualities, such as are time, night, day, peace, concord, love, contention, virtue, honour, health, rust, fever, and the like; which when they prayed for or against they prayed to, as if there were ghosts of those names hanging over their heads, and letting fall or withholding that good or evil for or against which they prayed. They invoked also their own wit by the name of Muses, their own ignorance by the name of Fortune, their own lust by the name of Cupid, their own rage by the name of Furies, their own privy members by the name of Priapus; and attributed their pollutions to Incubi and Succubæ: insomuch as there was nothing which a poet could introduce as a person in his poem which they did not make either a 'god' or a 'devil.'

The same authors of the religion of the Gentiles, observing the second ground for religion, which is men's ignorance of causes, and thereby their aptness to attribute their fortune to causes on which there was no dependence at all apparent, took occasion to obtrude on their ignorance, instead of second causes, a kind of second and ministerial gods, ascribing the cause of fecundity to Venus, the cause of arts to Apollo, of subtlety and craft to Mercury, of tempests and storms to Æolus, and of other effects to other gods; insomuch as there was amongst the heathen almost as great variety of gods as of business.

And to the worship which naturally men conceived fit to be used towards their gods, namely, oblations, prayers, thanks, and the rest formerly named, the same legislators of the Gentiles have added their images, both in picture and sculpture, that the more ignorant sort, that is to say the most part or generality of the people, thinking the gods for whose representation they were made were really included and as it were housed within them, might so much the more stand in fear of them; and endowed them with lands, and houses, and officers, and revenues, set apart from all other human uses, that is consecrated and made holy to those their idols, as caverns, groves, woods, mountains, and whole islands; and have attributed to them not only the shapes, some of men, some of beasts, some of monsters, but also the faculties and passions of men and beasts, as sense, speech, sex, lust, generation; and this not only by mixing one with another to propagate the kind of gods, but also by mixing with men and women to beget mongrel gods, and but inmates of heaven, as Bacchus, Hercules, and others; besides anger, revenge, and other passions, of living creatures, and the actions proceeding from them, as fraud, theft, adultery, sodomy, and any vice that may be taken for an effect of power or a cause of pleasure; and all such vices as amongst men are taken to be against law rather than against honour.

Lastly, to the prognostics of time to come, which are naturally but conjectures upon experience of time past, and supernaturally, divine revelation, the same authors of the religion of the Gentiles, partly upon pretended experience partly upon pretended revelation, have added innumerable other superstitious ways of divination, and made men believe they should find their fortunes, sometimes in the ambiguous or senseless answers of the priests at Delphi, Delos, Ammon, and other famous oracles, which answers were made ambiguous by design, to own the event both ways, or absurd, by the intoxicating vapour of the place, which is very frequent in sulphurous caverns: sometimes in the leaves of the Sibyls, of whose prophecies, like those perhaps of Nostradamus (for the fragments now extant seem to be the invention of later times), there were some books in reputation in the time of the Roman Republic; sometimes in the insignificant speeches of madmen supposed to be possessed with a divine spirit, which possession they called enthusiasm, and these kinds of foretelling events were accounted theomancy, or prophecy; sometimes in the aspect of the stars at their nativity, which was called horoscopy and esteemed a part of judiciary astrology; sometimes in their own hopes and fears, called thumomancy, or presage; sometimes in the prediction of witches, that pretended conference with the dead, which is called necromancy, conjuring, and witchcraft, and is but juggling and confederate knavery; sometimes in the casual flight or feeding of birds, called augury; sometimes in the entrails of a sacrificed beast, which was 'aruspicina'; sometimes in dreams; sometimes in croaking of ravens or chattering of birds; sometimes in the lineaments of the face, which was called metoposcopy; or by palmistry in the lines of the hand; in casual words, called 'omina'; sometimes in monsters or unusual accidents, as eclipses, comets, rare meteors, earthquakes, inundations, uncouth births, and the like, which they called 'portenta' and 'ostenta,' because they thought them to portend or foreshow some great calamity to come; sometimes in mere lottery, as cross and pile, counting holes in a sieve, dipping of verses in Homer and Virgil; and innumerable other such vain conceits. So easy are men to be drawn to believe anything from such men as have gotten credit with them and can with gentleness and dexterity take hold of their fear and ignorance.

And therefore the first founders and legislators of commonwealths among the Gentiles, whose ends were only to keep the people in obedience and peace, have in all places taken care, first to imprint in their minds a belief that those precepts which they gave concerning religion might not be thought to proceed from their own device but from the dictates of some god or other spirit, or else that they themselves were of a higher nature than mere mortals, that their laws might the more easily be received: so Numa Pompilius pretended to receive the ceremonies he instituted amongst the Romans from the nymph Egeria; and the first king and founder of the kingdom of Peru pretended himself and his wife to be the children of the Sun, and Mahomet, to set up his new religion, pretended to have conferences with the Holy Ghost in form of a dove. Secondly, they have had a care to make it believed that the same things were displeasing to the gods which were forbidden by the laws. Thirdly, to prescribe ceremonies, supplications, sacrifices, and festivals, by which they were to believe the anger of the gods might be appeased, and that ill success in war, great contagions of sickness, earthquakes, and each man's private misery, came from the anger of the gods, and their anger from the neglect of their worship or the forgetting or mistaking some point of the ceremonies required. And, though amongst the ancient Romans men were not forbidden to deny that which in the poets is written of the pains and pleasures after this life, which divers of great authority and gravity in that state have in their harangues openly derided, yet that belief was always more cherished than the contrary.

And by these and such other institutions they obtained in order to their end, which was the peace of the commonwealth, that the common people in their misfortunes, laying the fault on neglect or error in their ceremonies or on their own disobedience to the laws, were the less apt to mutiny against their governors, and, being entertained with the pomp and pastime of festivals and public games made in honour of the gods, needed nothing else but bread to keep them from discontent, murmuring, and commotion against the state. And therefore the Romans, that had conquered the greatest part of the then known world, made no scruple of tolerating any religion whatsoever in the city of Rome itself, unless it had something in it that could not consist with their civil government; nor do we read that any religion was there forbidden but that of the Jews, who, being the peculiar kingdom of God, thought it unlawful to acknowledge subjection to any mortal king or state whatsoever. And thus you see how the religion of the Gentiles was part of their policy.

But where God Himself by supernatural revelation planted religion, there He also made to Himself a peculiar kingdom, and gave laws not only of behaviour towards Himself but also towards one another; and thereby in the kingdom of God the policy and laws civil are a part of religion; and therefore the distinction of temporal and spiritual domination hath there no place. It is true that God is king of all the earth, yet may He be king of a peculiar and chosen nation. For there is no more incongruity therein than that he that hath the general command of the whole army should have withal a peculiar regiment or company of his own. God is king of all the earth by His power, but of His chosen people He is king by covenant. But to speak more largely of the kingdom of God, both by nature and covenant, I have in the following discourse assigned another place.

From the propagation of religion it is not hard to understand the causes of the resolution of the same into its first seeds or principles, which are only an opinion of a deity and powers invisible and supernatural that can never be so abolished out of human nature but that new religions may again be made to spring out of them, by the culture of such men as for such purpose are in reputation.

For, seeing all formed religion is founded at first upon the faith which a multitude hath in some one person whom they believe not only to be a wise man, and to labour to procure their happiness, but also to be a holy man, to whom God Himself vouchsafeth to declare His will supernaturally, it followeth necessarily, when they that have the government of religion shall come to have either the wisdom of those men, their sincerity, or their love suspected, or when they shall be unable to show any probable token of divine revelation, that the religion which they desire to uphold must be suspected likewise, and, without the fear of the civil sword, contradicted and rejected.

That which taketh away the reputation of wisdom, in him that formeth a religion or addeth to it when it is already formed, is the enjoining of a belief of contradictories, for both parts of a contradiction cannot possibly be true; and therefore to enjoin the belief of them is an argument of ignorance, which detects the author in that, and discredits him in all things else he shall propound as from revelation supernatural; which revelation a man may indeed have of many things above but of nothing against natural reason.

That which taketh away the reputation of sincerity is the doing or saying of such things as appear to be signs that what they require other men to believe is not believed by themselves, all which doings or sayings are therefore called scandalous, because they be stumbling-blocks that make men to fall in the way of religion, as injustice, cruelty, profaneness, avarice, and luxury. For who can believe that he that doth ordinarily such actions as proceed from any of these roots believeth there is any such invisible power to be feared, as he affrighteth other men withal for lesser faults?

That which taketh away the reputation of love is the being detected of private ends, as when the belief they require of others conduceth or seemeth to conduce to the acquiring of dominion, riches, dignity, or secure pleasure to themselves only or specially. For that which men reap benefit by to themselves they are thought to do for their own sakes, and not for love of others.

Lastly, the testimony that men can render of divine calling can be no other than the operation of miracles, or true prophecy, which also is a miracle, or extraordinary felicity. And, therefore, to those points of religion which have been received from them that did such miracles, those that are added by such as approve not their calling by some miracle obtain no greater belief than what the custom and laws of the places in which they be educated have wrought into them. For, as in natural things, men of judgment require natural signs and arguments, so in supernatural things they require signs supernatural, which are miracles, before they consent inwardly and from their hearts.

All which causes of the weakening of men's faith do manifestly appear in the examples following. First, we have the example of the children of Israel, who when Moses, that had approved his calling to them by miracles and by the happy conduct of them out of Egypt was absent but forty days, revolted from the worship of the true God, recommended to them by him, and setting up (*Exod.* xxxii, 1, 2) a golden calf for their god relapsed into the idolatry of the Egyptians, from whom they had been so lately delivered. And again, after Moses, Aaron, Joshua, and that generation which had seen the great works of God in Israel (*Judges* ii, 11) were dead, another generation arose and served Baal. So that, miracles failing, faith also failed.

Again, when the sons of Samuel (1 *Sam.* viii, 3) being constituted by their father judges in Bersabee, received bribes, and judged unjustly, the people of Israel refused any more to have God to be their king in other manner than He was king of other people, and therefore cried out to Samuel to choose them a king after the manner of the nations. So that, justice failing, faith also failed; insomuch as they deposed their God from reigning over them.

And whereas in the planting of Christian religion the oracles ceased in all parts of the Roman Empire, and the number of Christians, increased wonderfully every day and in every place by the preaching of the Apostles and Evangelists, a great part of that success may reasonably be attributed to the contempt into which the priests of the Gentiles of that time had brought themselves by their uncleanness, avarice, and juggling between princes. Also the religion of the Church of Rome was partly for the same cause abolished in England and many other parts of Christendom, insomuch as the failing of virtue in the pastors maketh faith fail in the people; and partly from bringing of the philosophy and doctrine of Aristotle into religion by the schoolmen, from whence there arose so many contradictions and absurdities as brought the clergy into a reputation both of ignorance and of fraudulent intention, and inclined people to revolt from them, either against the will of their own princes, as in France and Holland, or with their will, as in England.

Lastly, amongst the points by the Church of Rome declared necessary for salvation, there be so many manifestly to the advantage of the Pope and of his spiritual subjects residing in the territories of other Christian princes that, were it not for the mutual emulation of those princes, they might without war or trouble exclude all foreign authority as easily as it had been excluded in England. For who is there that does not see to whose benefit it conduceth to have it believed that a king hath not his authority from Christ unless a bishop crown him? That a king, if he be a priest, cannot marry? That whether a prince be born in lawful marriage or not must be judged by authority from Rome? That subjects may be freed from their allegiance, if by the Court of Rome the king be judged an heretic? That a king, as Chilperic of France, may be deposed by a pope, as Pope Zachary, for no cause, and his kingdom given to one of his subjects? That the clergy and regulars, in what country soever, shall be exempt from the jurisdiction of their king in cases criminal? Or who does not see to whose profit redound the fees of private masses and vales of purgatory, with other signs of private interest enough to mortify the most lively faith, if, as I said, the civil magistrate and custom did not more sustain it than any opinion they have of the sanctity, wisdom, or probity of their teachers?

So that I may attribute all the changes of religion in the world to one and the same cause, and that is, unpleasing priests; and those not only amongst Catholics but even in that Church that hath presumed most of reformation.

CHAPTER XIII

OF THE NATURAL CONDITION OF MANKIND AS CONCERNING THEIR FELICITY AND MISERY

NATURE hath made men so equal in the faculties of the body and mind, as that, though there be found one man sometimes manifestly stronger in body or of quicker mind than another, yet when all is reckoned together the difference between man and man is not so considerable as that one man can thereupon claim to himself any benefit to which another may not pretend as well as he. For, as to the strength of body, the weakest has strength enough to kill the strongest, either by secret machination or by confederacy with others that are in the same danger with himself.

And, as to the faculties of the mind, setting aside the arts grounded upon words and especially that skill of proceeding upon general and infallible rules called science, which very few have and but in few things, as being not a native faculty born with us, nor attained, as prudence, while we look after somewhat else, I find yet a greater equality amongst men than that of strength. For prudence is but experience, which equal time equally bestows on all men in those things they equally apply themselves unto. That which may perhaps make such equality incredible is but a vain conceit of one's own wisdom, which almost all men think they have in a greater degree than the vulgar, that is, than all men but themselves, and a few others whom by fame or for concurring with themselves they approve. For such is the nature of men that, howsoever they may acknowledge many others to be more witty or more eloquent or more learned, yet they will hardly believe there be many so wise as themselves, for they see their own wit at hand and other men's at a distance. But this proveth rather that men are in that point equal than unequal. For there is not ordinarily a greater sign of the equal distribution of anything than that every man is contented with his share.

From this equality of ability ariseth equality of hope in the attaining of our ends. And therefore, if any two men desire the same thing which nevertheless they cannot both enjoy, they become enemies; and, in the way to their end, which is principally their own conservation and sometimes their delectation only, endeavour to destroy or subdue one another. And from hence it comes to pass that, where an invader hath no more to fear than another man's single power, if one plant, sow, build, or possess, a convenient seat, others may probably be expected to come prepared with forces united to dispossess and deprive him not only of the fruit of his labour but also of his life or liberty. And the invader again is in the like danger of another.

And from this diffidence of one another there is no way for any man to secure himself so reasonable as anticipation, that is, by force or wiles to master the persons of all men he can so long till he see no other power great enough to endanger him; and this is no more than his own conservation requireth and is generally allowed. Also, because there be some that, taking pleasure in contemplating their own power in the acts of conquest, which they pursue farther than their security requires, if others, that otherwise would be glad to be at ease within the modest bounds, should not by invasion increase their power, they would not be able long time, by standing only on their defence, to subsist. And by consequence, such augmentation of dominion over men being necessary to a man's conservation, it ought to be allowed him.

Again, men have no pleasure, but on the contrary a great deal of grief, in keeping company where there is no power able to overawe them all. For every man looketh that his companion should value him at the same rate he sets upon himself, and, upon all signs of contempt or undervaluing, naturally endeavours as far as he dares (which amongst them that have no common power to keep them in quiet, is far enough to make them destroy each other) to extort a greater value from his contemners by damage, and from others by the example.

So that in the nature of man we find three principal causes of quarrel. First, competition; secondly, diffidence; thirdly, glory.

The first maketh man invade for gain; the second, for safety; and the third, for reputation. The first use violence, to make themselves masters of other men's persons, wives, children, and cattle; the second, to defend them; the third, for trifles, as a word, a smile, a different opinion, and any other sign of undervalue, either direct in their persons or by reflection in their kindred, their friends, their nation, their profession, or their name.

Hereby it is manifest that, during the time men live without a common power to keep them all in awe, they are in that condition which is called war, and such a war as is of every man against every man. For 'war' consisteth not in battle only or the act of fighting, but in a tract of time wherein the will to contend by battle is sufficiently known, and therefore the notion of 'time' is to be considered in the nature of war, as it is in the nature of weather. For as the nature of foul weather lieth not in a shower or two of rain but in an inclination thereto of many days together, so the nature of war consisteth not in actual fighting but in the known disposition thereto during all the time there is no assurance to the contrary. All other time is 'peace.'

Whatsoever therefore is consequent to a time of war where every man is enemy to every man, the same is consequent to the time wherein men live without other security than what their own strength and their own invention shall furnish them withal. In such condition there is no place for industry, because the fruit thereof is uncertain, and consequently no culture of the earth, no navigation nor use of the commodities that may be imported by sea, no commodious building, no instruments of moving and removing such things as require much force, no knowledge of the face of the earth; no account of time, no arts, no letters, no society, and, which is worst of all, continual fear and danger of violent death, and the life of man solitary, poor, nasty, brutish, and short.

It may seem strange to some man that has not well weighed these things that Nature should thus dissociate and render men apt to invade and destroy one another; and he may therefore, not trusting to this inference made from the passions, desire perhaps to

have the same confirmed by experience. Let him therefore consider
with himself, when taking a journey, he arms himself and seeks to
go well accompanied; when going to sleep, he locks his doors; when
even in his house, he locks his chests; and this when he knows
there be laws and public officers armed to revenge all injuries shall
be done him; what opinion he has of his fellow-subjects when he
rides armed; of his fellow-citizens, when he locks his doors; and of
his children and servants, when he locks his chests. Does he not
there as much accuse mankind by his actions as I do by my words?
But neither of us accuse man's nature in it. The desires and other
passions of man are in themselves no sin. No more are the actions
that proceed from those passions, till they know a law that forbids
them; which, till laws be made, they cannot know, nor can any
law be made till they have agreed upon the person that shall make it.

It may peradventure be thought there was never such a time nor
condition of war as this; and I believe it was never generally so
over all the world, but there are many places where they live so
now. For the savage people in many places of America, except the
government of small families the concord whereof dependeth on
natural lust, have no government at all, and live at this day in
that brutish manner as I said before. Howsoever, it may be perceived
what manner of life there would be where there were no common
power to fear, by the manner of life which men that have formerly
lived under a peaceful government use to degenerate into, in a
civil war.

But, though there had never been any time wherein particular
men were in a condition of war one against another, yet in all times
kings and persons of sovereign authority, because of their independency, are in continual jealousies and in the state and posture of
gladiators, having their weapons pointing, and their eyes fixed on
one another, that is, their forts, garrisons, and guns, upon the
frontiers of their kingdoms, and continual spies upon their neighbours: which is a posture of war. But because they uphold thereby
the industry of their subjects, there does not follow from it that
misery which accompanies the liberty of particular men.

To this war of every man against every man this also is consequent, that nothing can be unjust. The notions of right and wrong,

justice and injustice, have there no place. Where there is no common power, there is no law; where no law, no injustice. Force and fraud are in war the two cardinal virtues. Justice and injustice are none of the faculties neither of the body nor mind. If they were, they might be in a man that were alone in the world, as well as his senses and passions. They are qualities that relate to men in society, not in solitude. It is consequent also to the same condition that there be no propriety, no dominion, no 'mine' and 'thine' distinct, but only that to be every man's that he can get, and for so long as he can keep it. And thus much for the ill condition which man by mere nature is actually placed in, though with a possibility to come out of it, consisting partly in the passions, partly in his reason.

The passions that incline men to peace are fear of death, desire of such things as are necessary to commodious living, and a hope by their industry to obtain them. And reason suggesteth convenient articles of peace, upon which men may be drawn to agreement. These articles are they which otherwise are called the Laws of Nature, whereof I shall speak more particularly in the two following chapters.

CHAPTER XIV

Of the First and Second Natural Laws, and of Contracts

'The right of Nature,' which writers commonly call *jus naturale,* is the liberty each man hath to use his own power as he will himself for the preservation of his own nature, that is to say, of his own life; and consequently of doing anything which in his own judgment and reason he shall conceive to be the aptest means thereunto.

By 'liberty' is understood, according to the proper signification of the word, the absence of external impediments; which impediments may oft take away part of a man's power to do what he would, but cannot hinder him from using the power left him according as his judgment and reason shall dictate to him.

A 'law of Nature,' *lex naturalis,* is a precept or general rule found out by reason by which a man is forbidden to do that which is destructive of his life or taketh away the means of preserving the same, and to omit that by which he thinketh it may be best preserved. For, though they that speak of this subject use to confound *jus* and *lex,* 'right' and 'law,' yet they ought to be distinguished; because 'right' consisteth in liberty to do or to forbear, whereas 'law' determineth and bindeth to one of them; so that law and right differ as much as obligation and liberty; which in one and the same matter are inconsistent.

And because the condition of man, as hath been declared in the precedent chapter, is a condition of war of every one against every one, in which case every one is governed by his own reason, and there is nothing he can make use of that may not be a help unto him in preserving his life against his enemies, it followeth that in such a condition every man has a right to everything, even to one another's body. And therefore, as long as this natural right of every man to everything endureth, there can be no security to any man, how strong or wise soever he be, of living out the time which Nature ordinarily alloweth men to live. And consequently it is a precept or general rule of reason 'that every man ought to endeavour peace as far as he has hope of obtaining it, and, when he cannot obtain it, that he may seek and use all helps and advantages of war.' The first branch of which rule containeth the first and fundamental law of Nature, which is, 'to seek peace, and follow it.' The second, the sum of the right of Nature, which is, 'by all means we can, to defend ourselves.'

From this fundamental law of Nature, by which men are commanded to endeavour peace, is derived this second law, 'that a man be willing, when others are so too, as far-forth as for peace and defence of himself he shall think it necessary, to lay down this right to all things, and be contented with so much liberty against other men as he would allow other men against himself.' For as long as every man holdeth this right of doing anything he liketh, so long are all men in the condition of war. But if other men will not lay down their right as well as he, then there is no reason for any one to divest himself of his; for that were to expose himself to prey, which no man is bound to, rather than to dispose himself to peace. This is that law of the Gospel: 'whatsoever you require that others should do to you, that do ye to them.' And that law of all men, *quod tibi fieri non vis, alteri ne feceris.*

To 'lay down' a man's 'right' to anything is to 'divest' himself of the 'liberty,' of hindering another of the benefit of his own right to the same. For he that renounceth or passeth away his right giveth not to any other man a right which he had not before, because there is nothing to which every man had not right by Nature; but only standeth out of his way that he may enjoy his own original right without hindrance from him, not without hindrance from another. So that the effect which redoundeth to one man, by another man's defect of right, is but so much diminution of impediments to the use of his own right original.

Right is laid aside either by simply renouncing it, or by transferring it to another. By 'simply renouncing' when he cares not to whom the benefit thereof redoundeth. By 'transferring,' when he intendeth the benefit thereof to some certain person or persons. And, when a man hath in either manner abandoned or granted away his right, then is he said to be 'obliged' or 'bound' not to hinder those to whom such right is granted or abandoned from the benefit of it; and that he 'ought,' and it is his 'duty,' not to make void that voluntary act of his own; and that such hindrance is 'injustice' and 'injury' as being *sine jure,* the right being before renounced or transferred. So that 'injury' or 'injustice,' in the controversies of the world, is somewhat like to that which in the disputations of scholars is called 'absurdity.' For, as it is there called an absurdity to contradict what one maintained in the beginning, so in the world it is called injustice and injury voluntarily to undo that from the beginning he had voluntarily done. The way by which a man either simply renounceth or transferreth his right is a declaration or signification, by some voluntary and sufficient sign or signs, that he doth so renounce or transfer, or hath so renounced or transferred, the same, to him that accepteth it. And these signs are either words only or actions only, or, as it happeneth most often, both words and actions. And the same are the 'bonds' by which men are bound and obliged: bonds that have their strength not from their own nature, for nothing is more easily broken than a man's word, but from fear of some evil consequence upon the rupture.

Whensoever a man transferreth his right or renounceth it, it is either in consideration of some right reciprocally transferred to himself, or for some other good he hopeth for thereby. For it is a voluntary act; and of the voluntary acts of every man the object is some good 'to himself.' And therefore there be some rights which no man can be understood by any words or other signs to have abandoned or transferred. As first a man cannot lay down the right of resisting them that assault him by force to take away his life, because he cannot be understood to aim thereby at any good to himself. The same may be said of wounds, and chains, and imprisonment, both because there is no benefit consequent to such patience, as there is to the patience of suffering another to be wounded or imprisoned, as also because a man cannot tell when he seeth men proceed against him by violence whether they intend his death or not. And lastly the motive and end for which this renouncing and transferring of right is introduced is nothing else but the security of a man's person in his life and in the means of so preserving life as not to be weary of it. And therefore, if a man by words or other signs seem to despoil himself of the end for which those signs were intended, he is not to be understood as if he meant it or that it was his will, but that he was ignorant of how such words and actions were to be interpreted.

The mutual transferring of right is that which men call 'contract.'

There is difference between transferring of right to the thing and transferring or tradition, that is delivery of the thing itself. For the thing may be delivered together with the translation of the right, as in buying and selling with ready money, or exchange of goods or lands, and it may be delivered some time after.

Again, one of the contractors may deliver the thing contracted for on his part, and leave the other to perform his part at some determinate time after, and in the meantime be trusted; and then the contract on his part is called 'pact,' or 'covenant'; or both parts may contract now to perform hereafter; in which cases he that is to perform in time to come, being trusted, his performance is called 'keeping of promise,' or faith, and the failing of performance, if it be voluntary, 'violation of faith.'

When the transferring of right is not mutual, but one of the parties transferreth in hope to gain thereby the friendship or service from another or from his friends, or in hope to gain the reputation of charity or magnanimity, or to deliver his mind from the pain of compassion, or in hope of reward in heaven, this is not contract but 'gift,' 'free gift,' 'grace,' which words signify one and the same thing.

Signs of contract are either 'express' or 'by inference.' 'Express' are words spoken with understanding of what they signify, and such words are either of the time 'present' or 'past,' as 'I give,' 'I grant,' 'I have given,' 'I have granted,' 'I will that this be yours'; or of the future, as 'I will give,' 'I will grant,' which words of the future are called 'promise.'

Signs by inference are sometimes the consequence of words, sometimes the consequence of silence, sometimes the consequence of actions, sometimes the consequence of forbearing an action; and generally a sign by inference of any contract is whatsoever sufficiently argues the will of the contractor.

Words alone, if they be of the time to come and contain a bare promise, are an insufficient sign of a free gift, and therefore not obligatory. For if they be of the time to come, as 'to-morrow I will give,' they are a sign I have not given yet, and consequently that my right is not transferred, but remaineth till I transfer it by some other act. But if the words be of the time present or past, as 'I have given,' or 'do give to be delivered to-morrow,' then is my to-morrow's right given away to-day, and that by the virtue of the words, though there were no other argument of my will. And there is a great difference in the signification of these words *volo hoc tuum esse cras* and *cras dabo,* that is, between 'I will that this be thine to-morrow,' and 'I will give it thee to-morrow,' for the word 'I will,' in the former manner of speech, signifies an act of the will present, but in the latter it signifies a promise of an act of the will to come; and therefore the former words, being of the present, transfer a future right; the latter, that be of the future, transfer nothing. But if there be other signs of the will to transfer a right besides words, then, though the gift be free, yet may the right be understood to pass by words of the future; as, if a man propound a prize to him that comes first to the end of a race, the gift is free;

and, though the words be of the future, yet the right passeth; for if he would not have his words so be understood, he should not have let them run.

In contracts the right passeth not only where the words are of the time present or past, but also where they are of the future; because all contract is mutual translation or change of right, and therefore he that promiseth only because he hath already received the benefit for which he promiseth is to be understood as if he intended the right should pass, for, unless he had been content to have his words so understood, the other would not have performed his part first. And for that cause, in buying and selling and other acts of contracts, a promise is equivalent to a covenant, and therefore obligatory.

He that performeth first in the case of a contract is said to 'merit' that which he is to receive by the performance of the other, and he hath it as 'due.' Also when a prize is propounded to many which is to be given to him only that winneth, or money is thrown amongst many to be enjoyed by them that catch it, though this be a free gift, yet so to win or so to catch is to 'merit,' and to have it as 'due.' For the right is transferred in the propounding of the prize and in throwing down the money, though it be not determined to whom but by the event of the contention. But there is between these two sorts of merit this difference, that in contract I merit by virtue of my own power and the contractor's need, but in this case of free gift I am enabled to merit only by the benignity of the giver: in contract I merit at the contractor's hand that he should depart with his right; in this case of gift I merit not that the giver should part with his right, but that, when he has parted with it, it should be mine rather than another's. And this I think to be the meaning of that distinction of the schools between *meritum congrui* and *meritum condigni*. For God Almighty, having promised Paradise to those men hoodwinked with carnal desires that can walk through this world according to the precepts and limits prescribed by Him, they say he that shall so walk shall merit Paradise *ex congruo*. But because no man can demand a right to it by his own righteousness or any other power in himself, but by the free grace of God only, they say, no man can merit Paradise *ex condigno*. This, I say, I think is the meaning of that distinction; but, because disputers do not agree upon the signification of their own terms of art longer than it serves their turn, I will not affirm anything of their meaning: only this I say—when a gift is given indefinitely as a prize to be contended for, he that winneth meriteth, and may claim the prize as due.

If a covenant be made wherein neither of the parties perform presently but trust one another, in the condition of mere nature, which is a condition of war of every man against every man, upon any reasonable suspicion, it is void; but, if there be a common power set over them both with right and force sufficient to compel performance, it is not void. For he that performeth first has no assurance the other will perform after, because the bonds of words are too weak to bridle men's ambition, avarice, anger, and other passions, without the fear of some coercive power, which in the condition of mere nature, where all men are equal and judges of the justness of their own fears, cannot possibly be supposed. And, therefore, he which performeth first does but betray himself to his enemy, contrary to the right, he can never abandon, of defending his life and means of living.

But in a civil estate, where there is a power set up to constrain those that would otherwise violate their faith, that fear is no more reasonable, and for that cause he which by the covenant is to perform first is obliged so to do.

The cause of fear, which maketh such a covenant invalid, must be always something arising after the covenant made, as some new fact or other sign of the will not to perform; else it cannot make the covenant void. For that which could not hinder a man from promising ought not to be admitted as a hindrance of performing.

He that transferreth any right transferreth the means of enjoying it as far as lieth in his power. As he that selleth land is understood to transfer the herbage and whatsoever grows upon it; nor can he that sells a mill turn away the stream that drives it. And they that give to a man the right of government in sovereignty are understood to give him the right of levying money to maintain soldiers, and of appointing magistrates for the administration of justice.

To make covenants with brute beasts is impossible, because, not understanding our speech, they understand not nor accept of any translation of right; nor can translate any right to another; and without mutual acceptation, there is no covenant.

To make covenant with God is impossible, but by mediation of such as God speaketh to, either by revelation supernatural or by His lieutenants that govern under Him and in His name; for otherwise we know not whether our covenants be accepted or not. And therefore they that vow anything contrary to any law of Nature vow in vain, as being a thing unjust to pay such a vow. And, if it be a thing commanded by the law of Nature, it is not the vow but the law that binds them.

The matter or subject of a covenant is always something that falleth under deliberation, for to covenant is an act of the will, that is to say an act, and the last act of deliberation, and is therefore always understood to be something to come, and which is judged possible for him that covenanteth to perform.

And therefore to promise that which is known to be impossible is no covenant. But, if that prove impossible afterwards which before was thought possible, the covenant is valid and bindeth, though not to the thing itself, yet to the value, or, if that also be impossible, to the unfeigned endeavour of performing as much as is possible, for to more no man can be obliged.

Men are freed of their covenants two ways: by performing or being forgiven. For performance is the natural end of obligation, and forgiveness the restitution of liberty, as being a retransferring of that right in which the obligation consisted.

Covenants entered into by fear, in the condition of mere nature, are obligatory. For example, if I covenant to pay a ransom or service for my life to an enemy, I am bound by it, for it is a contract wherein one receiveth the benefit of life; and the other is to receive money or service for it; and consequently where no other law, as in the condition of mere nature, forbiddeth the performance, the covenant is valid. Therefore prisoners of war, if trusted with the payment of their ransom, are obliged to pay it; and, if a weaker prince make a disadvantageous peace with a stronger for fear, he is bound to keep it, unless, as hath been said before, there ariseth some new and just cause of fear to renew the war. And even in commonwealths, if I be forced to redeem myself from a thief by promising him money, I am bound to pay it, till the civil law discharge me. For whatsoever I may lawfully do without obligation, the same I may lawfully covenant to do through fear, and what I lawfully covenant I cannot lawfully break.

A former covenant makes void a later. For a man that hath passed away his right to one man to-day hath it not to pass tomorrow to another, and therefore the later promise passeth no right, but is null.

A covenant not to defend myself from force by force is always void. For, as I have shown before, no man can transfer or lay down his right to save himself from death, wounds, and imprisonment, the avoiding whereof is the only end of laying down any right; and therefore the promise of not resisting force, in no covenant transferreth any right, nor is obliging. For, though a man may covenant thus, 'unless I do so or so, kill me,' he cannot covenant thus, 'unless I do so or so, I will not resist you when you come to kill me.' For man by nature chooseth the lesser evil, which is danger of death in resisting, rather than the greater, which is certain and present death in not resisting. And this is granted to be true by all men, in that they lead criminals to execution and prison with armed men, notwithstanding that such criminals have consented to the law by which they are condemned.

A covenant to accuse oneself, without assurance of pardon, is likewise invalid. For in the condition of nature, where every man is judge, there is no place for accusation; and in the civil state the accusation is followed with punishment, which, being force, a man is not obliged not to resist. The same is also true of the accusation of those by whose condemnation a man falls into misery, as of a father, wife, or benefactor. For the testimony of such an accuser, if it be not willingly given, is presumed to be corrupted by nature, and therefore not to be received; and where a man's testimony is not to be credited he is not bound to give it. Also accusations upon torture are not to be reputed as testimonies. For torture is to be used but as a means of conjecture and light, in the further examination and search of truth; and what is in that case confessed tendeth to the ease of him that is tortured, not to the informing of the torturers, and therefore ought not to have the credit of a sufficient testimony, for, whether he deliver himself by true or false accusation, he does it by the right of preserving his own life.

The force of words being, as I have formerly noted, too weak to hold men to the performance of their covenants, there are in man's nature but two imaginable helps to strengthen it. And those are either a fear of the consequence of breaking their word, or a glory or pride in appearing not to need to break it. This latter is a generosity too rarely found to be presumed on, especially in the pursuers of wealth, command, or sensual pleasure, which are the greatest part of mankind. The passion to be reckoned upon is fear, whereof there be two very general objects: one, the power of spirits invisible, the other, the power of those men they shall therein offend. Of these two, though the former be the greater power, yet the fear of the latter is commonly the greater fear. The fear of the former is in every man his own religion, which hath place in the nature of man before civil society. The latter hath not so, at least not place enough to keep men to their promises; because in the condition of mere nature the inequality of power is not discerned but by the event of battle. So that before the time of civil society, or in the interruption thereof by war, there is nothing can strengthen a covenant of peace agreed on against the temptations of avarice, ambition, lust, or other strong desire, but the fear of that invisible power which they every one worship as God and fear as a revenger of their perfidy. All therefore that can be done between two men not subject to civil power is to put one another to swear by the God he feareth, which 'swearing,' or 'oath,' is 'a form of speech, added to a promise; by which he that promiseth signifieth that, unless he perform he renounceth the mercy of his God or calleth to Him for vengeance on himself.' Such was the heathen form, 'Let Jupiter kill me else, as I kill this beast.' So is our form, 'I shall do thus, and thus, so help me God.' And this, with the rites and ceremonies which every one useth in his own religion, that the fear of breaking faith might be the greater.

By this it appears that an oath taken according to any other form or rite than his that sweareth is in vain, and no oath; and that there is no swearing by anything which the swearer thinks not

God. For though men have sometimes used to swear by their kings, for fear or flattery, yet they would have it thereby understood they attributed to them divine honour. And that swearing unnecessarily by God is but profaning of His name; and swearing by other things, as men do in common discourse, is not swearing but an impious custom, gotten by too much vehemence of talking.

It appears also that the oath adds nothing to the obligation. For a covenant, if lawful, binds in the sight of God without the oath as much as with it: if unlawful, bindeth not at all, though it be confirmed with an oath.

CHAPTER XV

OF OTHER LAWS OF NATURE

FROM that law of Nature by which we are obliged to transfer to another such rights as, being retained, hinder the peace of mankind, there followeth a third, which is this, 'that men perform their covenants made'; without which covenants are in vain, and but empty words: and the right of all men to all things remaining, we are still in the condition of war.

And in this law of Nature consisteth the fountain and original of 'justice.' For, where no covenant hath preceded, there hath no right been transferred, and every man has right to everything; and consequently, no action can be unjust. But when a covenant is made, then to break it is 'unjust'; and the definition of 'injustice' is no other than 'the not performance of covenant.' And whatsoever is not unjust is 'just.'

But because covenants of mutual trust, where there is a fear of not performance on either part, as hath been said in the former chapter, are invalid, though the original of justice be the making of covenants, yet injustice actually there can be none, till the cause of such fear be taken away, which, while men are in the natural condition of war, cannot be done. Therefore, before the names of just and unjust can have place, there must be some coercive power to compel men equally to the performance of their covenants, by the terror of some punishment greater than the benefit they expect

by the breach of their covenant; and to make good that propriety
which by mutual contract men acquire in recompense of the universal right they abandon; and such power there is none before the
erection of a commonwealth. And this is also to be gathered out of
the ordinary definition of justice in the schools; for they say that
'justice is the constant will of giving to every man his own.' And
therefore where there is no 'own' there is no propriety, there is no
injustice; and where there is no coercive power erected, that is,
where there is no commonwealth, there is no propriety, all men
having right to all things: therefore, where there is no commonwealth, there nothing is unjust. So that the nature of justice consisteth in keeping of valid covenants; but the validity of covenants
begins not but with the constitution of a civil power sufficient to
compel men to keep them; and then it is also that propriety begins.

The fool hath said in his heart there is no such thing as justice,
and sometimes also with his tongue, seriously alleging that every
man's conservation and contentment, being committed to his own
care, there could be no reason why every man might not do what
he thought conduced thereunto; and therefore also to make or not
make, keep or not keep, covenants was not against reason when it
conduced to one's benefit. He does not therein deny that there be
covenants, and that they are sometimes broken, sometimes kept,
and that such breach of them may be called injustice, and the observance of them justice; but he questioneth whether injustice, taking away the fear of God, for the same fool hath said in his heart
there is no God, may not sometimes stand with that reason which
dictateth to every man his own good; and particularly then when it
conduceth to such a benefit as shall put a man in a condition to
neglect not only the dispraise and revilings, but also the power,
of other men. The kingdom of God is gotten by violence; but what
if it could be gotten by unjust violence? Were it against reason so
to get it, when it is impossible to receive hurt by it? And, if it be
not against reason, it is not against justice, or else justice is not to be
approved for good. From such reasoning as this, successful wickedness hath obtained the name of virtue, and some that in all other
things have disallowed the violation of faith, yet have allowed it when
it is for the getting of a kingdom. And the heathen that believed that

Saturn was deposed by his son Jupiter believed nevertheless the same Jupiter to be the avenger of injustice, somewhat like to a piece of law in Coke's *Commentaries on Littleton,* where he says, if the right heir of the crown be attainted of treason, yet the crown shall descend to him, and *eo instante* the attainder be void; from which instances a man will be very prone to infer that, when the heir apparent of a kingdom shall kill him that is in possession, though his father, you may call it injustice or by what other name you will, yet it can never be against reason, seeing all the voluntary actions of men tend to the benefit of themselves; and those actions are most reasonable that conduce most to their ends. This specious reasoning is nevertheless false.

For the question is not of promises mutual, where there is no security of performance on either side, as when there is no civil power erected over the parties promising, for such promises are no covenants, but either where one of the parties has performed already, or where there is a power to make him perform, there is the question whether it be against reason, that is against the benefit of the other to perform or not. And I say it is not against reason. For the manifestation whereof we are to consider, first, that when a man doth a thing which notwithstanding anything can be foreseen and reckoned on tendeth to his own destruction, howsoever some accident which he could not expect, arriving may turn it to his benefit, yet such events do not make it reasonably or wisely done. Secondly, that, in a condition of war, wherein every man to every man, for want of a common power to keep them all in awe, is an enemy, there is no man who can hope by his own strength or wit to defend himself from destruction without the help of confederates; where every one expects the same defence by the confederation that any one else does; and therefore he which declares he thinks it reason to deceive those that help him can in reason expect no other means of safety than what can be had from his own single power. He therefore that breaketh his covenant, and consequently declareth that he thinks he may with reason do so, cannot be received into any society that unite themselves for peace and defence but by the error of them that receive him; nor, when he is received, be retained in it without seeing the danger of their error; which errors a man cannot reasonably reckon upon as the means of his security; and therefore, if he be left or cast out of society, he perisheth; and if he live in society, it is by the errors of other men which he could not foresee nor reckon upon, and consequently against the reason of his preservation; and so, as all men that contribute not to his destruction, forbear him only out of ignorance of what is good for themselves.

As for the instance of gaining the secure and perpetual felicity of heaven by any way, it is frivolous; there being but one way imaginable; and that is not breaking, but keeping of covenant.

And, for the other instance of attaining sovereignty by rebellion, it is manifest that, though the event follow, yet, because it cannot reasonably be expected, but rather the contrary, and because by gaining it so, others are taught to gain the same in like manner, the attempt thereof is against reason. Justice therefore, that is to say keeping of covenant, is a rule of reason by which we are forbidden to do anything destructive to our life; and consequently a law of Nature.

There be some that proceed further, and will not have the law of Nature to be those rules which conduce to the preservation of man's life on earth, but to the attaining of an eternal felicity after death; to which they think the breach of covenant may conduce; and consequently be just and reasonable; such are they that think it a work of merit to kill or depose or rebel against the sovereign power constituted over them by their own consent. But, because there is no natural knowledge of man's estate after death, much less of the reward that is then to be given to breach of faith, but only a belief grounded upon other men's saying that they know it supernaturally, or that they know those that knew them, that knew others, that knew it supernaturally; breach of faith cannot be called a precept of reason or nature.

Others that allow for a law of Nature the keeping of faith do nevertheless make exception of certain persons as heretics and such as use not to perform their covenant to others; and this also is against reason. For if any fault of a man be sufficient to discharge our covenant made, the same ought in reason to have been sufficient to have hindered the making of it.

The names of just, and unjust, when they are attributed to men, signify one thing; and when they are attributed to actions, another. When they are attributed to men, they signify conformity or inconformity of manners to reason. But, when they are attributed to actions, they signify the conformity or inconformity to reason, not of manners or manner of life but of particular actions. A just man, therefore, is he that taketh all the care he can that his actions may be all just, and an unjust man is he that neglecteth it. And such men are more often in our language styled by the names of righteous and unrighteous than just and unjust, though the meaning be the same. Therefore a righteous man does not lose that title by one or a few unjust actions that proceed from sudden passion or mistake of things or persons; nor does an unrighteous man lose his character for such actions as he does, or forbears to do, for fear, because his will is not framed by the justice but by the apparent benefit of what he is to do. That which gives to human actions the relish of justice is a certain nobleness or gallantness of courage, rarely found, by which a man scorns to be beholden for the contentment of his life to fraud or breach of promise. This justice of the manners is that which is meant where justice is called a virtue, and injustice a vice.

But the justice of actions denominates men not just, 'guiltless'; and the injustice of the same, which is also called injury, gives them but the name of 'guilty.'

Again, the injustice of manners is the disposition or aptitude to do injury, and is injustice before it proceeds to act, and without supposing any individual person injured. But the injustice of an action, that is to say injury, supposeth an individual person injured, namely him to whom the covenant was made; and therefore many times the injury is received by one man when the damage redoundeth to another. As when the master commandeth his servant to give money to a stranger: if it be not done, the injury is done to the master, whom he had before covenanted to obey; but the damage redoundeth to the stranger, to whom he had no obligation, and therefore could not injure him. And so also in commonwealths. Private men may remit to one another their debts, but not robberies or other violences whereby they are endamaged, because the detaining of debt is an injury to themselves, but robbery and violence are injuries to the person of the commonwealth.

Whatsoever is done to a man conformable to his own will signified to the doer is no injury to him. For, if he that doeth it hath not passed away his original right to do what he please by some antecedent covenant, there is no breach of covenant, and therefore no injury done him. And if he have, then his will to have it done being signified is a release of that covenant, and so again there is no injury done him.

Justice of action is by writers divided into 'commutative' and 'distributive'; and the former they say consisteth in proportion arithmetical, the latter in proportion geometrical. Commutative, therefore, they place in the equality of value of the things contracted for; and distributive, in the distribution of equal benefit to men of equal merit. As if it were injustice to sell dearer than we buy, or to give more to a man than he merits. The value of all things contracted for is measured by the appetite of the contractors; and therefore the just value is that which they be contented to give. And merit, besides that which is by covenant, where the performance on one part meriteth the performance of the other part, and falls under justice commutative not distributive, is not due by justice, but is rewarded of grace only. And therefore this distinction, in the sense wherein it useth to be expounded, is not right. To speak properly, commutative justice is the justice of a contractor; that is, a performance of covenant in buying and selling, hiring and letting to hire, lending and borrowing, exchanging, bartering, and other acts of contract.

And distributive justice, the justice of an arbitrator; that is to say, the act of defining what is just. Wherein, being trusted by them that make him arbitrator, if he perform his trust he is said to distribute to every man his own; and this is indeed just distribution, and may be called, though improperly, distributive justice, but more properly equity, which also is a law of Nature, as shall be shown in due place.

As justice dependeth on antecedent covenant, so does 'gratitude' depend on antecedent grace, that is to say, antecedent free gift; and is the fourth law of Nature; which may be conceived in this form, 'that a man, which receiveth benefit from another of mere grace, endeavour that he which giveth it have no reasonable cause to repent him of his good will.' For no man giveth but with intention of good to himself; because gift is voluntary; and of all voluntary acts the object is to every man his own good, of which, if men see they shall be frustrated, there will be no beginning of benevolence, or trust, nor consequently of mutual help, nor of reconciliation of one man to another; and therefore they are to remain still in the condition of 'war,' which is contrary to the first and fundamental law of Nature, which commandeth men to 'seek peace.' The breach of this law is called 'ingratitude,' and hath the same relation to grace that injustice hath to obligation by covenant.

A fifth law of Nature, is 'complaisance,' that is to say, 'that every man strive to accommodate himself to the rest.' For the understanding whereof, we may consider that there is in men's aptness to society, a diversity of nature, rising from their diversity of affections, not unlike to that we see in stones brought together for building of an edifice. For as that stone which by the asperity and irregularity of figure takes more room from others than itself fills, and for the hardness cannot be easily made plain, and thereby hindereth the building, is by the builders cast away as unprofitable and troublesome, so also a man that by asperity of nature will strive to retain those things which to himself are superfluous and to others necessary, and for the stubbornness of his passions cannot be corrected, is to be left or cast out of society as cumbersome thereunto. For seeing every man, not only by right but also by necessity of nature, is supposed to endeavour all he can to obtain that which is necessary for his conversation, he that shall oppose himself against it for things superfluous is guilty of the war that thereupon is to follow; and therefore doth that which is contrary to the fundamental law of Nature, which commandeth 'to seek peace.' The observers of this law may be called 'sociable'—the Latins call them *commodi;* the contrary, 'stubborn,' 'insociable,' 'froward,' 'intractable.'

A sixth law of Nature is this, 'that, upon caution of the future time, a man ought to pardon the offences past of them that, repenting, desire it.' For 'pardon' is nothing but granting of peace, which, though granted to them that persevere in their hostility, be not peace but fear; yet not granted to them that give caution of the future time is sign of an aversion to peace, and therefore contrary to the law of Nature.

A seventh is, 'that in revenges,' that is, retribution of evil for evil, 'men look not at the greatness of the evil past but the greatness of the good to follow.' Whereby we are forbidden to inflict punishment with any other design than for correction of the offender or direction of others. For this law is consequent to the next before it, that commandeth pardon, upon security of the future time. Besides, revenge, without respect to the example and profit to come, is a triumph or glorying in the hurt of another tending to no end; for the end is always somewhat to come; and glorying to no end is vain-glory and contrary to reason, and to hurt without reason tendeth to the introduction of war, which is against the law of Nature, and is commonly styled by the name of 'cruelty.'

And because all signs of hatred or contempt provoke to fight, insomuch as most men choose rather to hazard their life than not to be revenged, we may in the eighth place, for a law of Nature, set down this precept, 'that no man by deed, word, countenance, or gesture, declare hatred or contempt of another.' The breach of which law is commonly called 'contumely.'

The question who is the better man has no place in the condition of mere nature; where, as has been shown before, all men are equal. The inequality that now is has been introduced by the laws civil. I know that Aristotle, in the first book of his *Politics,* for a foundation of his doctrine, maketh men by nature some more worthy to command, meaning the wiser sort, such as he thought himself to be for his philosophy, others to serve, meaning those that had strong bodies but were not philosophers as he; as if master and servant were not introduced by consent of men but by difference of wit, which is not only against reason but also against experience. For there are very few so foolish that had not rather govern themselves than be governed by others; nor, when the wise in their own conceit contend by force with them who distrust their own wisdom, do they always, or often, or almost at any time, get the victory. If Nature therefore have made men equal, that equality is to be acknowledged; or, if Nature have made men unequal, yet because men that think themselves equal will not enter into conditions of peace but upon equal terms, such equality must be admitted. And therefore for the ninth law of Nature I put this, 'that every man acknowledge another for his equal by nature.' The breach of this precept is 'pride.'

On this law dependeth another, 'that at the entrance into conditions of peace no man require to reserve to himself any right which he is not content should be reserved to every one of the rest.' As it is necessary for all men that seek peace to lay down certain rights of nature, that is to say, not to have liberty to do all they list, so is it necessary for man's life to retain some, as right to govern their own bodies, enjoy air, water, motion, ways to go from place to place, and all things else without which a man cannot live or not live well. If in this case, at the making of peace, men require for themselves that which they would not have to be granted to others, they do contrary to the precedent law, that commandeth the acknowledgement of natural equality, and therefore also against the law of Nature. The observers of this law are those we call 'modest,' and the breakers 'arrogant' men. The Greeks call the violation of this law πλεονεξία, that is, a desire of more than their share.

Also if 'a man be trusted to judge between man and man,' it is a precept of the law of Nature 'that he deal equally between them.' For without that the controversies of men cannot be determined but by war. He therefore that is partial in judgment doth what in him lies to deter men from the use of judges and arbitrators, and consequently against the fundamental law of Nature, is the cause of war.

The observance of this law, from the equal distribution to each man of that which in reason belongeth to him, is called 'equity,' and, as I have said before, distributive justice; the violation, 'acception of persons,' προσωποληψία.

And from this followeth another law, 'that such things as cannot be divided be enjoyed in common, if it can be; and, if the quantity of the thing permit, without stint; otherwise proportionably to the number of them that have 'right.' For otherwise the distribution is unequal and contrary to equity.

But some things there be that can neither be divided nor enjoyed in common. Then the law of Nature, which prescribeth equity, requireth 'that the entire right, or else making the use alternate, the first possession, be determined by lot.' For equal distribution is of the law of Nature, and other means of equal distribution cannot be imagined.

Of 'lots' there be two sorts, 'arbitrary,' and 'natural.' Arbitrary is that which is agreed on by the competitors; natural is either 'primogeniture,' which the Greeks call κληρονομία, which signifies 'given by lot' or 'first seizure.'

And therefore those things which cannot be enjoyed in common nor divided ought to be adjudged to the first possessor; and in some cases to the first born, as acquired by lot.

It is also a law of Nature 'that all men that mediate peace, be allowed safe conduct.' For the law that commandeth peace as the end, commandeth intercession as the 'means' and to intercession the means is safe conduct.

And because, though men be never so willing to observe these laws, there may nevertheless arise questions concerning a man's action; first, whether it were done or not done; secondly, if done, whether against the law or not against the law; the former whereof is called a question 'of fact,' the latter a question 'of right,' therefore, unless the parties to the question covenant mutually to stand to the sentence of another, they are as far from peace as ever. This other to whose sentence they submit is called an 'arbitrator.' And therefore it is of the law of Nature 'that they that are at controversy submit their right to the judgment of an arbitrator.'

And, seeing every man is presumed to do all things in order to his own benefit, no man is a fit arbitrator in his own cause, and if he were never so fit, yet, equity allowing to each party equal benefit, if one be admitted to be judge, the other is to be admitted also; and so the controversy, that is, the cause of war, remains against the law of Nature.

For the same reason no man in any cause ought to be received for arbitrator to whom greater profit, or honour, or pleasure, apparently ariseth out of the victory of one party than of the other; for he hath taken, though an unavoidable bribe, yet a bribe, and no man can be obliged to trust him. And thus also the controversy and the condition of war remaineth, contrary to the law of Nature.

And in a controversy of 'fact,' the judge, being to give no more credit to one than to the other if there be no other arguments, must give credit to a third, or to a third and fourth, or more; for else the question is undecided and left to force, contrary to the law of Nature.

These are the laws of Nature, dictating peace, for a means of the conservation of men in multitudes, and which only concern the doctrine of civil society. There be other things tending to the destruction of particular men, as drunkenness and all other parts of intemperance; which may therefore also be reckoned amongst those things which the law of Nature hath forbidden, but are not necessary to be mentioned, nor are pertinent enough to this place.

And though this may seem too subtle a deduction of the laws of Nature to be taken notice of by all men, whereof the most part are too busy in getting food and the rest too negligent to understand, yet, to leave all men inexcusable, they have been contracted into one easy sum, intelligible even to the meanest capacity; and that is, 'Do not that to another which thou wouldst not have done to thyself'; which showeth him that he has no more to do in learning the laws of Nature but when weighing the actions of other men with his own, they seem too heavy, to put them into the other part of the balance and his own into their place, that his own passions and self-love may add nothing to the weight; and then there is none of these laws of Nature that will not appear unto him very reasonable.

The laws of Nature oblige *in foro interno,* that is to say, they bind to a desire they should take place; but *in foro externo,* that is, to the putting them in act, not always. For he that should be modest and tractable and perform all he promises, in such time and place where no man else should do so, should but make himself a prey to others and procure his own certain ruin, contrary to the ground of all laws of Nature, which tend to Nature's preservation. And, again, he that, having sufficient security that others shall observe the same laws towards him, observes them not himself, seeketh not peace but war, and consequently the destruction of his nature by violence.

And whatsoever laws bind *in foro interno* may be broken, not only by a fact contrary to the law but also by a fact according to it, in case a man think it contrary. For, though his action in this case be according to the law, yet his purpose was against the law; which, where the obligation is *in foro interno,* is a breach.

The laws of Nature are immutable and eternal; for injustice, ingratitude, arrogance, pride, iniquity, acception of persons, and the rest, can never be made lawful. For it can never be that war shall preserve life, and peace destroy it.

The same laws, because they oblige only to a desire and endeavour —I mean an unfeigned and constant endeavour—are easy to be observed. For, in that they require nothing but endeavour, he that endeavoureth their performance fulfilleth them, and he that fulfilleth the law is just.

And the science of them is the true and only moral philosophy. For moral philosophy is nothing else but the science of what is 'good' and 'evil' in the conversation and society of mankind. 'Good' and 'evil' are names that signify our appetites and aversions, which, in different tempers, customs, and doctrines of men, are different; and divers men differ not only in their judgment on the senses of what is pleasant and unpleasant to the taste, smell, hearing, touch, and sight, but also of what is conformable or disagreeable to reason in the actions of common life. Nay, the same man in divers times differs from himself, and one time praiseth, that is calleth good, what another time he dispraiseth and calleth evil; from whence arise disputes, controversies, and at last war. And therefore, so long as a man is in the condition of mere nature, which is a condition of war, as private appetite is the measure of good and evil, and consequently all men agree on this, that peace is good, and therefore also the way or means of peace, which, as I have showed before, are 'justice,' 'gratitude,' 'modesty,' 'equity,' 'mercy,' and the rest of the laws of Nature, are good; that is to say, 'moral virtues'; and their contrary 'vices,' evil. Now the science of virtue and vice is moral philosophy, and therefore the true doctrine of the laws of Nature is the true moral philosophy. But the writers of moral philosophy, though they acknowledge the same virtues and vices, yet, not seeing wherein consisted their goodness, nor that they come to be praised as the means of peaceable, sociable, and comfortable living, place them in a mediocrity of passions; as if not the cause, but the degree of daring made fortitude; or not the cause, but the quantity, of a gift, made liberality.

These dictates of reason men used to call by the name of laws, but improperly; for they are but conclusions or theorems concerning what conduceth to the conservation and defence of themselves; whereas law, properly, is the word of him that by right hath command over others. But yet if we consider the same theorems, as delivered in the word of God, that by right commandeth all things, then are they properly called laws.

CHAPTER XVI

OF PERSONS, AUTHORS, AND THINGS PERSONATED

A PERSON is he 'whose words or actions are considered, either as his own or as representing the words or actions of another man, or of any other thing, to whom they are attributed, whether truly or by fiction.'

When they are considered as his own, then is he called a 'natural person'; and, when they are considered as representing the words and actions of another, then is he a 'feigned' or 'artificial person.'

The word person is Latin; instead whereof the Greeks have πρόσωπον, which signifies the 'face,' as persona in Latin signifies the 'disguise' or 'outward appearance' of a man, counterfeited on the stage, and sometimes more particularly that part of it which disguiseth the face, as a mask or vizard, and from the stage hath been translated to any representer of speech and action, as well in tribunals as theatres. So that a 'person' is the same that an 'actor' is, both on the stage and in common conversation; and to 'personate' is to 'act,' or 'represent,' himself or another; and he that acteth another is said to bear his person, or act in his name, in which sense Cicero useth it where he says: Unus sustineo tres personas; mei, adversarii, et judicis: I bear three persons: my own, my adversary's, and the judge's; and is called in diverse occasions, diversely: as a 'representer' or 'representative,' a 'lieutenant,' a 'vicar,' an 'attorney,' a 'deputy,' a 'procurator,' an 'actor,' and the like.

Of persons artificial some have their words and actions 'owned' by those whom they represent. And then the person is the 'actor,' and he that owneth his words and actions is the 'author,' in which case the actor acteth by authority. For that which in speaking of goods and possessions is called an 'owner' and in Latin *dominus,* in Greek κύριος; speaking of actions is called author. And as the right of possession is called dominion, so the right of doing any action is called 'authority.' So that by authority is always understood a right of doing any act, and 'done by authority,' done by commission or licence from him whose right it is.

From hence it followeth that, when the actor maketh a covenant by authority, he bindeth thereby the author no less than if he had made it himself, and no less subjecteth him to all the consequences of the same. And therefore all that hath been said formerly (chap. xiv) of the nature of covenants between man and man in their natural capacity is true also when they are made by their actors, representers, or procurators, that have authority from them, so far forth as is in their commission, but no further.

And therefore he that maketh a covenant with the actor or representer, not knowing the authority he hath, doth it at his own peril. For no man is obliged by a covenant whereof he is not author, nor consequently by a covenant made against or beside the authority he gave.

When the actor doth anything against the law of Nature by command of the author, if he be obliged by former covenant to obey him, not he but the author breaketh the law of Nature; for, though the action be against the law of Nature, yet it is not his; but, contrarily, to refuse to do it, is against the law of Nature, that forbiddeth breach of covenant.

And he that maketh a covenant with the author by mediation of the actor, not knowing what authority he hath, but only takes his word, in case such authority be not made manifest unto him upon demand, is no longer obliged, for the covenant made with the author is not valid without his counter-assurance. But if he that so covenanteth knew beforehand he was to expect no other assurance than the actor's word, then is the covenant valid, because the actor in this case maketh himself the author. And therefore, as when the authority is evident, the covenant obligeth the author, not the actor, so, when the authority is feigned, it obligeth the actor only, there being no author but himself.

There are few things that are incapable of being represented by fiction. Inanimate things, as a church, an hospital, a bridge, may be personated by a rector, master, or overseer. But things inanimate cannot be authors, nor therefore give authority to their actors; yet the actors may have authority to procure their maintenance, given them by those that are owners or governors of those things. And therefore such things cannot be personated before there be some state of civil government.

Likewise children, fools, and madmen, that have no use of reason, may be personated by guardians or curators, but can be no authors, during that time, of any action done by them longer than, when they shall recover the use of reason, they shall judge the same reasonable. Yet during the folly he that hath right of governing them may give authority to the guardian. But this again has no place but in a state civil, because before such estate there is no dominion of persons.

An idol, or mere figment of the brain, may be personated, as were the gods of the heathen, which, by such officers as the state appointed, were personated, and held possessions and other goods and rights, which men from time to time dedicated and consecrated unto them. But idols cannot be authors, for an idol is nothing. The authority proceeded from the state; and therefore before introduction of civil government the gods of the heathen could not be personated.

The true God may be personated. As He was, first, by Moses, who governed the Israelites, that were not his, but God's people, not in his own name, with *hoc dicit Moses,* but in God's name, with *hoc dicit Dominus.* Secondly, by the Son of man, His own Son, our blessed Saviour Jesus Christ, that came to reduce the Jews, and induce all nations into the kingdom of His Father, not as of Himself but as sent from His Father. And thirdly, by the Holy Ghost or Comforter, speaking and working in the Apostles, which Holy Ghost was a Comforter that came not of Himself, but was sent and proceeded from them both.

A multitude of men are made 'one' person when they are by one man or one person represented, so that it be done with the consent of every one of that multitude in particular. For it is the 'unity' of the representer, not the 'unity' of the represented, that maketh the person 'one.' And it is the representer that beareth the person, and but one person; and 'unity' cannot otherwise be understood in multitude.

And because the multitude naturally is not 'one' but 'many,' they cannot be understood for one, but many authors, of everything their representative saith or doth in their name, every man giving their common representer authority from himself in particular, and owning all the actions the representer doth, in case they give him authority without stint; otherwise, when they limit him in what and how far he shall represent them, none of them owneth more than they gave him commission to act.

And, if the representative consist of many men, the voice of the greater number must be considered as the voice of them all. For if the lesser number pronounce, for example in the affirmative, and the greater in the negative, there will be negatives more than enough to destroy the affirmatives; and thereby the excess of negatives, standing uncontradicted, are the only voice the representative hath.

And a representative of even number, especially when the number is not great, whereby the contradictory voices are oftentimes equal, is therefore oftentimes mute and incapable of action. Yet in some cases contradictory voices equal in number may determine a question, as in condemning or absolving, equality of votes, even in that they condemn not, do absolve, but not on the contrary condemn in that they absolve not. For when a cause is heard, not to condemn is to absolve; but, on the contrary, to say that not absolving is condemning is not true. The like it is in a deliberation of executing presently or deferring till another time; for when the voices are equal, the not decreeing execution is a decree of dilation.

Or if the number be odd, as three or more, men or assemblies, whereof every one has by a negative voice authority to take away the effect of all the affirmative voices of the rest, this number is no representative; because, by the diversity of opinions and interests of men, it becomes oftentimes, and in cases of the greatest consequence, a mute person and unapt, as for many things else; so for the government of a multitude, especially in time of war.

Of authors there be two sorts. The first simply so called; which I have before defined to be him that owneth the action of another simply. The second is he that owneth an action or covenant of another conditionally, that is to say, he undertaketh to do it if the other doth it not at or before a certain time. And these authors conditional are generally called 'sureties,' in Latin, *fidejussores,* and *sponsores,* and particularly for debt, *praedes;* and for appearance before a judge or magistrate, *vades.*